THE LIBRARY
ST. MARY'S COLLEGE OF MARYLAND
ST. MARY'S CITY, MARYLAND 20686

D1598514

*International Kierkegaard Commentary*

# International Kierkegaard Commentary

## Works of Love

edited by
# Robert L. Perkins

MERCER UNIVERSITY PRESS

ISBN 0-86554-685-1                          MUP/H505

International Kierkegaard Commentary
*Works of Love*
Copyright ©1999
Mercer University Press, Macon, Georgia 31210-3960 USA
All rights reserved
Printed in the United States of America

The paper used in this publication meets the minimum requirements
of American National Standard for Information Sciences—
Permanence of Paper for Printed Library Materials, ANSI Z39.48-1984.

*Library of Congress Cataloging-in-Publication Data*

Works of love / edited by Robert L. Perkins.
x+378pp. 6x9" (15x22cm.) — (International Kierkegaard commentary ; 16)
Includes bibliographical references and index.
ISBN 0-86554-685-1 (alk. paper).
1. Kierkegaard, Søren, 1813–1855. Kælighedens gerninger.
2. Spiritual life—Christianity. I. Perkins, Robert L., 1930– .    II. Series.
B4376.I58      1984 Vol. 16
[BV4505.K42]
198'.9 s—dc21
[241'.41]                                          99-36516
CIP

# Contents

# Acknowledgments

All the contributors to the volume would desire to make acknowledgments, but it is a privilege reserved for the editor. Those whom the contributors would have named will be content to have served their friends and colleagues.

I have the privilege of thanking a number of persons at Stetson University who have supported my work in general and the International Kierkegaard Commentary in particular: H. Douglas Lee, president of Stetson University; Grady Ballenger, dean of the College of Arts and Sciences; Donna Schick, secretary to the Department of Philosophy; and Jessica Ryder, student assistant.

The advisory board and the volume consultant read all the contributions, offered valuable insights into the articles, and also made some recommendations for changes. Dr. Ronald L. Hall of Francis Marion University also made helpful recommendations about one article. Dr. Julia Watkin of the University of Tasmania continues to be particularly helpful in suggesting possible authors and tracking down obscure allusions in Kierkegaard's texts. The interest of Mercer University Press and especially the efforts of Senior Editor Edmon L. Rowell, Jr. are deeply appreciated. Princeton University Press gave permission to quote from *Works of Love* and other translations to which they hold copyright.

The several contributors and I also thank our families for the lost evenings and other scattered hours while we pursued these tasks. Finally, I wish to thank my wife, Sylvia Walsh, for assistance at every stage of this project and for making our life together an unutterable joy.

*Robert L. Perkins*

# Sigla

AN    *"Armed Neutrality" and "An Open Letter."* Trans. Howard V. Hong and Edna H. Hong. Bloomington and London: Indiana University Press, 1968.

C    *The Crisis and a Crisis in the Life of an Actress.* See *Christian Discourses.*

BA    *The Book on Adler.* Trans. Howard V. Hong and Edna H. Hong. Princeton NJ: Princeton University Press, 1995.

CA    *The Concept of Anxiety.* Trans. Reidar Thomte in collaboration with Albert B. Anderson. Princeton NJ: Princeton University Press, 1980.

CD    *Christian Discourses* and *The Crisis and a Crisis in the Life of an Actress.*
C    Trans. Howard V. Hong and Edna H. Hong. Princeton NJ: Princeton University Press, 1997.

CI    *The Concept of Irony* together with "Notes on Schelling's Berlin Lectures."
NSBL    Trans. Howard V. Hong and Edna H. Hong. Princeton NJ: Princeton University Press, 1989.

COR    *The Corsair Affair.* Trans. Howard V. Hong and Edna H. Hong. Princeton NJ: Princeton University Press, 1982.

CUP    *Concluding Unscientific Postscript.* Two vols. Trans. Howard V. Hong and Edna H. Hong. Princeton NJ: Princeton University Press, 1992.

EO, 1    *Either/Or.* Two vols. Trans. Howard V. Hong and Edna H. Hong.
EO, 2    Princeton NJ: Princeton University Press, 1987.

EPW    *Early Polemical Writings.* Trans. Julia Watkin. Princeton NJ: Princeton
FPOSL    University Press, 1990.

EUD    *Eighteen Upbuilding Discourses.* Trans. Howard H. Hong and Edna H. Hong. Princeton NJ: Princeton University Press, 1990.

FPOSL    *From the Papers of One Still Living.* See *Early Polemical Writings.*

FSE    *For Self-Examination* and *Judge for Yourself!* Trans. Howard V. Hong and
JFY    Edna H. Hong. Princeton NJ: Princeton University Press, 1990.

FT    *Fear and Trembling* and *Repetition.* Trans. Howard V. Hong and Edna H. Hong. Princeton NJ: Princeton University Press, 1983.

JC    *Johannes Climacus or De omnibus dubitandum est.* See *Philosophical Fragments.*

JFY    *Judge for Yourself!* See *For Self-Examination.*

JP    *Søren Kierkegaard's Journals and Papers.* Ed. and trans. Howard V. Hong and Edna H. Hong, assisted by Gregor Malantschuk. Bloomington and London: Indiana University Press, (1) 1967; (2) 1970; (3) and (4) 1975; (5-7) 1978.

LD    *Letters and Documents.* Trans. Hendrik Rosenmeier. Princeton NJ: Princeton University Press, 1978.

NSBL    "Notes on Schelling's Berlin Lectures." See *The Concept of Irony*.

P       *Prefaces: Light Reading of Certain Classes as the Occasion May Require*. Trans. William McDonald. Tallahassee: Florida State University Press, 1989.

PC      *Practice in Christianity*. Trans. Howard V. Hong and Edna H. Hong. Princeton NJ: Princeton University Press, 1991.

PF      *Philosophical Fragments* and *Johannes Climacus*. Trans. Howard V. Hong
JC      and Edna H. Hong. Princeton NJ: Princeton University Press, 1985.

PV      *The Point of View for My Work as an Author*. Trans. Walter Lowrie. London and New York: Oxford University Press, 1939.

R       *Repetition*. See *Fear and Trembling*.

SLW     *Stages on Life's Way*. Trans. Howard V. Hong and Edna H. Hong. Princeton NJ: Princeton University Press, 1988.

SUD     *The Sickness unto Death*. Trans. Howard V. Hong and Edna Hong. Princeton NJ: Princeton University Press, 1980.

TA      *Two Ages: the Age of Revolution and the Present Age. A Literary Review*. Trans. Howard V. Hong and Edna H. Hong. Princeton NJ: Princeton University Press, 1978.

TM      *The Moment and Late Writings*. Trans. Howard V. Hong and Edna H. Hong. Princeton NJ: Princeton University Press, 1998.

TDIO    *Three Discourses on Imagined Occasions*. Trans. Howard V. Hong and Edna H. Hong. Princeton NJ: Princeton University Press, 1993.

UDVS    *Upbuilding Discourses in Various Spirits*. Trans. Howard V. Hong and Edna H. Hong. Princeton NJ: Princeton University Press, 1993.

WA      *Without Authority*. Trans. Howard V. Hong and Edna H. Hong. Princeton NJ: Princeton University Press, 1997

WL      *Works of Love*. Trans. Howard V. Hong and Edna H. Hong. Princeton NJ: Princeton University Press, 1995.

# Introduction

## Works of Love as a Philosophic Tract

To claim that *Works of Love* is an important philosophical essay is to assume a hazardous burden of proof. The book's title is an allusion to the Bible's injunction that we should love our neighbor as we love ourselves, a far cry, for instance, from Diotima's ladder of erotic desire up which we climb from the love of bodies until we catch a vision of that "single sea of beauty," beauty itself (Plato, *Symposium*). This contrast, given that some of our neighbors may not be particularly likable or one may even be a determined enemy, suggests immediately to some that a book with such an obviously religious title must be excessively moralistic and, at best, full of sermon helps for the harried clergy or, at worst, laden with rules for the unlearned laity. A casual perusal of a few paragraphs, however, shows these "put-down" views of the book to be unfounded.

The unrelenting critic could add that the idea of love being commanded is logically incoherent, or that loving enemies or people one does not like demonstrates a confused understanding of the passions. In any case, the very combination, "commanded love," is an oxymoron. Also, the idea that there is an antithesis in ethics, that ethics is an either/or, a universalizable normative claim and more than a perspective, smacks of revenge and resentment. Thus, briefly stated, run the prevailing forms of offence against the Christian ethic.

By contrast, several essays in this volume argue that the Judeo-Christian view of neighbor love, as presented by Kierkegaard in *Works of Love*, is a concept that challenges some of the most debatable features of modern ethical theory and offers important insights into perennial philosophic problems: the nature and extent of moral sentiment, the nature or limit of ethical concern (the subjugation of ethics to nosiness into other people's private lives or a mechanism of domination), the fundamental problems associated with ethical egoism, the relation of the individual to society, and the issue of relativism, to name only a few. Then too, how is the strange love that can be commanded related to eros, human desire? More fundamental still, for Kierkegaard at least, the relation of the divine to ethical discourse and action, if any, is one of the most important and enduring metaethical debates (Plato, *Euthyphro*, 9d-10a), and one that Kierkegaard addresses forthrightly. Raising these debatable philosophic issues in the context of Kierkegaard's insights in *Works of Love* suggests that the book is a philosophic text.

During a time that is characterized by an explosion of ethical issues that must be discussed in order to develop numerous decent and fair social policies and personal moral integrity, it is foolhardy to neglect any source of ethical insight. On the contrary, I submit that the philosophic appropriation of the Christian concept of neighbor love, a love that is not subject to our whims but which enables us to judge and evaluate our whims, could be a valuable source in the development of ethical theory and applied ethics in the next century and millennium.

These issues are raised, however, in an environment that many think to be hostile. What for Plato was a question to be discussed (the relation of piety and the gods) seems to be decided. Today some in the academy have simply written off religion as, at best, an academic subdiscipline in the departments of history or psychopathology. The pervasive temper on many campuses and in a large portion of the public is much like Nietzsche's: "Pious and merely churchgoing people seldom realize *how much* good will it requires nowadays for a German scholar to take the problem of religion seriously."[1] Though Nietzsche intended this to be an ironic criticism of the scholar as much as of religion, today the scholar is fully in charge and the opposition to the religious is widespread throughout the intellectual life, except when religion is treated academically, that is, as a historical-cultural event or as psychologically interesting. Though Nietzsche's comment may seem extreme, until very recently there has existed an Enlightenment or modernist prejudice against a philosophic criticism of religious ethics that amounts to dismissal, with the result that the concept of neighbor love is largely missing from ethical and metaethical discourse. The prejudice both results from and contributes to a pervasive ignorance of Kierkegaard's opposition to the "Christian-

---

[1]Friedrich Nietzsche, *Beyond Good and Evil*, trans. R. J. Hollingdale (Hammondsworth: Penguin Books, 1973) sect. 58, p. 65.

bourgeois" settlement and of his importance as a source of a constructive philosophical and ethical appraisal of late capitalism. Due to the lasting popularity of his ironic examination of the form modernity was taking in Denmark, expressed in his pseudonymous writings, and the relative neglect of his philosophical and religious writings in the academy, it is a safe guess that what could be called the "deconstructive side" of Kierkegaard is better known than the constructive. However, *Works of Love* demonstrates that Kierkegaard is not much of a deconstructionist, unless, that is, deconstruction can be or is upbuilding.

There is also an unjustifiable social prejudice that prevents a philosophically rigorous examination of this particular religious ethic. I refer to the banal expression, "We are all Christians," that Kierkegaard criticized with such passion. Now, of course, if we are all Christians in heart and mind, whatever we think of the love commandment is the truth of the matter. Since we are all Christians, our common life is a social expression of the Christian ethic. What I am suggesting is that the very permeation of Christian signs and symbols in our speech and common life leads to subtle complacency about it among some religious folk and outright rejection by those who note the difference between Christian ethical theory and bourgeois practice. Though many philosophers have recognized the simplicity of this banality, they have subtlety accepted the identity of the banality with the normative content of Christian ethics and have concluded that Christian ethical concepts are bankrupt and hackneyed, not worth another thought. It is precisely this reduction of the moral imperatives of the Christian religion to bourgeois self-satisfaction and complacency that Kierkegaard criticizes in *Works of Love* as he attempts to work out the grammar of the love command. The following essays attempt to present aspects of that grammar.

*Works of Love* is a thoroughly theocentric book, and Christianly theocentric at that. As Martin Andic points out in his article, "Love's Redoubling and Eternity's Like for Like," Kierkegaard stresses the differences rather than the connections and similarities between the Jewish and the Christian religions' ethical demands. And demands they are, austere and uncompromising, just as much so in the Hebrew scriptures as in the Christian. Andic takes us directly into the very heart of Kierkegaard's understanding of the divine command through his study of Kierkegaard's concepts of "redoubling" and "reduplication." For Kierkegaard a person's response to the neighbor-love command is the basis of a divine "redoubling": "God does unto you what you do unto others." God redoubles, but persons must "reduplicate." Reduplication is a task we must perform in time, for we must become what we profess. To love the neighbor is every moment a new demand and task to be performed each time we meet the neighbor.

Good Lutheran that he was, Kierkegaard understood that a person was never what he/she should be, that a person is *simul justus et peccator*, justified and sinner at the same moment, as Anthony Burgess emphasizes in his article, "Kierkegaard's Concept of Redoubling and Luther's *Simul Justus*." Because our thoughts and actions often express less than undiluted and uncompromised love toward others, we are sinners (*peccator*) and are driven to grace, everlastingly to grace. Our self-love cannot endure the divine's redoubling of it within ourselves; self-love turns into self-hatred and the person is driven to repentance. God is eternally loving to all sinners, and those who accept, understand, and repent of their condition as sinners, God justifies though they remain sinners. In justification God's love redoubles itself in them and enables them to overcome self-love and to love other people, whether they are lovable or not.

Paul Martens, in his article, "You Shall Love: Kant, Kierkegaard, and the Interpretation of Matthew 22:39," uses the command form of Jewish and Christian ethics to connect them both to the moral philosophy of another Lutheran, Immanuel Kant, who thought the categorical imperative, the keystone of his whole moral theory, to be a rational equivalent of the divine command to neighbor love. However, realist that he was, Kant also understood that he had to deal with the issue of moral failure; and he does so by the development of the concept of "radical evil." Kant rewrites the love command into a rational and universal duty which is the root of all action and which defines true morality. Martens sees Kierkegaard as addressing precisely Kant's missing emphasis upon love. Both Kant and Kierkegaard emphasize the rigor and universality of the command, be it the categorical imperative or the biblical command to love the neighbor.

Arnold Come refocuses the issues of redoubling and reduplication in his essay, 'Kierkegaard's Ontology of Love," in the realm of general ontology and philosophy of language. Kierkegaard's metaphysical language is strange, for it is metaphorical and in no way traditional; it is an interpersonal metaphysics of the divine-human encounter, the encounter with a singular God with singular persons, individuals who have defined themselves primarily in and through their understanding of the divine. The relations between the eternally personal and the humanly personal are faith and love, love being the fundamental, for God is love and love is God.

Whereas Come emphasizes the metaphysical structures of neighbor love, Anthony Rudd in his essay, "'Believing All Things': Kierkegaard on Knowledge, Doubt, and Love," examines the epistemological import of *Works of Love*. Rudd attempts to show how Kierkegaard's epistemological ideas, which seem to have little or no moral import, in fact underlie the priority of love and the two other theological virtues, hope and faith. Kierkegaard signals the epistemological import in the very title of the deliberation, "Love Believes All Things—and Yet Is Never Deceived," and he certainly got in the first lick against the "prophets of suspicion." Kierkegaard's view of knowledge is fully in keeping with the tradition from Descartes to Hume: knowledge is that of which we can be certain. Well and good, but those morsels are so slight and abstract as to be of little existential use. As a result, we for the most part act on belief. This rather skeptical epistemology, which permits and requires us to believe most things, also endorses a tolerance toward others, for it is soon realized that we do not have to pass a veridical or moral judgment on everything or everybody, for the simple reason that we are not qualified to do so. This last, again, is rather like the skeptical ataraxia. To avoid the judgmental, we must find the mitigating explanation, the most charitable explanation, for what seems to be an unloving act. This permits us to understand our outrage over such terrible events as the Holocaust: there is no possible mitigating explanation.

How all the above issues in redoubling, metaphysics, and epistemology relate the divine command to the material world is addressed by Lee Barrett in his article, "The Neighbor's Material and Social Well-Being in Kierkegaard's *Works of Love*," the term "material well-being" being used in the broadest sense to include "physical health, economic flourishing, possession of legal rights, and access to political power." Contrasting one reading of *Works of Love* which urges that social improvement is unimportant with another that holds it is a duty to promote the neighbor's material well-being, Barrett argues that this tension in Kierkegaard's text and in the variety of the readings that follow from it is explicable if one pays attention to the several goals he attempts to achieve in the book, goals which Barrett spells out.

Mark Dooley does not find the diverse readings of *Works of Love* that puzzled Barrett. In his article, "The Politics of Exodus: Derrida, Kierkegaard, and Levinas on Hospitality," Dooley argues that there is a close relationship between works of love and a Derridean "politics of exodus which has as its most fundamental objective the diminution of social injustice and inequality." Though these positions are Levinasian in tone, Dooley interestingly argues that Levinas is "insufficiently cognizant of the ethical imperative to privilege the oppressed over the oppressor." Joining forces with John Caputo, Dooley argues, much to the chagrin of the secular neo-Nietzschean scholars, that there is a religious dimension of Derrida's work which, though rooted primarily in Levinas, bears a fundamental resemblance to Kierkegaard.

Jamie Ferreira and Louise Carroll Keeley argue against the position of an earlier European thinker whose critique of Kierkegaard amazingly continues to be influential. In his response to the ninth deliberation in the second series, "The Work of Love in Recollecting One Who Is Dead," Theodor Adorno argues that "one may most accurately summarize Kierkegaard's doctrine of love by saying that he demands that love behave toward all men as if they were dead." Neither Ferreira not Keeley think Adorno's characterization is accurate, and their very different explorations are attempts to determine how Adorno got it so nearly entirely wrong.

In her article, " Mutual Responsiveness in Relation: The Challenge of the Ninth Deliberation," Ferreira first attempts to understand how Kierkegaard's text opens itself up to Adorno's interpretation, and then responds to Adorno that though a certain kind of reciprocity is condemned by Kierkegaard, "he leaves room for and even requires significant dimensions of mutual responsiveness within relationship, without which responsibility for the other would be emptied of its meaning." She also shows the broader implications of what is brought into question for any who either affirm or challenge the presence of reciprocity in human relations. What Adorno missed were the dialectical structures and the nuanced qualifications of Kierkegaard's argument.

Keeley sees the ninth deliberation as "a summary, a test, and a task" and argues that in spite of the title it is about life and living out love's essential requirements, contra Adorno, whom she criticizes in detail in her article, "Loving 'No One,' Loving Everyone: The Work of Love in Recollecting the Dead in Kierkegaard's *Works of Love*." Then she suggests the importance of Kierkegaard's use of "recollection" in the title, stressing its difference from memory and tying the text to Plato and to other parts of Kierkegaard's own oeuvre, exegeting his view of this particular work of love as a summary of the whole of neighbor love as well as an example of it. These reflections enable her to examine love as the test in regard to self-deception and as the task of recollection, using the Holocaust as an example.

Michael Oppenheim furthers the ongoing dialogue between Kierkegaard and the Jewish community in his essay, "Four Narratives of the Interhuman: Kierkegaard, Buber, Rosenzweig, and Levinas." Oppenheim focuses three issues in each of the authors before generalizing his conclusion. First he examines how each author characterizes the "natural state" of relations between persons based on a detailed description of the individual in the thought of each. Next, he characterizes the God-relation as presented in each author. Finally, he examines the character of the transformed interhuman that follows in the wake of the God-relation. In his conclusion Oppenheim provides comparative assessments of the three authors on the social nature of the self, the types of alienation, the divine as a means of passage from this condition, and the importance of the metaphor of God as person in each of the narratives.

Eric Ziolkowski, in his essay "The Child and Kierkegaard's 'One Who Loves': The Agapic Flip Side of Peter Pan," surprises us with a fresh and original treatment of the child in Kierkegaard's thought, emphasizing both positive and negative qualities attributed to children. The view of the child in Kierkegaard's authorship varies according to the dialectical needs of the concepts being discussed. The notion of childhood as a distinctive stage in human life was a relatively new thought in Kierkegaard's time, and the texts, *Works of Love* as well as others, indicate that Kierkegaard was fully aware of the shift in the concept of the child. Ziolkowski's treatment is thoroughly ecumenical and historical, emphasizing Jesus, St. Paul, St. Augustine, and Rousseau before locating Kierkegaard and his pseudonyms in relation to that history. *Works of Love* expresses the same bipolar views of the child evident in the contrasts between Paul and Jesus. Between these two poles we come to understand the child as paradigmatic of the complexity of human nature. Kierkegaard never succumbs to the conventional and sentimental view of the mother-child relationship, which after William Golden's *Lord of the Flies* and William March's *The Bad Seed*, should be quite dead. If one is not convinced of the death of the sentimental view of the mother/child relation by the literary references, then one can scan the daily newspapers for reports of the mayhem that parents are daily visiting upon their children. Kierkegaard attempted to give the age of childhood its due, avoiding both sentimentality and cynicism, and restoring the child as a neighbor.

Begonya Sàez Tajafuerce interprets *Works of Love* through modern discourse theory. The central theme of her paper, "Rhetoric in *Works of Love* or 'No Sooner Said Than Done,' " is that Kierkegaard has combined conceptual clarification and edification in the text, and the combination is a major reason for its power. She draws attention to Kierkegaard's concern for the task of communication to help a "deaf audience" hear so each individual can be "carried over" into a new way of life, a concern he planned to develop in a series of lectures on communication. Planning for these lectures interrupted the writing of *Works of Love*, a circumstance that reinforces the usefulness of the rhetorical reading Tajafuerce develops.

Having drawn a rhetorical and philosophical contrast between Christian love and romantic love, Kierkegaard proceeded to argue that the former transforms but does not replace the latter, just as marriage changes but does not replace erotic love. Ronald M. Green and Theresa M. Ellis in their paper, "Erotic Love in the Religious Existence-Sphere," examine several features of erotic love and how these are transfigured by the commanded love of Christianity. They then review the expression of love in the existence spheres before presenting alternative interpretations of *Works of Love*.

*Works of Love* is indeed a deep and rich book, one that deserves to be widely read and reflected upon. However, the aim of Kierkegaard's labor is not to increase reflection, though that may itself be a work of love, but rather to increase the works of love directed to the flesh-and-blood neighbor, the walking-down-the-street variety of human being.

This volume of essays is offered to our readers, who by criticism and better thinking we invite to become our teachers.

*Robert L. Perkins*

# 1

## Love's Redoubling
## and the Eternal Like for Like

### Martin Andic

In his Conclusion to *Works of Love*, Kierkegaard asks his reader to remember *"the Christian like for like, eternity's like for like,"* adding that this is "such an important and decisive Christian specification" that he could wish to end with it at least one, if not every one, of his books developing what is essentially Christian (WL, 376). He is pointing out an idea of *justice* that marks what is fully Christian by contrast with what is Jewish, and thus is characteristic of New Testament rather than Old Testament religion. As he goes on to explain, Christianity is misrepresented as soft and mild and easy, not hard and severe and strenuous; for there is a rigor to it [*strenghed*, strictness, austerity]. It has indeed given up the temporal and Jewish like for like, by which you are to take an eye for an eye; but it has replaced this with an eternal one, whereby God judges or blesses you as you judge or bless others. The old exigency concerned your outward or worldly relation to the human, but the new one concerns your inward relation to the Divine. For now your every relation to others is finally and essentially a relation to God, who looks on you in your conscience leniently or rigorously, exactly as you look on others: in a way God looks on you with your own rigor, or with a rigor that is leniency if you acknowledge and obey God by practicing God's equal, unconditional love.

> The Jewish, the worldly, the bustling like for like is: as others do unto you, by all means take care that you also do likewise unto them. But the Christian like for like is: God will do unto you exactly as you do unto others. In the Christian sense, you have nothing at all to do with what others do unto you. . . . You have to do only with what you do unto others, or how you take what others do unto you. . . . essentially you have only to do with

yourself before God. This world of *inwardness . . . is actuality.* The
Christian like for like . . . will turn you away from externality
(but without taking you out of the world), will turn you upward
or inward. In the Christian sense, *to love people is to love God, and
to love God is to love people*—what you do unto people, you do
unto God, and therefore *what you do unto people, God does unto
you.* . . . God *is* actually himself this pure like for like, the pure
rendition of how you yourself are. If there is anger in you, then
God is anger in you; if there is leniency and mercifulness in you,
then God is mercifulness in you. . . . God's relation to a human
being is at every moment to infinitize what is in that human
being at every moment. (WL, 383-84; emphases added)

When Kierkegaard contrasts the Jewish like for like with the
Christian one as "Do unto others as they do unto you" with "God
does unto you as you do unto others," he is opposing not only
human justice to divine justice, but two conceptions of divine
justice to each other. For he considers that in the Old Testament
God surely fulfills our unsure human justice, and sees to it that we
will get the prosperity or misery that we deserve;[1] whereas the
God of the New Testament prospers or punishes us not merely
outwardly and materially and sooner or later through the events
of the world, but inwardly and ethically and here and now by our
own intentions in acting, so that doing wrong worsens and harms
us and doing right improves and benefits us. Thus the Christian
God does not merely condemn those whom we condemn when
they wrong us, or forgive those whom we forgive when they
admit guilt and remorse and offer us amends; God forgives or
condemns *us* when we forgive or condemn one another. God does
not merely repay good for good and evil for evil to those who
benefit or harm us, but repays it to us as we pay it to each other:
it is the same thing, because what God gives or denies us *is* the
mercy that we give or deny to human beings.

Kierkegaard ignores passages in the Old Testament that
suggest or anticipate the Christian category.[2] He is close to Socrates

---

[1]Jeremiah 16:17-18; 17:10; Deuteronomy 28:1-68; 30:15-20; Isaiah 3:10-11; 33:1;
65:6-7. JP, 2:1899, 2217-25, 3:3098.

[2]"Good and upright is the LORD, / therefore he instructs sinners in the way.
/ He leads the humble in what is right"—that is to say, he guides them with
meekness, who receive it from God and regard men not in their own proud way

and the Stoics, but probably relying directly on the Gospel and on Augustine.[3] He does not spell out how this Christian like for like follows from his premises that inwardness is actuality so that we have always only to do with ourselves before God, and that to love people is to love God and to love God is to love people, or even how these premises can be true together. For it is hard to see at first how human beings shall be real to us if only God is to be real to us, and if these are two different loves or one and the same. Moreover, to say that "God is actually himself this pure like for like" seems to subjectivize the God who is the maker of heaven and earth. And to characterize God as relentless to the relentless seems to contradict the notion that God is Love that is perfect and equal and changeless, and loves everyone, just and unjust, saint and sinner alike.

I mean to clarify the idea that Kierkegaard is emphasizing here by relating it to a category that he has explicitly presented and relied upon in the argument of *Works of Love*. He generally calls it "redoubling" [*Fordoblelse*], and gives it a use different from the concept of "reduplication" [*Reduplikation*], which is only part of it and should be distinguished carefully from it; the idea of "eternity's like for like" also proves to be only part of it and not the whole.

---

but in *God's* selfless way. "[L]et him who glories glory in this, . . . that I am the LORD who practice steadfast love, justice, and righteousness in the earth"—that is, in the love and justice towards human beings of those who acquire it from Me to impart it to others in and through whom I practice it. (Psalm 25:8 and Jeremiah 9:24 RSV; see also Psalms 18:20-30; 23:1-6; 86:5; Isaiah 30:18; 40:11; 29-31.)

[3]Matthew 5:25; 6:12-15; 7:1-5; 8:5-13; 18:25-35. Augustine, *Confessions* 1.12, 3.8; and more explicitly "As you have been [to others], so is He with you . . . a helper if you have been good, an avenger if you have been evil." "If you would acquire God's mercy, be merciful yourself. If you deny humanity to man, though you yourself are a man, God will also deny you divinity. . . . Have pity on man, O man, and God will have pity on you . . . how can [you] demand a pitying heart of Him, who never will be pitiable? . . . you do give what you have received from God and yet you wish God to give you what He has not received from you." In the standard collection by Erich Pryzwara, *An Augustine Synthesis* (New York: Sheed and Ward, 1936) 719, 839. Kierkegaard read Shakespeare in Danish and German and may also have noted the passage about "twice blest" mercy in *The Merchant of Venice* 4.1.184-202; cf. *Measure for Measure* 2.2.75-79; *Henry V* 2.2.79-83. For his thorough knowledge and admiration of Augustine and Shakespeare, see Gregor Malantschuk's notes in JP, 1, p. 504 and 4, pp. 650-53.

The category belongs to religious metaphysics, or more exactly to religious psychology because it concerns not God as such but in relation to us; it belongs to dialectic too insofar as it describes communication. Kierkegaard mentions it mostly in the middle and later works, and I will propose that it focuses and replaces another puzzling category that has received more attention from scholars, namely, "repetition" (*Gjentagelsen*). Once this idea of redoubling has been fully stated, we can understand why he thinks that the Christian like-for-like is implied by the thought that inwardness is actuality and that the two loves are paired, and how this preserves the objectivity of God and neighbor and preserves the equality of divine love.

The structure of my discussion is as follows. First, I will show that Kierkegaard's uses of the phrase "like for like" elsewhere in the book indicate that he understands the divine like for like to be an element of redoubling, along with inwardness and reduplication; and that reduplication has for him a special meaning narrower than that of redoubling. Second, I will examine the "dialectical" redoubling and reduplication involved in the communication that is part of all redoubling, and note how this coinstantiation makes them extensionally the same and indiscernible, and how nevertheless even if they are thus one in being they are different in definition.[4] Third, I will explain how the redoubling of a human being, though it has an active element in inwardness, involves a passivity to the redoubling of God, and that it is God who actively redoubles us; Kierkegaard says emphatically that God is not only infinite redoubling but infinite subjectivity, and I will try to clarify this crucial idea. Fourth, I will explain the redoubling of human beings and spell out how the eternal like for like is implied in the understanding of inwardness as reality and of the unity of the love of God and the love of people. I will show that Kierkegaard is not committed to religious and ethical solipsism, nor to any "immanence" or anthropomorphism or subjectivism that reduces divine love to human love, or divine reality to its appearance to us, nor is he committed to the notion that divine mercy and grace are earned by the inward person who loves his or her neighbor. And

---

[4]Aristotle, *Physics* 3.3.202b19; *Psychology* 3.2.425b27.

I will briefly discuss the link between repetition and redoubling. Fifth and finally, I will consider whether God's "reversed echo" amounts to a dialectical reduplication in God or whether, as I suggest, Kierkegaard always understands reduplication to be for human beings to practice while redoubling is the act of God.

### Three Elements of Redoubling: Inwardness, Reduplication, and the Like for Like

For Kierkegaard the eternal like for like is a higher rigor or gravity than ours, whereby God regards us exactly as we regard one another. God is accusing when we are accusing and loving when we are loving, though infinitely more so because divine judgment is immeasurably more accurate and complete, and divine love boundlessly more fulfilling and sustaining and its loss immeasurably more devastating. The exactness, like the infinity, is not so much quantitative as qualitative. It is a second-order rigor about our rigor or mercy, in the sense that God is rigorously all mercy when we are merciful with others, and all rigor when we are rigorous with them.

There is thus a doubleness or ambiguity to it: a reversal and a unity of opposites whereby God's justice is mercy for those who let it move them and have the mercy that they give to others, just as gravity is lightness for those who lets it swing them in God's course.[5] This ambiguity is related to the "double mark" in everything decisively Christian, of which Kierkegaard reminds his reader at the end of Part One, namely that one collides thereby both inwardly with one's own natural inclination and outwardly with the disapproval of others: "the essentially Christian is always exactly the opposite of what the natural man most easily and

---

[5]The *glory* of the LORD (*kabod Yahweh*) that is divine presence, as in Ezekiel 1:28, is literally the *weight* or gravity of God; it is a burden of responsibility that Christ makes easy and light: Matthew 11:29-30. Thus Kierkegaard writes that conscience involves us in "the infinite weight of God" (WL, 143), but allows "soaring up to Heaven" (WL, 174), for "to hope is to make oneself light with the help of the eternal" (WL, 250); "The heavenly body soars lightly in the infinite— [because of its] gravity. But if it gets off its course, if it becomes much too light, then the lightness becomes heaviness, and it falls heavily—[because of its] lightness" (WL, 377).

naturally understands" (WL, 336).[6] It is natural to return good for good and evil for evil, like for like: good to friends who do us good, evil to enemies who do us harm. It is divine to return good for evil and love our enemies, to give and forgive, bear and forbear.[7]

Kierkegaard uses the phrase "like for like" in several other passages in his book, on love as a *debt*, as *building up*, as *hoping* all things, and as *selfless*. Thus he argues that (1) the more I love, the less [it is to me that] I give and the more [it is to me that] I receive and owe, so that love makes the giver feel the infinite smallness of the gift or service and the receiver its infinite greatness: "What marvelous like for like in this infinitude!" (WL, 181-82). Again, (2) the more I forgive and presuppose love in another person, the more I build up love and the more the other loves, so that as I believe in the other so the other comes to be: "there is no other relationship in which there is such a like for like, in which the result so accurately corresponds to what was presupposed" (WL, 219). And (3) the more I hope for another that he or she will love truly, the more I hope for myself that I will, and thus as I have and give or give up hope for another, so I have or lose hope for myself: "this is the infinitely accurate, the eternal like for like that is in everything eternal. Oh, wherever love is present, there is something infinitely profound!" (WL, 255). Finally, (4) love does *not* seek a return or know "how to watch out whether like is now given for like," but then "the wondrous thing occurs that is heaven's blessing on self-denying love . . . all things become his,

---

[6]WL, 191-204. Note the strong verbal parallel of WL, 191 and 376: in both passages he mentions "just one more thing," an important and decisive one, to remember at the end of this discourse lest there be a fundamental misunderstanding. (Cf. Plato, *Euthyphro* 13a, *Protagoras* 328e, 329b.) For Christianity's" inverse" use of human language, see JP, 3:2333, 3102, 4:4680, 4696.

[7]Similarly Socrates in Plato's *Crito* 49ad, *Gorgias* 469bc, 472e, *Republic* 1.331e-336ba, 2:368b, 366c, 6:500b-501b, 10:613ab. Cf. Isaiah 55:6-11; Matthew 5:38-45. Socrates would agree that it is also natural or human-all-too-human to *say* that it is always better to do right, in opportunistic hypocrisy, while despising as a fool or lunatic someone who does it even when one can do wrong to one's profit without others knowing and punishing, or can do it to save oneself from being wronged: *Republic* 1:344c, 2:360d, and generally 358c-62c.

his who had no *mine* at all" (WL, 269, 268), and thus the more I give away in love, the more I acquire.

The thought implied in such passages is unfolded further on in a discussion of love's *hiding many sins*, where Kierkegaard emphasizes love's double presence in the lover: outwardly in what one is to others and inwardly in what it is to oneself, so that "by giving one acquires and receives just the same as one gives" (WL, 282). He calls this double presence, love's "redoubling" (*Fordoblelse*), whereby love does to the lover what the lover does to others, for example, gives confidence and saves from death. Thus in speaking of love as a debt, he expressly says that like spirit "love is a redoubling in itself" (WL, 182). He seems to mean by this that because love is belonging and giving and owing ourselves, it has only what it gives, keeping nothing back but the debt that it continually acquires as it continually loves. Thus it is doubly present in the lover, or is to us what we are to others, like for like.[8]

Again, in the chapter on love's *conscience*, he says that there is a redoubling in its confidence: lovers confide themselves completely to one another (as in a ceremony of marriage) only if each has first confided himself or herself to God, thus making their love for each other "a matter of conscience," grounded in one's relation first to God and then to the other as a human equal before God.[9] For to confide yourself to another is to give yourself and belong to the other, to have nothing but what is now the other's, and to have it only as received from the one to whom you owe everything in acquiring the self that emerges through this love: how much more

---

[8]WL, 280-82; 1 John 4:17-18; James 5:20. *Fordoblelse* was rendered as "reduplication" in the Swensons' translation (1946) and in the Hongs' first one (1962); but this is wrong, as I will explain. It is rightly given as "redoubling" in the Hongs' second translation (1995), followed here.

[9]WL, 137-38, 151-53. Cf. 175-91: true and earnest love has all and only the love that it owes and gives, and owes it not only to human beings but still more to God, who *is* love: God is your guardian who has bound you to others and can alone truly judge your love for them; only by acknowledging God as such a guardian and creditor and judge can you abide in God, and only so can God in turn abide in you (WL, 190). 1 John 4:16.

do you owe everything to this love itself, and to the God who personifies it and gives it to you.[10]

For Christian love, which is to Kierkegaard the only true, fully earnest love, the other is your *neighbor* first, and only then your spouse, a neighbor whom you *shall* love as yourself. He remarks that "the concept of neighbor is actually a redoubling of your own self," and that "the commandment's *as yourself* is a redoubling" (WL, 21). He means that to see another human being as your neighbor is to address yourself to him or her as to someone who is truly, in the sight of God, exactly what you are: the *spirit* that each person in his or her own way can become before God in conscience, and this is the true self in each that is the other and double of the natural one, the *you* addressed eternally by God.[11] It is this that you shall love in each human being, and in yourself, because you love God above all, in relationship with whom each becomes what he or she truly is.

Kierkegaard is relying on the ideas of redoubling and like for like, without mentioning them explicitly, when he argues that the lover *believes all things* and so is never deceived, sc. out of the highest good, which is to love and believe in everyone, even the person who would deceive one into loving without return. There is at first sight a tangle in the reasoning, in that Kierkegaard quotes the words of Matthew 7:1, (a) "Judge not, lest you be judged in return," and adds that (b) to judge another is only to judge yourself; although he has just said that (c) to live is to judge and be judged (by "existence"), it is to choose to believe others to be loving and trustful or otherwise, and (d) you must not try to "sneak out of disclosing yourself in judging or in the way you judge" others (WL, 233, 227-28). It looks as if judging others is at once (a') *wrong* and risky, (b') *impossible*, (c') *inevitable*, and (d') ethically *necessary* and *right*. The resolution is surely this: (a") Do not judge others unlovingly, lest you reveal your own lack of love (and so bring down the eternal like for like). For (b") the true

---

[10]WL, 12, 107-108, 265-67. Cf. LD, 63, 82; CI, 30; EO, 1:49, 73, 401-402, 406. 1 John 4:19.

[11]WL, 56-58, 86-90, 138. Cf. "you must not call one a nobody to whom the king has spoken." George MacDonald, *The Princess and Curdie* (New York: Puffin Books, 1966) 62.

meaning of what you say and do is in the love or lack of love that
it reveals in you. (c″) To live is lovingly or otherwise to judge
human beings to be in good faith or not, and so it is willy-nilly to
reveal yourself to be loving and in good faith or not. But (d″) truly
to live as a human being among human beings is to submit yourself to God, to understand yourself in the judging that you *must* do
as choosing in God's presence what you shall be towards them,
and not pretend to yourself that your judging is merely a direct
and conclusive inference from what they outwardly do and say.
There is a redoubling here in that, because you judge and reveal
yourself by the way you judge others, you therefore have love, the
highest good, only as you presuppose that they too have it fundamentally. It is a like for like, in that "existence" or God judges you
loving or otherwise as you judge others so.

Putting all these passages together, we can relate the *self understanding* just mentioned, that you are before God and judged by
the measure you apply to others (WL, 233), to the *inwardness* that
is reality in the eternal like for like (WL, 384), and the *relationship
to God* in the confidence of conscientious love (WL, 151-53), in fully
earnest love as a debt (WL, 181-82), and in true love of self and
neighbor (WL, 21, 56-58, 86-90, 138). They variously present the
first of the three elements we can see in love's redoubling, as presented in the text from the chapter on love's hiding many sins
(WL, 280-82).[12] To focus this more sharply, let us look again at that
text.

If "the eternal is *in* a human being" (WL, 280), so that you
recognize its presence and relate yourself to it,[13] it is present (says
Kierkegaard) as one and the same thing both *out*wardly in what it
is through you to others (when it "goes beyond itself") and
*in*wardly in what it is in you by whom it acts (when it "turns back
into itself") so that, in other words, what *you* outwardly do to
others *it* inwardly does to you, and the other way. For example
"many sins are forgiven one who loved much—because the love
in him hides a multitude of sins" (WL, 282), which means both

---

[12]The first element is the presence of the eternal in you, the second is its
outward presence in what you are to others, and the third is its inward presence
in what it is to you.

[13]WL, 26-27, 143, 258, 280-82.

that you *receive* God's forgiveness when you forgive others (the "like for like") and also that you *give* to others what you receive from God (thus realizing it or proving its reality for you). Kierkegaard goes on here to emphasize the outward movement, by contrast with the inward one, because he says that he is dealing in this book more with the *works* of love than with love itself, with *human* love rather than divine. But as it is one and the same love that is present in these two different ways, it is really *God's* love that you both communicate to others and acquire for yourself.[14] It is human love only by appropriation, and by an active pathos in which you surrender yourself to it and so fulfill and deepen your inward relationship to God, who *is* this love.[15]

If we think of the eternal's presence as "inwardness" and "subjectivity," and its inward movement as "the like for like," then we can regard its outward movement as "reduplication" understood as making (religious and ethical) truth recognizable to people in your existence, or realizing it *out*wardly in what you are for others, and thus communicating it. It is manifestly being what you believe, or so existing in it that it is visible in how you act and live.[16]

----

[14]WL, 280-82; Luke 7:47; 1 Peter 4:8. Love's *in*coming movement is emphasized in the first of the *Two Discourses for the Communion on Fridays*, in *For Self-Examination*, trans. Walter Lowrie (London: Oxford University Press, 1941) 9-16: "When you love much, much is forgiven you—and when much is forgiven you, you love much. Behold here the blessed law of the progressive recurrence of salvation in love. First you love much, and much is forgiven you—oh, but see how love exerts its influence more powerfully, the fact that so much was forgiven elicits in turn more love, and you love much because much was forgiven you" (FSE, 15-16). See also the third chapter of the third section of *Upbuilding Discourses in Various Spirits*, in *The Gospel of Suffering*, trans. David Swenson and Lillian Swenson (Minneapolis: Augsburg, 1948): "the meek who humbly knows how heaven's forgiveness of himself depends on his forgiveness, really *needs* to forgive his enemy" (GS, 40).

"But in this little work we are continually dealing only with the works of love, and therefore not with God's love but with human love" (WL, 301); "with the works of love; therefore we are considering love in its outgoing movement" (WL, 282); "these are *Christian deliberations*, therefore not about [God's] *love* but about [our] *works of love*" (WL, 3).

[15]As we shall see, it is God who is agent, and God who redoubles us: we are redoubled by letting the Eternal redouble itself in us, and through us in others.

[16]CUP, 1:192. PC, 134, 123; JP, 1:484, 656, 6:6224.

Reduplication is one of Kierkegaard's favorite ideas,[17] and he shows tireless ingenuity in devising ways to formulate it. In the *Journal* he speaks, for example, of realizing the truth and fulfilling it, expressing it existentially and being its visible demonstration;[18] translating it into existence, bringing it into the world, proclaiming it with your life, acting to create the situation in which its visible actuality in you can awaken it in others;[19] it is being what you say, existing in it as food for others so that it occasions them to exist in it also;[20] making it present and contemporary;[21] communicating it by being the guarantee and only proof possible and necessary of its truth;[22] being its verification and testimony and witness;[23] showing your integrity and truth to it, your earnestness and honesty of ideality, and your right or authority to speak for it;[24] venturing your life for it, knotting the thread so that the stitch holds, and thus stepping out in character with what you say;[25] it is speaking personally and with existential transparency and primitivity;[26] and so on. He uses the idea, though not the word *Reduplikation*, in *Works of Love*, as when he speaks of obeying God, accomplishing the truth, expressing it, witnessing to it, and proclaiming it.[27] Nevertheless (as I will show in the next section) it is natural to identify reduplication with redoubling, as so many translators and scholars have done, because the one is a part of the other. The person redoubled in and by the truth will reduplicate it; existing

---

[17]He draws it mainly from Socrates and Diogenes and the Stoics, but also from the Bible. See, e.g., Plato, *Laches* 188c-189b; cf. Euripides, *Hecuba* 1186-89; Diogenes Laertius, *Life of Diogenes* 6.27-28; Epictetus 2.19, 3.21-22; *Manual* 46, 52. Matthew 7:5; 1 Timothy 4:15-16; cf. 2 Samuel 12:1-7.

[18]JP, 1:649-10, 4:4275, 4573; 3:3674; 1:484, 3:3479, 3666, 3669, 3685; 4:4966.

[19]JP, 3:3685, 3686, 3748, 3764; 1:649.27ff., 653.17, 656, 978, 3.3141, 4:4275, 4278.

[20]JP, 6:6224; 1:482, 4:4183, 1:656.

[21]JP, 1:761, 973; 3:2377, 3473.

[22]JP, 1, 484, 656; 3:3519, 4:4559; 3:3580. 3608, 4:4900.

[23]JP, 1:890, 3:3673; 4:3913; 2:1957, 4:4967.

[24]JP, 1:251, 4:4380, 3:3668; 1:379, 2:1853, 1812; 1:183, 2:1258: 4:3837.

[25]JP, 1:73, 2:3774, 4:4933; 3:3540, 3689; 3:3057, 3166, 3694, 4:4056, 4194, 4881, 4900.

[26]JP, 1:656, 3:3219, 3223-29, 4:4056; 1:995, 3:3105, 3228, 4561; 1:84, 3:2978, 3560-61.

[27]WL, 19-20, 46, 117, 196, 366.

in it, one will exist in it for other people, or communicate it so that they may exist in it too.

## *Dialectical Redoubling*

Let us turn our attention to the first element in redoubling, variously expressed as inwardness or subjectivity, relating oneself to God in conscience, and confiding oneself to God. Kierkegaard sometimes speaks of redoubling in other works as if it consisted fundamentally in this, in becoming *spirit*, in other words, becoming yourself, by humanly speaking working against yourself (CD, 43). Thus in *Christian Discourses* he writes that the bird of the air is simply what it is and does not attain the redoubling of the humble Christian who is not only what is he is before other people but also and first of all what he is before God.[28] The pseudonyms treat redoubling in a similar way. Anti-Climacus remarks that "a self is a redoubling, it is freedom," so that Christ draws one freely to one's own self, and then to himself (PC, 159); while in *Philosophical Fragments* Climacus says that (human) existence is said to contain "a redoubling [*Fordobling*], that is, a possibility of a second coming into existence within its own coming into existence," sc. coming before God, indeed becoming or acknowledging that one is a sinner.[29] Let us remember that in *The Concept of Anxiety*, Vigilius emphasizes that a human being is or is meant to become spirit, a synthesis of soul and body in which each element exists doubly, as temporal and as eternal, so that one comes to exist at once in time and in eternity (CA, 43, 85). But this has to be accomplished by God, as Anti-Climacus indicates in *The Sickness Unto Death*:

> A human being is spirit. But what is spirit? Spirit is the self. But what is the self? The self is a relation that relates itself to itself, or is the relation's relating itself to itself in the relation. . . . If the relation . . . has been established by another, then the relation indeed is the third [term], but this . . . is yet again a relation and relates itself to that which established the entire relation . . . in relating itself to itself and in willing to be itself, the spirit rests transparently in the power that established it. . . .

---

[28]CD, trans. Walter Lowrie (1940) 43.
[29]PF, 76; CUP, 1:584; cf. 267, 379, 573.

This formula in turn . . . is the definition of faith. (SUD, 13-14, 131)

That is to say, to become oneself is to become spirit, relating to oneself subjectively all that one temporally is, but to oneself as spirit transparently related to God by God who *is* relationship. Kierkegaard would therefore say that it is not oneself that redoubles a human being but God; or rather it is the Divine that redoubles itself in someone who consents that it be done in one and thus becomes nothing but this consent. This spirit or deeper self that one is to become is the other and doubling of one's natural self, the *you* whom the Divine has called into being and to whom it for ever speaks. It is the image of the Divine in one, the possibility of relationship with it and through it with every other human being as one's neighbor and equal before it. In the idiom of the chapter on love's upbuilding, spirit is the fundamental presence in someone of the love that one is to acquire by giving it to others as received from Love itself (WL, 215-19).[30]

To become spirit is to deny self and affirm God.[31] As Kierkegaard writes in *Attack upon Christendom*, a spiritual person must "endure a redoubling in himself" by willing what humanly offends and pains one; for one collides both with one's own natural inclination and with the mockery and contempt of people. (KAUC, 162; cf. WL, 192, 194.) And in *Judge For Yourself!* he says that "everything essentially Christian is a redoubling [*Fordoblelse*] or . . . is first of all its opposite": the Spirit gives life by killing or teaching us to die away from all that we usually live for; it exalts by humbling, inspires by sobering. God's ways are not man's ways, and divine truth is the reverse of human truth, only "inversely recognizable" with the ears and eyes of faith: with God subtracting (distance) is adding, demanding is giving (grace), and afflicting is loving.[32]

It follows that a spiritual person in expressing the life of spirit—declaring or communicating it, for example by speaking out

---

[30]For the failure of all attempts at self-redoubling without God, see JP, 1:188, 2:1793, 3.3660; SUD, 67-74.
[31]More precisely, it is to let God do this, let God turn one to nothing but an instrument of the divine will: JP, 2:2098-99, cf. WL, 86, 279, 360-65, cf. 209-10.
[32]JFY, 98. JP, 2:1425. 1432, 3:3664, 3102, 4:4680, 4690, 4696.

and writing about it—must "work against oneself," humanly speaking, by commending what people disapprove and not commending oneself for serving the truth in doing so. Thus Kierkegaard remarks in the chapter on love's praise that while Socrates was the ugliest man of all and could therefore praise love of the beautiful without fear of seeming to speak out of love of self, the Christian for his part must praise love for what is humanly ugly, the neighbor, as opposed to the friend or romantic lover (so that one praises the love that people find unnatural and uninviting, by contrast with the love to which they feel naturally drawn); and thus one seems to love oneself because one will not let people love themselves (WL, 371-74). In *The Point of View* Kierkegaard calls this a "dialectical redoubling" that "acts to counteract one's action—a redoubling that is seriousness, like the pressure on the plough"—implied in the "dialectical reduplication" of authorship, whereby one reflects the truth not just in one's actions fulfilling it but in one's way of presenting it, or what one has to say in how one says it (PV, 147n, cf. 16). More carefully, if *reduplication* is making truth audible in one's own actions and life whether or not they are listening, *dialectical reduplication* is making it audible in one's words (or silence!) by so awakening subjectivity in others (perhaps by irony making truth *in*audible) that they will listen and hear it and appropriate it in their own actions and life: it is typically verbal, and amounts for Kierkegaard to indirect communication. Likewise his pseudonym Anti-Climacus mentions a dialectical redoubling that one must use temporarily and "maieutically in order to avoid becoming [for the other] an object of faith" (PC, 142, cf. JP, 1:649-22, 653-24, 662).

One could then be excused for thinking that redoubling and re- duplication amount to the same, in that such dialectical redoubling seem to amount to the dialectical reduplication of reflecting what you mean to say in how you say it, namely, that the life of spirit must be freely chosen by each as a single individual. Thus Gregor Malantschuk seems to run together the two dialectical forms as "double reflection."[33] But let us consider what Anti-Climacus actually says in the first of the passages Malantschuk cites:

> Indirect communication can be an art of communication in redoubling the communication; the art consists in making oneself, the communicator, into a nobody, purely objective, and then continually placing the qualitative opposites in a unity. This is . . . the double reflection of the communication. For example, it is indirect communication to place jest and earnest together in such a way that the composite is a dialectical knot—and then to be a nobody oneself. If anyone wants to have anything to do with this communication, he will have to untie the knot himself. Or, to bring attack and defense into a unity in such a way that no one can directly say whether one is attacking or defending. (PC, 133)

This passage, however, is concerned not with *double reflection* as such but with *double reflection in communication*; the two are contrasted by Climacus in the *Postscript* as, first, the subjective thinker's thinking of oneself and one's own relation to the truth that one thinks, and, second, one's indirect communication of it to another:

> Whereas objective thinking is indifferent to the thinking subject and his existence, the subjective thinker as existing is essentially interested in his own thinking, is existing in it. . . .
> The reflection of inwardness is the subjective thinker's double-reflection. In thinking, he thinks the universal, but, as existing in this thinking, as acquiring this in his inwardness, he becomes more and more subjectively isolated.
> The difference between subjective and objective thinking must also manifest itself in the form of communication. . . .
> Just as the subjective existing thinker has set himself free by the duplexity, so the secret of communication specifically hinges on setting the other free, and for that very reason he must not communicate himself directly. (CUP, 1:72-74)

That is to say, if by double reflection one reflects on one's relation to what one reflects, so that *one* becomes it or makes it one's own (one realizes it inwardly and not just in outward actions), in double reflection in communication one reflects on its relation to how one says it to another (one realizes it outwardly

---

[33]See his notes in JP, 3, pp. 908-11, citing PC, 133 and JP, 3:3665; and his "Begrebet Fordoblelse hos Soren Kierkegaard," *Kierkegaardiana* 2 (1957) 42-53. See further n. 37 below.

and not just in thoughts about it), so that *the other* will become it and make it his or her own.[34] In the first case, one is concerned with oneself and one doubles one's reflection (redoubles it dialectically) in what one *is* oneself; in the second, one is concerned with others and one doubles one's reflection (reduplicates it dialectically) in how one *presents* it to them, sc. indirectly, since the truth that one presents is not an object but a life, not a result but a way, and cannot be received except by those who actively choose it and so acquire it for themselves. Such indirection means working against oneself so that they may make this choice freely and so stand alone—by one's help; or one may have to pretend to share their illusions in order to lead them to see the invalidity of these illusions for themselves and to choose the truth, in this sense deceiving them into it.[35]

Insofar as becoming spirit entails witnessing or otherwise presenting to human beings the conception of life as spirit, and loving implies building up love in others, and having means sharing,[36] redoubling includes reduplication or making the truth recognizable in one's existence, which is to say exemplifying it in what one is for others, in other words, communication. Consequently the double reflection in redoubling will always include a double reflection in communication, or dialectical reduplication, and it will be difficult at first to see any difference between them.[37]

We can distinguish them, nevertheless by saying that *dialectical redoubling* (or *double reflection* as such) means so understanding

---

[34]See generally CUP, 1:74-80, and 169, 192-20, 254-55; CA, 142-143; WL, 360-62; TDIC, 5, 74, 93-94. JP, 3:3668, 3672, 3686, 3107 citing Pascal, "Few speak humbly or humility, chastely of chastity, dubiously of skepticism." *Pensées*, trans. A. J. Krailsheimer (Baltimore: Penguin Books, 1966) #655. Cf. #928: "It is better not to fast and be humiliated by it than to fast and be self-satisfied . . . since the way a thing is done matters as much as doing it, and perhaps more so, since God can bring good out of evil, and without God we bring evil out of good."
[35]On dialectical reduplication see PC, 133. On truth as a way see PC, 202-209; CUP, 1:78, 379-80. On indirection see WL, 274-79, 365-74; PV, 27-41.
[36]JP, 1:81, 656, 2:1901, 4:4862; WL, 189-90, 212-13, 223; CD, 121.
[37]So it is in JP, 3:3665 where, because Kierkegaard is speaking of *authorship*, he seems to say that "to redouble the thought dialectically in existence" = a reduplication of one's thinking in "the dialectic raised to the second power" = "reduplication of such thinking [that] is action in life."

yourself in the truth that you understand, that this is reflected or approximated in what you are; whereas *dialectical reduplication* (or *double reflection in communication*) means so understanding yourself in the truth that you communicate, that this is reflected or approximated in the way that you communicate it. The one entails the other, because becoming spirit entails becoming spirit to or for others and helping them to become spirit. To that extent Malant-schuk is right to treat them as coming to the same in actuality; but they are distinct in definition.

Thus when Kierkegaard writes that living what you teach because you are convinced that it is true is a redoubling of your conviction but not authority to command the conviction of others (OAR, 110-11), he means that there is dialectical redoubling but not dialectical reduplication, because while you mean to communicate the truth, your concern is *your* appropriation of the truth. But when his pseudonym Anti-Climacus argues that truth is a redoubling of being not merely in thought but in life that strives to attain it and expresses it approximately and only so comes to know and explain it (PC, 205), it is both: for your concern is to explain the truth by fulfilling it so that *others* will appropriate it. Love's confidence (WL, 151-53) is both, at least when one lover confides himself or herself to another.

But what about confiding oneself to God? When Kierkegaard remarks (JP, 3:3667) that few "religious authors" reduplicate their thought, or speak to others with the understanding that "God also hears it" (thus understanding oneself in what one says about the Divine, as speaking to the same one that one speaks about), there is no question of helping God to appropriate or understand or be-lieve; nevertheless it is dialectical reduplication, because you mean not only to *be* what you say, but to *be understood* as saying what you yourself are. And what about God's confiding to us, in our conscience and in his resounding, infinitely magnified echo of what we say to and of others in mercy or condemnation (WL, 384-85)? Is this a dialectical reduplication in God? Because this question requires the completion of my analysis, I will defer discussion of it until the close of my essay.[38]

## Divine Redoubling

Returning to simple redoubling, we can summarize our discussion to this point as follows. Human redoubling consists in dying to self and the world, in order to become spirit and like to God: it is truly and fully acquiring human identity and individuality. It is at once activity and passivity. The activity is variously described by Kierkegaard as turning inward to God in subjectivity, coming before and confiding yourself to God, submitting yourself to judgment, acquiring a conscience (an understanding) with God, relating yourself to the eternal in true self-concern, earnestness, transparency. The passivity consists in allowing the divine will to be done in and through you, so that you hand on to others what you receive from God, and receive from God what you give to them, like for like. Divine redoubling, on the other hand, involves both divine love's fundamental presence in you but also, when and so far as you choose, its realization at once outwardly in what you do to others and inwardly in what it does to you, in a way that transcends and looks opposite to all human, sc. nonreligious thinking. All that you actually do is to make this choice to become subjective or turn inward to the Eternal to be transformed for its use. It takes only, but this is everything, a confidence that it will do the rest or enable you to. You must reduplicate, or be to others what you understand it to be to you—giving and forgiving, bearing and forbearing—but you are simply to let this happen, since it is the Eternal that redoubles in you. In fact even this consent is not quite your own to you, as you are before giving it, since it can scarcely be the work of your own raw sensual selfish self.[39]

---

[38]Redoubling tends to be dialectical in Kierkegaard's pseudonymous works, simple in the direct ones. But there are exceptions, e.g., at PC, 159; PV, 16-17, 147n., as well as PF, 76; BA, 179-80 just cited.

[39]EO, 2:215; CD, 67; JP, 2:2257, 3:3369, 3394, 4:4551, 6:6969. Psalms 119:36; 1 Corinthians 15:10; 2 Corinthians 3:5.

We can clarify the way the eternal "redoubles itself in" someone[40] by reference to this striking journal entry:

God is infinite subjectivity.

He has not an element of objectivity in his being, . . . but he relates objectively to his own subjectivity, but this again is simply a redoubling of his subjectivity, for in his being subjective there is no imperfection at all that should be taken away, nor is there anything lacking that should be added, as is the case with human subjectivity. . . .

God is infinite redoubling, which, of course, no man can be; he [sc. man] can neither completely transcend himself in such a way that he relates perfectly objectively to himself, nor can he become subjective in such a way that he can bring to full consummation what he in his objective transcendence has understood about himself; he cannot look at himself with unconditioned and perfect objectivity; even if he could, he still cannot unconditionally achieve subjective reproduction of this view of himself. (JP, 4: 4571)

That is to say, the Divine is "infinitely subjective" in that it is pure of objectivity, or has no "finite" worldly objectives or intentions to accomplish, nothing to do, for which it needs human beings.[41] It is nothing but love that loves nothing but love ("God is infinite subjectivity . . . [and] has not an element of objectivity in his being"); and when the Divine knows itself, that it seeks not its own finitely (God "relates perfectly objectively to himself," the Divine as it were treating itself as an other), it finds and enjoys its own infinitely ("brings it to full consummation" so that "this again is simply a redoubling of [God's] own subjectivity"). No human being is thus pure of self, so that one knows oneself to be nothing but God's living likeness; and so no human being is the "purely

---

[40]WL, 280. Love establishes itself in someone to form one's heart (WL, 12); Sylvia Walsh, "Forming the Heart," in *The Grammar of the Heart*, ed. Richard Bell (New York: Harper & Row, 1988) 234-56.

[41]JP, 4:4571, 1:251, 2:1431. Cf. Eckhart "God seeks not His own: He is perfectly free in His acts, which He does out of true love," "God acts without why and has no why," *German Sermons*, 3 vols., trans. Maurice Walsh (London: Watkins, 1979–1987) 1:56-57, 2:2; William Law, "Love is quite pure; it has no by ends; it seeks not its own; it has but one will, and that is, to give itself into everything, and overcome all evil with good," *The Spirit of Prayer and the Spirit of Love*, ed. Sidney Spencer (London: James Clarke, 1969) 125.

transparent subjectivity" that God is (JP, 2:1449), no one has "sheer purified subjectivity or pure transparency in willing solely what God wills, so that there is no residue of [one's] original [finite] subjectivity." (JP, 3:4384)

There is a similar thought in *Works of Love*, the chapter on love's selflessness and freedom, "Love Does Not Seek Its Own":

> But [God] who created man in his image so that [man] might be like him, might become perfect as he is perfect, and thus attain the perfection that is God's own, be like the image that is God's own—does he not seek his own? Indeed, he seeks his own, which is love; he seeks it by giving all things. . . . Love is a giving of oneself; that it seeks love is again love and is the highest love. . . . To be able to seek love and oneself to become the object of love, yet without seeking one's own, is reserved for God alone. But no human being *is love*. Therefore, if a human being seeks to become the object of another human being's love, he is deliberately and fraudulently seeking his own, inasmuch as the only true object of a human being's love is *love*, which is God, which therefore in a more profound sense is not any object, since he is Love itself. (WL, 264-65)

In other words, Divine Love alone loves itself in loving others (making them truly loving by helping them to love it); perfect love in human beings is to love not ourselves but God in loving one another (making one another truly loving by helping one another to love Love). But—to return to the *Journal* passage—we all too humanly misunderstand ourselves in this love and so do not find ourselves, as it were, in losing ourselves to love others in God.

The Divine *is* infinitely and eternally what we are called to be and are when and so far as we allow it to be present in us, namely a redoubled selfless love that loves nothing but love. To follow, imitate, and obey God is to unite ourselves to and appropriate this selfless love, to purify ourselves and become transparent to it, letting it flow in and through us to the world.

### Human Redoubling

We can now see why Kierkegaard writes that divine love has a *double* presence in human beings, and why he treats *the eternal like for like* as a conclusion from the premises that *inwardness is actuality,* and that *the love of human beings implies the love of God and is implied by it.*

First, when Kierkegaard says that *inwardness is actuality,* he means that you have no concern with what others do to you but only with what you do to them, or how they receive what they do to you, and thus only with yourself before God: for us, that *is* actuality. This is not ethical solipsism, the view that only you exist, in your relation to the Divine, or even that to you the Divine, or your relation to it, is the only actuality, so that other human beings, or your relations to them, are not actuality. Rather, Kierkegaard is declaring the primacy of the ethical and religious. It is the connection with the Divine that counts first in human existence and relationships, and shall transform them so that you exist for others on the basis of equality before it. Inwardness is actuality, then, in the sense that to turn in toward the Eternal to be centered on it, and related to it first of all, is authentic human existence; it is true individuality and selfhood as spirit in relation to each and every other human being as spirit. It is subjectively and conscientiously understanding the Divine as Source and Judge, and yourself as addressed by it about yourself in all that you hear, and receiving from it all that you receive, but also as doing and saying in its presence and to it all that you say, to be measured by your own actions and words. And so the eternal like for like is "at home" in this new world of inwardness: for it is, or is involved in, what you understand in being turned in toward the Eternal.

Second, turning to the Eternal is turning *with* it to human beings, and turning to them is turning *with* them to it: in other words, *loving people is loving God, and loving God is loving people.* Kierkegaard emphasizes this thought all through his book, beginning with the first chapter on "Love's Hidden Life and Its Recognizability by Its Fruits": the words refer to this grounding of human love in the love of God, and its expression in works of love toward people, grounded (that is to say) in an inward conscientious understanding with the Divine; but the point is not simply that we shall love the Divine first and best. Kierkegaard does repeatedly say that true self-love is love of God, and love of people is helping them to love God, and being loved is being helped, while on the other hand to love God is to love people, because this is how we cling to and show our love for God. But the special point here is rather that only with God's equal "infinite" love, free of "finite" worldly distinctions and directed to each human being as such as our neighbor—only by turning to and embracing all, giving all that we have and are and all our love to make others loving—can we become like God, who is what we truly love because God *is* love, selfless, impartial, unconditional.[42] Kierkegaard develops this in commenting on the First Letter of John 4.19: you learn what it is to love by loving God whom you do not see, and prove that you really do this by loving the brother whom you do see. It is not the other way,

> as if God were envious of [the brother] and of [his] being loved, instead of the blessed God's being merciful and therefore continually pointing away from himself, so to speak, and saying, "If you want to love me, then love the people you see; what you do for them, you do for me." God is too exalted to be able to receive a person's love directly. . . . If you want to show that your life is intended to serve God, then let it serve people, yet continually with the thought of God. God does not have a share in existence in such a way that he asks for his share for himself. . . . God does not ask for anything for himself, although he asks for everything from you. (WL, 160-61)[43]

We cannot love God, who is love itself, except by becoming part of what God does and is. As Kierkegaard explains in connection with love as a debt, love "turns outward toward people where indeed it has its object and its tasks," and God "brings up love in a person," not simply so that God may enjoy seeing it but "to send love out into the world, continually engaged in the task."[44] And because loving is belonging, the task is to *belong* in love to human beings, and thus continually to *owe* ourselves to them, not merely because we have *given* ourselves to God but because we have *been*

---

[42]On love's grounding see WL, 8-10, 137-40. On true love, WL, 67-75, 106-107, 121-22, 140. On likeness to God, WL, 62-63, 69, cf. Matthew 5:43-48. On God as love, WL, 3-4, 9-10, 264-65.

[43]For a striking parallel see the *Dialogue* of Catherine of Siena (1347–1380), trans. Suzanne Noffke (New York: Paulist, 1980) 121, 164-65.

[44]WL, 189-190. Cf. Isaiah 55:10-11; John 21:15-17; Shakespeare, "Rather rejoicing to see another merry, than merry at anything which professed to make him rejoice; a gentleman of all temperance," *Measure for Measure* 3.2.249-50; see also 3.1.203, 1.1.33-36.

*given* ourselves by God who gave us love, and who in teaching us love has taught us identity. Consequently, we *have* the love of God only as we have it *for others*, a debt we owe boundlessly to them because we owe it boundlessly to God. This is a debt that we cannot repay directly to the Eternal, because we cannot do for it what it has done for us, give it itself with the understanding of what love truly is, thus creating it, freely; nor can we love the Eternal except by loving, since it *is* the love with which we love one another. This is why love is a redoubling: whoever truly loves, *has* the love of God insofar as one has it *for* one's neighbor. As Kierkegaard says, to love human beings is the only proof that we love God, the only true life, and the only way in which God can love us.[45]

Precisely this is the eternal like for like, that *you do to God what you do to human beings, and so God does to you what you do to them.* The key to it is the divine subjectivity, that God *is* our loving one another (WL, 3: "so that one who loves is what he is only by being in You"). This means not that the Divine is no more than we are, but the other way, that we have no being or love but from the Divine: for it is the lover in all our loving, and it is our beloved only when it has become our love. If we can repay the Divinity who gave us love and identity only by doing for others what it does for us—give them love and identity by helping them to acquire love from it, continually owing as we continually acquire by giving—then love is acquired only by the lover, so that we *have* God's love only as we *give* it or direct it to one another.[46]

Let us note the paradox in saying that the God who is love that is given freely and expects no return, expects and requires a return of love that we can make to God only in our neighbor, whom God also loves. If God needs nothing, and gives love *freely*—gives it without being compelled or obliged to, without regard to our

---

[45]On belonging and owing, see WL, 12, 107-108, 148-49, and 101-102, 271-72. On being given love and identity, WL, 24-25, 110, 126, 364. On the love of God for others, WL, 233, 190; cf. 1 John 4:13. On proof see WL, 160-61, 375-76. On true life, WL, 5-6, 234-35, 311-12. On God's love for us, WL, 190, 301-302.

[46]God is our love and our life: cf. John 1:3; 4:16, 14; 6:52-56; Revelation 1:17-18. CUP, 1:200: "God is a subject and hence only for subjectivity in inwardness." On love acquired by giving it see WL, 176-77, cf. 160-61, 190.

merit, and even before our asking it, and leaves us free to accept it with thanks and return it, or not—then how can God claim a *debt* of us, even if we accept this love?

Kierkegaard would answer, I think, that a true, earnest lover needs to love and to be loved in return, though not to be loved as a condition of loving: one needs to love even without being loved, and can do without the return of love or even reject it if one ought to, or if this is the cost of making both truly loving.[47] On the other hand, a lover feels that one continually receives everything, even love itself and with it oneself, from the person to whom one belongs in love, and still more from God who is love. It follows that even if love *claims* no debt, it *undertakes* one nevertheless: so that someone who is given love, or helped to become loving, will acknowledges a debt of love, or else one has not acquired *love* which is precisely a debt.[48] Moreover, since "God does not ask for anything for himself, although he asks for everything from you" (WL, 161), perhaps there is a way in which love claims a debt too. For if love seeks to make itself known, it is because it seeks, not only to be known or acknowledged in the lover by the other, but also to be known *in* the other, to be communicated to him or her so that this other person in turn becomes loving: and thus a true, earnest love "does not seek its own," but simply to see itself come alive in the other, who shall acknowledge a debt not to the lover but to *God*. This means that such love seeks no "finite" like for like, but only an "infinite" one: it seeks *love* for love, yet seeks that the other shall love not merely the lover in return as his or her one and only object of passionate preference, but shall love God who is love and the true lover and giver of love. God and the true

---

[47]For example, Kierkegaard might say, by breaking an engagement, as he himself did with Regine Olson. But he did this, his critics have said, for his own sake not hers. Although he meant to put his God-relationship first, he ignored or did not think enough of his relationship with her.

[48]On the paradox see WL, 264-69, 160-61. On the need for love, WL, 10-11, 39-40, 107-109, 154-55, 273. On love's receiving everything, WL, 12, 174-91. In God freedom *is* indebtedness or duty, since in giving us love God undertakes to owe us everything, that is to say everything that we need for our good.

lover, then, do seek a return of love, but one that is payable to the *neighbor*, the first human being one meets who has need of it.[49]

It is not two loves but one, and that one God's own, that is in question. It is so to say the love with which the Divine loved us even before we were born and with which it called us into being, called to be ourselves to one another before it, with which we are to love the Divine by loving one another. This fully human love is evidently not a second best to, but a fulfillment of, divine love, and the neighbor to whom we are to pay it is not a mere proxy for, but the human presence of, the Divine.

This is the reason why Kierkegaard says that God's love is our own as we make it our own gift to one another, and most clearly as we love our enemy, the most humanly unlovable. It becomes our own only by our taking part as lovers in God's equal unconditional love for every single individual, that is, for the spirit that each equally but uniquely may become, the authentic self in each of us that is the redoubling of the merely natural one, the "you" eternally singled out by God (who tells us "*You* shall love"). Becoming the hearer of this "you" means understanding that God is in you what you are to others. Thus,

> forgiveness *is* forgiveness . . . your forgiveness of another is your
> own forgiveness; the forgiveness you give [to your neighbor] is
> the forgiveness you receive [from God] (WL, 380),

for they are the same thing. On the other hand, make God your judge of another's wrongs, and you make God *your* judge; and then there are two cases, the other's and yours. Your task then is not to judge and repay the wrongs done to you; it is to be judged, not by yourself but by God before whom you act in all that you do and from whom or by whose permission you receive all that you have from others. As you receive these wrongs as a gift from God given to prove the reality of forgiveness for you and in you—to prove that you truly believe in it—so you have forgiveness, the

---

[49]On love's seeking to be known see WL, 10-14. On seeking love, WL, 52-60, 154-57, 264-70, 212-13, 274-79. On seeking love of neighbor, WL, 51-52, 69.

very same with which you forgive others and make them forgiving. For this is the only way in which God can give it to you.[50]
When Kierkegaard goes on to say that

> God is actually himself this pure like for like, the pure rendition of how you yourself are. If there is anger in you, then God is anger in you. . . . God's relation to a human being is at every moment to infinitize what is in that human being at every moment (WL, 384),

it should now be clear that this is not "immanence" or anthropomorphism, the view that God is made by man and not the other way. It is rather the view that man is the measure, not of the reality of God, but of its inward appearance to him: that a person knows God not the way God is but only the way the person is.[51] God is to you the rendition in vengeance or mercy of what you are in your own relations with human beings. To you the Divine is "infinitely," not just inwardly and spiritually but equally or impartially and unconditionally, what *you* are to people: for just as before the Divine you are a judgment on or a blessing to them, so for you is the Divine a judgment or a blessing; but Divinity is this evenly to all and so likewise to you, since it can be for *you* only what you allow it to be in you for *everyone*, as you become divine love, acquiring it by giving it to others, or as you refuse to do this. God is a God of loving mercy, not of relentless vengeance; but the relentless person has a relentless God, for God is merciful *only* to those who are merciful to others, and so acquire this mercy.

---

[50]Thus the famous prayer attributed to Francis of Assisi: "Lord, make me an instrument of thy peace. Where there is hate, let me bring love. Where there is offense, let me bring forgiveness. . . . Let me seek, O Lord, not so much to be understood, but to understand; not to be loved, but to love. For it is in giving that one receives . . . in forgiving that one is forgiven. . . . "

[51]Cf. Goethe in *The Pantheist*: "As a man is so is his God; that is what has made God ridiculous. The God a man worships is his own inmost being turned inside out," in *Goethe*, trans. David Luke (Baltimore: Penguin, 1964) 282; JP, 2:1311, 3:2573; CUP 52, citing Boethius' principle (*Consolation* 5.4) that knowledge depends on the power of the knower, so that you know something not as *it* is but as *you* are, or as it is or appears to you. Similarly Paul says that God is truly known by love that acknowledges *God's* knowledge: 1 Corinthians 13:12; 8:3, Galatians 4:9; John quotes Christ to the effect that love of neighbor acquires the knowledge of God: John 14:21, 23. JP, 2:1351, 2299.

That is not to say that divine mercy is earned, Kierkegaard insists in closing (WL, 385-86). The love of God is a grace freely given and not a reward for your merit. You have not deserved it by giving it to others, but simply shown that you believe in it and desire it and open yourself to share in what God wants to give to everyone.

This is the infinite gravity or rigor of God, and the decisively Christian category [of] eternity's like for like, that "God just repeats everything you say to and do to other people . . . with the magnification of infinity" (WL, 384); for "in these areas there is always the reversed [sc. rebounding] echo" (JP, 2:1413). "The magnification of infinity" is not quantitative but qualitative; it is a heightening of meaning and value, thus a truer redefinition and revaluation of what we are and say and do. "Eternity's like for like" thus turns out to be a dimension of the divine redoubling and the divine subjectivity: God is the true subject of our love as well as its true object, so that we acquire God's love, or unite ourselves to it, by making it our own gift to one another. What we receive from God (in "subjectivity") we give to human beings, and what we give to human beings (in "reduplication") we receive from God (in the "like for like"). Our human works of love thus *presuppose* divine love and *acquire* it for us, or prove its reality in us. It is *doubly* present in us because it is ours only for the giving, as something we *owe*, since we receive ourselves (in our continually renewed identity as lovers) by giving it: we acquire by giving precisely what we give by acquiring it from God.

If reduplication is a kind of *unity*, wholeness, or integrity, a continuity between what we inwardly understand and what we outwardly are and communicate, or again (in its dialectical form) a continuity between what we say and how we say it, then redoubling is a kind of *symmetry* in giving and receiving, but a higher symmetry that is unity in the sense that the same thing is given and received when the more love we give the more we have, and the more we have the more we owe.

Kierkegaard's category of *repetition* (resumption, taking again, literally asking and receiving again, sc. from God, as *his*) seems to be an anticipation and early form of redoubling and reduplication, and superseded by them and especially by redoubling. (E.g., "repetition is the daily bread that satisfies with blessing," "if God had not willed repetition, the world would not have come into existence," "for him the repetition is the raising of his consciousness to the second power," "Here is a redoubling; here it is a matter of repetition.") In the *Journal* he refers to two treatises on categories by Adolf Trendelenburg and remarks:

> What I have profited from Trendelenburg is unbelievable; now I have the apparatus for what I had thought out years before. . . . There is no modern philosopher from whom I have profited so much. . . . At the time I wrote *Repetition* I had not read anything of his—and now that I have read him, how much more lucid and clear everything is to me.[52]

He means, I suggest, everything about repetition, a category that scholars have found elusive and difficult to pin down in a single simple definition. I suggest further that it is in redoubling that Kierkegaard has got repetition into sharper focus. It is something that especially is now much more lucid and clear to him. He gives it a new name, and in the Conclusion to *Works of Love* he applies it, linking it to divine justice, the eternal like for like.

### God Redoubles, Human Beings Reduplicate

I close with a further comment on the like for like and the reversed or rebounding echo, to clarify further the difference between redoubling and reduplication and why it is important for the understanding of Kierkegaard's religious metaphysics and psychology to distinguish them carefully.

If (a) the Divine speaks personally with each human being about himself or herself, and (b) it is itself what it says to each, the love and spirit and truth that it communicates in the words that each hears subjectively, then does this mean that there is a *redupli-*

---

[52]On repetition see R, 132, 133, 229, 275, cf. 212, 220-21, 137; CUP, 1:121, 164, 203, 248, 263, 312-13, 351; CA, 17-19, 89-90, 106, 149, 151; JP, 1:972, 2:1246, 4:3795. On Trendelenburg see JP, 5:5977-78; and Arnold Come, *Trendelenburg's Influence on Kierkegaard's Modal Categories* (Montreal: Inter Editions, 1991). Come does not, however, mention repetition here or in his later *Kierkegaard as Humanist, Discovering My Self* (Montreal: McGill-Queens, 1995), where he identifies redoubling with reduplication, e.g., at 359, 363-69; similarly *Kierkegaard as Theologian: Recovering My Self* (Montreal: McGill-Queens, 1997) e.g., 62, 70-79.

*cation* in the Divine, or being outwardly what it knows itself inwardly to be, perhaps indeed a *dialectical* reduplication, or being in its communication to us what it invites us to be?

But (a') if the Divine is eternal and changeless, then it does not talk with us, presenting one thought after another, for in its Word it has said once and for all what it has to say to us; that we hear it as spoken to us personally characterizes *us* in relation to the Divine rather than it in relation to itself. Thus when it repeats our own thought to us "with the magnification of infinity," this is a feature of the like for like and of *our* subjectivity rather than its own.

And (b') while *redoubling* is a perfection for ever achieved in the Divine, which thus for ever is itself "infinitely" by denying itself "finitely," *reduplication* seems to be a task that we perform in time: for it is becoming what we know or truly say, to the best of our ability, as we strive to accomplish or approximate it; whereas in the Divine all is for ever complete that is only more or less manifest in our temporal existence. To us love is a new debt at any moment, but in the Divine "all" moments are one single present, in which its redoubling of its subjectivity is infinitely consummated. Thus if the Divine reduplicates, then it too has a task to perform in and throughout time. But that may not be entirely illogical and unthinkable, insofar as its eternity is not timelessness so much as ceaseless temporality, and insofar as it *is* our love, as Christ, and as Spirit.[53] Reduplication in the Divine would also mean that it does to others what is done to it, or gives on to them what it itself receives. Does it undergo the actions of others, or receive anything from them? In a way this is true of it precisely as Christ the Mediator. Kierkegaard does say that "what you do unto people, you do unto God, and therefore what you do unto people, God does unto you." But Kierkegaard never calls this God's *reduplication*, but only God's like for like, or *redoubling*.

Weighing all this together, we may put Kierkegaard's position like this. *We are redoubled in God by reduplicating what we thereby*

---

[53]See the great edifying discourse of 1855, "The Unchangeableness of God," in *For Self-Examination*, trans. Walter Lowrie (London: Oxford University Press, 1941) 221-240. On God's presence in time see WL, 3-4, 6, 9-10, 215-16, 280, 300-14, also JP, 1:251, 571, 832-34, 2:1412, 1433, 3:3410.

*receive.* In other words, God redoubles us and we reduplicate. *We* are redoubled by allowing God to make us nothing and to create us anew. But *the Divine* redoubles itself, in boundlessly communicating itself or what it itself is, and so for ever and continuously acquires what it gives; our highest perfection is to become nothing but an instrument of divine redoubling.[54]

---

[54]WL, 94, 260-62; EUD, 297-326.

# 2

## Kierkegaard's Concept of Redoubling and Luther's Simul Justus

### Andrew J. Burgess

Kierkegaard and Luther make a puzzling combination. Although Kierkegaard himself insists he has "never really read anything by Luther" before 1847 (JP, 3:2463), many passages throughout Kierkegaard's works betray deep affinities.[1] One such passage is the chapter in *Works of Love* (1847) on the text "Love Hides a Multitude of Sins." While never mentioning Luther's name, the chapter draws from a distinctive motif in Luther, summed up in the slogan that the Christian is *simul justus et peccator* ("at the same time justified and a sinner"). The plan here will be to look first at the preface to the chapter in *Works of Love* dealing with the concept of redoubling (*Fordoblelse*), then within the discourse itself at the paradox of "hiding sins," and finally at the fit between the chapter and Luther's teaching.

### The Concept of Redoubling

The preface in the first two pages of the chapter on hiding sins provides a good introduction to the concept of redoubling. The length of the preface, a mere two pages, belies its importance. In effect, these pages outline the ontological structure for *Works of Love*, connecting the discourse that follows to the book as a whole.

---

[1]See, e.g., the illuminating study by Craig Quentin Hinkson, "Kierkegaard's Theology: Cross and Grace: The Lutheran and Idealist Traditions in His Thought" (diss., University of Chicago, 1993). One of Hinkson's main sources is the classic article by Eduard Geismar, "Kierkegaard und Luther," *Monatschrift für Pastoraltheologie* 25 (October–November 1929): 227-41.

Although the concept of redoubling is one of Kierkegaard's most original notions, it appears only in isolated references in his writings. For the most part early translators pay little attention to the Danish word and translate it with English terms such as "reduplication" (JP, 3:909nn.). Part of the problem may be that, in one of the most familiar passages using the word, Kierkegaard takes up a merely apparent case of the concept. The context for the passage is in *Concluding Unscientific Postscript* (1846), as part of a critique of the effort to define truth as the agreement of thinking with being or being with thinking (CUP, 1:189-92). This effort understands being (*Vaeren*) as "the abstract rendition or the abstract prototype of what being *in concreto* is as empirical being" (CUP, 1:190). Since an abstraction is a kind of thinking, however, all this supposed agreement produces is a bare tautology, that thinking is a kind of thinking. The only "redoubling" that takes place is in "an entirely abstract sense" (CUP, 1:190).

Where the concept of redoubling is used in its proper sense it builds on the distinction between the temporal and the eternal. A temporal thing does not in itself have the possibility of redoubling, whereas the eternal does. How this distinction works out can be partially pieced together from scattered references in writings of various periods. Even the birds of the air hymned in *Christian Discourses* (1848) lack redoubling (CD, 40-41), since they are merely temporal. Yet human beings, who do have the capability for redoubling, are also temporal beings. A human being, he says in *Philosophical Fragments* (1844), can have a double kind of existence, both temporal and eternal. Not only do humans come into existence like all other temporal things, but they have also the possibility of a second coming into existence within this first coming into existence (PF, 76). In *Christian Discourses*, the eternal is identified as righteousness, and the redoubling of the eternal in time is seen in the difference between right and wrong (CD, 208). In fact, as he says later in *Practice in Christianity* (1850), to be a self is to be a redoubling, and thereby to have freedom, in that one posits a choice (PC, 159).

Happily, Kierkegaard has not left readers without any clues to the concept of redoubling beyond these isolated references but has provided a relatively extensive passage about redoubling in its religious sense, the preface to the discourse in *Works of Love*. In his

classic treatment of the concept of redoubling (*Fordoblelse*), Gregor
Malantschuk points to *Works of Love* as the clearest place for
studying the religious use of the concept, and he praises in
particular the preface to this chapter for its plainness and clarity.[2]
The passage he cites begins the preface:

> The temporal has three periods and therefore does not ever
> actually exist completely or exist completely in any of them; the
> eternal *is*. A temporal object can have many various characteris-
> tics, in a certain sense can be said to have them simultaneously
> insofar as it is what it is in these specific characteristics. But a
> temporal object never has redoubling [*Fordoblelse*] in itself; just as
> the temporal vanishes in time, so also it is only in its characteris-
> tics. When, however, the eternal is in a human being, this eternal
> redoubles in him in such a way that every moment it is in him,
> it is in him in a double mode: in an outward direction and in an
> inward direction back into itself, but in such a way that this is
> one and the same, since otherwise it is not redoubling. The
> eternal is not only in its characteristics but is in itself in its char-
> acteristics. It not only has characteristics but is in itself in having
> the characteristics. (WL, 280)

Plain and clear these sentences may be, as Malantschuk says, but
they are also highly compressed. At the core of the passage is the
distinction between the eternal, which has redoubling in itself, and
a temporal thing (such as a human being), which does not but
may receive the capacity for redoubling from the eternal. When the
eternal gives this capacity, a human being redoubles itself in two
ways, outwardly, toward other things, and inwardly, toward itself.

The paragraph that follows illumines this first passage by identifying love (*Kjærlighed*) as an example of such redoubling. "What
love does, that it is; what it is, that it does—at one and the same
moment" (WL, 280). Love redoubles itself both outwardly and
inwardly. "When we say 'Love gives bold confidence,' we are
saying that the one who loves by his nature makes others boldly
confident. Wherever love is present, it spreads bold confidence
(WL, 280). This is love's outward redoubling. On the other hand,
"when we say 'Love gives bold confidence,' we are at the same
time saying something else, that the one who loves has bold con-

---

[2]"Begrebet Fordoblelse hos Søren Kierkegaard," *Kierkegaardiana* 2 (1957): 46.

fidence" (WL, 281). Love makes the lover boldly confident, and this is love's inward redoubling.

Not until two paragraphs later, however, does Kierkegaard make the key identification that the initial passage of the preface requires: "God is Love" (WL, 281). Divine love is what he means here by "the eternal" that has redoubling in itself and that redoubles itself in human beings. Only when this specific kind of love (Kjaerlighed) is present in human beings are they enabled to become inwardly loving and to show true love outwardly to others. As he has shown earlier in the book, self-love cannot endure redoubling. It cannot accept the command "You shall love your neighbor as yourself," because "the commandment's as yourself is a redoubling" (WL, 21). Kjærlighed, on the other hand, is recognizable by its self-denial and by its refusal to exclude any people from love (WL, 52), whether they are what we are apt to call "lovable" or not.

Without this initial identification Kierkegaard's argument in the preface will not work. Love is not the only attitude that works in a double mode. If hate rather than love had been the attitude Kierkegaard used as his example, the argument would start out right—when hatred "redoubles" itself in human beings, hateful people are hateful in themselves, and in hating others bring about hatred in them—but the argument in the rest of the chapter would run all awry. No, trying to begin from the bare premises of the initial paragraph in this way is a mistake. Whatever it looks like, Kierkegaard's passage does not really start from such abstract metaphysical principles to get to its conclusion about divine love. Instead, the basic, though unstated, premise of the whole passage is given at the end rather than at the beginning. That premise is, that "God in heaven, or love" (WL, 281) is "the eternal" that redoubles itself in human beings. When this kind of divine love is present in a human being, that person is changed and begins to relate to other people also with this new kind of love. Beginning with that premise the rest of Kierkegaard's argument follows logically; without it, the argument goes nowhere.

The preface sketches the basic structure of Works of Love, in terms of such primary ontological categories as the eternal, the temporal, simultaneity, the inward, the outward, and of course redoubling. Works of Love carries out its analysis within the realm of the redoubling of the eternal in the temporal. God's love redoubles itself in human love in its inward and outward directions; particularly the latter, since, as he says: "In this little book we are continually dealing with the works of love; therefore we are considering love in its outward direction" (WL, 282). The theme of redoubling is tied to the notion of love's reciprocity (love's "like for like"), which helps to structure the whole book.[3] Redoubling God's love is both that which makes a person truly human and the highest human task; it is both an ontological and an ethical matter. As Malantschuk writes, redoubling is closely related to its sister concept of "reduplication" (*Reduplikation*), "in that redoubling signifies a reduplication already completed. Here the weight is on the ontological, that is, on being, which already exists, whereas in his use of the word 'reduplication' Kierkegaard points to the ethical task that must first be actualized."[4]

What makes reading this preface so difficult is that Kierkegaard mixes abstruse ontological argumentation with sermonic illustrations. It is an approach he takes increasingly in the following years. In a later work, *The Sickness unto Death* (1849), Kierkegaard starts out with a warning that readers may find the style of exposition strange; "it may seem to them too rigorous to be upbuilding and too upbuilding to be rigorously scholarly" (SUD, 5). That same warning could well have been affixed to the preface of the present chapter in *Works of Love*, which leads off with heavy metaphysics and then switches abruptly to homiletical examples about love in action. The task for the interpreter is to smooth out the differences between the two parts of the preface and to find the upbuilding in the scholarly rigor, and the scholarly rigor in that which seems to be merely upbuilding.

The preface to *Works of Love* foreshadows *The Sickness unto Death* in another respect as well, in that the redoubling structure of the Christian self fits in with the better-known definition of the

---

[3]Timothy Houston Polk, *The Biblical Kierkegaard: Reading by the Rule of Faith* (Macon GA: Mercer University Press, 1997) 97-98n.10; cf. Bruce Kirmmse, *Kierkegaard in Golden Age Denmark* (Bloomington: Indiana University Press, 1990) 307.

[4]Gregor Malantschuk, *Nøglebegreber i Søren Kierkegaards Taenkning*, ed. Grethe Kjaer and Paul Müller (Copenhagen: C. A. Reitzels, 1993) 130; trans. in JP, 3, p. 910nn.

self in the later work. *The Sickness unto Death* describes the human self positively as "in relating itself to itself and in willing to be itself, the self rests transparently in the power that established it" (SUD, 14). This formula begins from the situation of the self, and both the self and the eternal ("the power that established it") are described in terms of the situation of the self. Although *The Sickness unto Death* does not use the language of redoubling here, it would not be hard to translate its famous formula into those terms; and in fact the other book by Anti-Climacus, *Practice in Christianity*, has a passage that makes a move in this direction (PC, 159). The key passage discussed from *Works of Love*, however, differs from both of these passages in the two later books, in that it stresses that the initiative is with the eternal: "When . . . the eternal is in a human being, this eternal redoubles in him in such a way that every moment it is in him, it is in him in a double mode" (WL, 280). Like *Works of Love*, *The Sickness unto Death* describes the self as a synthesis of opposites, but in the later work these opposites are described more fully than before: "a synthesis of the infinite and the finite, of the temporal and the eternal, of freedom and necessity" (SUD, 13). The conceptual terrain described in both books is the same, only the perspective is different. *The Sickness unto Death* describes the synthesis from the point of view of the human struggle against despair, while *Works of Love* sees the synthesis as a gift from the eternal that opens up new possibilities for human love. *The Sickness unto Death*'s concept of despair is another way of presenting the nature of sin, in psychological terms, and *Works of Love*'s concept of the eternal redoubling itself is, in ontological terms, another way of describing the action of divine grace.

### "Love Hides a Multitude of Sins"

The discourse on "Love Hides a Multitude of Sins" moves in the opposite direction from its preface. Whereas the preface starts from God's love and then interprets it in human terms, the main part of the discourse (WL, 289-96) starts with cases of human love that need to be understood in terms of divine love. The style, too, is different. The preface develops its argument first in an abstract, scholarly tone before supplying upbuilding examples, while the main section of the discourse begins casually with advice for upbuilding and only gradually exposes the conceptual issues involved.

The reason for the differences between the preface and the discourse is that the preface presents divine love, and its human counterpart, in general, while the discourse takes up a particular form of love, forgiveness, the love that "hides a multitude of sins." The main topic of the discourse is how Christians should forgive others' sins by "hiding" them in various ways. For the most part the discourse offers practical advice on forgiving sins, always keeping in mind the example of Christ, the ultimate "prototype" (WL, 288) for such forgiveness.

Close in the background of the main topic of the discourse lies another, secondary one with a distinctly Lutheran flavor, a paradox in the concept of forgiveness itself. Forgiveness seems a simple concept, suitable more for sermons than for scholarship. Yet the concept of forgiveness has its puzzling sides too. If sins are merely "hidden" by forgiveness, are they not still there, in some hidden mode? And if the sins remain, what value has the forgiveness? These are the issues with which the discourse struggles increasingly as it develops its argument.

The biblical text about love hiding a multitude of sins (1 Peter 4:8b) is one of Kierkegaard's favorites. He uses it with two discourses (EUD, 55-78) near the beginning of his main writing period in 1843 and in the very last set of discourses he publishes (WA, 181-88) in 1851, as well as in the chapter of *Works of Love* here under scrutiny, which comes out midway between those dates, in 1847. The text's metaphor of "hiding" constrains Kierkegaard to struggle with the categories of sin and forgiveness in similar ways in each of the discourses. In both of the two 1843 discourses, for example, the text gets a perfectly straightforward reading that lends itself well to homiletical purposes. The first 1843 discourse on the text contrasts love's blindness to sin, as the biblical text treats it, to the claim of the "common sense" or "understanding" (*Forstand*) that the number of sins stays just as great whether or not love discovers it (EUD, 62). The second discourse grants that love may discover a multitude of sins, by making a person no longer satisfied with the deeds of the past; but love also hides the sins of that same person (EUD, 72-74). Thus both of these 1843 discourses speak of hiding sins in a perfectly straightforward way: sins may be hidden, but they are still there. The discourse on this text in Kierkegaard's last collection of discourses, *Two Discourses at Communion on Fridays* discusses how Christ's own love hides a multitude of sins. Christ's love, he says, does not have the "double sense" of the love analyzed in *Works of Love* (WA, 181), since Christ himself is without sin.

The central section of the discourse in *Works of Love* (WL, 289-96) begins from a point very similar to that in the two 1843 discourses, keeping to the metaphor of hiding. Does the number of sins remain the same whether or not love hides them? Not necessarily; if the jaundiced eye of an evil understanding discovers the sins, the number may actually become greater (WL, 286-87; cf. 296-97). Then, however, Kierkegaard changes the context and discusses three strategies by which love can cut down on the number of sins. (1) Love can keep the number of sins from increasing by using silence, which stops rumor (WL, 289-91). (2) Again, love can sometimes find a way to make the number of sins smaller, by finding a mitigating explanation for some of them (WL, 292-94). (3) Finally, love can remove the sins that cannot be denied to be sin, by forgiveness. There seems to be a slight discrepancy here, however, in that, while all three of these strategies are described as showing how love hides a multitude of sins, this third "most notable way" (WL, 294) does not merely hide sins but removes them; "forgiveness takes the forgiven sin away" (WL, 294).

The following two paragraphs sharpen the difficulty with an analogy of forgiveness with faith, which "always relates itself to what is not seen" (WL, 294). When forgiveness removes sin it "takes away that which does indeed exist. . . . The one who loves sees the sin he forgives, but he believes that forgiveness takes it away" (WL, 294-95). Both faith and forgiveness deal with the unseen: "Just as one by faith *believes* the *unseen into* what is seen, so the one who loves by forgiveness *believes away* what is seen. Both are faith. Blessed is the believer, he believes what he cannot see; blessed is the one who loves, he believes away that which he indeed can see!" (WL, 295). This analogy only points up the difficulty without resolving it. Do the sins continue to exist, but unseen, after they are believed away? If they do, they are merely hidden and not removed. If they do not, they are removed and not hidden. A further difficulty in which this passage involves the argument has to do with the nature of belief and the will. The phrase "believes away what is seen" conjures up the image of getting rid of objects that are plainly before the eyes simply by resolutely refusing to believe in them. Still, perhaps this difficulty is only apparent. After all, that human forgiveness cannot completely remove sin does not greatly matter, since in ordinary human circumstances a person would be happy to have one's sins charitably ignored. But cannot the almighty God remove sins completely? At this point Kierkegaard introduces a new metaphor for forgiveness, and it is applied first and foremost to God: God forgets sins (WL, 195-96). Kierkegaard starts by using again the metaphor of hiding sins—"what God forgives, it is hidden behind his back" (WL, 295; cf. Isaiah 38:17)—and then, without warning, he begins to discuss what it means for God to forget sins as well. The change of metaphor, however, does not bridge over the difference between hiding sins and removing them. In normal usage forgetting is like hiding, but not like removing. That is to say, when someone forgets or hides something, that thing continues to be there, only unnoticed; whereas when something is removed the thing is gone.

Kierkegaard next seems to suggest a way out of the puzzle, but then he goes ahead and blocks off that exit too. He proposes a special sense of the term ("this highest sense," he calls it) in which the opposite of "forgetting" is not "recollecting" but "hoping" (WL, 296). "To hope is in thinking to give being [*Tilvaer*]; to forget is in thinking to take away being [*Tilvaer*] from that which nevertheless exists [*er til*], to blot it out" (WL, 296). The context for this notion of hope comes in an earlier chapter of *Works of Love*, entitled "Love Hopes All Things," where he indicates that "hope"—in its true sense, not in what we in ordinary speech call "hope" (WL, 250)—"relates to the future, to possibility" (WL, 249). Hope in this highest sense means to "relate oneself expectantly to the possibility of the good," that is, the eternal (WL, 249). On the basis of this specialized definition, Kierkegaard's concept of hope turns out to mean that, by hoping, a human being gains some new future possibility of the eternal. The corresponding concept of forgetting, then, would be for a human being to lose some future possibility. That God forgets sins, accordingly, means that one of their possibilities has been taken away. Nonetheless, with the same sentence in which he proposes the special sense of "forgetting" that "blots out" sin, Kierkegaard also includes a phrase to show that the sins still remain. Forgetting, he says, takes "away being from that which nevertheless exists" (WL, 296). The sins still exist, only without one of their future possibilities.

The climax of this passage in the discourse draws on a metaphor that seems to exclude in the strongest possible terms the existence of forgiven sins—and then the passage goes on to describe those sins as existing "behind God's back." "Forgetting," he writes, "when God does it in relation to sin, is the opposite of creating, since to create is to bring forth from nothing, and to forget is to take back into nothing" (WL, 296). The nothingness of forgiven sins is like the nothingness from which God created the world, and what could be more thoroughly "nothingness" than that? Yet even after this extreme metaphor Kierkegaard continues right on to speak of the sins continuing to exist after the one who loves has forgiven and forgotten them: "in love he turns toward the one he forgives; but when he turns toward him, he of course cannot see what is lying behind his back" (WL, 296).

The further Kierkegaard goes in this section of the discourse (WL, 289-96), the deeper he is enmeshed in a basic paradox. From the start Kierkegaard is working with two conflicting sets of metaphors. On the one hand, sins are forgiven, removed, blotted out, and brought to a nothingness as complete as that before the creation of the world; on the other hand, all those same sins still remain, though hidden, covered over, and placed behind God's back. What begins as simple puzzles about human forgiveness ends up as an apparently irresolvable paradox about divine forgiveness, that all the sins removed by God's forgiveness continue to exist behind God's back. But what can this paradox possibly mean?

## Luther and Kierkegaard

Although Kierkegaard's paradox in these pages of *Works of Love* sounds strange, its very strangeness provides an interpretive clue, since it points to a distinctive historical precedent, Luther's famous slogan *simul justus et peccator*: the Christian is at the same time

justified and a sinner. To answer the particular question of Kierkegaard's use of the simul justus paradox in *Works of Love* will
require looking both at the meaning of Luther's *simul justus*
formula and the possible fit or lack of fit shown here between the
ideas of the two men.

Like Kierkegaard's concept of redoubling, Luther's *simul justus*
phrase is rarely mentioned explicitly in his writings, and then in
diverse contexts, so that a reader of Luther might easily not recognize its importance as technical terminology. Moreover, one of the
main sources for the expression is Luther's *Lectures on Romans*
(1515), which was not rediscovered and published until 1908.[5] Thus
it is only since Kierkegaard's time that the phrase has become a
standard expression among scholars, including Roman Catholic
writers.[6]

Luther expresses the *simul justus* formula in two main forms,
in a "partial" and a "total" sense of the phrase:

(1) As early as his 1515 *Lectures on Romans* Luther uses the
*simul justus* formula in the "partial" sense, which says that the
saints are partly righteous and partly sinful. Sin is the *terminus a
quo* and righteousness the *terminus ad quem* of the Christian life, he
writes: "Therefore if we always are repentant, we are always
sinners, and yet thereby we are righteous and we are justified; we
are in part sinners and in part righteous, that is, we are nothing
but penitents."[7] This sense is not distinctively Lutheran but is
found in Augustine and belongs to the common heritage of
Western Christianity.[8] When Kierkegaard's discourse in *Works of
Love* opens with quantitative strategies for keeping the number of
sins down, he is drawing on this first analysis of the relation of sin
and righteousness.

---

[5]Martin Luther, *Lectures on Romans*, trans. and ed. Wilhelm Pauck, Library of
Christian Classics 15 (Philadelphia: Westminster, 1961) xxiv.

[6]For example, Hans Küng, "Simul Iustus et Peccator," *Justification: The Doctrine
of Karl Barth and a Catholic Reflection* (New York: Thomas Nelson, 1964) 236-48;
Karl Rahner, "Justified and Sinner at the Same Time," *Theological Investigations*,
vol. 6 (London: Darton, Longman, and Todd, 1974) 218-30.

[7]Martin Luther, *Lectures on Romans*, ed. Hilton C. Oswald, *Luther's Works*, vol.
25 (St. Louis: Concordia, 1972) 434. Translated from the standard German edition,
the *Weimarer Ausgabe* 56:442.

[8]Pauck in Luther, *Lectures on Romans*, xliv.

(2) In the second sense of the *simul justus* formula, on the other hand, the saints are at the same time totally righteous and totally sinful. That is why, Luther says in the Romans commentary, the saints confess not only their past sins but also their present sins: "Is it not that they know that there is sin in them but that for the sake of Christ it is covered and is not imputed to them, so that they may declare that all their good is outside of them . . . ?"[9] This latter sense of the formula is intimately connected to Luther's distinctive teaching of justification by faith alone. Before God (*coram Deo*[10]) the saints find themselves totally sinful, but their sins are entirely covered by Christ's righteousness. Directly before God there can be no quantitative judgment of "more or less sinful," or "more or less righteous," but only a qualitative judgment of total sinfulness and total righteousness.

The paradoxical situation Kierkegaard describes at the end of the passage in *Works of Love*, where the sin is forgiven but "nevertheless exists," echoes the paradox in the second sense of Luther's *simul justus* phrase. As Kierkegaard writes later in *The Sickness unto Death*, "what makes sin so terrible is that it is before God," and "because sin is against God it is infinitely magnified" (SUD, 80). The Christian standing before God is therefore not just partially guilty but infinitely guilty.

Where Kierkegaard diverges from Luther, however, and even more from the movement of Lutheran orthodoxy that follows Luther,[11] is in the way Kierkegaard shies away from the courtroom (that is, what is traditionally called "forensic") terminology to describe the situation of the Christian before God. It is significant that, in this passage from *Works of Love*, Kierkegaard omits the characteristically Lutheran metaphor of God the judge "imputing" righteousness to the sinner. In an earlier work, *Concluding Unscientific Postscript*, Kierkegaard protests against Lutheran orthodoxy's use of just this sort of courtroom metaphor, saying that it gives the appearance of an externality, "a court, a tribunal, a third party,

---

[9]Luther, *Lectures on Romans*, ed. Oswald, 267; *Weimarer Ausgabe* 56:280.

[10]This phrase from Luther is taken as the title of part 2 of Gordon Rupp, *The Righteousness of God: Luther Studies* (London: Hodder and Stoughton, 1953).

[11]See, e.g., Karl Hase, *Hutterus Redivivus* (Leipzig: Breitkopp und Härtel, 1839) ¶109.

which hears and votes in the case between God and man" to "that which essentially pertains to the individual specifically in his isolation before God" (CUP, 1:530). The problem with putting divine forgiveness into a courtroom setting is that doing so promotes an external and quantitative rather than an inward and qualitative picture of the sinner before God. A human "third party" will see the sinner as more or less guilty, rather than totally guilty as the sinner is who stands directly before God. By abandoning the courtroom metaphor, however, Kierkegaard is not thereby ignoring Luther's basic insight on justification by faith alone. On the contrary, Kierkegaard fully accepts the Lutheran position even in the "total" *simul justus* sense, but he sets out to explicate it in a more consistent way than before, through the metaphor of God turning in love toward the one he forgives and thereby not seeing the sins hidden behind his back.

1847, the year when Kierkegaard is writing *Works of Love*, marks a turning point in his relation to Luther. During that year Kierkegaard begins a regular ("according to plan," JP, 3:2465) reading of Luther's devotional sermons (*Huuspostiller*) that continues most of the rest of his life. Kierkegaard had of course read Luther earlier as well,[12] and he had also learned much from reading such figures as Johann Georg Hamann.[13] Nevertheless, Kierkegaard's 1847 remark that he has "never really read anything by Luther" (JP, 3:2463) has the ring of truth, since Luther had never before mattered to him personally as much as he does now. Kierkegaard does not always agree with Luther. In the journals of his last years he never tires of berating the Danish church for listening only to Luther's words of comfort and getting too complacent to hear God's stern judgment. For Kierkegaard, Luther's soothing words to the penitent with an anguished conscience in the sixteenth century are seldom the right message for the patron of the Danish established church three centuries later. Nonetheless, whether praising Luther or attacking him, Kierkegaard is after 1847 no longer able to take him for granted.

---

[12]Johannes Sløk, "Kierkegaard and Luther," *A Kierkegaard Critique*, ed. Howard A. Johnson and Niels Thulstrup (New York: Harper, 1962) 86.

[13]Hinkson, "Kierkegaard's Theology," chap. 3, "Johann Georg Hamann as Likely Mediator of Luther's *Theologia Crucis* to Kierkegaard," 95-120.

Accordingly, at the same time as Kierkegaard is thinking through the discourse on hiding sins, during the period leading up to his Easter experience of forgiveness in 1848, he also comes to have a personal stake in Luther's struggles over sin and grace. The theme of God's forgiving and forgetting sin surfaces in his journals on August 16, 1847, the day after he sends in the manuscript for *Works of Love*, when he writes of his deciding not to take a trip at that time:

> Up to now I have armed myself against my depression with intellectual activity which keeps it away—now, in the faith that God has forgotten in forgiveness whatever guilt I have, I must try to forget it myself, but not in any diversion, not in any distance from it, but in God, so that when I think of God I may think that he has forgotten it and in that way myself learn to dare to forget it in forgiveness. (JP, 5:6043)

By this point in his life, he admits to himself, he has a faith that God has not only forgiven but even forgotten his guilt—but not so strong a conviction that he could forget the guilt himself.

That Luther influences Kierkegaard on issues relating to the paradox of forgiveness suggests that Luther's writings may also have a bearing on the primary topic of the discourse on hiding sins, which is practical advice for showing God's kind of forgiving love to others. Here help comes from an unexpected quarter, because Luther and Kierkegaard largely share the same lectionary of prescribed sermon texts. Among the devotional sermons in Luther's collection of *Huuspostiller* is a sermon on nearly the same scripture text as Kierkegaard's discourse, a sermon which Kierkegaard would almost certainly have read. Luther preaches on the full pericope (1 Peter 4:7-11) rather than the mere fragment of a verse (1 Peter 4:8b) Kierkegaard uses. For this reason there is only a small area of overlap between the two interpretations of the text, and it would be hard to show any direct borrowing by Kierkegaard. Only one paragraph in Luther's sermon[14] takes up the strategies for hiding sin that occupy almost all of Kierkegaard's discourse. Still, there are at least two passages in Luther's sermon

---

[14]Martin Luther, "Sunday after Ascension Day," *Sermons of Martin Luther*, vol. 7, ed. John Nicholas Lenker (Minneapolis: Luther Press, 1909) ¶31, p. 317.

that show a similar general orientation in their ways of interpreting scripture. The first is Luther's introduction to the sermon, where he writes that he preaches for the person "who, through faith, has obtained redemption from sin and death and has a place in the kingdom of grace and of eternal life," to exhort such a person "to live henceforth in a manner indicative of the fact that he has apprehended the treasure of salvation and is become a new man."[15] This is precisely the theology that lies in the background of Kierkegaard's discourse. The second passage comes where Luther distinguishes between God's forgiveness of our sins and our forgiveness of others' sins, and then he says that the text from 1 Peter clearly focuses on the latter kind of forgiveness.[16] Kierkegaard, too, makes this kind of distinction, and this is why he writes that his discourse on forgiveness will be on love "in its outward direction" and on the "works of love" (WL, 282).

While Luther would not likely have written a discourse in the way Kierkegaard does here, Kierkegaard's discourse is unthinkable apart from its Lutheran background. The polemical context of the Reformation summons Luther to champion "justification by faith in Christ alone," so that he has less energy than otherwise to write on the "works of love." Nonetheless, Kierkegaard shows himself in this discourse an apt pupil of Luther, even, and perhaps especially, where he shuns courtroom metaphors in an effort to improve the consistency of his master's teachings.

### Simul Justus and Redoubling

At the basis of the ties between Luther and Kierkegaard in the discourse on hiding sins lies a fundamental similarity in the structures of their ways of thinking. Luther's slogan *simul justus et peccator* implies a theology[17] that resembles the thought structure outlined in the preface on "redoubling" that introduces Kierkegaard's discourse.

---

[15]Ibid., ¶1, p. 303.
[16]Ibid., ¶29, p. 316.
[17]Such a theology has in fact been articulated by Kjell Ove Nilsson, *Simul: Das Miteinander von Göttlichem und Menschlichem in Luthers Theologie* (Göttingen: Vandenhoeck & Ruprecht, 1966).

One way in which the structure of Luther's theology can be defined is in terms of his *simul justus* formula. The two apparently contradictory senses of the formula operate in two different dimensions of human life.[18] The relationship of total sinfulness and total righteousness works in the vertical dimension of life, before God, as the Christian daily submits in full surrender to God's judgment and daily receives God's full grace, whereas the partial sinfulness and partial righteousness takes place in the horizontal dimension of life, as the forgiven sinner grows increasingly Christlike in relationships to other people.

When *simul justus* is interpreted in terms of two dimensions, it fits with Kierkegaard's delineation of the structure of divine love in his preface on the concept of redoubling in *Works of Love*. In the vertical dimension, all the initiative belongs to the eternal, God, who graciously enters into human life to transform it. This is the first "redoubling" Kierkegaard describes in the preface. But then from that redoubling arises a second redoubling, within human life, when human beings, transformed by grace, show forth that love in a double way, inwardly, by becoming more loving, and outwardly by showing this love toward other people. While both Luther and Kierkegaard grant priority to the vertical dimension, "before God," Kierkegaard's concept of a second redoubling fills out the ethical implications of the horizontal dimension. Kierkegaard's discourse shows concretely what it means for human love to mirror divine love. The love of God, who "hides a multitude of sins," first redoubles itself in human beings; and then, a second redoubling takes place, and these human beings gratefully become, like God, not only forgiving in themselves but also forgiving toward others.

Kierkegaard's indebtedness to Luther in this chapter of *Works of Love* would be easy to overlook, because he makes no effort to appeal to Luther's authority. His analysis of the paradox of forgiveness is in any case only secondary to the main topic of the discourse. For that matter, the explicit parallel between Luther's *simul justus* and Kierkegaard's concept of redoubling would not

---

[18]Paul Althaus, *The Theology of Martin Luther* (Philadelphia: Fortress, 1966) 244-45.

even have been available in Kierkegaard's day, long before the
Luther renaissance helped make the *simul justus* phrase into a
shibboleth of Reformation theology.

Yet the depth of Kierkegaard's debt to Luther in this discourse
is all the more impressive for being unobtrusive. The parallel
between the two men on *simul justus* lies at the personal roots of
their theologies. The common bond between them does not grow
only out of Kierkegaard's childhood memorization of Luther's
catechism, his attention to countless sermons from Lutheran
pulpits, or even his reading of Luther's works for his seminary and
doctoral training, important as all of these may be; it arises out of
a shared experience. Kierkegaard discovers his kinship to Luther
on the topic of forgiveness of sin through sharing with Luther an
overwhelming conviction of sin, together with an experience of
astonished joy at God's forgiving and forgetting it, and it is at this
level that Kierkegaard and Luther are most at one concerning the
message of God's hiding their sins.

# 3

## *"You Shall Love":*
## *Kant, Kierkegaard,*
## *and the Interpretation of Matthew 22:39*

### Paul Martens

[Jesus] said to him, " 'You shall love the Lord your God with all your heart, and with all your soul, and with all your mind.' This is the greatest and first commandment. And a second is like it: 'You shall love your neighbor as yourself.' On these two commandments hang all the law and the prophets."

(Matthew 22:37-40 NRSV)

Late in his life, Karl Barth acknowledged the reveille that Kierkegaard provided as a cock whose crowing "seemed to proclaim from near and far the dawn of a really new day."[1] However, the charity expressed by Barth, in the 1963 Copenhagen address, seems quite at odds with the remarks in the *Church Dogmatics* referring to Kierkegaard's understanding of the command to love.

Following the completion of the second edition of his *Römerbrief*, Barth's appreciation for Kierkegaard began to wane. Nowhere is this as evident as in his comparison of Kierkegaard's understanding of the command to love the neighbor, found in Matthew 22:39, to his particular understanding of Kantian ethics. Speaking directly of *Works of Love*, Barth suggests that it is perhaps possible to sense what Kierkegaard has in mind, but that his manner of stating it is quite false.[2] He defines the distinctively Kierkegaardian "unlovely, inquisitorial, and terribly judicial" character of *Works of*

---

[1]Karl Barth, "A Thank You and a Bow: Kierkegaard's Reveille," trans. H. Martin Rumscheidt, *Canadian Journal of Theology* 11 (1965): 5.

[2]Karl Barth, *Church Dogmatics*, vol. IV, *The Doctrine of Reconciliation (2)*, trans. and ed. G. W. Bromiley and T. F. Torrance (Edinburgh: T. & T. Clark, 1958) 782.

*Love* as contrasting the "creative, generous, liberating love of God." Finally, to complete the criticism of Kierkegaard's attempt to expound the duty to love, Barth states, "And it is not the case that a love which is imposed and enforced as a duty—however it may be understood—can ever be more than an *eros* with its back to the wall as it were."[3]

The following essay will deal with the problems Barth poses regarding Kierkegaard's understanding, if indeed it is problematic. Does Kierkegaard, in *Works of Love*, provide an understanding of the duty to love that is parallel to, or grounded in, the writing and thought of Immanuel Kant? If not, how, and to what extent do their readings differ? Ronald Green has recently asked very similar questions, and he has gone on to state that his own work, in the deepest sense, serves to show that what is true for Kant is also true for Kierkegaard.[4] In order to provide a differing solution to these questions, first, Kant's treatment of the command to love the neighbor will be presented within its context. Then the same shall be done with Kierkegaard's extensive exposition. Thirdly, several important similarities between their interpretations will be drawn out. Lastly, I will demonstrate that Kierkegaard and Kant do, in fact, provide very different ways of reading the commands. The significant differences will be shown to be due, in a large part, to the role of God in their variant conceptions of the *ordo salutis*.

*Fear and Trembling* has frequently been used to champion Kierkegaard's advocacy of the teleological suspension of the ethical, and to challenge the Kantian categorical imperative.[5] However, *Works of Love* provides a unique locus for the discussion, in relation to *Fear and Trembling*, for several important reasons. Firstly, *Works*

---

[3]Barth, *Church Dogmatics* IV/2:782.

[4]Ronald M. Green, *Kierkegaard and Kant: The Hidden Debt* (Albany: State University of New York Press, 1992) 222.

[5]Ronald M. Green, "ENOUGH IS ENOUGH! *Fear and Trembling* Is *Not* about Ethics," *Journal of Religious Ethics* 21 (1993): n.1. We must also recognize that there are several recent proponents for reading *Fear and Trembling* as a revision and enlargement of ethics in order to embrace the universal in the proper spirit. See Edward Mooney, "Getting Isaac Back: Ordeals and Reconciliations in *Fear and Trembling*", in *Foundations of Kierkegaard's Vision of Community: Religion, Ethics, and Politics in Kierkegaard* (hereafter *FKVC*), ed. George B. Connell and C. Stephen Evans (New Jersey: Humanities Press, 1992).

*of Love* belongs to his explicitly Christian "second authorship" and is signed by his own name. Secondly, it appears to formulate a reading of Matthew 22:39 which stands much closer to a Kantian understanding of the categorical imperative. Lastly, it provides a much more nuanced clarification of the relationship between the human being and God in the duty to love. However, before moving to a direct comparison between the two, a few words need to be said regarding Kant's treatment of the issue.

### 1. The Command to Love the Neighbor in Kant's Writings

The duty to love is treated in several of Kant's writings, but it is developed differently for different reasons. In *Grounding for the Metaphysics of Morals*, Kant attempts to do nothing more than seek out and establish the supreme principle of morality, namely, the categorical imperative. Scriptural commands are not central to Kant's formulation of the categorical imperative, but he does go out of his way to suggest that the command to love one's neighbor is an appropriate expression of practical love which arises from duty and conquers the propensities of inclination.[6]

In the *Metaphysics of Morals*, published twelve years later, the discussion of love towards one's neighbor is again reassessed, leading to a much more amplified statement. In this text, Kant provides a structure of duties that can be given in external laws (duties of right) and duties that cannot (duties of virtue). Under the discussion of duties of virtue, Kant argues that in the intelligible moral world, love and respect are the two laws of duty which draw us closer together and keep us at a distance. These two provide the poles from which Kant constructs the duties of virtue to others. Practical love is defined as a maxim of benevolence which is opposed to feeling or delight.[7] Further, Kant clarifies

---

[6]Immanuel Kant, *Grounding for the Metaphysics of Morals*, trans. James W. Ellington (Indianapolis: Hackett Publishing Co., 1981) 12. A similar treatment of the command—"to obey it from duty and not from a spontaneous inclination"—is given in *Critique of Practical Reason*, trans. Lewis Beck White, Library of Liberal Arts (New York: Macmillan Publishing, 1993) 86-88.

[7]Immanuel Kant, *The Metaphysics of Morals*, trans. Mary Gregor, Cambridge Texts in the History of Philosophy (Cambridge: Cambridge University Press, 1996) 199-206.

several duties subsumed under the general, and inappropriate, term love: beneficence, gratitude, and sympathy.

Between the publishing of these two texts stands *Religion within the Boundaries of Mere Reason*.[8] In a letter, dated May 4, 1793, Kant openly declares that *Religion* was an attempt to address the question "What may I hope for?" In describing what can be hoped for, Kant proposes a possible union of Christianity with the purest practical reason.[9] The structure of *Religion*, therefore, leads us through the hopelessness inherent in the human condition towards a hope firmly grounded in the gradual establishment of the good on earth.[10] The text forms a systematic analysis of the redemptive process of morality with a moral goal in mind.

Kant begins the text by placing humans in a natural state of evil; further, he places humans in a state of radical evil. There is a tremendous contest between our *predisposition* to good (prior to any exercise of freedom) and our *propensity* to evil (subjective ground of the possibility of an inclination) (*Rel*, 74-79). However, he maintains that the root of one's ability to do good arises in its possibility, which in turn, is guaranteed simply because the command that "I ought" resounds unabated in our souls. Willful choice can overcome propensities. The idea of the prototype of moral perfection[11] requires that we conform to it though it is nowhere visible in the physical world. Because it appears in our reason (not necessarily

---

[8]When referring to Immanuel Kant's *Religion within the Boundaries of Mere Reason*, I will be using the recent English translation of Greorge di Giovanni in *Immanuel Kant: Religion and Rational Theology*, ed. Allen W. Wood and George di Giovanni, Cambridge Edition of the Works of Immanuel Kant (Cambridge: Cambridge University Press, 1996). I will be referring to this work as *Religion* in my text, and as *Rel*, with appropriate page numbers, in notes and references.

[9]Immanuel Kant, "To C. F. Stäudlin, May 4, 1793," *Kant: Philosophical Correspondence, 1759–1799*, trans. Arnulf Zweig (Chicago: University Press of Chicago, 1967) 205.

[10]Gordon E. Michaelson, Jr. has recently brought out the importance of recognizing the framework of *Religion* as an explication of Kant's soteriology in *Fallen Freedom: Kant on Radical Evil and Moral Regeneration* (Cambridge: Cambridge University Press, 1990) 7.

[11]In deference to Christian terminology, Kant allows that the personified idea could possibly be considered the "Son of God." However, for practical purposes, the idea has complete reality within itself (*Rel*, 104-105).

in history), the moral prototype breaks the hold of evil and profoundly demonstrates that human corruption cannot be overcome except through the resources of our original predisposition within ourselves.

Although moral perfection can potentially be accomplished individually, Kant proposes an ethical union into which people would voluntarily submit to the laws of virtue alone. Kant is speaking about the church, but it is a fundamentally altered one which would be governed by moral laws alone. He is speaking of the one true religion. Once the parameters of the newly defined "Kingdom of God" are set, Kant proceeds to describe the appropriate ways to serve God in the Christian religion as a natural religion. In this context, the command to love the neighbor is radically rewritten.

Kant is well aware of the biblical account of Jesus Christ which is important to the Christian religion, but he interprets the Jesus of the biblical narrative as the first advocate of a pure and compelling religion in defiance of the dominant ecclesiastical faith which was oppressive and devoid of moral scope. He refers to Jesus as the founder of the pure church, and referring to one of the major roles of this founder, Kant states:

> Finally, he sums up all duties (1) into one *universal* rule (which includes the internal as well as the external moral relation of human beings), namely, Do your duty from no other incentive except the unmediated appreciation of duty itself, i.e. love God (the Legislator of all duties) above all else; (2) and into a *particular* rule, one namely that concerns the human being's external relation to other human beings as universal duty, Love every one as yourself, i.e. promote his welfare from an unmediated goodwill, one not derived from selfish incentives. (*Rel*, 182)

Kant does not cite any reference to the biblical parallel for the above quotation, but his distinctions within the discussion bear similarities to Matthew 22. There is a universal rule; there is a particular rule. Both of these rules sum up the duties of the universal religion of reason. The first rule, a universal rule, has two aspects, namely, the internal and external moral relations of human beings. The internal relation is the unmediated appreciation of duty itself as the sole incentive for humans to do their duty. Similarly, all external relations must be governed by duty as the sole incentive

and this definition is "clarified" by the example of "love God
(Legislator of all duties) above all else." The almost parallel use of
the terms "duty" and "God" appears confusing at first, and will be
dealt with later. Further, "unmediated" seems to communicate the
manner in which one becomes aware of duty. One becomes aware
of the duty through the "I ought" inscribed on every human heart
that becomes unlocked by reason alone.

The second rule, a particular rule, is nearly identical to the universal, except the external relations of human beings are slightly
elaborated. There is a striking similarity between the particular rule
and Kant's formulations of the categorical imperative.[12] None of
the formulations mention the concept of duty, though it undergirds them all.

Kant uses the term "unmediated goodwill" in the second rule
to describe the moral state which opposes selfish incentives in the
promotion of another's welfare. However, the parallel between
goodwill and loving another "as yourself" is not obvious. One
would expect that any self-love, for Kant, would be merely inclination not governed by moral law, yet he defines self-love in two
differing ways: the love of good pleasure and the love of good
will.[13] Only the latter definition can clarify Kant's reading of the
command to love your neighbor as yourself found in Matthew
22:39.

Therefore, Kant rewrites the biblical language of love into the
rational language of duty and it is the rootedness of all actions in
duty which defines true morality. Love ceases to exist as an important term in Kant at this point. Acting solely from duty is the only
way to restore a human's original predisposition to good. In this
manner, the commandments contained in Matthew 22 represent,
almost entirely, the hope for human restoration to moral goodness.

---

[12]Though Kant presents several variations on the categorical imperative, its
simplest form is: "Act only according to that maxim whereby you can at the same
time will that it should become a universal law." *Grounding for the Metaphysics of
Morals*, 30.

[13]Kant refers to this as *rational love* of oneself which prevents any adulteration
of incentives by other causes of contentment. This denotes respect for the law, but
he suggests that speaking in terms of self-love merely renders a more difficult
understanding of the principle (*Rel*, 90-91).

Kant outlines the integral part the essence of the command plays in the future hope of humanity:

> The restoration [of the original predisposition to good] is therefore only the recovery of the *purity* of the law, as the supreme ground of all our maxims. . . . The original good is *holiness of maxims* in the compliance to one's duty, hence merely out of duty, whereby a human being, who incorporates this purity into his maxims . . . is nonetheless upon the road of endless progress toward holiness. (*Rel,* 91)

Kant's formulation of the command to love the neighbor cannot be properly understood outside of its context of the restoration of humanity to original goodness. The vast scope of *Religion* provides the backdrop to Kant's interpretation of a central Christian command. Ronald Green has recently argued that those interested in deepening their understanding of the meaning of Christian neighbor-love will not "do badly" by starting with Kant. With this I heartily agree, but he also mentions that there may be some specifically religious dimensions of love missed by Kant.[14] It is these specifically religious dimensions of love that Kierkegaard addresses. Kant is a great thinker that cannot be easily challenged, but Kierkegaard does exactly that. It is the religious dimension of the command which Kierkegaard introduces, and amplifies; it is the religious dimension that ultimately reverses the placement of the command in Kierkegaard's treatment of Christian ethics. Kant uses the command to bring the human into original goodness; Kierkegaard uses the command to demonstrate the inability to achieve goodness.

## 2. The Duty to Love the Neighbor in Works of Love

*Works of Love* was written by Kierkegaard in 1847, near the beginning of his explicitly Christian authorship. The text is centered not on love, but on *works of love.* In order to accomplish this, Kierkegaard selects certain, very familiar, biblical passages and presents them in a unique, and often startling way. One of

---

[14]Ronald M. Green, "Kant on Christian Love," in *The Love Commandments: Essays in Christian Ethics and Moral Philosophy,* ed. Edmund N. Santurri and William Werpehowski (Washington DC: Georgetown University Press, 1992) 277.

these familiar passages comes from Matthew 22:39. The second chapter is the largest in the book and it addresses this small portion of Scripture. This chapter also falls into the first of two series of discourses which make up *Works of Love*. Very generally, it can be argued that the first series defines the works of love the Christian must accomplish; the second series celebrates what love accomplishes apart from what we, as humans, are capable of doing. Kierkegaard first presents the rigorous requirements, and their inherent impossibilities, which the duty to love Christianly entails. Then he moves through love's possibilities in dialectical fashion, concluding the work with a more mediated position. It is important that we notice not only the place in which the "duty to love" is discussed, but also what place it holds in Kierkegaard's formulation of the order of salvation.

In a Journal entry of 1851, Kierkegaard crystallizes the progression from duty to a mediated position which I suggest is already evident in *Works of Love*. He states:

> *Christianly* the emphasis does not fall so much upon to what extent or how far a person succeeds in meeting or fulfilling the requirement, if he actually is striving, as it is upon his getting an impression of the requirement in all its infinitude so that he rightly learns to be humbled and to rely upon grace.
>
> To pare down the requirement in order to fulfill it better (as if this were earnestness, that now it can all the more easily *appear* that one is earnest about wanting to fulfill the requirement)—to this Christianity in its deepest essence is opposed.
>
> No, infinite humiliation and grace, and then a striving born of gratitude—this is Christianity. (JP, 1:993)

In addressing the command to love, Kierkegaard focuses on three major themes. Each theme roughly correlates to a separate subsection of the chapter. The first is the security contained within the duty to love. Because the biblical text assumes that humans love themselves, Kierkegaard argues that people can love their neighbors appropriately only if they love themselves in a Christian way (WL, 22-23). To achieve this appropriate love, the duty to love must be understood as a word of *royal law*. This love stands polemically against conceptions of erotic love and friendship described by the poet. It is made free from inclinations and change; it is eternally made free in blessed independence; it is happily secured against despair. Christian love stands or falls, therefore, with the eternal, and Kierkegaard fervently argues that it becomes the eternal's responsibility to make sure it can be done.

In the second part, Kierkegaard introduces God as the middle term between all relationships. The chasm separating passionate love and Christian love seems to be split so wide that to bridge them becomes an impossibility. In partially addressing this problem he introduces the spiritual aspect of Christian love. The idea of loving one's neighbor as spirit appears unusual, but in qualifying his assertion, Kierkegaard states that in erotic love the I (of oneself) is defined as sensate-psychical-spiritual, and in friendship, the I is psychical-spiritual (WL, 56-57). To love one spiritually means, then, to love one without regard to the sensate-psychical aspects of the neighbor. This understanding is fundamental to loving Christianly because Kierkegaard bluntly states, "Ultimately, love for God is the decisive factor; from this originates love for the neighbor" (WL, 57). God becomes the Christian's ultimate love and the middle-term in all relationships, for only in loving God first, and above all else, can one love the neighbor who is the other human being. God, therefore, comes between all humans in relationship. Kierkegaard expresses this diagramatically as human-God-human. As such, the neighbor, as a spiritual equal before God, is only defined within the context of a relationship with God.

Lastly, Kierkegaard uses the third part of the chapter to further develop the relationship between the eternal and earthly relationships. However, he now casts the relationship between humans in light of the perfection of the eternal. Within interpersonal relations, Kierkegaard argues for both kinship and individuality. Kinship is eternally and unforgettably stamped through standing as equals before God; individuality is rooted in standing before God singly, as on a mountain peak looking down on the clouds. The neighbor is eternity's mark on every human being; before Christ there is no mass or aggregate.

It is important to note that Christian equality does not look at all like earthly likeness. Earthly preferences for distinctions cannot be eradicated, according to Kierkegaard. However, he goes further and affirms erotic love and friendship, but not without qualification. Instead, he suggests that they must be held in check through the duty to love the neighbor. He states:

[L]ove the beloved faithfully and tenderly, but let love for the neighbor be the sanctifying element in your union's covenant with God. Love your friend honestly and devotedly, but let love for the neighbor be what you learn from each other in your friendship's confidential relationship with God! Death, you see, abolishes all dissimilarities, but preference is always related to dissimilarities; yet the way to life and to the eternal goes through death and through the abolition of dissimilarities—therefore only love for the neighbor truly leads to life. (WL, 62)

A Christian is required to *lift oneself up* above distinctions (WL, 72). To love the neighbor Christianly, Kierkegaard is inevitably led to the discussion of loving God. He points continually to the impossibility of loving one's neighbor without God, yet the apparent contradiction of duty to *lift oneself up* rings of Kant's exhortation. The particular chapter devoted to Matthew 22:39 can be understood, on its own, in differing manners. One option would be to emphasize the individual's responsibility to heed the royal law as the final word. Emphasis here would yield a rather harsh yoke. I have chosen to emphasize, rather, the easier yoke of the duty to love by highlighting the role which God has, even within the limited discussion of Matthew 22:39. Whether I am correct to do so will be borne out once we look at the similarities and differences between Kant's and Kierkegaard's interpretations.

### 3. Similarities and Kierkegaard's Alleged Debt to Kant

The conversation between Kierkegaard and Kant is very broad, and it always needs to be recognized that time and other issues stand between them. However, when the conversation is limited to the command to love the neighbor, there are at least three recognizable points of convergence between Kant and Kierkegaard: a) the fallen state of humanity;[15] b) the validity of the duty to love; and c) an understanding of God as the lawgiver.

---

[15]I am using the term "fallen" loosely. Kant uses the terminology of evil and radical evil, while Kierkegaard uses the language of despair and sin. However, I have followed Michaelson's lead and used "fallen" to represent the broad umbrella under which these stand.

A. *Fallen Humanity and a Possibility of Goodness.* As we have already seen, Kant gives extended attention to the "natural" state of humanity. Humanity is evil in that people cannot incorporate goodness into their maxims, and this evil is an internal condition which every human being is predisposed to from birth. Kierkegaard, similarly, addresses the state of humanity before the "you shall" of Christian love is appropriated by stating, "Anyone who has not undergone this change *is* in despair" (WL, 40).[16] In *Works of Love*, despair is primarily a condition which is perpetuated by natural love, or, all love which is not transformed into duty. Both Kant and Kierkegaard presume an internal evil opposed to, or in disharmony with, moral goodness.

However, as Kant provides the germ of the return to goodness by claiming a predisposition to good, Kierkegaard also provides a means through which goodness is imparted to humanity. He believes that the love God has implanted within each human is the foundation upon which Christian love is built. Both thinkers attribute a certain aspect of humanity's ontological reality as the ground upon which the command can be followed.[17] For Kierkegaard, love, God's love, is deeply rooted in human nature, and this stands at the core of Kierkegaard's understanding of neighbor. It is "eternity's light" which shines through earthly distinctions and dissimilarity. Paul Roubiczek rightly recognizes that the fundamental equality of all humans is grounded in this love. It explains the concept of neighbor, and only because of it can love be commanded. Only by its acceptance can we obey the command.[18]

Though the return to "goodness" follows differing paths for Kierkegaard and Kant, the path, for both, passes through the narrow gate of the duty to love. In a very real sense, the duty to

---

[16]Here in *Works of Love*, like *Sickness unto Death*, Kierkegaard defines despair as a misrelation in a person's innermost being (WL, 40; SUD, 15).

[17]One must notice, however, that Kant's understanding of the predisposition to good is concerned with grounding the possibility of loving the neighbor in one's own predisposition with respect to the law while Kierkegaard's assumption that love is present in all humans places the possibility of loving the neighbor in the relationship between oneself, God and other individuals.

[18]Paul Roubiczek, *Existentialism: For and Against* (Cambridge: Cambridge University Press, 1964) 71.

love found in Matthew 22:39 is a necessary and valid command for both writers.

B. *The Validity of the Command to Love.* The fact that both work the biblical passage into their writing demonstrates that it is considered to be important to both Kierkegaard and Kant. In general, they both recognize that humans are often given to the influence of feelings, drives, inclination, passions, and in short, the powers of immediacy (WL, 25). The duty to love is intimately tied to salvation from these powerful influences against moral purity. However, a little more clarification is necessary.

As we have seen, Kant presupposes a predisposition to good innate within each individual. In order to harness and guide this goodness against evil, he introduces the simple process of maxim making. In subordinating and redefining the commands to love in terms of duty, Kant provides the ultimate maxims, his two-pronged formulation of the duty to love, which are compatible with his understanding of Christianity. Therefore, the command to love one's neighbor plays an integral role in the progress of overcoming evil.

Kierkegaard, on the other hand, argues that those in despair reject the necessity to love the neighbor because they are entirely given to earthly passions and inclinations. However, love can be Christianly performed only when one has the proper understanding of God's love implanted within each and every individual, including the neighbor. One can come to practice Christian love for the neighbor only when it becomes a duty.[19] Therefore, Kierkegaard believes the command to love the neighbor is fundamental to overcoming despair.

One further footnote to this section is their common understanding of the free will in being able to choose to practice love as a duty. Also, neither of them specifies particular expressions and actions as appropriate love; the disposition of the will (or heart) is what qualifies an action as good or evil; the fruit of love can be

---

[19]Phillip L. Quinn, "The Divine Command Ethics in Kierkegaard's *Works of Love*," in *Faith, Freedom, and Rationality: Philosophy of Religion Today*, ed. Jeff Jordan and Daniel Howard-Snyder (Lanham MD: Rowman & Littlefield, 1996) 44.

hidden. For Kant, to be free is to be a morally responsible person.[20] His understanding of *propensity* to evil allows for the ability to choose goodness. Each moment of action can be approached as if there is no influence of prior habit or tendency to do evil. With each failure to realize one's duty, one newly enters evil (*Rel*, 87). Therefore, habit has a place in moral action neither for Kant nor for Kierkegaard.

Whether Kierkegaard radicalizes and exaggerates Kant's understanding of individual freedom cannot be resolved here,[21] but we must recognize that Kierkegaard assumes that one can choose to, or not to, heed God's call to make love one's duty. However, we must also recognize that Kierkegaard redefines freedom by suggesting that until love becomes duty, it is not free (WL, 37-39, 147-49). At least partially parallel to the goal of the categorical imperative, Kierkegaard's formulation of the *royal law* of the command to love seeks to achieve true freedom from enslavement to one's inclinations. One final point of convergence now arises. Both see God as the administrator of the law.

C. *The Conception of God as the Lawgiver.* God does not play a central role in Kant's *Religion*. However, Kant cannot entirely drop God from the progress to moral perfection. God is necessary, but an understanding of him arises from the necessity to assume a higher, moral, most holy, and omnipotent being who can unite the good as a Legislator of duties (*Rel*, 58). To Kant, this definition sums up three subsidiary roles: (1) holy lawgiver; (2) benevolent ruler and moral guardian; and (3) just judge and administrator of laws (*Rel*, 165-66). Kierkegaard, too, is similar to Kant in that he assumes the royal law of the commands is administered by God. At this point, however, the similarities begin to disappear. Green's argument that Kierkegaard's God "turns out to be very similar to Kant's" appears strained, at best, if limited to the commands to love.[22] In the following section, I will attempt to draw out the

[20]See Roger Sullivan, *Immanuel Kant's Moral Theory* (Cambridge: Cambridge University Press, 1989) 46.

[21]This is the charge leveled by George Schrader in "Kant and Kierkegaard on Duty and Inclination," in *Kierkegaard: A Collection of Critical Essays*, ed. Josiah Thompson (New York: Anchor Books, 1972) 340.

[22]Green, *Kierkegaard and Kant: The Hidden Debt*, 127.

differences in Kant's and Kierkegaard's understandings of God as they relate to the commands to love. In doing so, I will demonstrate that, although Kant and Kierkegaard have several similar conceptions which frame the context of the command, their understandings of God, and his role in the drama of human redemption, radically drives them in separate directions.

### 4. God, Duty, Love, and their Differing Roles in Human Redemption

Though we have seen that there are marked similarities between Kant and Kierkegaard thus far, the root and fulfillment of the command to love are explicated in profoundly differing ways. The three main points of contention are: (1) the foundation of the command; (2) Christ as the prototype of dutiful love; and (3) the definitions of love and duty. As we analyze these issues, we see that Kierkegaard owes some of his conceptions and formulations to Kant, but he also radically injects a religiousness into the commands through his understanding of God.

A. *The Foundation of the Command.* For Kant, the whole of morality is grounded in the "I ought" which resounds unabated in the soul. From this innate understanding of perceived morality, Kant proceeds to construct the basic principles of moral living. Further, he goes to great lengths to demonstrate that no book, whatever its authority, can substitute for the holy law within which already has made it a duty to answer for everything. Therefore, the biblical account of Jesus giving the command can only serve as a fortification for what is already known a priori.[23]

Although Kant argues that his God is not entirely remote, it appears that he does not allow God to impose on, or interact with, the phenomenal world. Reading *Religion* sympathetically, John Hare suggests that Kant requires us to make room for such

---

[23]Kant, "To J. C. Lavater [after April 28, 1775] [sic]," *Philosophical Correspondence,* 82. In this letter Kant states, "My presupposition is that no book, whatever its authority might be . . . can substitute for the religion of conscience. The latter tells me that the holy law within me has already made it my duty to answer for everything I do. . . . Because of this presupposition, I seek in the Gospels not the ground of my faith but its fortification, and I find in the moral spirit of the Gospels a clear distinction between . . . my duty and that which God has done for me."

assistance in our belief, even if we, as humans, cannot do anything about it.[24] However, even Hare agrees that Kant does not, and cannot, reconcile belief in supernatural assistance with his pure religion of reason.[25] This is one of the continual tensions within *Religion*. Kant suggests that there may be some supernatural cooperation to become good or better, which he describes as a "positive increase of force," yet he demands that humans make themselves antecedently worthy of receiving it. Further, he argues that divine blessedness is the crowning hope of humanity's final moral success. Kant's doctrine of divine blessedness contains the concept of an object which we represent to ourselves as a cause supplementing our incapacity with respect to the moral end. However, he makes it very clear that this blessedness is merely a means of achieving a virtuous human disposition. It is clear that God's blessedness holds out expectation of the final end, yet it is powerless to guarantee or achieve it (*Rel*, 89-90; 200-201). What we are left with in Kant's explanation of the human-divine interaction returns once again to the human striving to love the Law. He states, "The highest goal of the moral perfection of finite creatures, never completely attainable by human beings, is, however, the love of the Law."[26]

Therefore, the command to love arises within the human heart. If the biblical account also makes the claim that the command is valid, Kant also allows it to stand to fortify his a priori moral understandings. Further, since God cannot be the source of the command, his role in helping it become actualized becomes unclear at best, and incoherent at worst.

---

[24]This is Hare's paraphrase of *Religion*, 96-97. John E. Hare, *The Moral Gap: Kantian Ethics, Human Limits, and God's Assistance*, Oxford Studies in Theological Ethics (Oxford: Clarendon Press, 1996) 27, 52.

[25]Hare, *The Moral Gap*, 60-65.

[26]*Rel*, 170. In a footnote, he recounts his understanding of the idea "God is love." This love is enacted by judging. Instead of judging guilty/not guilty, Kant's loving God judges according to the designations worthy/unworthy so that a person's merit can be valued. Only the worthy receive salvation, and this judgment would proceed out of love. However, we must be reminded, once again, that Kant also argues that this is merely an intellectual exercise used to evaluate one's own moral worth (*Rel*, 113-17).

Kierkegaard approaches the command from the opposite direction. He invests all of the binding power of the command within the authority of the revelation by God in Scripture. Repeatedly, he asserts that humans could not have come up with the Christian understanding of love, as a duty, on their own. God, breaking into history, issues this royal law. Its authority rests simply on the fact that it was God who issued the command. It is not hard to understand; but its offensiveness will surprise and disturb. However, it is important to note that the Scripture, as it recounts the command, is not merely an external, objective fact; it is worth nothing until there is a relationship between the Word of Scripture and the obedient heart of the listener or reader.[27] In stating this, Kierkegaard clearly defines the validity of the command to love only in the context of a relationship between God, as the giver of the command, and the individual, as the receiver of the command. Once again, we return to Kierkegaard's description of God as the middle term in all Christian interactions.

A brief reading of the opening prayer of *Works of Love* reveals how important God is as the source of love. In it, Kierkegaard not only celebrates that God is love, but further that God is the source of all love in heaven and earth, "so that one who loves is what he is only by being in you!" (WL, 3). However, the prayer does not only focus on God as the source of love; the Trinitarian structure of the prayer also addresses the revealer of love in Christ.[28] Christ's role in understanding love is praised heartily by Kierkegaard, as well as Kant, yet the specific role that Christ plays forms another critical juncture at which they diverge significantly.

B. *Christ as the Prototype and Fulfillment of Dutiful Love.* For Kierkegaard, it is imperative to recognize that Christ is the manifestation of God's love. Only in a historical existence could God's love and sacrifice be demonstrated. Only in a historical existence could the law be fulfilled. Only in a historical existence could God present an example for humans to learn from and seek to imitate.

---

[27]Stephen N. Dunning, "Who Sets the Task? Kierkegaard on Authority," in *FKVC*, 22.

[28]See Michael Plekon for a brief analysis of the Trinitarian structure of the opening prayer in "Kierkegaard the Theologian: The Roots of His Theology in *Works of Love*," in *FKVC*, 7-8.

Only in a historical existence could God issue the commands to love God and neighbor (WL, 99-101). One does not need to refer to *Philosophical Fragments* to understand the importance Kierkegaard attaches to the historical existence of the revealer of love. *Works of Love* spells it out very clearly.

There is only one way through the severity, and boundlessness, of the law. The love of Christ fulfills the law. He describes the use of the law as teaching us our downfall. Christ then became the downfall of the law because he was what it required. Christ came to fulfill the law, and in doing so, he saves us and presents an example of Christian love; he did not come to set an example. The term "presents" means that the necessity to completely mimic Christ is impossible, but his example does serve as the goal to which we strive. Setting an example, to Kierkegaard, would require complete imitation. This distinction, found in an 1849 journal entry, attempts to describe a qualitative difference between two ways of viewing Christ's life. Later in the same entry, Kierkegaard states:

> And in our striving to approach the prototype, the prototype itself is again our very help. It alternates; when we are striving, then he is the prototype; and when we stumble, lose courage, etc., then he is the love which helps us up, and then he is the prototype again.
> It would be the most fearful anguish for a person if he understood Christ in such a way that he only became his prototype and now by his own efforts he would resemble the prototype. Christ is simultaneously "the prototype," and precisely because he is that absolutely he is also the prototype who can be approached through the help of the prototype himself. (JP, 1:334)

It appears that close attention to the fine distinction Kierkegaard makes between the two roles of Christ begins to answer the charge by James Farris that Kierkegaard does not provide an appropriation of Christ as a model and enabler in the unfolding of a kingdom of righteousness.[29] For Kierkegaard, the law exists first, but Christ can be appropriated as the blessing which satisfied the hunger of the law. Christ reveals what love is, yet Kierkegaard confidently also calls him the Savior and Redeemer (WL, 3). More

---

[29]James Farris, "Christ as Prototype," *Toronto Journal of Theology* 8 (1992): 294.

than merely setting an example, Christ injects grace into the redemption story and the Spirit continuously reminds the believer of this love-sacrifice (WL, 4).

Kant cannot follow Kierkegaard into this territory. As stated earlier, Kant's Christ is the founder of the church, and as such, is the ideal of moral perfection. Further, the historicity of Christ is irrelevant, since the prototype of pure morality is a rational ideal. As a rational ideal, Christ becomes the standard against which humans judge themselves in moral development (Rel, 104). It can in no other way impose itself upon one's existence. The gulf between Kant and Kierkegaard on the foundation and communication of the command to love appears to be ever widening. Up until now, I have been using the terms "love" and "duty" in the same way for both writers. However, as we come to understand the different foundations of the command, we are finally enabled to see their language and grammar are dependent on these differences.

C. *Definitions of Love and Duty.* The use of the terms love and duty are widespread and often contradictory between Kierkegaard and Kant. For Kant, the emphasis is on duty; for Kierkegaard, the emphasis is on love. Kant primarily defines love as inclination and passion, and therefore, love cannot serve as a guide to morality. Therefore, he translates the command in terms of duty alone. Kierkegaard retains the use of love, but provides a new "grammar" of its own by which it is understood and known.[30] Love is the term that denotes content; duty is the term used to describe how love is expressed.

Duty is used in several ways by Kant. First, it is the requirement laid down by the law, that is, doing one's duty. The thrust of this definition is obedience to a law that is understood through reason. In this sense, God is also seen as the legislator of all duties. However, he also appears to use duty to represent the entire system of laws and requirements, that is, for the sake of duty. In this case, the law is not a particular action, but rather an abstraction of the concept of law. Duty is then understood only with refer-

---

[30]Sylvia Walsh, "Forming the Heart: The Role of Love in Kierkegaard's Thought," in *The Grammar of the Heart: New Essays in Moral Philosophy and Theology*, ed. Richard Bell (San Francisco: Harper & Row, 1988) 235.

ence to the laws of morality or the divine Legislator. In the first definition, specific actions are required, but the second definition is abstract. The command can then easily be interpreted to state that one should do one's duties through an appreciation for duty.

Kierkegaard performs almost the same sequence of definition. First, he uses the term "love" in terms of pure action, that is, the life of Christ.[31] This action is not necessarily empirical, but often exists only spiritually; this spiritual qualification makes it Christian. Love is also used to refer to God, since God is love. Therefore, Kierkegaard can formulate the command in the same way as Kant; the formulation is simply love is acted out through an appreciation of Love.

Although the commands are reformulated almost identically, love and duty, according to Kierkegaard, cannot be used interchangeably. Kierkegaard makes it manifestly clear that, humanly speaking, it is impossible to fulfill the boundless ocean of requirements which the duty to love entails. However, love, Christ's love, covers a multitude of sins. The sinner, who is unable to fulfill one's duty, can find comfort and eternal defense through Christ from the judgement of God. Kierkegaard does not reject the idea that the law should be followed, but he does reject the idea that a human can follow it without Christ.[32] Though this idea is ever present in *Works of Love*, it is clearest expressed later in *Judge for Yourself* with the following prayer:

> Help us all, each one of us, you who both will and can, you who are both the prototype and the Redeemer, and in turn both the Redeemer and prototype, so that when the striving one droops under the prototype, crushed, almost despairing, the Redeemer raises him up again; but at the same moment you are again the prototype so that he may be kept in the striving. O Redeemer, by your holy suffering and death you have made satisfaction for everyone and everything; no eternal salvation either can or shall be earned—it has been earned. (JFY, 147)

---

[31]Kierkegaard maintains a definition of erotic love, which is given to passions and inclinations, but this is self-love, not Christian love (WL, 50).

[32]Though Kierkegaard is not exactly systematic (and perhaps a bit "cagey" about the doctrine of God's assistance), I think Hare rightfully argues from *Either/Or* that Kant's version of the ethical life must break down internally (*The Moral Gap*, 191, 205).

When love hides a multitude of sins, there is also hope. Kant speaks of hope, and his hope for the good's victory over evil is grounded in the ability to accomplish good before any talk of grace. Virtue is the expression of obedience to duty, but grace is unseeable, unknowable, unreliable, but hoped for. For Kierkegaard, love takes upon itself the work of hope. One's hope in eternity is rooted in the relationship with God. In this relationship, we learn to love and we learn to hope. One who love's the neighbor hopes for the possibility of the good in the neighbor, and therefore in oneself (WL, 260). This reflexive relationship of love gives rise to hope. It appears that Kierkegaard would reject the possibility of any reason for hope being found in Kant's understanding of the commands to love.

We have now come to the point at which we can see that Kant and Kierkegaard do not view God, Christ, the commands, or love in the same way. It is difficult, if not impossible, to claim that they are saying the same thing, or seeking to accomplish the same goal. If anything has been accomplished by this essay, hopefully it has demonstrated that Kant and Kierkegaard do not interpret Matthew 22:39 in the same way. For Kant, ultimate moral responsibility is on humanity:

> So far as morality is based on the conception of the human being as one who is free but who also, just because of that, binds himself through his reason to unconditional laws, it is in need neither of the idea of another being above him in order that he recognize his duty, nor, that he observe it, of an incentive other than the law itself. (*Rel*, 57)

For Kierkegaard, moral responsibility ultimately rests in God:

> And when eternity says, "You shall love," it is responsible for making sure that this can be done. What is all other comfort compared with that of eternity! What is all other spiritual care compared with that of eternity! (WL, 41)

### 5. Conclusion

Let us return once again to Karl Barth. I have attempted to demonstrate, in closely reading the interpretations of the command to love, that Kierkegaard's understanding of the duty to love is not as he claims. It is not *eros* with its back against the wall, and it is not "unlovely, inquisitorial and terribly judicial." In fact, I believe that Kierkegaard also answers Barth's criticism that he does not know God's "*Yes.*" It appears that Barth wrongly suggests that those schooled in Kierkegaard can not find comfort in what the majesty of God's free grace has done, is still doing, and shall do conclusively.[33] Kierkegaard, like Kant, is revolted by the thought of cheap grace appropriated without cost, and there is no way one could confuse him with a universalist. However, I suggest that Kierkegaard's thought is infused with a sense of hope and assurance that Barth does not recognize.

Kant powerfully argues for a vision of morality which is grounded on "reason alone," and in some ways it looks very much like Kierkegaard's treatment of ethics. However, Kant fails to see that from a position of radical evil, practical progress in the individual and communal moral life, without a fundamental dependence upon God's direct intervention into the phenomenal world, is impossible. Fortunately, the end of the story is not the duty to love, but "Beloved, let us love one another." Kierkegaard, himself, did not think that he had reached the perfection of the Apostle John's intermediate mood. Nevertheless, the goal of Christian love is not to remain in the rigorousness of duty, nor is it to move beyond the necessity to love. The poet himself states it best, "There is something transfigured and beatific in these words, but there is also a sadness that is agitated over life and mitigated by the eternal" (WL, 375).

Kierkegaard, as a specifically Christian interpreter of the command, has not solved all the issues inherent in the discussion of Christian love. However, he does provide a foundation for analysis and evaluation of strictly moral readings of the commands to love. Kierkegaard's descriptions of the self-lover are strikingly similar to the aesthete found in some of the pseudonymous works, and in *Works of Love* he designates the necessary requirements for progress, through the ethical, towards the religious life. The spiritual dimension brought out in his exegesis prescribes a Chris-

---

[33]Karl Barth, "Kierkegaard and the Theologians," trans. H. Martin Rumscheidt, *Canadian Journal of Theology* 13 (1967): 65.

tian solution to being tossed upon the despairing waves of poetic love; it provides a shelter from the boundless assault of the law.

And so we return to the opening prayer at the beginning of the text. Clearer than anywhere else, it is here that Kierkegaard challenges a purely moral understanding of the command to love the neighbor. He states:

> How could one speak properly about love if you were forgotten, you God of love, source of all love in heaven and on earth; you who spared nothing but in love gave everything; you who are love, so that one who loves is what he is only by being in you! How could one speak properly about love if you were forgotten, you who revealed what love is, you our Savior and Redeemer, who gave yourself in order to save all. (WL, 3)

# 4

## Kierkegaard's Ontology of Love

### Arnold B. Come

[W]hat, in the spiritual sense, is the ground and foundation of the spiritual life that is to bear the building? It is love. Love is the source of everything [*Alt*] and, in the spiritual sense, love is the deepest ground of the spiritual life. (WL, 215)

[*B*]*efore God* to be oneself, . . . this is the source and origin of all distinctiveness [*Eiendommelighed*]. . . . To have distinctiveness is to believe in the distinctiveness of everyone else [*enhver Anden*], because distinctiveness is not mine but is God's gift by which he gives being [*at være*] to me, and he indeed . . . gives being to all [*Alle*]. (WL, 271)[1]

In these passages from two different discourses in *Works of Love*, Kierkegaard is taking a position within the enigmatic sphere of being, and thereby implies his own positions on some of the puzzling questions that beset the general field of ontology.

Kierkegaard rarely uses the term "ontology."[2] Of course he was familiar with the problem of being from his extensive readings in and about Greek philosophy, but he never makes a thorough analysis and direct treatment of that problem. He was probably (and wisely) unsure how to organize his thoughts in this field, but basically he refused on principle to become involved in an abstract,

---

[1]The word *Alt* in this context means every aspect of the human being, including its finitude (sensuousness, temporality, sociality, historicality, etc), in fact can designate the universe. But the word *Alle* in this context clearly means simply other selves like oneself.

[2]There are three passages in his notes from lectures and readings (*Papirer* II C 20 in 1837; JP, 5:5598 and 1:197 in 1843); one in *The Concept of Irony* (CI, 45-46) and one in *Stages on Life's Way* (SLW, 476-77); two in background notes for *Postscript* (*Papirer*, VI B 29, p. 109; JP, 1:199); and one in his journals (JP, 3:3089 from early 1847). Their content will be used where relevant below.

speculative approach to any problem because he considered it to be an illusionary way to grasp the truth of human existence. So he says, "a logical system can be given, but a system of existence cannot be given" (CUP, 1:109). And even in his major treatment of "logical problems" in *Postscript*, he spends only a couple of pages specifically contrasting the "empirical" and "idealistic" definitions of the relationship between thinking and being (CUP, 1:189-90) (which we will look at later). And he asserts that great confusion has been caused by "modern speculative thought" when it explains necessity in terms of world history, whereas "*necessity* must be treated by itself" (CUP, 1:343). Indeed, he says, "What our age needs most to illuminate the relationship between logic and ontology is an examination of the concepts: possibility, actuality, and necessity" (JP, 1:199).[3]

In spite of his reluctance to attack this field directly, Kierkegaard had worked out some rudimentary views on the general problems of being before he developed what I call his "ontology of love" in *Works of Love*. And in *Practice in Christianity* there is one key passage that provides a crucial concept of being that I believe already informed everything he wrote in *Works of Love*. It is requisite that we summarize this material first, because today the words ontology and ontological are being freely, and often loosely, used in both philosophical and religious writing, even while some decry all attempts at any ontological formulation whatsoever. Therefore we must know what Kierkegaard himself means by *being* when, in *Works of Love*, he speaks of love as the being of God and hence the source of all other being. I will try to be as brief as possible so that we can get on with the major concern of this essay.

---

[3]The latter is a background note for *Postscript*. As he says in *Postscript* (1:343), he had briefly treated this theme in *Fragments* (PF, 73-75). For an extended explication of Kierkegaard's treatment of this theme see my *Kierkegaard as Humanist* (Montreal: McGill-Queen's Press, 1995) chap. 5; also my *Trendelenburg's Influence on Kierkegaard's Modal Categories* (Montreal: Inter Editions, 1991). It is important to note that Kierkegaard's rejection of a system of *human* existence does not imply that he was an empirical skeptic. See Thomas C. Anderson's excellent commentary on this issue in his article, "Kierkegaard and Approximation Knowledge," in *IKC: Concluding Unscientific Postscript to "Philosophical Fragments,"* ed. Robert L. Perkins (Macon GA: Mercer University Press, 1997), 187-203.

### Kierkegaard'S General View of Being

As I just noted, Kierkegaard rarely uses the terms ontology/ ontological, but he did use the information gleaned from university lectures and readings to begin a formulation of his own thoughts in the field while writing *Philosophical Fragments* and *The Concept of Anxiety*. He gets at his own concept of being by analyzing the ancient Greek concept of nonbeing. In *Concept of Anxiety* Haufniensis takes the Eleatics to task because for them "nonbeing was conceived ontologically" in the purely *negative* sense of "that which is not," that is, τὸ μὴ ὄν is τὸ κενόν, nonbeing is the empty void, and "only being is." He says that Plato and modern philosophy refute this position, but Christianity goes further to insist that "nonbeing [*Ikke Værende*] is present everywhere as the nothing [*Intet*] from which things were created, as semblance, . . . as sensuousness removed from spirit, as the temporal forgotten by the eternal; consequently, the task is to do away with it in order to bring forth being [*Værende*]" (CA, 82-83).

In *Fragments* Climacus provides a more detailed analysis of what happens in this transition. He says, "This change is not in essence [*Væsen*] but in being [*Væren*], and is from not existing [*ikke at være til*] to existing. But this nonbeing [*Ikke Væren*] that is abandoned by that which comes into existence [*det Tilblivende*] must also exist." And what is the character and status of this being that yet is nonbeing? It is "possibility, and a being that is being is indeed actual being or actuality." And this transition of "coming-into-existence" [*Tilblivelse*] of possibility "demonstrates that it is not necessary. . . . All coming into existence occurs in freedom, not by way of necessity," and "point[s] back to a freely acting cause" (PF, 73-75).

Obviously, the "actual being" that Climacus is talking about is that of *human* being, and of human being not in its merely physical and temporal factuality but in its hidden "illusiveness" of freedom. It is the being that cannot escape the fact that "[a]ll coming into existence is a *suffering*," the suffering involved in the annihilation of both "the possibility that is accepted" and the possibility "that is excluded" (PF, 74), but also the suffering involved in believing that "the transition from nothing, from nonbeing, and from the multiple possible *'how'* " has occurred, in spite of the claims of "immediate sensation and cognition" to provide the adequate explanation of the transition (PF, 81-82).

From this material two things are clear. First, the "nothing," from which human actuality comes into existence or actuality, is not emptiness or vacuity, but a set of circumstances that provide the occasion for a possibility and potentiality or "essence" which already has a kind of "being" or existence. So the alleged "elimination" of nonbeing in the transition to being (CA, 83) and the alleged "annihilation" of possibility in its transition to actuality (PF, 81) is accomplished in bringing sensuousness into accord with spirit and temporality into accord with eternity. So, sensuousness and temporality continue to exist but not as such; they are transformed in their very being by their new context of spirit (self) and eternity.

This kind of transition in being, this ontological event, is what Anti-Climacus has in mind when, in *Sickness*, he says that the self is a synthesis or relation of infinitude and finitude, and that this "relation, . . . even though it is derived [i.e., created], relates . . . to itself, which is freedom. The self *is* freedom" (emphasis added, and I believe "relates to" is preferable to "relates *itself* to"). "But freedom is the dialectical aspect of the categories of possibility and necessity" (SUD, 29). In these words we find an *abstract* ontological definition of human being as sheer freedom, but there immediately follows a *concrete* ontological definition that lodges that freedom integrally in the dialectic of possibility and necessity and, by implication, in the dialectic of eternity and temporality. Kierkegaard generally will have nothing to do with a purely abstract ontology of sheer substance, essence, concept, ideal, but always struggles to clarify a dynamic "being" that is present and operative in the enactment of spiritual possibility within the limitations of concrete finitude and of both an inner and outer necessity.

### Kierkegaard's Method of Ontological Formulation

The second thing clearly emphasized in these materials of *Concept of Anxiety* and *Philosophical Fragments* is that the kind of being that comes into existence in the sphere of the spiritual/ eternal cannot be grasped or explicated within the concepts and procedures of immediate sensation and purely rational cognition. Truth in the sphere of spirit (self) is of a different order than truth in the purely sensate/rational sphere. Throughout his entire authorship, Kierkegaard repeatedly asserts that the truth of religious faith and of the understanding that comes with it neither consist of nor are reducible to a set of statements or concepts or doctrines. Rather, this truth consists of a kind of living expressed in actions in relationship with oneself and with other beings who are also spirit.

One of the crucial implications of this kind of truth and being (for Kierkegaard) is that it requires a language peculiar to itself and quite different from the languages used for sensate experience and for rational cognition. His most direct statement of this view is in one of his discourses on love. He says that all human beings are spirit from the moment of birth but "become conscious as spirit" only later, after living for a period on the purely senate-psychical level. "But this first portion is not to be cast aside when the spirit awakens." Rather, it is taken over and "becomes the metaphorical." Hence for the realm of the spirit, the words are the same but "all human speech . . . about the spiritual is essentially metaphorical. . . . There is a world of difference between the two." And this fact is the basis of a great confusion between those who remain living at the purely sensate-psychical level and those who have "made the transition . . . to the other side," because "just as the spirit is invisible, so also is its language a secret" (WL, 209-10).

For Kierkegaard, this distinction between two kinds of language also implies that no word, no image, no metaphor, no concept or idea actually contains or captures truth when the truth of being spirit is being talked about, because this truth resides in living active relationships of conscious subjects with their complex, diversified environment, including other conscious subjects. So a continuing concern throughout the authorship is an exploration of the nature of indirect communication, because it is the only medium through which human beings can communicate as subjective beings. And indirect communication as a distinct medium implies that the pursuit of truth in the realm of human spirit (self) requires not only its own language but its own methodology. Put succinctly in Kierkegaardian terms, it requires subjective reflection rather than objective reflection.

By this terminology he means that one can speak about this truth only out of one's own subjective experience, with its inwardness, isolation and the uniqueness of the individual self. The truth that involves being conscious spirit cannot be caught in the impersonal, abstract generalizations secured through disinterested objective observation. Furthermore, when one human subjective self wishes to share this kind of truth with another such self, it requires the other person's own personal appropriation of that truth as meaningful in terms of her/his own inner self. In such intercourse there must be both a willingness to share and to give, as well as a willingness to receive and to accept. This sharing between and among personal subjects requires and involves love, or one might say that this kind of sharing *is* love, because in its essence this kind of sharing is the act of affirming and encouraging each individual to explore and to be and to become his or her own unique self. And of course there is no love of this kind without freedom. For want of a better designation, one may call this method phenomenological—in a specialized sense of that term.[4]

*The Role of Categories in Ontological Formulation*

Kierkegaard clearly relates this entire view of truth to the question of ontology in a brief journal entry early in the year of 1847 as he began writing *Works of Love*. In the entry, he calls upon all *"human* science [*Videnskab*]" (meaning both philosophy and natural science) to acknowledge that there is "something [it] can clearly understand that [it] cannot understand." In other words, it must recognize that there is a dimension to being (truth) that remains "the inexplicable" (*det Uforklarige*). If science "will take the trouble to understand itself, it must straightway posit the paradox." And he then declares that the inexplicable or paradoxical "is not a concession [i.e., an insignificant detail] but a category, an ontological qualification, which expresses the relationship between an existing cognitive spirit and the eternal truth" (JP, 3:3089).

---

[4]For a treatment of subjective/objective reflection, see my *Kierkegaard as Humanist*, 77-107; for a defense of Kierkegaard as phenomenologist, see my "Kierkegaard's Method: Does He Have One?" in *Kierkegaardiana* 14 (1988): 14-28.

In this brief statement Kierkegaard has revealed several significant aspects of his own developing ontology. First, he interrelates
"category" and "ontological determinant," and thus implies that
the use of certain categories is one way to explore the nature of
being, and hence they can be called "ontological" determinants or
definitions (*Bestemmelse*). At the time of this entry, he was also
writing *The Book on Adler*, and there he uses similar language when
he asserts that Christian awakening and Christian emotion must
be "controlled by conceptual definitions [*Begrebs-Bestemmelser*], and
when the emotion is transformed into or expressed in words in
order to be communicated, this transformation must continually
take place within the conceptual definitions" (BA, 113). He continues: "What is required for a Christian awakening is on the one
hand the Christian emotion and on the other firmness and definiteness of conceptual language [*Begrebs-Sprogets*]" (BA, 114-15).[5]
Hence I am suggesting that Kierkegaard was in search for a
language of categories or concepts, to be used in a "metaphorical"
way, which would develop through a cyclic or circular interplay
with the concrete spiritual experience of the truth, so that this
language would not only repeatedly be shaped and reformed by
that experience but also serve as a means for controlling, enriching
and communicating that experience.

Kierkegaard displays an intense interest in categories throughout his authorship, and it was encouraged by his reading of
Trendelenburg's *Geschichte der Kategorienlehre* (History of the Doctrine of Categories) early in 1847. The latter's statement that "the
doctrine of categories will come to its goal when the origin of the
concept and the emergence of the thing progress with each other."[6]
And this statement supports a second significant aspect of Kierkegaard's ontology as indicated in the journal entry under consideration (JP, 3:3089), namely, that categories as "ontological determinants" or "conceptual-determinants" are not abstract eternal truths

---

[5]For an extended discussion of Kierkegaard's use of this language and the
safeguards he puts upon it, see my *Kierkegaard as Theologian* (Montreal: McGill-
Queen's University Press, 1997) 28-34.
[6]Friedrich Adolf Trendelenburg, *Geschichte der Kategorienlehre* (Hildesheim:
Georg Olms Verlagsbuchhandlung, 1963; photographic reproduction of the Berlin
1846 ed.) 189.

in and of themselves, but are expressions of "the relation between an existing cognitive spirit [that is, a human self] and the eternal truth." So the "being" that concerns Kierkegaard is the mode of the presence of eternal truth within the existence of the cognitive spirit, and the categories are "ontological determinants" or definitions that point to, give expression to, and even help shape that interrelationship of eternal truth and human existence.[7]

### The Nature of Eternal-Being and Its Encounter with Human-Being

All these points, however, leave untouched the question: what is "the truth," or what is the nature of the eternal being to which the individual human self (spirit) relates? The clearest answer comes in Anti-Climacus' *Practice in Christianity*. He asks what Christ means when he says that he "will draw all to myself" (John 12:32). He remarks, "whatever truly can be said to *draw to itself* must first be something in itself, or must be a something that is in itself." This is certainly not the case "with the sensate, the secular, the momentary, the multiple, [because] in itself it is nothing [*Intet*], is empty." Now "when that which is to be drawn is in itself a self, then truly to draw to itself means *first* to help it truly to become itself in order *then* to draw it to itself. . . . What, then, is it to be a self? . . . [A] self is a reduplication,[8] is freedom; therefore in this relation truly to draw to itself means to posit a choice. . . . So it is

---

[7]It is interesting that each of the points made in the last several pages about Kierkegaard's developing ontology are also characteristics of that of Martin Heidegger's ontology, at least as the latter is analyzed by Richard Schmitt in his *Martin Heidegger on Human Being* (New York: Random House, 1969). But increasingly in what follows, it will become clear that one of Kierkegaard's continuing primary concerns was with the uniqueness of Being-in-and-for-Itself, that is, with the Being of the Eternal or God, as God is present and active within the dimensions of human existence. Heidegger finally turned to this subject only late in life, but he never resolved its contradictions with his earlier attempt at a purely human ontology (see Schmitt's last chap., esp. 232-34).

[8]*Fordoblelse* (see PC, 159) I translate as "reduplication" instead of "redoubling" (as the Hongs do) because Kierkegaard also uses *Reduplication* as a Danish word, and I cannot discern any difference in his meanings. In English, to "redouble" means literally to make twice as great or, broadly, to intensify, whereas with both words Kierkegaard clearly means to reduplicate or repeat. *Fordoblelse* can mean to redouble but also to reduplicate.

when truth draws to itself, for truth is in itself, is *in-and-for-itself*—and Christ is the truth" (emphasis added). So Christ wants to draw the human being to himself but "only as a free being, that is, through a choice." And this condition requires that the truth encounter the human being in a "composite" (*Sammensat*), "true God and [true] man,"[9] in the "duplexity" (*Dobbelthed*) of the simultaneous "lowliness and loftiness" of Jesus as the Christ, because this fact, "that both parts are there, make it impossible to be drawn to him without a choice. . . . [N]othing, no natural force, nothing on earth draws to itself in this way . . . ; only spirit can do that, and in turn only in this way can spirit draw spirit to itself" (PC, 158-60).

Several points made or implied by Anti-Climacus in this passage of *Practice* must be highlighted. (1) He defines being as "something . . . in and for itself." But this kind of being is peculiar to selfhood, in contrast to the sphere of the sensate and the momentary, of natural forces. (2) To be self means to be capable of "reduplication" or freedom. This is the being that eternal truth (God) shares with the sensate temporal being of the human being. (3) But for human being to become self, it must be in continuous touch with eternal being, which can encounter human being only in the ambiguous relationship of indirection (simultaneously transcendent/immanent), in order to preserve and to evoke the freedom (being for itself) of the human self. How, then, does this happen?

The answer comes in a later section of the same discourse:

Christ is the truth in the sense that to *be* the truth is the only explanation [*Forklaring*] of what truth is. . . . This means that the truth . . . is not a sum of statements, not a definition, etc., but a life. The being of truth is not the direct redoubling of being in relation to *thinking* [emphasis added], which gives only thought-being. . . . No, the being of truth is the redoubling [of truth] within you, . . . that your life . . . expresses the truth approximately in the striving for it, . . . just as the truth was in Christ a *life*, for he was the truth. (PC, 205)

---

[9]In this passage Kierkegaard does use "man [*Mand*]" instead of "human being [*Menneske*]," but as I have shown in *Kierkegaard as Theologian* (22n.53), this is his only slip on this issue and he corrects it in two other passages in *Practice* (182, 202).

Then Anti-Climacus draws the direct implication that it is totally mistaken to think that this kind of truth can be "known" (*vide*), that is, abstractly "grasped" (*begribe*) in the intellect purely as a concept, "because knowing the truth is something that entirely of itself accompanies being the truth,.. not the other way around." Hence, "no human being knows more of the truth than what he is of the truth," not even Christ. So he warns against "the monstrous mistake" of "didacticizing Christianity," that is, "the view that truth is cognition, knowledge" that comes simply from "comprehending, speculating, observing," rather than "the view that truth is a being" (PC, 205-206).

Finally, then, we are left with the question as to what categories or conceptual-determinants Kierkegaard would consider the best for expressing this "being" that is "a life," a being that consists in living in a certain kind of *relationship* with transcendent eternal truth itself. He uses two such categories: love and faith. The interaction and interdependence between the two is very complex in the Kierkegaard exposition.[10] But one thing is clear: Kierkegaard never says, "God is faith," but he bluntly asserts, "God is love," and "love is God" (WL, 364-65, 121). The faith quality of the God-relationship is required by the character of the human self as derived and as located in space and time. The love quality of the God-relationship is rooted in the very being of God's own selfhood, of love in-and-for-itself.

I have previously drawn this important distinction between faith and love by saying that love is a personal, passionate relation reflecting an essential kinship of human being with God's being, while faith reflects our struggle to know, understand and believe in God because of our essential difference of dependent finitude.[11] Hence love is a relationship of continuity with the ontological reality and dynamic power of God's own being, while faith involves a relationship of possible discontinuity because of our fallibility and instability.[12] One could say that while love turns toward God's own nature, faith moves off toward knowledge

---

[10]I have explored this topic at length in *Kierkegaard as Theologian*, esp. at 305-37.

[11]In *Kierkegaard as Theologian*, 305-306.

[12]*Kierkegaard as Theologian*, 315.

issues. Climacus supports this point when he argues that human thought and knowledge are only in the realm of possibility and hence are approximations to the truth. And this is true even in our knowledge of another human being. (CUP, 1:194, 316, 320-21)[13] So when Kierkegaard speaks of God's act of "reduplication" in the creation of human being in God's image, it is the central, definitive human capacity for love and need of love that he has in mind.

Finally, we can now turn to Kierkegaard's ontology of love as expounded in *Works of Love.*

### Givenness as Key to Kierkegaard's Ontology of Love

Basic to everything that follows, we must stress again Kierkegaard's methodology and the role of language within it. The focal point of his ontology is a single phenomenon: the "givenness" of my total existence and of my potentiality as human self in particular. Another mode of the appearance of this quality of my being takes the form of my coming to some awareness of what Kierkegaard repeatedly calls the human being's "eternal validity [*Gyldighed*]" (e.g., EO, 2:188-89, 211), or occasionally, the human being's "eternal dignity [or worth: *Værdighed*]" (e.g., EO, 2:250; WL, 41). I discover this infinite self-worth as something simply "being there," as I come to consciousness of the unrelenting demand that I transcend my life of immediacy and struggle to become spirit/self (see EO, 2:188-89, UDVS, 152). This I did not create or make up, rather it comes to me from elsewhere, it has its ground in the beyond, and it asserts itself as integral to my own most central and inner being.

Therefore, according to Kierkegaard, this phenomenon does not present itself to my consciousness as an object or an objective fact to be observed and described, to be theorized and demonstrated. Rather, it is a dynamic moving, living reality to be explored in and through all the diverse levels and spheres and qualities of the human spirit (self). There is no one language, no one set of categories that is adequate to its reality. We can and must speak of its aesthetic, ethical and religious dimensions, of its expression in our

---

[13]Cf. Thomas C. Anderson's treatment of this point in his article, "Kierkegaard and Approximation Knowledge" (IKC: CUP, 187-203, esp. sect. I).

feeling, our thinking, our willing. We are forced to resort to metaphors, analogies and concepts in order to come to some understanding or to achieve some mutual sharing of its mysteries. And ultimately we will come to its true meaning only as we act it out in our living, in vital interactive relationships with every dimension of our existence, but especially with other beings who also are defined by selfhood. This is Kierkegaard's methodology as incarnated in his entire authorship.

Unlike Heidegger's characterization of human existence as "being thrown" (*Geworfenheit*), "givenness" does not connote an accidental, indifferent, impersonal event but a purposive, caring, personal act. Consciousness of one's givenness inevitably gives rise to musings of "Whence?" and even "From whom?" In response to these questions, Kierkegaard's most common terms are "the eternal" and "God." But these are general, indefinite, and nonspecific. His two regulative terms for speaking about the eternal are one analogy, "God is love" (WL, 364-65), and one concept, "God is this—that everything is possible" (SUD, 40). I propose that the dimension of possibility in the self and in the self's relationship with God has to do primarily with human freedom and with the God-relationship as faith.[14] But in *Works of Love*, Kierkegaard insists that underlying the fact of human freedom and the relationship of faith is the more fundamental reality of love.

When Kierkegaard says that "distinctiveness is not mine but is God's gift, by which he gives being to me and . . . gives . . . being to all [or everyone]," he immediately adds, "This [act] is the unfathomable fountain [or spring: *Væld*] of goodness in God's goodness" (WL, 271). He introduces this image in the opening pages of *Works of Love*. There he is asserting that to deprive oneself of love "is an eternal loss," one has "forfeited everything," because "What is it . . . that connects [*forbinde*] the temporal and eternity, what else but love, which for that very reason is before everything and remains after everything is gone" (WL, 6). So "Where does love come from," what is the "origin and its source . . . from which it flows? . . . There is a place in a person's innermost being; from

---

[14]I have developed this point at some length in chaps. 4, 5, and 6 of *Kierkegaard as Humanist*.

this place flows the life of love" (WL, 8). But this place is hidden, cannot be seen, because it

> is in an unfathomable connectedness [*Sammenhæng*] with all existence. Just as the quiet lake originates deep down in hidden springs [*Kildevæld*] no eye has seen, so also does a person's love originate even more deeply in God's love. . . . [T]he mysterious origin of love in God's love prevents you from seeing its ground. . . . [T]he quiet lake can dry up if the gushing spring [*Væld*] ever stops; the life of love, however, has an eternal spring. (WL, 9-10)

### The Gift: Selfhood

So the "being" that is given to me and to every other human individual has the definitive quality of "love," because its mysterious origin is a hidden connectedness of my existence with eternal being, and "God is love." And what does it mean, "to love?" It means that Love (God),

> "the *Omnipotent One*, yet gives in such a way that the receiver acquires distinctiveness, that . . . [the One] who creates out of nothing yet creates distinctiveness, so that the creature in relation to . . . [that One] does not become nothing even though it is taken from nothing and is nothing but becomes . . . [distinctiveness]. (WL, 271-72)

And this unfathomable hidden connection between my being and that of the eternal also integrally involves a connectedness of my being with all existence. So this introductory discourse on "Love's Hidden Life" is immediately followed by a three-part discourse on "You Shall Love the Neighbor." Kierkegaard posits a "kinship" between human being and human being that "is secured by each individual's equal kinship with and relationship to God" (WL, 69; cf. SUD, 120, 125).

In summary, then, Kierkegaard is intimating that the phenomenon of my givenness is revelatory of three profound mysteries about the ultimate dynamic that permeates and qualifies everything that "is." The three are distinct and yet indivisible. Firstly, givenness posits my own being as a unique-identity of eternal validity and dignity. I must love my self. Secondly, this identity is grounded in and flows from a connection (unity, kinship) with an eternal, unfathomable, inexhaustible, and continuing source. I must love God. Thirdly, this eternal source is present in me in such a way that it demands that I recognize and affirm this same validity and dignity in every other human being. I must love my neighbor. Kierkegaard's ontology neither is an abstract conceptualization of eternal verities that totally transcend the exigencies of temporal, spatial existence, nor is it a merely "regional" ontology of an anthropological type.[15] Rather, in his "Christian reflections (deliberations)" in *Works of Love*, he explores a dynamic, living "being" that ties everything together, and for him the ultimately adequate designation for it can only be: Love. God, the original and continuing source, is "Love Itself" (WL, 301), or one can say, "Love is God" (WL, 121).

Let me repeat and emphasize that "love" in this context means, first, the act in which God gives me being so that I, "directly before God, do not become nothing, . . . but become distinctiveness" (my translation; cf. WL, 271-72), that is, become a self (cf. CUP, 246-47). Secondly, "love" means the act in which I come to know and to affirm that another human being is also a focused center of self-consciousness, as unique and private and self-determining as my own self, and then to make it a law of my being to extrapolate and to affirm the mystery of truly *other* selfhood to every single individual of the human race, my neighbor whom I love (in this way) even as (I love) my own self.[16]

But this definition of love leaves us with a serious problem. The definition works for God's relation toward all human beings and for the relation among human beings. It does not work for our relation of love toward God. God's own selfhood does not stand in need of affirmation or assistance from human beings. We obviously mean something else when we speak of our love of God. We mean what Kierkegaard repeatedly calls worship, that is, a profound attitude of gratitude, mixed with fear and trembling, as we

---

[15]I have obviously changed my mind since I suggested that Kierkegaard assumes only a regional ontology in *Kierkegaard as Humanist*, 468.

[16]Similarly in *The Sickness unto Death*, Anti-Climacus says that faith is not "believing in God" but the fact that "the self in being itself and in willing to be itself rests transparently in God" (SUD, 82; see also 14, 30, 49, 131). So both the love relation and the faith relation have to do with affirming and achieving the selfhood of the individual human.

seek the courage, before God, to be and to become what God has given us, what God has shared with us: to be spirit, to be self, in God's own "image so that . . . [the human being] might be like . . . [God], might become perfect as . . . [God] is perfect" (WL, 264).[17]

### The Being of Love-Itself

In this contrast Kierkegaard is positing a radical ontological thesis: in our consciousness of the phenomenon of the givenness of our being there is a clear and forceful communication that the Source and Origin of our being is essentially different in its own being from our being, in spite of a certain kind of fundamental "likeness" and "kinship." This topic was clearly in the mind of Kierkegaard as he wrote *Works of Love*, because at the same time he was also writing *The Book on Adler* in which he first made the formulation of "an eternal essential qualitative difference" between God and the human being (BA, 181).[18] And he picks this phrase up and uses it in *Sickness* as a controlling notion for all that he writes there. I find no use of this phrase or anything like it in *Works of Love*, but the point is made in several different ways, primarily in the use of the notion of being-in-itself (a shortened form of being-in-and-for-itself: *Iogforsigværende*) and of the notion of reduplication, in order to speak about God or the eternal.

In developing this distinction between divine and human being, Kierkegaard is making the radical claim that contained in and revealed through the phenomenon of our givenness is the presence of being-itself, the claim that the transcendent source and origin of all things does not find being present in and related to existence (in finite time and space) to be contradictory or excluded. Being-itself can be thus present, and still retain its freedom, identity, and independence (transcendence, of a sort). As mentioned in note 7 above, Heidegger attempted in his later writings to explore such a possibility, but his attempt is indecisive and lost in a fog of

---

[17]For an extended discussion of the topics of this and the previous paragraphs, see my *Kierkegaard as Humanist*, sections entitled "Love's Triad" and "Love Presupposes Love" in chap. 7.

[18]For an account of the development of this idea, see my *Kierkegaard as Theologian*, 66-70.

ambiguous images when compared to that of Kierkegaard. So let us see how Kierkegaard provides further clarity and content or shape to the term love through his use of these notions of being-in-itself and of reduplication.

The interrelationship of the two terms and concepts is briefly suggested in one key passage in *Works of Love*. Kierkegaard is contrasting temporal existence with the eternal. "A temporal object [i.e., a human being] can have many various characteristics," but because it is involved in the dialectic of past, present, and future, "it *is* only in its characteristics" (emphasis added). In contrast, the "eternal *is* . . . in itself" (WL, 280). Earlier in *Works of Love*, Kierkegaard notes that the human being can have either "qualities for oneself" or "qualities for others." Such things as wisdom and talent are "being-for-itself [*forsigværende*] qualities" but "Love is not a being-for-itself quality but a quality by which or in which you are for others" (WL, 223). Again in contrast, the eternal has qualities, but "the eternal is not only in its characteristics but is in itself [*in sig selv*] in its characteristics. It not only has characteristics but is in itself [*i sig selv*] in having [simultaneously: *idet*] the characteristics." And this distinction within the eternal, between "being in itself" and "having qualities," manifests itself in a very significant form "when the eternal is in a human being," namely, "the eternal is reduplicated in [the human being]" in that "it is in [the human being] in a double mode: in an outward direction and in an inward direction back into itself." Then Kierkegaard makes his point:

> So also with love. . . . At the same moment it goes out of itself (the outward direction), it is in itself (the inward direction); and at the same moment it is in itself, it goes out of itself, . . . one and the same. (WL, 280)

This kind of movement is the dynamic that is characteristic of the eternal as "being-in-and-for-itself," and that pervades, shapes, guides all things. And its name is "love." Kierkegaard's ontology of love is not regional; it is total.

This qualitative distinction between temporal and eternal being (while assuming an intimate compatibility and interrelationship) is drawn even more sharply in *Christian Discourses*, which Kierkegaard wrote immediately after finishing *Works of Love*. In one discourse he says that God is the "only one who completely knows himself, who in and for himself [*i og for sig selv*; translation corrected] knows what he himself is." But the human being cannot be himself unless he is "before God," that is, "one is oneself only by being in the One who is in [and for] himself." And only then can a human being "be in others or before [for?] others, but one cannot be oneself merely by being before [or for] others" (CD, 40). Clearly, Kierkegaard has in mind his assertion that for human beings, "Love is not a being-for-itself quality but a quality by which or in which you are for others" (WL, 223). So, because "God is love," God is simultaneously both a being-for-others and a being-in-and-for-itself, both a going out of itself and a returning back into itself. But "no human being *is love*"; yet, "he is, if he is in love [*Kjerlighed*], one who loves" (WL, 264, 301). As we shall emphasize later on, the implication here is that love is triadic.

Now, this is tortuous language, but I think Kierkegaard is making one simple point. The human being does have a certain centered, relatively independent and free being, which can be called "being-for-itself." But this human being is what Kierkegaard calls "derived" or "created" and "dependent" being. It is not "being-*in*-and-for-itself," which only the eternal is. As noted (two paragraphs above) Kierkegaard views "being-for-itself [*forsig-værende*] quality" as characteristic of the human. Hence he can say that the self as "a relation which relates to itself" is a "being-for-itself [*for sig værende*] relation" (my translation; cf. SUD, 14). But in some journal entries written in 1854 (JP 2:1449, 2079; 4:4918), Kierkegaard makes absolutely clear that he has always meant "being-in-and-for-itself" to be descriptive only of the eternal.[19] One can hardly assume that the more sophisticated view of being as stated in these entries (seven years after *Works of Love* was completed) is implicit in the ontology of love as contained in *Works of Love*. But, as we shall see, there are themes in this later view that are consonant with and that help to enlighten certain aspects of that ontology.

---

[19]In *Kierkegaard as Theologian* (70-75) I trace Kierkegaard's interest in this phrase from its beginnings in *The Concept of Irony* and *Either/Or*, and show its connections with his later notions of God as subjectivity, reduplication, and personhood.

In two of these entries he is deriding those Christians who argue that God needs them in order to fulfill the divine cause and purpose, but only "up to a point" (JP, 2:1449, 4:4918). In the first one he declares that God is "the Unconditioned [*det Ubetingende*], the Being-in-and-for-itself [*det Iogforsigværende*]" who has no purposes, for which he would require "means" to which "he must adapt himself." Indeed, "God is sheer subjectivity, has nothing of an objective being in himself. . . . Only that which infinitely subjectively has its subjectivity in its power as subjectivity, only that has no intentions."[20] And in another entry he explains that "everything with such objectivity comes thereby into the realm of relativities," whereas God is unconditioned (JP, 3:2570; translation modified). But then he elaborates this position in still another entry by saying that although God "has not an element-of-objectivity [*Objektivt*] in his being, . . . yet he relates objectively to his own subjectivity, but this again is simply a reduplication of his subjectivity, because in his being subjective there is no imperfection . . . nor anything lacking. . . . God is infinite reduplication." In contrast, "no human being . . . can transcend [*overlegen*] himself in such a way that he perfectly relates objectively to himself," that is, no human being can "become subjective in such a way that he can bring to full consummation what he in his objective transcendence has understood about himself" (JP, 4:4571).

## How Do We Know God as Being-in-and-for-Itself?

Obviously, an urgent question presents itself: how does this character of God, the hidden transcendent source and ground of our human being, manifest and communicate itself to us in the phenomenon of our givenness? Or is it simply a rational speculation or inference that Kierkegaard yielded to in some of his final musings? The clue to Kierkegaard's answer lies in his identification of being-in-and-for-itself with the unconditioned. He had explained this identification in several journal entries two years earlier (1852). In one entitled, "Being-in-and-for-Itself—and My Task," he

---

[20]The Hongs blur this point when they translate the passage (quoted two paragraphs above) from *Christian Discourses* (40). Where Kierkegaard speaks of God as "in and for himself," they translate simply as "in himself."

declares that in our day "what it means to be a man" has qualitatively changed from "the whole concept of life contained in the
New Testament," in that "being-in-and-for-itself, the unconditioned, has completely gone out of life, and 'reason' [Forstand] has
been substituted." The evidence is that "instead of unconditional
obedience" we have "obedience by virtue of reasons [Raisone-
ments]" (JP, 1:536).

In another entitled, "Only the Unconditioned Can Support a
Human Being," he argues that most humans "willingly work for
the good" only if they can see what they will get out of it. If asked,
they will say, "Why?" that is, what's in it for me? And if you
answer that it is for posterity, so the world will get better, this
"will not motivate a human being really to stake his life for the
good." But if in faith I truly risk everything, then "I have no 'why'
at all; I am controlled simply and solely ty this unconditional; I
must do it, I cannot do otherwise." In other words, "no ends-in-
view consideration can actually get him to venture everything. We
urgently need the unconditioned again. In the unconditioned all
teleology vanishes" (JP, 4:4901).

In still another entry entitled, "Being-in-and-for-Itself—'Faith,' "
Kierkegaard directly asks our question, "How is it known whether
or not someone is related to a being-in-and-for-itself, . . . in the
form of the unconditioned? It is known by this, that one holds fast
to this being-in-and-for-itself, even though one suffers because of
the relationship." Of course, not all suffering is evidence of this
relationship, but "wherever this suffering is not, unconditioned
faith is not." And it is not the suffering as such that "proves that
you are truly relating in faith to the being-in-and-for-itself, . . . no,
faith is the assurance, there is no other assurance." One sure
negative sign is this: "if someone wants to relate to a being-in-and-
for-itself and also have the things of this world, then this is a
duplicity" (JP, 4:4902).

The common theme of these journal entries is simply this: in
my sense of the givenness of my being as human spirit/self, there
appears to me an unequivocal, unconditional, absolute demand
that I use my gift in a certain way, in correspondence and
harmony with the Source and Ground of this gift. The gift comes
with the Spirit of Love, and it speaks in the Word of Love as a
"new commandment, . . . that you love one another as I have

loved you" (John 13:34). There can be no "Why?" or "What will I get back?" To say that the Giver of my being "*is* love" means that there is no other principle or condition or force beyond or outside of Love in terms of which to explain or to account for Love. It is "for-itself" in that It relates to itself, that is, comes to conscious resolve when it acts, so is free. And Love is "in-itself" in that, unlike human being, Love relates only to *itself* when it resolves what to do. Being-*in*-and-for-itself is not derived or created or dependent being. Since, then, in the phenomenon of my givenness, I come to know that Being-in-and-for-itself "*is* love," therefore, as one created in Its image, Love is the principle of my being and makes the absolute demand, without any possible conditions, "love your neighbor as [you love] your self." This is the ultimate, the absolute and the only good.

That Kierkegaard thought of this character of the phenomenon of givenness in ontological terms is stated clearly in another section of *Christian Discourses* (CD, 207-208, the entire passage should be read). He says, "the truth and perfection of eternal life are eternally to show the difference between right and wrong with the rigorousness of eternity. . . . What, then, is the eternal? It is the difference between right and wrong." All other distinctions are transitory, but this distinction "remains eternally as he remains, the Eternal One, who established this difference *from eternity.*" Then Kierkegaard asks the key question:

> How can the eternal be a difference? To be a difference—is it not a much too imperfect being [*Væren*] to be able to be [*til at kunne være*] the eternal? Well now, the eternal is not the difference either, the eternal is righteousness. But the being [*Væren*] of righteousness has this perfection, that it contains a redoubling; this redoubling that it has within itself is the difference between right and wrong. A being that has no difference whatever within itself is a very imperfect being. . . . The eternal, righteousness, has the difference within itself, the distinction between right and wrong. (CD, 207-208)

Here Kierkegaard is saying that the one who gives us our being is the eternal, the one who "remains;" indeed, "the one who rolls up the heavens like a garment changes everything, but never Itself—and therefore never changes this either, eternity's distinction."[21] In these images and concepts Kierkegaard is giving the ontological groundwork for a theme that is emphasized throughout his whole authorship, that human beings are not free to determine or even to judge what is right and what is wrong, but only the freedom to do, or not to do, what they know is the right. "Righteousness" simply indicates that there is an ultimate "being-in-and-for-itself" that establishes what is "true" and "good" for everything else that exists. But it also indicates that the gift of personal being to dependent creatures means that they are free to violate or rebel against what *is*, but not with impunity. The "wrong" is the impossible nonbeing or the loss of being that results when free creatures attempt to live contrary to the authentic being which they have been given to become in freedom.

In *Works of Love*, however, Kierkegaard stresses that a more adequate designation of "righteousness" is love. It is more adequate because his extensive analysis of the nature of love gives substance or content to *what* is righteous or good, namely, love as the gift and affirmation of the being of selfhood. In fact, Kierkegaard came to the conclusion that "to have a self, to be a self, is the greatest concession, an infinite concession, given to man [*Menneske*, not *Mand*], but it is also eternity's claim upon him" (SUD, 21), because the given self has the task of becoming itself, and that task is accomplished only when a self, in response to God's love, learns to love every other human being in the same way.

### Is God (Love) Really Changeless?

However, we have seen that, for Kierkegaard, love as being-in-and-for-itself is not a static mathematical structure that permeates all reality, not a blind force like gravity and electro-magnetism that irresistibly shapes all things and events in the universe, not an abstract conceptual principle or ideal that informs and guides human living. Rather, love is a personal, proactive, dynamic, moving, living, relational being. And for Kierkegaard to say that the eternal "changes everything but never itself" is difficult to apply to God defined as love. Kierkegaard is aware of this

---

[21]I have changed Kierkegaard's masculine pronouns for God, but tried to preserve his recognition of the personal nature of God.

problem. From the earliest serious treatment of love in *Philosophical Fragments*, he struggles with the question: in what sense does God "need" to love, or need the beloved? And in WL we have heard him describe Love (God) as inherently involved in the double movement of an "outward direction" toward others and an "inward direction" back into itself. We have heard him say that love as such "is not a being-for-itself quality but a quality . . . [of being] for others" (WL, 223), and again he says that God as love

> seeks his own, which is love; he seeks it by giving all things. . . . Love is a giving of oneself; that it seeks love is again love and is the highest love. That is, this is the way it is in the relationship between God and humanity [*Menneske*]. (WL, 264)

So we need to look at the claim that God as *being*, that is in-and-for-itself, that lacks nothing and contains no imperfection (JP, 4:4571), that remains unchanged, is yet propelled by this very being in an outward direction toward an object of love that is not God's own being, not an emanation in continuity with God's being, but that is a something that is "being-for-itself" in God's own image, created by God out of nothing. What is it, in the phenomenon of our givenness, that leads Kierkegaard to speak of "God's Unchangingness" (*Guds Uforanderlighed*),[22] while still insisting that, in our givenness, God reduplicates divine being in us and enables us to love one another? I have considered this question at some length in *Kierkegaard as Theologian* (298-305). But the present analysis of Kierkegaard's ontology of love brings some fresh insights for an answer.

Climacus (in chapter 2 of *Fragments*) explores this question in the story of the king's love for a lowly maiden, but he keeps conflating the languages of teacher-learner, king-maiden, God-human being. For our purposes here, let us assume that teacher and king are God, while learner and maiden are the human. While

---

[22]The title of a discourse Kierkegaard wrote in May 1851 but not published until 3 September 1855; the new Hong translation is in *Kierkegaard's Writings* 23: *The Moment and Late Writings* (MLW), 263-81. In a translation of 1944, David Swenson translated *Uforanderlighed* as "unchangeableness." In MLW, the Hongs use "changelessness." Both of these terms suggest a given abstract quality like "immutability," but I think "unchangingness" suggests a dynamic, personal quality, which is what I think Kierkegaard has in mind.

granting that "no human situation can provide a valid analogy" to the God-human relationship, yet he proposes that the story of love between a king and a maiden may serve "to awaken the mind to an understanding of the divine" (PF, 26).

In both the story and his introduction to it, Climacus presents some apparently conflicting material on the issue of God's transcendent unchangingness. On the one hand, we hear that "the god needs [behøver] no pupil in order to understand himself." So it is God alone that "moves him[self] to make his appearance" (in time, that is). So "there of course is no need [Trang: inner desire or craving for something] that moves him. . . . But if he moves himself, and is not moved by need [Trang], what moves him then but love, for love does not have the satisfaction of need outside itself but within." So God's resolve, "out of love," to appear in time "must be from eternity, even though fulfilled in time. . . . [B]ut just as love is the basis [Grund], so also must love be the goal [Maal], for it would indeed be a contradiction for the god to have a basis of movement and a goal that do not correspond to this. The love, then, must be for the learner, and the goal must be to win him, for only in love is the different made equal, and only in equality or in unity is there understanding" (PF, 24-25).

On the other hand, within the story itself this cool Aristotelian logic gets profoundly disturbed when the omnipotent king is faced with fulfilling this eternal love with a concrete and very humble human person living within the restrictions of a space/time psyche. The human being who is "the object of God's love" is fallible and prone to misunderstanding, in fact knows nothing of God's love. This is the occasion for God's "unfathomable sorrow," because "god's concern is to bring about equality" which emerges when the two come to understand each other. But there will be neither understanding or equality unless God can instill "bold [open]-confidence (Frimodighed) in the beloved." If this fails, "the love is unhappy" (PF, 28).

The whole relationship "makes understanding so difficult," because in this intimate relationship with the divine, "god's love . . . must be not only an assisting love but also a procreative love by which [God] gives birth to the learner, . . . meaning the transition from 'not to be' to 'to be.' " Will the learner (beloved) understand and gladly accept the fact that, before God, "he becomes nothing and yet is not annihilated; that he owes [God] everything and yet becomes boldly confident; that he understands the truth, but the truth makes him free," or will the learner be overwhelmed and flee away (PF, 30-31)? In this crucial "moment" the eyes of omnipotent God, standing upon the earth, "rest anxiously on humankind" lest the beloved be offended, because God knows that "the tender shoots of an individual life may be crushed as easily as a blade of grass. Such a life—sheer love and sheer sorrow. To want to express the unity of love and then not to be understood, to be obliged to fear for everyone's perdition and yet in this way truly to be able to save only one single person. . . . [W]hat if he [the learner] made a mistake, what if he became weary and lost his bold confidence!" In this moment, even the omnipotent sustainer of the universe must wait; "even though the learner is the lowliest of persons," God waits "to ask anxiously: do you now really love me" (PF, 32-33; partly Hong and partly Swenson's beautiful paraphrase)?

In other words, within the very nature of my givenness, God is present to me in this dual perspective. On the one hand, it is my very given nature as a free but dependent and fallible being beloved of God, owing my very creation to God and now in need of re-creation, that is the source and revelation of the very tenuousness and uncertainty of my relationship with God in this critical moment. Will I understand and accept this unbearable situation as an expression of love? Why does not divine love pervade me and transform me and draw me to God as an irresistible power? Why is God so tentative and indirect? On the other hand, this uncertainty is at the same time the source and revelation of the unchangingness, the absoluteness, the unconditionality of God, of Love-itself. That is to say, love cannot compromise itself and yet be love. Love *is* only between equals, when it is free "to be" or "not to be." The opposite of being-in-love is not-being, is the denial, the deluding and so the loss of self. It is not loving to ignore this corruption of self that leads to death of self. Precisely because God *is* love, God must bear "the possibility of offense of the human race when out of love one became its savior!" (PF, 32).

Kierkegaard intensifies this latter point as his second authorship develops, and gives it passionate expression in the closing pages of *The Sickness unto Death*. Here he says that in the "infinite love and merciful grace" of God's becoming a human being,

> [God] makes one condition: [God] cannot do otherwise. . . . [God] cannot remove the possibility of offense. Ah!, singular work of love [*Kjerlighedens Gjerning*], ah!, unfathomable grief of love, that even God cannot—as in another sense neither will God, nor can God will, but even if God wanted to—cannot make it impossible for this act of love to turn into just the opposite for the human being, to be the utmost misery. . . . And Christ cannot, 'love' cannot, make this impossible. . . . Oh! unfathomable contradiction in love! But still, in love he cannot find it in his heart not to complete this act of love. (Cf. SUD, 126).[23]

It is precisely this character of the Being of Love that Kierkegaard anticipates when he says that the eternal will show eternally "the difference between right and wrong with the rigorousness of eternity" (CD, 207-208), and that he confirms later when he says that God "relates objectively to his own subjectivity" (JP, 4:4571). Subjectively, God as "righteousness" is love, and as love-itself God needs and long's for the love of his creatures; objectively, God cannot and will not act otherwise, that is, out of love God must negate the "wrongness," the emptiness, the loss of being that occurs in all unloving. It is this God, with the eternal distinction within the divine being-itself, who appears and is present with me in the phenomenon of the givenness of my being. In this specific sense, I know and must be grateful for "God's Unchangingness," because that means that God's love is a love that will never annihilate me, that loves forth bold confidence in me, that sets me free to become my self in loving others—and that yet must leave open the possibility that I will take offense and be lost.

### The Implications of Love's Triad

While in this sense, therefore, "there is no imperfection . . . nor anything lacking" in God's subjectivity in so far as God also relates

---

[23]The words here are partly those of Alastair Hannay from his translation of *The Sickness unto Death* (London: Penguin Books, 1989). I think the complexity of Kierkegaard's own language in this sentence is important to preserve in the translation.

objectively to divine subjectivity, at the same time it is precisely God's goodness as *love* that defines God as "being for others," that moves God in an "outward direction," that expresses itself in reduplication of God's being within my being. Hence Love moves, not in eternity but in space and time, to fulfill what in another sense is lacking, namely, to create and to recreate the human being who can freely love God in return, and who can also reduplicate God's love and thereby "love forth love" from other human beings. So just as "when the eternal is in a human being, this eternal is reduplicated in him" (my translation; cf. WL, 280), it is also true that "the concept 'neighbor' is actually the reduplication of your own self; 'the neighbor' is what thinkers call 'the other,' that by which the selfishness in self-love is to be tested, . . . [because] what self-love unconditionally cannot endure is reduplication, and the commandment's [love your neighbor] *as yourself* is a reduplication" (my translation; cf. WL, 21). Just as authentic self-love in the human being *needs* "the other" for the fulfillment of love, God as love *needs* the creature in the divine image for the fulfillment of divine love. Therefore, along with the human lover and the human beloved there is always the eternal "third," Love-Itself. In the endless process of this eternal triad we find the ultimate ontology of love. As Kierkegaard puts it: "Every person . . . dare not belong to anyone in love unless in the same love he belongs to God and dare not possess anyone in love unless the other and he himself belong to God in this love" (WL, 107-108).

To put it another way, the final subtlety of this ontology, which Kierkegaard does not make explicit, is this: love-itself (God) is never present to and with any human being *except* when one human being loves another human being. No human being has a love relationship which is strictly one-on-one with Love-itself, no matter how inward, spiritual, subjective, personal, and private that relationship may be.[24] So Being-in-and-for-itself, which is infinitely and qualitatively different from all derived or created being, is involved ontologically and eternally in this process of loving self-reduplication in beings who are guaranteed the "something" of their being-for-themselves by the gift of living in space/time. And

---

[24]See my treatment of this idea in *Kierkegaard as Humanist*, 370-71.

the ontological question that is inherent in this situation, and that
Kierkegaard never directly explores, is this: does God's involvement in this process carry with it a kind of implicit development,
and therefore some kind of change, in Being-in-and-for-itself—a
change that is yet subject to control by no other conditions than
those set by the eternal unchanging character of Love-itself? In
other words, is the "fulfillment of divine love" (previous paragraph) something new and different for God?

Even though Kierkegaard does not directly explore this
question, I contend that it is lurking at the fringes of his thinking,
and we do not have to engage in speculation in order to discern
an implicit answer. He provides relevant perspectives on the God-
human relationship in the form of two central concepts which
suggest an answer. They are: (1) "Since with God all things are
possible, God is this: that all things are possible; . . . or that all
things are possible is God" (my translation; cf. SUD, 40).[25] (2) "The
change of coming-into-existence is the transition from possibility
to actuality," and "This change is not in essence but in being, and
is from not existing to existing" (PF, 74, 73). This latter notion of
Climacus continues to inform Kierkegaard's thinking as we see in
*Sickness unto Death*:

> The self is κατὰ δύναμιν [potentially] just as possible as it is
> necessary, for it is indeed itself, but it has the task of becoming
> itself. Insofar as it is itself, it is the necessary, and insofar as it
> has the task of becoming itself, it is a possibility." (SUD, 35)

Clearly, the immediate sense of the "possibility" that is being
talked about in both instances is that of *human* being. So, the
actualization of all my human possibilities (as a self created κατὰ
δύναμιν) depends upon my being "with God" or "before God."
Also, it is I as a human being who must experience the transition

---

[25]The Hongs accurately translate Kierkegaard's Danish when they use
"everything is possible," and that Danish is also what Kierkegaard found in the
version of the Bible in his study. But it is a mistranslation of the Greek, and
another Danish version in use in Kierkegaard's day has the correct translation. I
also use "*with* God" because "for" is an inaccurate translation of the Greek παρά
and is misleading about the meaning of the statement by Jesus (Mark 10:27,
Matthew 19:26). Also, Hong's phrase, "being of God," is not in the Danish.

"from not existing to existing." And yet there is the underlying implication that it is the very nature or being of God to be oriented toward and concerned about possibility. So in *Sickness* it is said that for the fatalist "God is necessity," while for the human being who prays "there must be a God, a self—and possibility—or a self and possibility in a pregnant sense" (SUD, 40). The ruling, defining presence of possibility in human existence is actually the presence of and relationship with the eternal (or God) in the very structure of the human self.

Therefore, with this formula in *Sickness* Kierkegaard is assuming Haufniensis' thesis that "the possible corresponds exactly to the future," and "the future . . . is . . . the first expression of the eternal and its incognito" (CA, 91).[26] This thesis clearly ties the eternal into the human process of time because "the future [and hence possibility] is the incognito in which the eternal, even though it is incommensurable with time, nevertheless preserves its association with time" (CA, 89). And this tie between the eternal and time is even accentuated when, in *Works of Love*, Kierkegaard identifies the eternal as love, because love is by definition a movement outward toward the other (WL, 223, 280). In the latter case, he is also clearly building upon Climacus' thesis that "of course there is no need [*Trang*] that moves [God]," so "[God] moves himself," that is, "what else moves [God] but love, because love does not have the satisfaction of need [*Trang*] outside itself but within itself." In other words, being loving toward the other is its own reward. But then Climacus immediately seems to contradict himself when he adds, "[God's] resolve [to make his appearance] . . . must be from eternity, even though *fulfilled* in *time*" (emphasis added) (PF, 24-25). Obviously, creaturely time is "outside" God, and the notion of fulfillment outside must mean that the eternal resolve of Love is to fulfill its inherent "need" for expression by moving in the "outward direction" toward its dependent other and thus by participating in all the complexities of the ongoing process of creaturely existence.

---

[26]Little wonder, then, that Haufniensis concludes *The Concept of Anxiety* with the declaration that "only he who is educated by possibility is educated according to his infinitude. Therefore, possibility is the weightiest of all categories" (CA, 156).

Haufniensis struggles to soften this contradiction by arguing that the eternal's appearance in time comprises an annulment of the succession of time, because it creates a new "present" or "moment" that is the "fullness of time, but the fullness of time is the moment as the eternal, and yet this eternal is also the future and the past" (CA, 86, 90). Thus "the moment is not properly an atom of time but an atom of eternity" (CA, 88). In this way God maintains an "association with time" even though time as such is "incommensurable with the eternal" (CA, 89). But I believe that I have shown in the foregoing that, in contrast to Climacus and Haufniensis, Kierkegaard himself moves on in *Works of Love*, *Christian Discourses*, *Sickness*, and *Practice* to a significantly altered view of the whole relation of the eternal (Being-in-and-for-itself, God) to the creaturely life in time and space.

This view is the product of his determination "to advance further in the direction of . . . discovering the Christianity of the New Testament" (MLW, 66), when he felt called by God to enter into the whole second authorship that followed the *Corsair* affair (see JP, 5:5962, 5966). As this view develops, two major differences appear. On the one hand, Kierkegaard sees and describes, in contrast to the preceding pseudonymous works, a more immediate, intimate and active presence of God in the human being of Jesus, in the loving obedience of Jesus' disciples, and in the capacity and power of one human being to love another when Love-Itself is present to them. On the other hand, he increasingly and ever more *overtly* asserts the inescapable destiny of every serious follower of Jesus to proclaim and to enact the love of God in such a way as to confront and to challenge every form of greed, envy, hatred, hypocrisy, duplicity, small-mindedness, and lust for power as they manifest themselves at every level and in every area of our personal, social and political lives.

The latter point, although essentially entailed in the former, is beyond the scope of my exploration of the present topic. But in order to show how radically new is this view of the presence of the eternal God according to Kierkegaard's second authorship (especially in *Works of Love*), I will now interrelate and interweave three of the main themes I have developed above, add a fourth, and in so doing, show how they comprise Kierkegaard's ontology of love.

### Conclusion

The three themes are: (1) God as Eternal or as Love is involved essentially in a double movement, both outward and inward; (2) this outward movement effects a reduplication of the Eternal/ Love in the human being; (3) Love is unconditional, even when reduplicated within the finitude and fallibility of the human being.

The interdependence of the three themes is obvious. Kierkegaard says, "when the eternal is in a human being, this eternal . . . [reduplicates] within him in such a way that every moment it is in him, it is in him in a double mode: in an outward direction and in an inward direction back into itself. . . . So also with love" (WL, 280). In other words, when God as eternal love moves out of itself toward the other, this movement is not an emanation or extension of God's own being but a reduplication of God's kind of being in the human individual. And (as noted above) in *Practice in Christianity* Kierkegaard makes clear the significance of this point: "A self is a redoubling, is freedom; therefore in this relation truly to draw to itself [as Christ does] means to posit a choice" (PC, 159). And again as we have heard, God as love never violates this freedom even when the human being in freedom takes offense, refuses God's love, and is in danger of being "lost." Love is unconditional, because the eternal distinction between right and wrong is grounded as a reduplication within God's own eternal being (CD, 207-208).

What I wish to stress here, however, is that "this outward going and this returning, this returning and this outward going are *simultaneously one and the same*." That is, "[w]hat love *does*, that it *is*; what it *is*, that it *does*" (WL, 280; emphasis added). This point is definitive of Kierkegaard's ontology, and the implications are startling. It means that the Eternal or Love-Itself—as Being-in-and-for-itself, in its "infinite qualitative difference" from human being—always *is* only in intimate indivisible relationship with the "other" of its outward movement, even though this other is a creation out of nothing and has no being *in* itself. To put it in temporal terms (as Kierkegaard would say, "to speak foolishly"), there never was (or is) a time when God or Being was (or is) alone, in pure isolation.

Hence transcendence and infinite-qualitative-difference do not entail, or mean for us, inherent disrelationship or sheer impenetrable mystery. Rather, all terms of difference and all images of transcendence mean that the ordinary categories and concepts and language of our spatial/temporal world are incongruent with the reality of Being, of Love, of God. So rational, abstract concepts do not grasp the reality of God/Being. The only way of coming to "know" and to "understand" Being is by sharing in a form of living together whose relationship can be pointed to only in a metaphorical use of the language of our temporal/spatial/personal existence. So Love-Itself, in which "there is no imperfection . . . nor anything lacking" (JP, 1:536), is nevertheless continually going outward toward the other and reduplicating itself in the other.

This latter fact carries another momentous ramification, namely, the triadic relationship of love. In the passage that speaks about the eternal's going out of itself and reduplicating in the other, Kierkegaard immediately talks about how this character of love also operates in the human-to-human relationship (WL, 280-81). And he had already made it clear that this continuation of the outgoing character of love, from that of God toward the human being to that of human being for human being, is indeed a continuation of the process of reduplication. As we have heard above, "the concept 'neighbor' is actually the redoubling of your own self; 'the neighbor' is what thinkers call 'the other,' that by which the selfishness in self-love is to be tested," because "what self-love unconditionally cannot endure is . . . redoubling, and the commandment's [love your neighbor] *as yourself* is a . . . redoubling" (WL, 21). The radical meaning of this view of the continuation of the outward going and reduplication of Being-Itself (Love-Itself) is this: the so-called "incarnation" of Love that took its decisive form in Jesus as the Christ takes a continuing form in the love that Jesus' disciple is able to manifest to "the neighbor." Kierkegaard clearly asserts that Jesus is unique and that disciples are not reduplications of him. But what is central in the life of Jesus, namely, the presence of God-as-Love, is reduplicated in the lives of Jesus' followers.

The difference between Jesus and his disciples is not easy to state and is certainly open to different definitions. But without the reality of this continuing process, there would be no such thing as Christian ethics: the following or imitation of the life of Christ by his disciples. There would be nothing for the disciples to do but to sit around waiting for the apocalyptic "return" of Jesus. Clearly in both *Works of Love* and *Practice in Christianity* Kierkegaard vigorously rejects such a conclusion. In a journal entry, when he was almost finished writing *Practice*, he adjures each of us "to maintain . . . the thought of God-present-with-me," to "remember that God is love" and to "bring love of God ablaze. . . . Remember that God at any moment has 100,000 possibilities for helping you, and . . . this thing God has allotted to you is still at this very moment the best." So "pray to God for having help in always having work to do, . . . holding fast to the thought of God within your work. No dreaming! because God is pure act" (JP, 2:2008).[27]

It is this understanding of the Being of God, present to the being given us by God, that Kierkegaard had in mind when he corrects Climacus' statement that "possibility is *annihilated* by actuality" (PF 74). In contrast, Anti-Climacus says, "Admittedly, thinkers say that actuality is annihilated possibility, but that is not entirely true; it [actuality] is the consummated, the active [or activated: *virksomme*] possibility" (SUD, 15). So it is the infinite possibilities of God present in and to us that are fulfilled in the work that God puts to our hands here and now, today, this moment. And the consummate possibility that God has given us to enact, to bring into actuality, is to live in the relationship of love both with God and with our fellow human beings. All human creativity, in its myriad variety of forms, is finally but "a noisy gong or a clanging symbol" when it does not support or express that love, glorying in the wonders of God's creation and especially in the wonder of humans loving each other. So, is not this work a fulfillment for God also, for the God "with whom all things are possible," for God who must be present as the third party (Love-Itself) in every authentic human relationship of love?

I can only answer "yes" to this question on the basis of Kierkegaard's phenomenological analysis of the meaning of God's gift of being to us, as beings created for living in love of God and

---

[27]Note that in the last five paragraphs we see illustrated and at work the main elements of Kierkegaard's ontology as analyzed in this article's introductory section on "Kierkegaard's General View of Being."

neighbor. Does the role of human creativity in bringing the possibility of love into actuality diminish the role of God's creativity and imply that God needs us to do something that is impossible for God? Hardly! when I remember that

> This is the unfathomable fountain of goodness in God's goodness that he, the *Omnipotent One*, yet gives in such a way that the receiver acquires distinctiveness, . . . so that the creature in relation to God does not become nothing even though it is taken from nothing and is nothing but becomes a distinctive individuality. (WL, 271-72)

In other words, in loving God and neighbor I am doing what I have been made to do, fulfilling both God's "infinite concession given to man" and "eternity's claim upon him" (SUD, 21).

The statement in *Works of Love* reflects a journal entry Kierkegaard made the year before where he says, "God's omnipotence is therefore his goodness. For goodness is to give oneself away completely, but in such a way that by omnipotently taking oneself back one makes the recipient independent. . . . [O]nly omnipotence can make [a being] independent, can form from nothing something which has continuity in itself through the continuing withdrawing of omnipotence" (JP, 2:1251). And two years after *Works of Love* Kierkegaard draws the only possible conclusion in another entry: "Freedom really *is* only when, in the same moment, . . . it rushes with infinite speed to bind itself unconditionally by the choice of attachment, the choice whose truth is that there can be no question of any choice" (JP, 2:1261). So if freedom is given simply and only *for* loving, then using freedom to be free *from* love is no longer finding and gaining one's self but losing one's self. So in the moment of "fulfilling" the possibility in the actuality of love, there is no inclination of the human being to glory in oneself but only in the glory of God's loving gift of love.

In the end, however, there is, in Kierkegaard's total picture, one shadow cast upon God's omnipotence and so also on the notion that humankind's fulfillment of God's goal of love is simply the working out of God's own will or "eternal resolve." We have seen that when Anti-Climacus states that "God is: that all things are possible," this precisely does not mean that all things are necessary. And it is in *Works of Love* that Kierkegaard recognizes this shadow and does not know quite what to do about it.

In this book Kierkegaard does not use the phrase, "with God all things are possible," but he treats the same theme in a discourse on "Love Hopes All Things."[28] To assist in making my point in this regard, I will provide a few key quotations:

> To hope relates to the future, to possibility, which in turn, unlike actuality, is always a duality, the possibility of advance or of retrogression, of rising or falling, of good or of evil. The eternal *is*, but when the eternal touches the temporal or is in the temporal, they do not meet each other in the *present*, because in that case the present would itself be the eternal. . . . Therefore, when the eternal is in the temporal, it is in the future. . . . [E]ternally, the eternal is the eternal; in time, the eternal is the possible, the future. . . . [I]n possibility the eternal always relates equally to its duality.
>
> On the other hand, when a person to whom the possible pertains relates equally to the duality of the possible, we say: He *expects*. . . . To relate oneself expectantly to the possibility of the good is to *hope*. . . . To relate oneself expectantly to the possibility of evil is to *fear*. . . . [B]y the decision to choose hope, one decides infinitely more than it seems, because it is an eternal decision. . . . [I]n the differentiation (and the choice is indeed differentiating) the possibility of the good is more than a possibility, because it is the eternal. (WL, 249-50)

So when Kierkegaard says in *The Sickness unto Death* that "God is this—that everything is possible" (SUD, 40), he of course means what he had said in *Works of Love*, that the eternal is "the possibility of *good*." The question that casts the shadow is this: what happens if a human being chooses the possibility of evil? Does God give up on the human and let him/her slip into the emptiness of nonbeing? Or does omnipotent love always win out by always winning over the one who fears? In *The Sickness unto Death* we have also heard that "God does not want, . . . cannot want, . . . Christ cannot, 'love' cannot" remove the possibility that the human being will take offense—this is the "unfathomable conflict in love" (SUD, 126). What then? is love in a sense defeated by the one who takes offense at the offer and demands of love, and so ends in

---

[28]By the time the Hongs translated this book in 1995, they decided to translate *Alt* as "all things" instead of "everything" as in *Sickness unto Death*.

despair? Anti-Climacus does not even attempt to entertain this question, but in "Love Hopes All Things" Kierkegaard does. He describes glowingly how,

> eternity, . . . taking upon itself the form of the future, the possible, with the help of hope, [the eternal] brings up temporality's child (the human being), teaches him to hope. . . . By means of the possible, eternity is continually *near* enough to be available and yet *distant enough* to keep the human being in motion forward toward the eternal, to keep him going, going forward. (WL, 252-53)

So also in human relationships, "the loving one . . . continually holds possibility open with an infinite partiality for the possibility of the good" (WL, 253). But

> Alas, . . . [t]he person in despair also *knows* what lies in possibility, and yet he gives up possibility (to give up possibility is to despair) or, even more correctly, he is brazenly so bold as to *assume* the impossibility of the good. . . . [And] when someone is so bold as to *assume* the impossibility of the good, possibility dies for him altogether. (WL, 253-54)

So at the conclusion of the discourse, Kierkegaard asks, "Is it not possible for a person to be eternally lost?" And if so, would not the one who loved such a person be put to shame? For example, what if the prodigal son "had died in his sins and therefore was buried with shame," would not the father who continued to hope all things also be put to shame? Kierkegaard answers,

> I should think that it was the son who had the shame, . . . but . . . the father, indeed, must have the honor. . . . If there were no salvation for the prodigal son beyond the grave, if he were eternally lost . . . would [the father] then be put to shame in eternity? . . . No, eternity . . . purges as something disgraceful the sagacity that wants to talk only about the extent to which one's expectancy was fulfilled but does not at all consider what the expectancy was. In eternity everyone will be compelled to understand that it is not the outcome that determines the honor or the shame, but the expectancy in itself. . . . [H]onor belongs to the loving one. . . . [I]n eternity the cry of the mocker is not heard . . . since only blessedly happy voices are heard in eternity! And in eternity no envy will tamper with the wreath of honor that the loving one wears with honor— . . . envy does not extend from hell to paradise! (WL, 263)

This is a strange conclusion for a treatment of hope. Kierkegaard himself notes that "surely the concerned father [of the
prodigal son] is thinking least of all about honor!" Then, what
about our "heavenly Father?" What is God the Eternal thinking
about when confronted with the human being who boldly assumes
"the impossibility of the good" so that "possibility dies for him
altogether" (WL, 253-54)? Does possibility also die altogether for
God? Note that Kierkegaard does not himself assert that a person
can be eternally lost because there is no salvation beyond the
grave. He only asks the question. Is this viewpoint consistent with
the "unfathomable conflict in love" as depicted by Anti-Climacus
(SUD, 126)? For my conclusion of this article, I propose that Kierkegaard's ontology of love suggests the possibility of still another
line of thinking on the questions I have been raising.

Later in *Works of Love* there is a discourse that has a different
perspective on the whole issue, "The Victory of the Reconciling
Spirit in Love."[29] Kierkegaard's main point is that in most battles
between right and wrong, the good seeks simply to vanquish and
subjugate the evil. This is not the true victory of goodness. Love
seeks not simply to vanquish or remove the evil ones but rather "is
fighting *reconcilingly* for the good to be victorious in the unloving
person, . . . struggling *to win the one overcome*. Thus the relationship
between the two is no longer an outright conflict-relationship,
because the loving one is fighting on the side of the enemy for his
benefit." From the very beginning love does not fight "*against* the
enemy" but fights "*for* the enemy. . . . [T]his is loving, or this is the
reconciling spirit in love!" (WL, 335).

How is this victory accomplished? Is it simply by forcing the
evil doer to recognize that he is in the wrong and you are in the
right so that he begs for forgiveness? This is not the way love
works, says Kierkegaard.

> Certainly it is the one who did wrong who needs forgiveness, but
> the loving one who suffered the wrong needs to forgive or
> [rather] needs agreement [or reunion: *Forligelse*], reconciliation,

---

[29]The Hong translation uses "the Conciliatory Spirit," but that English word
smacks of compromise and appeasement whereas the discourse is clearly talking
about forgiveness and reconciliation—as we shall see.

words that, unlike the word 'forgiveness,' which reminds us of right and wrong, do not make such a distinction but lovingly make a mental note that both are in need. (WL, 336)

In spite of the eternally reality of that distinction, in spite of the fact that love cannot remain love (with freedom and equality) and yet remove the possibility of offense, yet love forgets that distinction totally in seeking to win the unloving one, and thinks only of the desired goal and *mutual* need of harmony in reconciliation.

So Kierkegaard concludes that we are not just concerned with forgiveness, but

we are speaking about fighting in love so that the other will accept forgiveness, will allow himself to be reconciled. Is this not Christianity? . . . [I]t is not human beings who say to God, "Forgive us." No, God loved us first. . . . [T]he true conciliatory spirit is this: when the one who does not . . . *need* forgiveness is the one who offers reconciliation. (WL, 336; emphasis added)

And when and how do we know that it is time to give up the battle? In our human-to-human relationship, the answer is: Never! This Kierkegaard had emphasized in the discourse on hope, four times in three pages. If you possess the love that hopes all things, then you "never unlovingly give up on any human being or give up hope for that person, since it is possible that . . . even the most embittered enemy . . . could again become your friend" (WL, 254). Again, "it is one thing to despair oneself and something else to despair over someone else. . . . [T]o give up on another as hopelessly lost . . . is evidence that one is not oneself a loving person and thus is the one who despairs, who gives up possibility" (WL, 255). Furthermore, "to give up on [a human being] is to give up your love for him . . . but if you give up your love for him, then you yourself cease to be the one who loves" (WL, 255). And in this case, "the one who was the object of love loses, but the one who has 'given up his love for this person,' . . . is the loser. . . . I am not entitled to the adjective 'loving' if I have given up my love" (WL, 256).

If it is true that authentic love in a human person never gives up even on one's worst enemy, even on the most vile and evil human being, then how much more must this be true of God who is from all eternity Love-Itself! And if this character of love is true for the human being "to the very 'last day,' because not until then is hope over" (WL, 258), then surely the One who is eternal love, the Being which is love-in-and-for-itself, the Being in which there are no restrictions of time or space, must also *never give up on any one* of its dearly beloved offspring, its children to whom Being-Itself has given being, has given freedom to return love to Love-Itself and to love each other. Surely, eternal Love does not cease to be loving. "[I]n time, the eternal is the possible, the future." But "eternally, the eternal is the eternal" (WL, 249). There is no "last day" for Love-Itself. Then what is eternity for but for God to continue to confront the worst of sinners with the "100,000 possibilities for helping?" Surely, with God's help the being/life of the most wayward child will not "collapse" (JP, 2:2008). As Haufniensis points out, "reconciliation" (in the Christian under-standing) is precisely the task of "doing away with" the "nonbe-ing" of "sensuousness removed from spirit" (CA, 83). Does God, as Being-in-and-for-Itself, ever give up on this task? Does God admit defeat?

These questions do not rest on logical deductions or inferences but on phenomenological insights that emerge (as questions) from our own experience of the presence of God-as-Love in our own self-consciousness. We *know* that God will never desert us:

> Whither shall I go from thy Spirit? . . .
> if I make my bed in Sheol, thou art there! . . .
> If I say, "Let only darkness cover me,
>     and the light about me be night,"
> Even the darkness is not dark to thee. . . .
>                               (Psalm 139:7a, 8b, 11-12a RSV)

On the basis of this experience of our profound ontological connection with the source of all being as Love-Itself, some (such as Karl Barth) have made the deduction that God as Love is ulti-mately victorious over all enemies, and hence all unloving and all unbelieving is vanquished because in Jesus Christ, the eternal Son of God and hence "God's-Humanity" [*Menschlichkeitgottes*], sin and death have been permanently conquered, all have been reconciled and hence all will be redeemed into eternal life with God.

But this deduction ignores what some philosophers and theologians have called "radical evil," the persistence of the human heart in resisting all pleas to abandon its self-centered attempt to manipulate, dominate, oppress and use all other human beings simply as means for one's own self-satisfaction and aggrandize-ment. Kierkegaard's analysis of the forms of despair in *The Sickness unto Death* is an exploration of the diverse ways in which humans thus "lose" their given potentiality to become spiritual selves, "the most intensive form" being "demonic despair" which is simply a "hatred toward existence," a "rebelling against all existence" and against "the power that established it" (SUD, 73). On what grounds can anyone hope or expect that this conscious despair will ever yield to the power of infinite eternal love? In the "New Testament Christianity" that Kierkegaard took as the source and norm of his second authorship, Jesus does not hesitate repeatedly to warn that "all evildoers" will be thrown "into the furnace of fire" or "into the outer darkness" where "humans will weep and gnash their teeth" (see Matt. 13:41-42; 25:30; I do not think that SK restricted "New Testament" to the Sayings Gospel and to Q).

Furthermore, if even in eternity, the eternal holds open a future of possibility for those still in despair, it would still be true, as Kierkegaard says, that "in possibility the eternal always relates equally to its duality" of "advance or retrogression, . . . good or evil" (WL, 249), because as we have heard, "the difference between right and wrong remains eternally, just as he remains, the Eternal One. . . . [T]he Eternal One . . . changes everything, but never himself—and therefore never changes this either, eternity's difference" (CD, 208). And the "wrong" for human beings is precisely the refusal of love and to love. And just because of the very nature of love as the positive possibility, the Eternal will not and cannot remove this negative possibility of refusal. So again, this fact is the "unfathomable [inscrutable, impenetrable] grief [sorrow, anxiety] of love" or "the unfathomable conflict in love" (SUD, 126). Clearly then, Kierkegaard does not accept Barth's deduction of universal salvation.

To conclude, this note of sorrow within the Eternal Being of Love, a sorrow and conflict that is inscrutable within the limits of our understanding, is what casts the shadow on our understanding of the omnipotence of God. How can Love-Itself, which has created us with and for the potentiality of becoming lovers in God's image, be satisfied when so many human beings fail to fulfill that goal set for us? But the presence of this conflict in God is also what suggests that when the human heart does respond with joyous gratitude to God's loving forgiveness and reconciliation and thus is enabled to become itself in the fullness of all of its own unique creative powers, then God the Eternal also finds a fulfillment and a joy not present before. As Jesus said, "There will be more joy in heaven over one sinner who repents than over ninety-nine righteous persons who need no repentance" (Luke 15:7). And the joy is not over the repentance but for the unimaginable and untold riches that flow from the self's becoming itself and therein finding fulfillment in the creativity that comes with love from God and with love of God and neighbor.

Near the end of his life Leonard Bernstein wrote:

> In the beginning was the note,
> And the note was with God.
> And whosoever can reach that note,
> Reach high and bring it back to us on earth,
>     to our earthly ears,
> He is a composer,
> And to the extent of his reach
> Partakes of the Divine.[30]

And (I would say) the Divine partakes of the human.

The paradox of sorrow and love in eternal Love-Itself is one that we can only wonder at and muse about. Surely, all loving parents know that there comes a time when they must let the child slip away from them, to discover and to become its own self, waiting in terror as the child inevitably knows failure and thereby (we hope) to find oneself through losing oneself. And do not all loving parents continue to love in sorrow even the child who wanders into darkness?

Kierkegaard does not come to any clear conclusion or systematization on the question of whether God's love is omnipotent over all opposition in the end, or on the issue of God's need for fulfillment in human love and creativity. He did not ever argue toward an already received position. He followed relentlessly and

---

[30]I heard this recited by Bernstein on a television biography of Bernstein entitled, "Leonard Bernstein: Reaching for the Note," written and directed by Susan Lacy, and produced for the series, "American Masters," by WNET, New York, for the Educational Broadcasting Corp., 1998.

fearlessly the evidence of the Christian experience of truth wherever it might lead, even to paradox and mystery.

And given the options of *either* being an inevitable natural process without pain or possibility, *or* being a conscious self with the possibility of freedom, love and creativity matched with the possibility of ghastly failure, corruption, and despair, most humans would not hesitate to choose the latter.

But the mystery of human failure is not one that we can or need to resolve in any ultimate sense if we believe and hence understand that all our ways are designed to lead us to fulfillment in love. So Paul the apostle, when he was trying to explain the "mystery" of how Israel could be both God's chosen and God's enemy, finally had to cry out, "O the depth of the riches and wisdom and knowledge of God! How unsearchable are his . . . [God's] judgments and how inscrutable . . . [God's] ways!" (Romans 11:33 NRSV). Then he paraphrases the prophet Isaiah: "For who has known the mind of the Lord, or who has been God's counselor?" (cf. Isaiah 40:13-14). And he might also have quoted the book of Job, where "the LORD answered Job out of the whirlwind: 'Who is this that darkens counsel by words without knowledge?' . . . 'Where were you when I laid the foundation of the earth?' " (Job 38:1-2, 4 NRSV).

In the end the best we can do is to feel profound gratitude when God inspires us with love, and to share God's sorrow when any of our fellow human beings (or we ourselves) seem to be beyond the reach of God's love.

# 5

## "Believing All Things":
## Kierkegaard on Knowledge, Doubt, and Love

### Anthony Rudd

In part 2 of *Works of Love* are two discourses, "Love Believes All Things—and Yet Is Never Deceived" and "Love Hopes All Things—and Yet Is Never Put to Shame." These titles are taken from St. Paul's hymn to love in 1 Corinthians, and are intended to show how, as Paul asserts, love is greater than faith (belief) or hope in that it includes, or, better, serves as the condition for them. In developing his line of thought, Kierkegaard makes essential use of premises that are in themselves neither ethical nor theological, but epistemological. In this essay, I want to bring out the way in which Kierkegaard gives an ethical application to epistemological ideas that seem at first sight to be quite abstract and remote from ethical concerns. And I hope by so doing to demonstrate something of the unity of Kierkegaard's thought, and to shed some light on the vexed issue of the status of his pseudonymous writings.

### I

*Love believes all things.* Kierkegaard starts by making it quite clear that we do not have an initial, general understanding of what it is to believe all things and then note that this is something that love does. It is essential to "believing all things" in Kierkegaard's sense that it is *love* that does so. And it is only this loving belief that is incapable of being deceived. "Truly, not everyone who believes all things is therefore one who loves, and not everyone who believes all things is on that account secured against every deception" (WL, 225). Kierkegaard spells out the point with a series of contrasts:

> Light-mindedness, inexperience, naiveté believe everything that
> is said; vanity, conceit, complacency believe everything flattering
> that is said; envy, malice, corruption believe everything evil that
> is said; mistrust believes nothing at all; experience will teach that
> it is most sagacious not to believe everything—but love believes
> all things. (WL, 226)

It soon becomes clear that Kierkegaard is not primarily concerned with belief or disbelief in indifferent matters, for example,
of history or natural science, but with the assessment of moral
character, with what we should believe about one another's
motives and intentions. These are, often at least, far from transparent. (Even our own motives are often not transparent to us.)
Naiveté fails to realize this, and takes everything at face value.
Mistrust, on the contrary, is all too well aware of the possibility of
different interpretations of people's actions, noting how quick we
are to believe well or ill of people according to the way we want
to think about them, and how we will then tend to ignore any
contrary evidence. The mistrustful person takes pride in his or her
knowledge and cleverness. He or she realizes that someone's
apparent virtue may be a sham; that one cannot simply infer the
reality of someone's moral state from the appearance he or she
presents to the world. Mistrust does not conclude—as malice
would—that the apparent virtue *is* a sham; rather, that we cannot
tell, and therefore should come to no conclusion. Mistrust aims to
secure itself against the possibility of being deceived, not by
believing all things, but by believing nothing.

What underlies this attitude is, according to Kierkegaard, a
fundamental confusion, or even dishonesty. The mistrustful person
is quite right to see that people's actions can always be variously
interpreted, but then goes on to assume that the conclusion he or
she draws from this objective fact—that one should be mistrustful—follows from it as a necessary consequence. But it doesn't.
That conclusion is an existential choice, which the mistrustful one
refuses to admit he or she is making.

> What mistrust says or presents is really only knowledge; the
> secret and the falsity lies in this, that it summarily converts this
> knowledge into a belief and pretends that nothing has happened
> . . . as if it were therefore eternally certain . . . that when knowl-
> edge is given, then how one concludes is also given. (WL, 227)

It is true that any human action can be differently interpreted. But what follows from this? That we are not forced by objective knowledge into interpreting it one way rather than another. We are free to interpret the data differently, and this means that the interpretations we do make reveal what our own fundamental outlook on life is. So the malicious person puts the worst construction on any actions; the mistrustful refuses to make any conclusion at all; but the one who loves is free to interpret the actions lovingly.

> Just because existence has to test *you*, test *your* love . . . with the help of the understanding existence confronts you with the truth and the deception in the equilibrium of the opposite possibilities so that as *you* now judge, that is, as you now in judging *choose*, what dwells in you must become disclosed. (WL, 227)

The cynic notes that what appears to be the noblest or most altruistic behavior could be concealed selfishness or vanity. But he fails to notice the opposite possibility; that "even something that appears to be the vilest behavior could be pure love" (WL, 228). The lover differs from the naive or inexperienced person in that he or she is fully aware of all the possible interpretations that could be placed on anyone's actions. Faced with this objective uncertainty, the lover chooses to believe, and by so doing reveals the love that is in him or her. The cynic, who has precisely the same objective knowledge, chooses not to believe, and thus reveals his or her mistrust.

The mistrustful person, however, is unable to really maintain an equidistance between love and malice. Such a person aims to believe neither good nor ill of anyone. But "to believe nothing at all is the very border where believing evil begins" (WL, 234). Goodness is bound up with a willingness to trust, so the refusal to do so is a defiance of the good, and is therefore a turning to evil. "Mistrust cannot maintain knowledge in equilibrium; it defiles its knowledge [by appealing to it to justify mistrust] and therefore verges on envy, malice, and corruption, which believe all evil" (WL, 234).

Love, by contrast, believes all things; it puts the best construction on all actions. But surely in so doing, it often will be deceived? Kierkegaard concedes that "in a childish and poor sense," or on "a lower conceptual sphere," the lover may be deceived (WL,

235-36). But in a deeper sense, he or she is never deceived. For in this deeper sense, "*to be deceived simply and solely means to refrain from loving*" (WL, 236). The lover may be wrong about this or that particular matter, but the only essential deception would be if he or she were deceived into thinking that one should not love. Hence love cannot, by definition, be deceived.

Kierkegaard's treatment of hope is closely analogous. Like true belief (belief based on love) true hope (hope based on love) should not be confused with "a wish, a longing, a longing expectation now of one thing, now of another" (WL, 250). A loving hope is one that hopes for others, and primarily hopes that, however badly someone is behaving, that person may still repent and turn to the good. Hope shares with despair a knowledge of possibility. Even if—contrary to Kierkegaard's view—one could know for sure what the moral state of another person is now, it would still remain true that one could not know how he or she will turn out in the future. A good person may go to the bad, so despair advises us never to rely on anyone, never to hope that anyone will stay true, for one would thereby only be inviting disillusionment.

But hope, while acknowledging that, points out that the opposite also holds; however badly someone is acting now, there is always room to hope for a change for the better. "Objective" knowledge cannot rule this out; it can only tell us that anything is possible. It is up to the individual whether he or she takes this as a justification for never losing hope, or for never having hope. And, like belief, true hope is never disappointed, never put to shame. For true hope is identical with love, and the only way that a lover could be "put to shame" would be if she lost hope, that is, if she ceased to love, ceased to always believe that the good is still possible for anyone, even those who now seem to be the worst of people.

## II

*Works of Love* is primarily a book of edification, rather than philosophy. But it is clearly intended for the edification of an intellectually sophisticated readership. Such readers are, in Kierkegaard's eyes, particularly liable to certain temptations, such as that of using their cleverness to make themselves think that they, being more knowing, should be more suspicious, more distrustful than others. The attitude of "knowingness," of worldly-wise cynicism, of suspicion of others' motives, is certainly not confined to the intelligentsia, but it may not be unfair to suggest that they—we—are particularly susceptible to it. Certainly the "hermeneutics of suspicion," influenced by a combination of Nietzsche, Marxist ideology critique, and psychoanalysis, is a major academic industry, whose practitioners specialize in stripping away facades of supposed virtue in order to expose the corrupt realities that they conceal. And it is difficult to deny that in so doing, they reveal at least as much about themselves—their own will to denigrate and deny—as they do about their subject matter. (Though perhaps if I had really taken Kierkegaard's injunction to heart, I would not make such an uncharitable judgment, for their activity may be "pure love.")

Kierkegaard attempts to combat this kind of skepticism by taking it further than its own practitioners do. That is, he argues that nothing is certain, that there is always room for alternative interpretations of any phenomenon, and therefore room for generous as much as for cynical interpretations. And so the claim made by the suspicious that their attitude is justified objectively by the facts is itself revealed as self-deception. Marxist and psychoanalytic judgments rest on thoroughly dubious dogmatic presumptions which a serious skepticism will have little trouble undermining. Nietzsche is more deeply skeptical, and does turn his skepticism back upon itself; he leaves us with the paradox that his "Will to Truth," after swallowing everything else up, at last consumes itself. What remains is, of course, the Will to Power. Kierkegaard would have said, the Will to Mistrust.

One can choose to will in this way, but one can also choose not to. One can choose to believe lovingly. But clearly this whole argument rests on an epistemological claim to the effect that there is no objective certainty, that everything can be interpreted in an undecidable multiplicity of ways. And this claim itself is hardly uncontroversial. Since *Works of Love* is not, or not primarily, a book on philosophy, one cannot expect Kierkegaard to break off his discourse in order to give a detailed defense of his epistemological premises. Still, the question cannot be ignored. How can this crucial premise of Kierkegaard's ethical argument be supported? If this challenge were put to Kierkegaard himself, I think it is clear how he would have answered: by referring the inquirer to the *Philosophical Fragments* and *Concluding Unscientific Postscript*. For it is in these works that the epistemology used as a premise in *Works of Love*, but not argued for there, is expounded and defended at length. This fact tells us some important things, I shall argue, about the unity of Kierkegaard's thought and the status of his pseudonyms—or, at any rate, of Johannes Climacus.

## III

In *Works of Love*, knowledge is described in a way that might at first seem strange to contemporary epistemologists: Kierkegaard claims that it has to do only with possibilities. All that is knowable is that there are such and such possibilities. That any of them is realized is for Kierkegaard a matter of *belief*, not knowledge. Clearly, he uses these terms in a somewhat unusual and technical sense, but it is in fact one that the epistemologists should not find so unfamiliar. The terminology is basically Cartesian/Humean, in that "knowledge" is used by Kierkegaard to mean what we can be certain of. That such and such combinations of phenomena are possible we can know, but there is always room for doubt as to whether any of them is actual. Hence, in matters of empirical fact, we can only have belief, and not knowledge:

> Knowledge places everything in possibility and to that extent is outside the actuality of existence in possibility. The individual first begins his life with "ergo," with *belief*. But most people live so negligently that they do not notice at all that in one way or another, every minute they live, they live by virtue of an "ergo," a belief. There is no decision in knowledge; the decision, the determination and the firmness of personality are first in the "ergo," in belief. Knowledge is the infinite art of equivocation . . . at most it is simply a placing of opposite possibilities in equilibrium. (WL, 230-31)

Anyone who knows the Johannes Climacus writings will find these ideas familiar. In the *Fragments*, Climacus expresses his agreement with the Greek skeptics that everything (except "immediate sensation and immediate cognition" [PF, 81]) can be doubted. Any conclusion that I try to draw from immediate sense data may be mistaken. The skeptics were right about this; there is no intellectual refutation of skepticism.[1] However, it does not follow from this that we *should* doubt. The skeptics *chose* to do so: "they doubted not by virtue of knowledge, but by virtue of will. . . . This implies that doubt can only be terminated in freedom, by an act of will, something that every Greek skeptic would understand . . . but he would not terminate his skepticism, precisely because he *willed* to doubt" (PF, 82).

Even in ordinary empirical statements about the natural world, we have possibilities of doubt or belief which, just like love or mistrust in *Works of Love*, are chosen attitudes, neither of which simply follows from objective knowledge. One can no more intellectually refute skepticism than one can prove mistrust to be objectively mistaken. But it remains up to us whether we chose to doubt or mistrust, because those attitudes are not forced on us by knowledge, which, in itself, remains "infinite indifference" (WL, 231).

These ideas are articulated further, and at considerable length, in the *Postscript*. There Climacus explains that a logical system is possible—and certainty obtainable within it—precisely because it abstracts from existence and is concerned only with possibilities (CUP, 1:109-18). There cannot, however, be an existential system (CUP, 1:118-25). In respect to ordinary empirical judgments, truth, defined as "the agreement of thinking with being" becomes "a desideratum, and everything is placed in the process of becoming" (CUP, 1:189). One can only advance hypotheses and see how well they are confirmed by the evidence, but one can never obtain all the relevant evidence, or be sure what results future experience may bring. Climacus does recognize that one hypothesis can be better supported than another, and that it is rational for us to provisionally accept and rely on those theories which currently have the greatest evidential backing. But he insists that certainty in empirical matters can never be obtained. And Kierkegaard makes exactly the same (proto-Popperian) point in *Works of Love*: "an assumption can indeed explain a great number of instances very well and thereby confirm its truth and yet show itself to be

---

[1] I have more to say about this in my paper "Kierkegaard and the Skeptics," *British Journal for the History of Philosophy* 6 (1998): 71-88.

untrue as soon as the instance comes along that it cannot explain" (WL, 229).

Objective thinking, knowledge properly speaking, has only a "hypothetical" relation to reality. "All knowledge about actuality is possibility" (CUP, 1:316). And Climacus goes on to apply this epistemological thesis to ethics. He points out, in respect of the injunction, "Judge not that you be not judged," that although it is presented "as an admonition . . . it is also an impossibility. One person cannot ethically judge another, because the one can understand the other only as a possibility. Thus when someone is occupied with wanting to judge another, this is a manifestation of his weakness, that he is only judging himself" (CUP, 1:322).

The discourses from *Works of Love* that I have been discussing are essentially attempts to bring out the edification implicit in this line of thought. And Kierkegaard does indeed refer there to the same Scriptural injunction that Climacus comments on, and notes that it is so phrased that "it seems as if at times one could judge without being judged in return. But this is not the case. In the very same minute when you judge another person . . . you judge yourself" (WL, 233). I could continue to cite evidence, but it should be apparent to any attentive reader of the *Fragments* and *Postscript* that the epistemology employed in *Works of Love* is precisely that worked out by Climacus in those works.[2]

*IV*

This has some importance for the continuing debate in Kierkegaardian scholarship about the significance of the pseudonyms.

---

[2]The fullest and most systematic account of Kierkegaard's epistemology in English is a Ph.D. dissertation by M. G. Piety: "Kierkegaard on Knowledge" (McGill University, 1994). Piety's account draws on the whole range of Kierkegaard's published writings, pseudonymous and signed, and on the *Papirer*, and by so doing convincingly demonstrates the unity and coherence of his epistemological thinking. See also Piety's essays, "The Place of the World in Kierkegaard's Ethics," in *Kierkegaard: The Self in Society*, ed. George Pattison and Steven Shakespeare (Basingstoke: Macmillan; New York: St. Martin's, 1998) and "The Reality of the World in Kierkegaard's *Postscript*," in *International Kierkegaard Commentary: Concluding Unscientific Postscript to "Philosophical Fragments,"* IKC 12, ed. Robert L. Perkins (Macon GA: Mercer University Press, 1997) 169-86.

Not that it is particularly helpful to generalize about "the pseudo-nyms"; it is, to put it mildly, far from obvious that Kierkegaard was doing just the same thing with, for instance, Johannes the Seducer, Nicholas Notabene, Vigilius Haufniensis, and Anti-Climacus. Perhaps the most interesting debates have revolved around the Climacus writings. Many commentators have assumed that Climacus does represent Kierkegaard's own views, but others have argued that he is cunningly "set up" by Kierkegaard to present a point of view that eventually undermines itself, thus showing the futility of all philosophizing—even "existential philosophizing"—at least in respect of ethicoreligious matters.[3]

I am inclined to believe that the more traditional interpretation is broadly correct,[4] and I think this view is strongly supported by

---

[3]There exist various interpretations of this sort. A systematic account of the pseudonymous literature in these terms can be found in M. Holmes Hartshorne, *Kierkegaard: Godly Deceiver* (New York: Columbia University Press, 1990). But per-haps the most challenging "ironic" reading of the Climacus works, and particular-ly the *Postscript*, is due to James Conant: see his papers, "Putting Two and Two Together; Kierkegaard, Wittgenstein, and the Point of View for their Work as Authors" in *Philosophy and the Grammar of Religious Belief*, ed. Tessin and Von der Ruhr (Basingstoke: Macmillan, 1995) and "Kierkegaard, Wittgenstein, and Non-sense" in *Pursuits of Reason*, ed. Ted Cohen, Paul Guyer, and Hilary Putnam (Texas: Texas Technical University Press, 1993). See also S. Mulhall, *Faith and Reason* (London: Duckworth, 1994) esp. chap. 3. For some effective criticisms of Conant, see J. Lippitt, "A Funny Thing Happened to Me on the Way to Salvation: Climacus as Humorist in Kierkegaard's *Concluding Unscientific Postscript*," *Religious Studies* 33 (1997) and J. Lippitt and D. Hutto, "Making Sense of Nonsense: Kierke-gaard and Wittgenstein," *Proceedings of the Aristotelian Society* (1998). I have some further criticisms of Conant and Mulhall in my paper, "On Straight and Crooked Thinking: Why the *Postscript* Does Not Self-Destruct," in *Anthropology and Authori-ty in Kierkegaard*, ed. P. Houe, G. Marino, and S. H. Rossel (Amsterdam/Atlanta: Editions Rodopi, forthcoming).

[4]It is worth noting that if the "ironic" interpretations were right, then one would have to accept that the Climacus writings represent a colossal failure to communicate on Kierkegaard's part. For a century and a half no one understood what their true meaning was, until now, at last, "a Professor" has arrived who is clever enough to see what Kierkegaard was really getting at! In the meantime, poor, literal-minded dummies like Heidegger, Sartre, Jaspers, Tillich, et al. had revolutionized European thought by taking what were really ironically self-destructive texts at face value.

the considerations adduced above.[5] Kierkegaard, writing under his own name, states in summary form—and relies upon in an essential way for developing his ethical argument—exactly the epistemological doctrines worked out at length in the Climacus writings. This makes it clear that he cannot have intended us to take these parts of the Climacus works ironically. Of course, the possibility remains that there are other things in those works Kierkegaard does not intend us to accept, but it seems to me that the epistemology is so central to them that it becomes quite implausible to claim that Kierkegaard means us to accept that (which he clearly does, given his own reliance on it) but to reject what is said, for instance, about truth as subjectivity, or the Paradox and the possibility of Faith or Offense which goes with it.[6] These discussions are interwoven too closely with the epistemological themes set out above to be plausibly disentangled from them.

Moreover, we can read the discourse "Love Believes All Things" as providing an implicit explanation of the pseudonymity of, at any rate, the Climacus literature—one which allows a serious point to the pseudonymity without requiring us to suppose that Climacus is saying things with which Kierkegaard would have disagreed. There is a passage in the discourse, extending over three paragraphs (WL, 228-30), which is in quotation marks. It summarizes the epistemological points that Kierkegaard has made elsewhere in the discourse, stating that behavior that is in fact evil may appear to be good and vice versa; so that there is no objective

---

[5]In rejecting what I call the "ironic" interpretations, I do not of course mean to deny that the Climacus works are full of irony (as well as humor and sarcasm). Nor am I denying that the *Fragments* in particular is a very unstraightforward and in many ways puzzling work. All I am rejecting here is the idea that Kierkegaard set Climacus up to assert things that Kierkegaard himself considered confused.

[6]Conant and Mulhall do in fact try to distinguish between those parts of the *Postscript* that we are meant to take at face value and those we are not. In so doing they get into a whole series of muddles, some of which I have tried to indicate in my "On Straight and Crooked Thinking." In a longer paper, I would try to show that Kierkegaard's entire "edifying" literature presupposes an understanding of truth as subjectivity of the sort that is articulated discursively by Climacus in the *Postscript*. Such a demonstration would obviously strengthen the support for my claim about the relation of the Climacus works to Kierkegaard's religious writings, but I shall not attempt it here.

way of judging another's actions. Kierkegaard then asks (in his own voice):

> Now, can you tell me who said this? No, it is an impossibility. It is completely equivocal; in the capacity of a knower, the most mistrustful and the most loving person could equally well have said it. . . . It is knowledge, and knowledge as such is impersonal and is to be communicated impersonally. (WL, 230)

This helps us to see at least part of the reason Kierkegaard did not publish his epistemological writings under his own name. It was not that he disagreed with them, thought them self-refuting, or anything like that. The point is that they are in themselves indifferent to existential concerns. Kierkegaard appears to have taken a conscious decision[7] to publish only directly religious works under his own name, that is, works that fully and clearly represented his own fundamental beliefs. Works containing conceptual clarifications, even though they were of importance for his religious project, were to appear pseudonymously, since the points they had to make could be accepted by clearheaded opponents as well as adherents of his own ethicoreligious views.[8] Conceptual clarification was essential for those intellectuals who had been bewitched by Hegelian or other muddled thinking: they needed to clear their minds before they could come to understand ethics and religion as the existential challenges that they are. But such an understanding cannot prescribe how one will respond to the challenge. There is no way to be an epistemologically clearheaded Hegelian, but one can perfectly well accept all Kierkegaard's epistemological views and still opt for doubt, mistrust, or offense as existential stances.

---

[7]It can, I suppose, be dated to 1844 when, after completing the *Fragments* and *The Concept of Anxiety*, Kierkegaard abandoned his original plan to publish them under his own name and, after making only a few trivial changes to the texts, issued them under pseudonyms.

[8]Hence the pseudonyms "Haufniensis" and "Climacus" are used for an essentially different purpose than those employed in the more "literary" works. The latter are used by Kierkegaard to express existential stances different from his own, rather than philosophical positions which are neutral as between the different stances.

This being the case, Kierkegaard wishes to separate clarification clearly from edification, and he uses the device of pseudonymity to do so. By doing this, he can avoid cluttering up religious works with epistemological investigations which are not directly edifying and which would distract the reader from the main point; and he can avoid cluttering his philosophical works with religious exhortations which might make readers suspicious, or make them fear that he had a prior design on them. The separation of skeptical epistemology from ethicoreligious exhortation is clearly demonstrated by the section of *Works of Love* just referred to. Had it been longer, the passage in quotation marks might have been attributed to a pseudonym in its own right. As it is, it serves, in its context, as a brief reminder of the results established by the Climacus writings; and as a reminder that, although entirely valid in their own right, they do nothing to determine what existential attitude one should go on to adopt.[9]

## V

This is not the place to discuss in detail the objections that may be raised to Kierkegaard's epistemology. However, it may be worth trying to clear up one misunderstanding, which concerns his voluntarism.[10] Surely, it may be said, we don't have to make a con-

---

[9]I should perhaps say that, although I think this is in general the right way to see the role of the pseudonymity, I am not suggesting that everything in the Climacus writings or elsewhere can be explained in terms of a simple master plan. On the contrary, I think Kierkegaard was less consistent and more opportunistic in his use of the pseudonyms than has often been assumed.

[10]There has been a good deal of debate about this, though it has tended to focus on Kierkegaard's—or Climacus's—views on the rationality or otherwise of religious and specifically Christian belief. But his secular epistemology has been discussed, at least as a background to the religious issues. See, e.g., C. Stephen Evans, *Kierkegaard's "Fragments" and "Postscript": The Religious Philosophy of Johannes Climacus* (Atlantic Highlands NJ: Humanities Press, 1983) esp. chaps. 11 and 12; also Evans's *Passionate Reason: Making Sense of Kierkegaard's "Philosophical Fragments"* (Bloomington: Indiana University, 1992) esp. chaps. 5-8; M. Jamie Ferreira, *Transforming Vision: Imagination and Will in Kierkegaardian Faith* (Oxford/New York: Oxford University Press, 1991); Louis P. Pojman, *The Logic of Subjectivity: Kierkegaard's Philosophy of Religion* (University: University of Alabama Press, 1984); and Terence Penelhum, *God and Skepticism: A Study in Skepticism and*

scious decision in order to believe that our friends are telling us the truth, or even that there is a coffee cup on the table, and so forth? So how can it be right to describe belief as an act of will? This objection is based on a misunderstanding. Kierkegaard nowhere suggests that ordinary belief involves a conscious effort of the will. Rather, we start out with a natural tendency to believe. However, the cynicism-inducing course of ordinary experience, the acquisition of practical worldly wisdom, and, for some, the influence of philosophical (or sociological or psychoanalytic) skepticism may lead us to adopt an attitude of mistrust. If, having become aware of the possibilities of doubt, we are to continue to believe or to trust, then that is by virtue of a refusal to accept the possibilities of doubt that we know to exist. "The individual first begins his life with 'ergo,' with *belief*" (WL, 230). Our natural starting point is an attitude of trust. It is only after the possibility of doubting has arisen that we can be conscious of believing *despite* the possibility of doubt.

The loving person needs a degree of this self-consciousness. For he or she is not the naive person who isn't aware that human behavior can be differently interpreted. The loving person is able to remain loving precisely because he knows that even what looks like very bad behavior might not be what it seems. Thus Kierkegaard commends those who have "taken the time and effort to develop the infinite, equal sense for possibilities . . . and bring them into equilibrium" (WL, 231). This sounds very like the description of Pyrrhonean Skepticism given by one of its' practitioners: "Skepticism is an ability to place in antithesis . . . appearances and judgments and thus—because of the equality of force in the objects and arguments opposed—to come first of all to a suspension of judgment, and then to mental tranquillity."[11] Kierkegaard does not want to stop at the suspension of judgment, which is all that purely intellectual inquiries can produce; he wants to recom-

---

*Fideism*, Philosophical Studies 28 (Dordrecht and Boston: Kluwer, 1983) chaps. 4 and 5.

[11]Sextus Empiricus, *Outlines of Pyrrhonism*, I/iv, in *Selections from the Major Writings on Skepticism, Man, and God* (by Sextus Empiricus), new rev. ed., trans. Sanford G. Etheridge, ed. Philip Paul Hallie, new foreword and bibliography by Donald R. Morrison (Indianapolis: Hackett, 1985) 32-33.

mend an actively loving judgment. But a training in skepticism, in learning how variously all things—and in particular human actions—can be interpreted may be a spiritual discipline of great value to the would-be lover. To believe all things is a *work* of love, "a task" (WL, 226); it isn't something that we can just do, like snapping our fingers. Part of the task is to realize the impossibility of purely objective judgment, so that a devotion to skeptical argumentation may itself be a "work of love" in Kierkegaard's sense.[12] (Though of course, it might not be. Here too, objective uncertainty prevails.)

## VI

Finally, and too briefly, I should say a word about the plausibility of what Kierkegaard recommends as an ethical ideal. There is, after all, a natural response to what he says which might be put like this:

> Whatever the theoretical possibility of interpreting all human behavior in different ways, it is often clear enough what is really going on; the possibility of doubt *is* only theoretical, or even sophistical. How can one really doubt the evil of a Hitler or Stalin? Moreover, much of the time we are placed in positions where we have a responsibility to act in such a way as to prevent people doing harm to others; in such circumstances we have to make judgments about people's intentions and decide on the basis of probabilities how to act to thwart those intentions that we judge to be evil. And often, we are faced with a choice between believing two people. If x makes an allegation about y, and y replies that this is a slander, surely we cannot believe well of both x and y? Even if it is on the basis of probability rather than certainty, we still cannot avoid having to judge matters as best we can. And it may even be to the benefit of a wrongdoer that we don't give him the benefit of the doubt. How can anyone come to repent and reform, if no one will point out to him how badly he is acting?

These are all good points, and I don't think Kierkegaard would be committed to rejecting any of them. Admittedly, it does seem

---

[12]This can throw some interesting new light on the relationship between religious faith and philosophical skepticism, which might be relevant for an understanding of thinkers such as Montaigne and Bayle as well as Kierkegaard.

a bit sophistical to insist on the possibility of doubt in cases like those of Hitler, and it is a significant weakness of Kierkegaard's account that he does not provide concrete examples of apparently appalling acts that can be given plausibly generous interpretations. The discourse stays on a rather suspiciously high level of generality.[13] However, Kierkegaard nowhere denies that we need to act on the basis of probability. If it seems to me that someone has bad intentions, is aiming to harm others, and that I can thwart him, then I should do so. But in acting on the basis of reasonable probability, I can still allow for the possibility that I might be mistaken; or that, whatever the likely effect of the other's actions, he had no real intention to do harm; or that he was just lashing out blindly at what seemed to him a hostile world (the abused going on to abuse). In other words, I need not be forced to condemn anyone in my heart as simply evil. In any case, even if they may be, that is none of my business.[14]

Kierkegaard would therefore, I think, go along a good way with those who try to excuse or explain all criminal or antisocial acts as the effects of circumstances, bad upbringing, and so forth. Where he would differ from the archetypal modern sociological liberal is in refusing to abandon the notion of moral responsibility. For anyone else, I should make all the excuses I can, not hold them to be corrupt or evil. But with myself, I should be ruthless, allow no such excuse. I (any I) can say of others "They cannot be blamed." But I (any I) cannot say of (or to) myself, "I cannot be blamed." As Kierkegaard put it in the journals: "Most men are subjective toward themselves and objective toward all others, frightfully objective sometimes—but the task is precisely to be ob-

---

[13]This can be a problem with skepticism in general. It is quite easy to carry conviction in saying "Perhaps all our mathematical judgments are wrong," considerably harder to sound convincing in particular cases. ("2+2=4. Show me how I could be mistaken about *that*.")

[14]There is a further complication here: Kierkegaard, as a believer in Original Sin, *is* committed to supposing that everyone is in a sense radically evil. But the crucial point for him is that each of us is a sinner *before God*. And that is a matter for that person and for God; it is not for me to intervene in their relationship or to usurp God's role by trying to condemn or judge another person.

jective toward oneself and subjective toward all others" (JP, 4:4542).

All this applies particularly to those who occupy official positions where they are required to pass judgments and act to protect society from actual or potential evildoers. Kierkegaard refers to "the servant of justice [who] is not defiled by knowledge because he is better informed about all shady dealings than the criminal" (WL, 233). This "servant of justice" presumably acts rightly in preventing crime or punishing criminals; Kierkegaard was no anarchist. But it is possible—at least, one hopes it is—for the officer to do so without losing respect for the humanity of the criminal, and, indeed without forgetting that, whatever the evidence, the accused might after all not be guilty. The police and the courts have to act on the basis of probabilities, but their agents need not inwardly judge, condemn, and despise apparent offenders, whatever action they might be required to take against them.

# 6

# The Neighbor's Material and Social Well-Being in Kierkegaard's Works of Love: Does It Matter?

Lee C. Barrett III

Søren Kierkegaard's *Works of Love* raises vexing questions concerning the relationship of two crucial foci of traditional ethics: the cultivation of virtuous dispositions and the duty to promote the well-being, including the material and social well-being, of other human beings. (In this essay "material well-being" will be used in the broadest sense to include physical health, economic flourishing, possession of legal rights, and access to political power.) Although it would seem that these two concerns should be different sides of the same coin, they can point in divergent directions and even come into conflict with one another. The emphasis of one aspect can lead to the eclipse of the other. Kierkegaard's text accentuates the tension between them to the maximum degree. One trajectory in the book seems to suggest that because the duty to promote love in oneself and others overshadows all other duties, and because love can flourish in any social and material circumstances, it follows that the amelioration of social and material problems is unimportant. However, other features of the text, including Kierkegaard's illustrations of loving behavior, often seem to imply a positive duty to promote the neighbor's social and material well-being. The complexity of this tension in the text is evident in the fact that it has inspired widely divergent readings. According to some interpreters, Kierkegaard's attention to the interiority of love fosters a kind of spiritual narcissism and a cavalier indifference to the concrete needs of the neighbor. According to others, Kierkegaard's description of active love, and his rejection of spiritualizing dualisms, must lead to some sort of engagement with the total situation of the neighbor. Both interpretations can point to genuine aspects of the text to justify their positions.

I propose to explore a possible way to resolve this apparent discrepancy in *Works of Love*. I shall sort through the seemingly discordant themes in the text, considering their interactions in the light of Kierkegaard's various purposes. I shall argue that the tension in the text, and the possibility of diverse interpretations, is due to Kierkegaard's employment of different rhetorical strategies to achieve very different goals. These goals are by no means mutually exclusive, even though Kierkegaard himself does not synthesize them. His refusal to integrate them is entirely in keeping with the purpose of his authorship, which is to stimulate the reader's recognition of the need to synthesize concepts not on paper but in the reader's own existence. As we shall see, in the lives of receptive readers, his focus on the primacy of love as a disposition can motivate a certain kind of concern for the neighbor's social and material circumstances and even legitimate certain projects of social, political, and economic reform.

In order to appreciate the complexity of the multiple theses in the text, we must examine more closely the claims of the divergent interpretations. First we will consider the readings which detect in *Works of Love* a pernicious incentive to neglect the material well-being of the neighbor. This suspicion that Kierkegaard's book undermines any basis for a constructive socioeconomic ethic comes in several varieties and has several different aspects. The most sweeping version of this objection stretches back to the work of Martin Buber,[1] who claimed to detect a disjunction in Kierkegaard's works between the relation of the individual to God and the relation of the individual to anything else[2]. According to Buber,

---

[1]Martin Buber, "The Question to the Single One," in *Between Man and Man* (New York: Macmillan, 1965) 52-65.

[2]See Robert L. Perkins, "Buber and Kierkegaard: A Philosophic Encounter," in *Martin Buber: A Centenary Volume*, ed. Haim Gordon and Jochanan Bloch (New York: KTAV Publishing House, 1984) 275-303. "The Politics of Existence: Buber and Kierkegaard," in *Kierkegaard in Post/Modernity*, ed. Martin Matustik and Merold Westphal (Bloomington and Indianapolis: Indiana University Press, 1995) 167-81. M. Jamie Ferreira, "Otherworldliness in Kierkegaard's *Works of Love*," *Philosophical Investigations* 22/1 (January 1999).

Kierkegaard's emphasis on the individual's solitary relationship to God renders the world, including human sociality and physicality, spiritually inessential. W. T. Adorno's influential critique is a bit more nuanced.[3] According to Adorno, it is not so much the valorization of the individual/God relationship in itself which is the source of the problem; rather, it is the focus on the interiority of love which promotes an acosmic, otherworldly neglect of the neighbor's this-worldly needs. The accusation of acosmism is based on the alleged identification of "love" with the self-cultivation of purely internal attitudes. In this view, Kierkegaard's concern for the individual's pathos directs attention away from the world, thereby encouraging sociopolitical passivity and indifference to oppression. The danger is that Kierkegaard's remarks can function as reactionary advice to the lower classes to refrain from rocking the socioeconomic boat. Louis Dupré, although much more sympathetic to Kierkegaard's project, continued this interpretive trajectory, suggesting that Kierkegaard's early works tended to reduce ethics to an "inwardness" which could be outwardly indistinguishable from philistinism[4]. This can foster an indifference to the external forms which love takes. (Dupré does note that in *Works of Love* Kierkegaard began to move toward a more publicly enacted ethics, stressing the active imitation of Christ in the acceptance of suffering.) Louis Mackey, taking a different tack, locates the source of Kierkegaard's "loss of the world" in his view of "freedom," impervious to necessitating conditions.[5] The fact that

---

[3]T. W. Adorno, "On Kierkegaard's Doctrine of Love," *Studies in Philosophy and Social Science* 8 (1940): 413-29.

[4]Louis Dupré, *Kierkegaard as Theologian: The Dialectic of Christian Existence* (New York: Sheed and Ward, 1963) 158-64.

[5]Louis Mackey, "The Loss of World in Kierkegaard's Ethics," in *Kierkegaard: A Collection of Critical Essays*, ed. Josiah Thompson (Garden City NY: Anchor Books, 1972). See also Gene Outka, "Equality and Individuality: Thoughts on Two Themes in Kierkegaard," *The Journal of Religious Ethics* 10/2 (Fall 1982): 171-203. For a response to Mackey, see Louise Carroll Keeley, "Subjectivity and Loss of World in *Works of Love*," in *Foundations of Kierkegaard's Vision of Community*, ed. George B. Connell and C. Stephen Evans (Atlantic Highlands NJ: Humanities Press, 1992), and also M. G. Piety, "The Reality of the World in Kierkegaard's *Postscript*," in *International Kierkegaard Commentary: Concluding Unscientific Postscript to "Philosophical Fragments"* (Macon GA: Mercer University Press, 1997)

the radically free individual cannot be ultimately morally harmed or supported by external influences, including human communities, isolates the moral agent in its own autonomy. Other interpreters have seen Kierkegaard's apparent disinterest in the consequences of love as a lack of concern to actually help concrete neighbors[6]. We see that suspicions have been raised by several different aspects of *Works of Love*, most notably by Kierkegaard's emphasis of the individual/God relationship, his focus on interior pathos, his injunction against identifying love with externals, his allegedly isolating understanding of moral freedom, and his refusal to stress the attainment of beneficial results.

There certainly are passages in *Works of Love* which seem to support these suspicions that Kierkegaard lacks a full-bodied sociopolitical ethic. At times, Kierkegaard does appear to distance Christian love from any attempt to tamper with social structures. In one section, he claims that Christianity does not seek to take away the distinctions of status, position, circumstances, or education; rather, "with the calmness of eternity it (Christianity) surveys equably all the dissimilarities of earthly life but does not divisively take sides with any single one" (WL, 70). This refusal to "take sides" certainly does not sound like liberationist enthusiasm for "God's preferential option for the poor." The lack of reformist zeal is evident in Kierkegaard's claim that Christianity does not seek to initiate changes concerning the subservient marital roles of women (WL, 138). Moreover, some of his remarks do seem to be exhortations to the poor and lowly to remain content with their miserable lot. After praising a poor charwoman for diligently doing her job "for the sake of conscience," Kierkegaard declares that Christianity proclaims to everyone: "Do not busy yourself with changing the shape of the world or your situation, as if you, . . . instead of being a poor charwoman, perhaps could manage to be called 'Madame'" (WL, 136). He who loves his neighbor should be "content with the dissimilarity of earthly life allotted to him" (WL, 84). After all, earthly distinctions of wealth and status are like

---

169-86.

    [6]See Gilbert Meilaender, *Friendship: A Study in Theological Ethics* (Notre Dame IN: University of Notre Dame Press, 1981) 42.

inconsequential actors' roles which will be forgotten in eternity (WL, 87). Kierkegaard's recommendation that the disadvantaged should "show mercy" to the advantaged could be read as an attempt to keep the disadvantaged in their place (WL, 326). Moreover, Kierkegaard's insistence that the "world" stands in inveterate opposition to Christian love suggests that material results could not be expected even if they were desired.

At times Kierkegaard's language goes beyond an ostensible indifference to social reform to an apparent lack of concern for all material needs. For example, Kierkegaard observes that while "temporality" feels obligated to "do something to remedy the need" of the poor and wretched, eternity declares that the cultivation of mercifulness is more important that money or hospitals (WL, 326). Kierkegaard goes so far as to propose: "From the point of view of eternity, that someone dies is no misfortune, but that mercifulness is not practiced certainly is" (WL, 326). Some of his language does suggest an insouciance about the tangible benefits which might result from acts of love. For example, at one point Kierkegaard maintains that the inwardness of love is most clear and pure when there is no externality, when nothing at all can be done for the neighbor (WL, 330).

In spite of such passages, other commentators discover themes in Kierkegaard's works in general and in *Works of Love* in particular which counteract this alleged "acosmism" and even provide a rationale for an active concern for the material well-being of the neighbor which goes beyond the private into the public sphere. According to these expositors, the individual and society are more interdependent in Kierkegaard's writings than initially meets the eye, in that the life of love can be fostered or damaged by social influences and does involve social responsibilities. Kierkegaard, in this more recent reading, does not reject the social character of human being. Merold Westphal and Robert Perkins have argued that Kierkegaard's critique of philosophical systems is part of an exposé of societal self-deification which has profound implications for social and political practice.[7] Similarly, Bruce Kirmmse has

---

[7]See Merold Westphal, *Kierkegaard's Critique of Reason and Society* (Macon GA: Mercer University Press, 1987). See also Robert Perkins, "Kierkegaard's Critique

argued that Kierkegaard did indeed have a political vision, that of a liberal dissolution of the synthesis of Christianity and culture.[8] Arnold Come and Timothy Polk maintain that *Works of Love* in particular does imply a definite sociology and politics, and does furnish a positive motivation to transform human organizations.[9] By exposing the way that preferential self-love pervades the structures of class, nation, and church, *Works of Love*, according to Polk, should wreak havoc with the nation state.[10] Others, including Sylvia Walsh and David Gouwens, have reexamined Kierkegaard's descriptions of love, suggesting that the previously alleged indifference to social and material conditions is not supported by all dimensions of the text.[11] The seeming opposition of Christian love and the socially embodied natural loves in such writings as *Works of Love* is mitigated by the recognition that neighbor love expresses itself through the concrete responsibilities of eros, friendship, and other forms of human association. Continuing this trend, M. Jamie Ferreira has taken a closer look at specific particularly troubling passages in *Works of Love* concluding that attention to Kierkegaard's rhetorical strategies shows that Kierkegaard does not rule out a concern for the neighbor's material well-being.[12]

As is evident, the differences between the "acosmic/apolitical" readings and the "social/political" readings are profound, suggesting that the text which inspired them is intricately multilayered. I

---

of the Modern State," *Inquiry* 27 (1984): 207-18.

[8]Bruce Kirmmse, *Kierkegaard in Golden Age Denmark* (Bloomington: Indiana University Press, 1990).

[9]Arnold B. Come, *Kierkegaard as Theologian: Recovering My Self* (Montreal and Kingston: McGill-Queen's University Press, 1997) 338-59. See also Timothy Polk, *The Biblical Kierkegaard* (Macon GA: Mercer University Press, 1997) 31-47.

[10]See Polk, *The Biblical Kierkegaard*, 43.

[11]Sylvia Walsh, "Forming the Heart: The Role of Love in Kierkegaard's Thought," in *The Grammar of the Heart*, ed. Richard Bell (San Francisco: Harper & Row, 1988) 234-56, and *Living Poetically: Kierkegaard's Existential Aesthetics* (University Park: Pennsylvania State University Press, 1994) 262-66. See also David Gouwens, *Kierkegaard as Religious Thinker* (Cambridge: Cambridge University Press, 1996) 186-208.

[12]Ferreira, "Otherworldliness in Kierkegaard's *Works of Love*." See also "Equality, Impartiality, and Moral Blindness in Kierkegaard's *Works of Love*," *Journal of Religious Ethics* 25/1 (Spring 1997): 65-85.

propose to reexamine *Works of Love,* seeking to discover how the text can inspire a concern for the social and material needs of the neighbor, as these recent interpreters have maintained, while also seeming to express an apparent disregard for the neighbor's social and material well-being. In order to do this, attention must be paid to the particularities of purpose, rhetorical force, authorial voice, implied audience, and literary context. Kierkegaard says different things to different people in different contexts in order to pursue different ends. I will conclude that Kierkegaard weaves together different "upbuilding" purposes, seeking to elicit different virtues, dispositions, and attitudes in the reader. In order to do this, he utilizes different textual tactics. Some of these, if considered in isolation, would tend to devalue concern for social and material well-being, while others do endorse such a concern. The ultimate coherence of Kierkegaard's project depends upon the possibility that the virtues and attitudes he strives to encourage can cohere in the living of an individual life.

Kierkegaard's different purposes must first be disentangled in order to see how such final coherence may be possible. First we shall consider the way the lover's interiority interacts with the other-regarding character of love, then at the way the nondecisiveness of consequences interacts with the active, teleological nature of love, and finally at the way love as the highest good interacts with a concern for lesser goods, including the social and material dimensions of human well-being.

### Interiority and the "Other"

Certainly, Kierkegaard does highlight the "interiority" of the lover so much that at times the importance of effective public action seems to be jeopardized. Kierkegaard's focus on the individual's inclinations, dispositions, emotions, and intentions should not be surprising; the transformation of the reader's deepest passions is the book's main concern and basic purpose. Throughout, Kierkegaard strives to move the reader to assume responsibility for the reader's own passional life, particularly by encouraging the habit of self-critical examination of desires, intentions, and motivations. Self-reflection and self-critique are fostered by clarifying the daunting nature of the ideal which the assumed reader professes to value, exposing the distance between that ideal and the reader's actual life. This intention is evident in the book's self-description as a set of "deliberations," for deliberations are intended to "awaken," "provoke," and "sharpen thought" (JP 1:641). Kierkegaard writes, "Therefore a deliberation must first fetch them (the readers) up out of the cellar, call to them, turn their comfortable way of thinking topsy-turvy with the dialectic of truth" (JP 1:641). *Works of Love* is an exercise in conceptual clarification, emphasizing the distinctive characteristics of Christian love so that the reader will be forced to deal with his or her failure to instantiate them. Kierkegaard employs this strategy because the assumed reader, the bourgeois citizen of "Christendom," has confused the pathos of the Christian life with the performance of self-serving social roles. Kierkegaard also assumes that the reader, professing a commitment to Christianity, will be distressed to discover the disparity between authentic Christian love and the regnant ideology. The revelation that authentic Christianity not merely recommends but rather "commands" a way of life alien to the reader's current ethos should further destabilize the reader and trigger even deeper pathos.

However, this self-examination which the text hopes to inspire is not intended to be a narcissistic fascination with the individual's own emotional life nor a self-interested obsession with the purity of the individual's own moral character. Quite the contrary, Kierkegaard is adamant that love does not concentrate upon itself, but is directed away from the self toward the neighbor. Kierkegaard insists that "love in all its expressions turns outward toward people" (WL, 189). Much of the chapter "Our Duty to Remain in Love's Debt" is a warning that love must never begin to "dwell on itself" (WL, 179). Authentic love does not pause to evaluate itself in relation to the love exhibited by others, or to admire the quality of its deeds. In fact, if an individual were to convert his or her own love into an object for contemplation, that individual would "lose the moment" of action and cease to be loving. Kierkegaard warns, "As soon as love dwells on itself, it is out of its element" (WL, 182). Moreover, the examination of one's own passional core should never be motivated by a desire for moral self-satisfaction. No one's love can ever honestly be regarded as meritorious because the infinite requirement to love the neighbor at every opportunity can never be satisfied. The inexhaustibility of the duty to love the neighbor serves as a prophylactic against smug self-containment. Throughout the text Kierkegaard exposes the subtle ways in which putative acts of love are motivated by self-serving interests, including the desire to win the approval of others and one's own self. For example, not even the desire to be charitable to the poor is an instance of genuine love if it is not motivated by empathy for the poor as fellow human beings (WL, 83). Love is defined in such a way that not only is its object the "other," but its motivation must be concern for the other. Kierkegaard paradoxically urges the reader to look inward in order to make sure that the reader is looking outward. This inward movement is warranted by the suspicion that the reader is not properly motivated by other-regarding dispositions. Introspective scrutiny is not an end-in-itself but is a remedial strategy required by the reader's failings. *Works of Love* is certainly not intended to deflect attention permanently away from the needs of the concrete neighbor.

This concern for other-regarding motivations is no minor aspect of Kierkegaard's text; rather, it is an expression of the book's most foundational theme. This love for the neighbor as "other" is rooted in the very nature of God. Kierkegaard repeats at crucial junctures that God's love is the ultimate source of human love for human neighbors. "God has priority" is a recurrent refrain (WL, 149). It is significant that the book's opening reflection, "Love's Hidden Life," emphasizes the fact that God is the font of all love, the "hidden springs no eye has seen" in which originates the "quiet lake" of human love (WL, 9). Kierkegaard writes, "Just as God dwells in a light from which flows every ray that illumines the world, yet no one can force his way along these paths in order to see God, since the paths of light turn into darkness when one turns toward the light—so love dwells in hiding in the innermost being" (WL, 9). God's hidden love expresses itself indirectly through the "works" of human lovers. This initiates Kierkegaard's overall strategy of deriving the description of genuine human love from the description of God's love. In fact, God is not only the foundation but also the ultimate object of love. Kierkegaard writes, "This the world can never get into its head, that God in this way not only becomes the third party in every relationship of love but really becomes the sole object of love, so that it is not the husband who is the wife's beloved, but it is God" (WL, 121-22). Kierkegaard can describe God as both source and object because God is defined essentially as love. As Arnold Come has shown, Kierkegaard here departs from his more abstract descriptions of God as "being in-and-for-itself" or "infinite subjectivity" to identify God more concretely as "love itself."[13] God's "external" loving actions in creating, redeeming, and sustaining the cosmos are outpourings of God's internal life.[14] God is love in God's own self even apart from the existence of the universe. To underscore the book's foundation in the inner life of God, Kierkegaard's opening prayer invokes each of the persons of the Trinity as different aspects of God's loving nature (WL, 3-4).

It is the nature of God's love which determines the shape of human love and grounds its radically other-regarding qualities. All the characteristics of human love for the neighbor which Kierkegaard discusses are reflections of God's love. Most importantly, God's love is directed away from itself (WL, 160). God's love is not content to remain "in-itself," but resolves to be essentially "for others." This love flows out of itself in creating, as it secures the independent existence of a genuine "other," and then flows back to itself in reconciling, as that other returns the love. Consequently, the nature of all genuine love is to go beyond itself. God's love "redoubles" itself in human beings as they love their neighbors. The love of humans for one another is a reflection of God's love for humanity. We humans are designed to be discontent with self-containment; fulfillment comes only through going out to the neighbor. This "image of God" in humanity determines the basic structural features of human love. Just as God lovingly brought forth from nothing an "other," so also should humans love the sheer "otherness" of their neighbors. Just as God limits God's self in giving independent existence to the other, so also humans must "deny" themselves in order to promote the existence of the neighbor. Just as God's love is not motivated by need gratification,

---

[13]See Come, *Kierkegaard as Theolgian*; 70-77, 303.

[14]See Michael Plekon, "Kierkegaard the Theologian: The Roots of his Theology in *Works of Love*," in *Foundations of Kierkegaard's Vision of Community*, ed. George B. Connell and C. Stephen Evans (Atlantic Highlands NJ: Humanities Press, 1992) 2-17.

so neither should human love be rooted in utilitarian self-interest or self-seeking desire. Just as God's love is not based on the perfection of the beloved object, so neither should human love be contingent upon the perception of laudable qualities in the neighbor. Just as God's love is not preferential, so neither should human love exclude those we might not prefer. Just as God loves individuals as they are, so also human love should avoid judging neighbors harshly. Just as God's love is not contingent upon being returned, so neither should human love require reciprocity. Just as God's love is the uncompelled fruit of God's free resolve, so also should human love to the neighbor be freely and intentionally given. Just as God's love is inexhaustible, so also should human love for the neighbor be unstinting. Just as God's love takes the risk of rejection, so also should human love be willing to accept the inevitable hostility of the world. In all these ways the Christian life is a kind of *theosis*, a growth in God-likeness. The pervasiveness of this dynamic accounts for many other motifs in the text. It inspires Kierkegaard's invocation of Christ's life, the incarnation of God's love, as the pattern for Christian love (WL, 110). It also undergirds the distinction of Christian love and such natural loves as eros and friendship, which are critiqued as forms of self-love, motivated by the loved object's perceived capacity to satisfy some need or desire. The natural loves, being self-interested, possessive, preferential, and mutable, fail to reflect God's love. The theme of genuine human love as a reflection of God's other-regarding love is so integral to the structure of *Works of Love* that its importance cannot be seriously doubted.

The theme of the reflection of God's love for God's other (the human person) in the human person's love for its other (the neighbor) is so important to Kierkegaard that he insists that love for God cannot be expressed without loving the human neighbor. To grow in love for love-itself (God) necessarily involves becoming more loving to one's fellow humans. As Kierkegaard remarks,

a person should begin with loving the unseen, God, because then he himself will learn what it is to love. But that he actually loves the unseen will be known by his loving the brother he sees; the more he loves the unseen, the more he will love the people he sees. It is not the reverse, that the more he rejects those he sees,

> the more he loves the unseen, since in that case God is changed
> into an unreal something, a delusion. (WL, 160)

Human love is irreducibly triadic, involving self, God, and neighbor. One simply cannot have a relationship with God unmediated by relationships with the neighbor. According to Kierkegaard, there is no immediate way to express love for God through external devotional practices (WL, 161). The futile attempt to do that had been the mistake of monastic piety. Christian love can never be abstract, but necessarily moves toward the concrete other. The accusations of Buber, Adorno, and others that Kierkegaard encourages an asocial interior piety can only be sustained if one ignores this most basic pattern in the text.

### Anticonsequentialism and Active Benevolence

So far, we have seen that the concern to foster interiority does not jeopardize the other-regarding character of love. However, a wary critic could object that even if love, according to Kierkegaard, is other-oriented, it still might be nothing more than a passive attitude. The affirmation of the other-regarding quality of love is not enough by itself to demonstrate that *Works of Love* can legitimate the active promotion of the neighbor's well-being. One could hold the neighbor in high esteem, take delight in the neighbor's independent existence, and even lose oneself in rapt contemplation of the neighbor, but still not manifest that love in concrete action on behalf of the neighbor. Perhaps one can love the neighbor in the way that mountain enthusiasts love the Grand Tetons. As we have seen, some commentators have claimed to detect in *Works of Love* such a tendency to reduce love to a purely passive affirmation of the neighbor. The most often-cited bits of textual evidence for this contention are Kierkegaard's claims that love cannot be identified with any particular external acts and that genuine love can assume the form of a "mercifulness" which does not do anything.

However, such an inert love would run counter to the main theme of the book evident in its very title: "works of love." As we have seen, the book is structured according to the movement from the hidden essence of love in the depths of God to the outward expression of that love. Love necessarily strives toward externalization. The only way it can achieve this externalization is by producing concrete fruits. The thrust of the crucial first chapter which sets the agenda for the entire book is that love must become recognizable through its fruits. Kierkegaard maintains that the "one important thing" is that love has "fruits, and therefore can be known" (WL, 14). Love demands deeds, not panegyrics about love. Love is not a mood or a feeling to be aesthetically savored. An individual cannot love in theory. Although Kierkegaard himself does not directly exhort the reader to get busy and produce fruits (an appropriate restraint, given the fact that the book is a "deliberation" rather than a sermon or edifying discourse), he repeatedly reminds the reader that the Gospel does issue such an injunction in no uncertain terms. The Gospel's call to the individual to be fruitful should be unmistakable. Having made his point, Kierkegaard leaves the reader alone with the Gospel imperative, hoping that the encounter will inspire the obedient response of active love.

Of course, Kierkegaard does resist the reduction of love to particular external "works." In spite of all his talk of love's "recognizability" by its fruits, the recognizability is qualified by the fact that the source of love remains concealed. In order for a specific work to count as an act of love, it must flow from the appropriate motivation and the proper intentionality. A genuine act of love must be inspired by an enthusiasm for and commitment to love in general, and must intend the good of the neighbor without reference to the good of the lover. No single deed or set of deeds can be conclusive proof that such motivations and intentions are present. Not even the specifics of the particular context in which a deed is performed can sufficiently demonstrate the presence of love. Apparently benevolent acts can be motivated by the desire to win plaudits from an ethicoreligious community, to conform to the expectations of civil society, to earn spiritual merit for onself, to promote one's self-image as a "good" person, and a host of other ignoble concerns. Therefore, the conclusive interpretation of a supposed act of love is impossible.

However, these considerations in no way contradict the insistence that love must be active. By presenting the reader with a "strict definition" of love's inward requirements, Kierkegaard invites the reader to examine critically the reader's own motivational life. Kierkegaard assumes that many of his readers will be inclined to congratulate themselves on the performance of certain acts, which, while appearing benevolent, actually issue from self-serving motives. Kierkegaard in no way wants to suggest that humanity should refrain from benevolent activity. His attempts to arouse discontentment with selfish motivations does not entail an indifference to other-regarding action. On the contrary, this strategy presupposes that love should be active.

However, attention to the specifics of the literary context of these passages shows that this "anticonsequentialism" is part of Kierkegaard's strategy of emphasizing the universality and obligatory nature of the love commandment. The obligation to be loving is not contingent upon the ability to produce results. A formal similarity to a feature of Kant's ethics is evident here. Sometimes Kierkegaard argues that because "ought" implies "can," the equality of obligation to love the neighbor implies equality of ability to love the neighbor. Obviously, not all individuals possess equal resources or enjoy equal opportunities to improve the neighbor's empirical situation. Therefore, the ability to produce beneficial results cannot be part of the essence of love.[15] Adverse contingencies of social circumstances, biological endowments, and other constraining factors cannot destroy the possibility that an individual can exercise love. This conviction enhances the scope and force of the love commandment by foreclosing the possibility of excuses based on external circumstances beyond the individual's control. It also protects the love commandment from the discouragement which could result from the realization that, given the likely hostility of the world to the Gospel's view of love, loving efforts will often not meet with success. These considerations suggest that the independence of love from the ability to secure results is not symptomatic of an indifference to the fate of the neighbor. Kierkegaard's anticonsequentialism does not mean that an authentic lover of humanity need not intend results beneficial to the neighbor. The lover must strive as vigorously as possible to effect a felicitous outcome for the neighbor.

This insistence on the universality of the love commandment accounts for the tone and content of some of Kierkegaard's more

---

[15]See Ferreira, "Otherworldliness in Kierkegaard's *Works of Love*."

troubling passages, particularly his remarks to the poor. For example, his admonition that the poor should refrain from envying the rich does not function as a recommendation to acquiesce to oppression. Rather, the warning about envy is an expression of the universal scope of the duty to love and its universal difficulty. Just as the rich and powerful must struggle with their particular temptation, the haughty refusal to see the poor as neighbors, so also must the poor struggle against their particular temptation, the envious refusal to see the rich as neighbors. Similar passages can also function as good news for those with minimal resources.[16] In the chapter "The Duty To Be Merciful," the fact that the "you" in "you shall love your neighbor" admits of no exceptions legitimates its application to every position on the advantaged/disadvantaged spectrum. This empowers the poor and lowly, who have as much ability to love as do the rich and powerful (WL, 326). They are not excluded from loving by lack of resources. In regard to mercy, quality of love cannot be correlated with quantity of material resources, and growth in compassion cannot be correlated with advance in social status. The good news is that when it comes to the one thing that makes life worth living, the rich have no advantage. Neither poverty nor social oppression can destroy the ability to love. Such considerations account for Kierkegaard's surprising claim that one can be merciful even if circumstances prevent one from doing anything at all.

### The Independence of Love from Material Conditions

As we have seen, careful attention to Kierkegaard's particular purposes shows that he does not want to promote asocial self-absorption, or passive feelings of good will, or action without concern for beneficial results. Kierkegaard can be exonerated of the charges of acosmism and interiority. He does not seek to foster an ethic which discourages specific action toward concrete individuals. However, this conclusion in itself is not sufficient to justify any claim that *Works of Love* points to an ethics of concern for the neighbor's material well-being. In regard to the assessment of the

---

[16]See Ferreira, "Otherworldliness in Kierkegaard's *Works of Love*" for a convincing elaboration of this point.

significance of the material dimensions of the neighbor's situation, a problem may still exist. There may be one more possible theme in *Works of Love* which could function as a disincentive to the alleviation of the physical, social, and economic suffering of the neighbor. This final factor concerns Kierkegaard's view of what the neighbor really needs.

The problem is this: the neighbor's material needs might not be very important. If love intends the well-being of the neighbor, then the enactment of love must be governed by an understanding of the exact nature of the neighbor's well-being. What is it that the neighbor really needs? Kierkegaard's answer is loud, clear, and consistent: the neighbor needs what all people need, to become more loving. The attainment of a loving heart is the final telos of a human life. Kierkegaard insists that through loving the neighbor one possesses that which is "best," including all "comfort and joy" (WL, 64-65). This theme has been the whole point of the book. The neighbor's well-being is the neighbor's growth in love. Therefore, to really love someone is to help that person to grow in love. Again and again Kierkegaard repeats the refrain: To love another person is to help that person to love God (WL, 107, 114, 121, 130). Because God's love is essentially "redoubling," all genuine human love primarily seeks to "build up" love in others. Such love can only be encouraged by helping the other person to stand alone, to attain the psychological independence necessary for the free and responsible commitment to a life of love. It is significant that the chapter entitled "Love Builds Up" introduces the entire second series of discourses, framing the text with this motif. In fact, *Works of Love* as a whole is an instantiation of this kind of love for the neighbor. The book is the quintessential work of love in that its sole purpose is to help stimulate the reader to grow in love. The potential problem with all this is that Kierkegaard stresses the importance of helping the neighbor to grow in love so much that all other kinds of help are eclipsed. It begins to appear that the duty to help the neighbor is exhausted by nurturing psychological independence and responsible, intentional love in the neighbor.

The heart of the problem is that the love which is to be encouraged in the neighbor seems to be radically independent of the neighbor's material well-being. Kierkegaard has insisted that the neighbor should be exhorted to grow in love in any material circumstances. The more Kierkegaard stresses the ultimacy of growth in love, and the more he stresses its independence from all material circumstances, the less important it becomes to express love by attending to the neighbor's social, economic, and political situation. After all, the neighbor cannot be decisively harmed by adverse material circumstances. If not even physical debilities, economic misfortune, or political oppression can irreparably damage the capacity to love, then the motivation to alleviate these woes is greatly reduced. The disincentive is not due to any ontological mind/body dualism allegedly lurking in Kierkegaard's pages. Rather, it is the prioritization of love, the absolute good, over all lesser goods, and its independence from them, that devalues those other dimensions of human flourishing. When one has helped improve the neighbor's socioeconomic situation, one has not done anything of much importance. No improvement in material circumstances can make a person more loving.

This theme is not a peripheral feature of *Works of Love*. It partly accounts for Kierkegaard's disparagement of the inflated promises of political reform movements. The envisioned reforms cannot secure the one thing needful: growth in love. Consequently, there can be no political solution to the most significant issues in human life (WL, 70). In order to keep individuals focused on the real task of helping the neighbor to grow in love, Kierkegaard debunks the pretensions of political ideologies. He particularly criticizes the illusory expectation that economic, social, and political equality will produce the kind of felicity which Christianity desires. Besides ultimately disappointing the individual, trust in political solutions would divert an individual's energies away from the essential task of personally appropriating love. Too much investment in the social and political contexts militates against the task of differentiating one's own self from the "crowd" and attaining the independence necessary for the free giving of the self in love. Grand political projects tend to distract the individual from personal transformation by redirecting attention to world-historical consequences. Political struggles also tend to engender unloving attitudes, particularly fostering envy and fear of the opposition.

So does *Works of Love* encourage indifference to the neighbor's material needs and to unjust socioeconomic conditions after all? Is the final message that one should help the lowly to grow in love but leave them in their lowliness? Such conclusions should not be drawn too hastily. *Works of Love* contains other trajectories which point in other directions. At least three dynamics in the text suggest that the neighbor's material circumstances and even the institutional structures which impinge upon the neighbor's life must be addressed by love. As we shall see, all three of these dynamics are related to the crucial theme of the duty to "build up" the neighbor in love.

## The Duty to Maintain the Material Substratum of Love

The first of these dynamics is the least controversial and the most obvious. Unfortunately it only leads to the most minimal sort of social or political ethics. In a variety of ways, *Works of Love* does imply that love for the neighbor includes attention to the neighbor's survival needs. It is significant that, when citing examples of acts which could count as loving if the right motivations are present, Kierkegaard frequently uses such biblical examples as feeding the hungry, aiding the destitute, and comforting the sick. The neighbor cannot grow in love if the neighbor is debilitatingly diseased, malnourished, or dead. Kierkegaard's claim that one has an obligation to preserve oneself so that one can love is extended to the neighbor; one should preserve the neighbor's life so that the neighbor can grow in love. Throughout the book Kierkegaard acknowledges that the "sensate-psychical" dimensions of human life are at the very least a precondition for "spiritual" growth (WL, 209). Minimal biological functioning, including the capacity for self-consciousness and intentionality, is a necessary condition for growth in love. Kierkegaard does not elaborate exactly what the well-being of the "sensate-psychical" substratum of spirit involves. At least he leaves open the possibility that functionality may go beyond the mere maintenance of biological life and cognitive activity.

This recognition of the existence of some material preconditions for growth in love also points to the possibility that the neighbor's ethicoreligious development could be negatively affected by social, political, and economic factors. Societal institutions and dynamics which could harm the neighbor's capacity for intentionality should be resisted by neighbor love. This could provide a rational for opposition to economic policies which contribute to the inadequacy of food supplies, political arrangements which legitimate an unfair distribution of medical services, and a host of other life-endangering historical practices. Although Kierkegaard himself does not elaborate any of these possibilities, he does imply them through his recognition that "spirit" has a material substratum rooted in a social world.

Even if this trajectory can be legitimately inferred from the text, it must be qualified by a countervailing theme. It must be remembered that biological survival is only a precondition for the truly important thing in human life: growth in love. Kierkegaard repeatedly warns the reader that material flourishing should not become an end-in-itself. *Works of Love* is constantly on guard against the temptation to reduce the vision of well-being to longevity, physical health, and economic prosperity. As a result, Kierkegaard cannot give unqualified praise to programs of social and material amelioration. It must never be forgotten that attention to the material survival of the neighbor is only the beginning of love. It is only a preliminary condition for the possibility of the proper task of eliciting the love latent in the neighbor.

### The Duty to Remove Impediments to Love

A second trajectory can be discerned in *Works of Love* which could lead to a broader concern for the material substratum of human life and even to a more robust ethic of social, political, and economic reform. A major clue to this second trajectory can be found in Kierkegaard's examples of love and in his polemics against specific impediments to love. His illustrations suggest that other "temporal" factors in addition to threats to minimal biological functioning could inhibit growth in love. Kierkegaard implies that even if love can be developed in all circumstances, some circumstances unnecessarily make such development more difficult. Throughout the text Kierkegaard presents examples of the ways in which adverse socialization can erode growth in love. Various aspects of the "world" are structured to miseducate, teaching the individual "to forget God" (WL, 127). Kierkegaard condemns specific patterns of "upbringing" which reinforce the tendency toward unloving selfishness. For example, he criticizes the use of parental authority to instill a love of money in children. Such specific behaviors as a father's willingness to stay home from church on Sundays in order to avoid parting with the offering money can corrupt the young and impressionable (WL, 321). He laments, "This is how we are brought up; from earliest childhood we are disciplined in the ungodly worship of money" (WL, 320). Similarly, Kierkegaard condemns the way that society's praise of exclusivistic romance and friendship has led many astray, teaching them to devalue love for God and neighbor (WL, 128). Kierkegaard's catalogue of corrupting influences goes beyond family systems and interpersonal transactions to include broad cultural dynamics. He dwells at length on the ways in which slanderous journalism (WL, 320), busyness (WL, 98, 247), benefaction as a strategy of social domination (WL, 275), cultural snobbery (WL, 59), small-minded intolerance of distinctiveness (WL, 271, 273), and exclusivistic classism (WL, 81) all contribute to the creation of a cultural environment inhospitable to growth in love. Many of these dynamics tend to stifle the individual's freedom from the sensibilities of the dominant culture which is a prerequisite for the commitment to the life of love. Out of desire to help the neighbor, one should strive to remove such unnecessary impediments to growth.

Kierkegaard is well aware that these unloving cultural attitudes are often embodied in political and economic practices and institutions. Sometimes it is the very existence of these practices and institutions themselves which teach the damaging lessons. For example, the standard activities of "financiers" and those who "trade in commodities" encourage an uncharitable fear of being deceived (WL, 238). The institutionalized dissemination of irresponsible slander makes it difficult to believe in the loving potential in one's neighbors (WL, 291). The fact that the world rewards calculating sagacity discourages the buoyant hopefulness of love (WL, 261). Small-minded persons form social alliances in order to propagate the suspicion of distinctiveness (WL, 272). Many of these spiritually deleterious dynamics are the standard operating procedures of capitalism, mass journalism, etc. If such political, social and economic practices and institutions put unnecessary impediments in the way of growth in love, the loving individual should refuse to participate in them and perhaps even resist them.

Here an implicit motivation to engage in projects of social and political reform is emerging in the text.[17] Kierkegaard himself discerns this possibility. For example, he clearly calls for nonparticipation in social practices that reinforce classism. This nonparticipation must be a public activity, designed to alert people to the pernicious nature of class-based exclusivity. The public nature of the opposition to classism cannot be shirked; it is not permissible to seek seclusion and obscurity in order to avoid social opprobrium (WL, 85). One's life should "contain an admonition" to those who reduce love to class loyalty (WL, 127). Kierkegaard maintains that "the one who did his part to make people aware, the distinguished or the lowly, the one who, teaching, acting, or striving, existed equally for all people" benefits others by helping them to "become aware" (WL, 85). Of course, Kierkegaard could not entertain much hope that resistance to these practices would actually bring about desirable social transformations. His apprehension of the world's inveterate hostility to love was too deep for him to be sanguine about the prospects for social reform. Nevertheless, the individual is called to witness publicly. The person who responds to this call can "say consolingly to his soul, 'I have done my part; whether I have achieved anything, I do not know, whether I have benefited anyone, I do not know; but that I have existed for them, that I do know, and I know it because of their derision'" (WL, 85). Once again, the unlikelihood of success does not absolve the individual from the responsibility of trying.

This nascent critique of social, political, and economic practices may seem to conflict with Kierkegaard's simultaneous contention that love can be developed under any circumstances. His advocacy of a politics of eloquent noncooperation with spiritually hurtful social practices may seem difficult to reconcile with his suspicion of some reform movements. However, it must be remembered that Kierkegaard often says different things in different contexts in order to achieve different purposes. The distinction of these purposes may help resolve the apparent discrepancy. To those who

---

[17]See Walsh, "Forming the Heart: The Role of Love in Kierkegaard's Thought," 249, for a discussion of the way in which Kierkegaard's analysis of love should have led to a critique of patriarchal social arrangements.

are uncertain and insecure about their ability to love, Kierkegaard says reassuringly: "Do not despair. The good news is that you can still attain the highest thing in human life; you can still love." But to those who need instruction concerning the implications of the love commandment, Kierkegaard advises: "Refuse to cooperate with a system which puts unnecessary stumbling blocks and temptations in your neighbor's path." To those with the capacity to effect social changes he may even be saying: "Strive to correct those practices which are counterproductive to the encouragement of love."

### The Duty to "Upbuild" the Neighbor
### through Material and Social Means

These first and second trajectories of *Works of Love*, the duties to maintain the neighbor's life and to oppose unloving societal practices, only point to the removal of physical and societal impediments to love. They merely suggest that some environmental factors, including material conditions and cultural dynamics, can harm the neighbor's capacity to love. They imply an ethical principle of "do no harm" to your neighbor's growth in love. But a third trajectory in the text suggests that something more positive can be accomplished through attention to the neighbor's social and material condition. Perhaps some environmental factors can actually help foster the growth of love.

Kierkegaard's appreciation of the possibility that the individual could receive positive help from the individual's environment should not be a surprise. Clearly Kierkegaard believed that some interventions and environmental factors can positively contribute to the upbuilding of love in the neighbor. If that were not true, the writing of a book like *Works of Love* would have been pointless. The availability of such maieutic pedagogy is obviously an environmental advantage. It is not as evident that some environmental aids to the growth of love can be of a material and social sort. However, certain aspects of Kierkegaard's description of the exact nature of "upbuilding" do suggest that some types of attention to the neighbor's material needs can positively contribute to the neighbor's growth in love.

In order to grasp the motivation of this third type of material and social concern for the neighbor, it will be necessary to take a closer look at what "upbuilding" the neighbor in love involves. To do this, we must examine more carefully the way Divine love uses human agency as an instrument to elicit love in others. It is important to remember that no human being can "upbuild" love in another person's heart by directly implanting it. Because only God is the source of all genuine love, love must be brought forth by God's love (WL, 48). For our purposes the significant thing is the unique way in which God does this. God stirs up the love latent in the person by "presupposing it," by expressing confidence that love really is present in the individual. God preserves the genuine independence of God's human other by inviting rather than coercing a loving response. Kierkegaard underlines the centrality of this theme of "presupposing love" by repeating it like a litany at least a dozen times in the pivotal chapter "Love Builds Up" (WL, 216-24). Consequently, all human upbuilding efforts must "presuppose" that God has created the basis of love in the neighbor and is secretly working to bring that love to fruition.

God's "upbuilding" work is complicated by the fact that God's activity of "presupposing" love in a human heart is not directly perceivable. Significantly, *Works of Love* introduces the central topic of the book with a reflection on the hiddenness of God's love and the consequent difficulty of believing in that love (WL, 5-16). This hiddenness jeopardizes the efficacy of God's upbuilding activities. Upbuilding love must be perceived in order to be effective; an individual must recognize that his or her capacity for love is being affirmed. In order to have an impact, God's upbuilding love becomes recognizable through the upbuilding "works" of human lovers, which "witness to" or "reflect" God's love. Human works of love are the "instruments" of God's love which help make the love of God recognizable (WL, 86).

Kierkegaard's description of the way human love performs this function follows from his description of God's love. Just as God's love is an elicitation of a loving response in the human other, so also human upbuilding can only be a maieutic drawing forth of love. An individual human being can only hope to do for others what Socrates did for his dialogue partners or, even more significantly, what Jesus did for Peter. Human upbuilding efforts are only the occasions for the growth of love and not the source of it. Most importantly, human love, like God's love, works by "presupposing" love in the neighbor. The human lover must believe in the neighbor's "inner glory," the latent love in the neighbor, trusting in its potential for growth. Kierkegaard explains, "The one who loves presupposes that love is in the other person's heart and by this very presupposition builds up love in him" (WL, 216-17). To further emphasize this point he elaborates, "If anyone has ever spoken to you in such a way or treated you in such a way that you really felt built up, this is because you very vividly perceived how he presupposed love to be in you" (WL, 222). In this way one "loves forth love" in the neighbor (WL, 217). The need to clarify the various dimensions of this project sets the agenda for chapters II through VI of the second part of *Works of Love*. For example, "presupposing" love in the neighbor involves "believing all things" about the potential virtue of the neighbor, "hoping all things" for the neighbor's growth in love, and remaining faithful to the neighbor even if the neighbor backslides into selfishness.

We see that God's trust and confidence in the neighbor's loving potential is expressed through human trust and confidence. But here a further complication arises. Even human trust and confidence cannot be directly expressed, and certainly not by exclusively verbal means. It is not sufficient for a would-be "upbuilder" to declare to a neighbor: "I presuppose a capacity to love in you." Kierkegaard warns, "But one should not love in words and platitudes, and neither should one recognize love by them" (WL, 12). He continues, "There is no word in human language, not one single one, not the most sacred one, about which we are able to say: If a person uses this word, it is unconditionally demonstrated that there is love in that person" (WL, 13). Consequently, trust in the neighbor's capacity to love must be shown indirectly and ambiguously through the specifics of one's diverse dealings with the neighbor. The crucial conclusion is that the work of eliciting love must be pursued through concrete actions in the public world.

Some visible demonstration of concern for the neighbor must occur in order for upbuilding love to be recognizable and therefore effective. Of course, no particular deed or type of deed could conclusively express an affirmation of the love latent in the neighbor. But all sorts of actions can potentially contribute to this "upbuilding" project, as long at the specifics of their contexts and the manner in which they are performed can plausibly suggest that the agent is presupposing love in the neighbor. Ordinary deeds and interactions can be indirect ways of stimulating the neighbor's capacity to love by expressing confidence in it. Kierkegaard writes that "every human being by his life, by his conduct, by his behavior in everyday affairs, by his association with his peers, by his words, his remarks, should and could build up and would do it if love were really present in him" (WL, 213). Sometimes he even claims that almost any work can do this, depending on "how the work is done" (WL, 13). As an example of an upbuilding interaction Kierkegaard cites Christ's telling glance at Peter, his disciple and friend who had just denied him (WL, 170). Because it was not a repelling or dismissive look, that glance preserved the relationship and helped Peter become a more faithfully loving person. Christ's simple nonverbal gesture expressed a conviction that Peter was still worth loving in spite of his imperfections. Similarly, lovingly "hiding the sins" of those who have wronged us can function as a manifestation of God's affirming love (WL, 298-99).

This implies that "upbuilding love," particularly its crucial manifestation as faith in the neighbor's love, can and must express itself through the diverse obligations and responsibilities ingredient to specific human relationships. Upbuilding love does not exist as a separate form of love; consequently, it must be indirectly expressed through our ordinary relationships with "those at hand," including those whom we "naturally" love. "The spirit's love" can and should "lie at the base of and be present in every other expression of love" (WL, 146). This pivotal theme that "spirit" must be communicated through a "sensate-psychical" vehicle sets the stage for the second half of Works of Love (WL, 209). Upbuilding efforts borrow the language of the natural loves, transforming their verbal and physical expressions into metaphors of God's love. This metaphoric potential of the natural loves accounts for their importance. Preferential relationships like eros and friendship are not eliminated by neighbor love, but are transformed into vehicles for the "God-relationship" (WL, 112). As a result, an individual can express upbuilding love by fulfilling the particular obligations of specific social roles. Kierkegaard advises that one must remain "in the world of actuality as the task assigned to one" (WL, 161). Christians can marry but will love each other differently than do worldly-minded spouses. Kierkegaard writes, "Your wife must first and foremost be to you the neighbor: that she is your wife is then a more precise specification of your relationship to each other" (WL, 141).

These role-specific obligations involve care for the beloved's general well-being, including specific concerns for the beloved's material circumstances. For example, the concern shown by a parent for the physical health of a child can express the parent's valuation of that child as a bearer of God's image. Kierkegaard's text abounds in examples of this. A "housewife's loving solicitude" in frugally providing for her family "builds up" love by manifesting maternal faith in the eternal value of the children (WL, 214). In the biblical parable, the father's invincible hope in the reformation of his son builds up love in the wayward prodigal (WL, 221). A mother who endures the naughtiness of her child builds up by assuming "that the child still loves her and that this will surely show itself" (WL, 221). In all of these examples, actions are performed that express concern for the well-being of those to whom the agent has specific role-determined responsibilities. These actions have value by building up love in these particular neighbors.

Such examples suggest a way to discern upbuilding possibilities in more public types of action addressing the neighbor's political, economic, or social condition. Upbuilding potential need not be restricted to the private spheres of friendship and family. Political action, if done in the appropriate manner in the appropriate circumstances, could express a valuation of the neighbor as bearer of God's image. Although Kierkegaard does not explicitly draw this conclusion, some of his illustrations do point in this direction. For example, Kierkegaard suggests that, in resisting classism, one should manifest publicly the fact that one sees the image of God in both the high and the low, without distinction. Kierkegaard observes, "He (the genuine lover) neither cravenly avoids the more powerful but loves the neighbor, nor superiorly avoids the more lowly but loves the neighbor and wishes essentially to exist equally for all people" (WL, 84). This public embrace of the lowly, in defiance of social conventions, can function as an affirmation of their God-given value, their capacity to love. This does more than remove an impediment to love, as was the case with the second trajectory we have examined; this can positively "build up" by expressing confidence in the neighbor. In the proper circumstances, such affirmation could also be expressed through the enactment of concern for the neighbor's political rights and economic well-being.

Again, a caveat is in order. The ultimate goal of these projects would not be to increase the range of the neighbor's earthly opportunities as an end-in-itself. Rather, these activities would be a means to the end of eliciting love in the neighbor. Of course, they would need to be pursued in such a way as to make it clear that material flourishing is not the highest good in human life. Utopian rhetoric, extravagant aspirations, exclusive allegiances, demands for unquestioning loyalty, and totalizing ideologies would have to be assiduously avoided. Moreover, the reform efforts would have to protect themselves from the temptation to valorize success and exaggerate the importance of historical consequences. But, granted these qualifications, movements of social reform could have genuine instrumental value in "building up" the neighbor in love.

### Conclusion: The Tensive Dimensions of Love

*Works of Love* does contain important themes which authorize an active concern for the neighbor's material and social well-being. These themes are not arbitrary intrusions into an otherwise spiritualizing text, but follow naturally from Kierkegaard's analysis of what it is to "build up" the neighbor in love. Given the way Kierkegaard derives his understanding of human love from God's love, he must regard love as other-regarding, active, and concerned about benefiting the neighbor. Although the main benefit intended for the neighbor is the elicitation of love, this elicitation has material and social aspects. At least two trajectories in the text point to duties to remove material and social impediments to the neighbor's maturation in love, and one trajectory points to the "upbuilding" potential of active concern for the neighbor's material and social well-being. Textual indications even suggest that these trajectories could motivate the reform of social, political, and economic institutions and practices. The priority of love as the highest good does not require the rejection of lesser social and material goods. In fact, these lesser goods can contribute to the pursuit of the ultimate goal. These dynamics in *Works of Love* can be reconciled with Kierkegaard's focus on interiority and his anticonsequentialism, which serve to ensure that love for the neighbor will be grounded in the proper motivations and intentions.

However, not all the strands in *Works of Love* weave together this neatly. The above themes do stand in tension with Kierkegaard's continuing reminders to the reader that material and social circumstances cannot decisively damage the capacity to grow in love. Kierkegaard never retracts his claim that love, the one thing that everyone really needs, can be cultivated and enacted in any situation. If not actually contradicting himself, Kierkegaard is at least engaging in a very paradoxical literary strategy. On the one hand he talks as if material and social factors are important for love, but on the other hand he asserts that they are not.

This tension in *Works of Love* is no accident. It is not as if Kierkegaard were guilty of an inadvertent inconsistency or a confusion of purpose. The tension must be in the text, because the tension exists in human love, as Kierkegaard understands it. The two thematic poles, the rootedness of love in a social and material environment and the autonomy of love from environmental constraints, are linked in Kierkegaard's view of love. Both emphases are required to do justice to the nature of love. As we have seen, for Kierkegaard love involves resolute commitment to the other, so much so that the other's well-being becomes the genuine lover's vital concern. As such, love is both passionately heartfelt and actively other-directed. The dimension of passion and resolution requires the intensive focus on interiority which inspired the accusations of acosmism. The dimension of other-regarding activity requires the analysis of the neighbor's needs, which, in a somewhat circuitous way, leads to the attention to the neighbor's material and social situation. The focus on responsibility, resolution, and passion tends to distance love from its social and material context, while the focus on the upbuilding of the neighbor tends to resituate love in a social and material context. Inevitably, a tension is generated between the autonomy of love and its susceptibility to environmental influences.

For some, this tension may raise urgent metaphysical questions concerning the relation of freedom and necessity. In *Works of Love* Kierkegaard emphatically does not attempt to alleviate the tension by developing an explanatory metatheory. In fact, such a speculative endeavor would count as an evasion of the task of actually getting on with loving the neighbor. Rather than seek a theoretic answer, Kierkegaard aims at a more pragmatic resolution. Self-contradiction and confusion are avoided by gaining clarity concerning when to say what to whom. Sometimes Kierkegaard stresses one aspect of love, and sometimes another, depending on the requirements of the context. To those who need to reform their desires, intentions, and motivations, Kierkegaard emphasizes the rigorous requirements of interiority. Here the language of freedom from environmental constraints is part of the strategy of fostering self-criticism and the self-ascription of responsibility. To those who need courage and hope concerning their fledgling capacity to love, Kierkegaard offers the reassurance that love is possible in any circumstances, including their own. Here the language of freedom is part of a strategy of encouragement. To those who need instruction concerning the concrete ways to love their neighbor, Kierkegaard stresses the importance of attending to material and social circumstances. Here the language of environmental influences functions to heighten sensitivity to all the subtle ways one can harm or help the neighbor's maturation in love. The tensions among these emphases are resolved by sorting out which theme to employ in which circumstances. The prospect of a synthesis resides in the possibility that an individual life could be informed both by the assumption of responsibility for one's own life of love and by sensitivity to the difficulty and complexity of building up love in others.

# 7

## The Politics of Exodus:
## Derrida, Kierkegaard, and Levinas
## on "Hospitality"

### Mark Dooley

### *Hospitality as Love*

If Kierkegaard has a politics, a politics which can act as a viable alternative for those of us struggling to make sense of our lives in a "postmodern" world, it is surely to be found in his much ignored text, *Works of Love*. For Kierkegaard, a genuine *work* of love amounts to an unconditional affirmation of the singularity of the Other, whoever that other may be. This is not a politics of the conventional type, not a paradigm founded on divine right, natural law, or social contract, but one which privileges mercy above retribution. To love demands that we respond to those whose voices have been silenced by the established order; it instructs us to take the side of the least among us as a means of shaking the prevailing order from its dogmatic indolence and inertia. Kierkegaardian love, that is, privileges lowliness above loftiness, the Other above the same, the exception above the rule. In the language of *Fear and Trembling*, to love is to sacrifice ("teleologically suspend") the universal in the name of singularity.

Such is what I wish to call, following Jacques Derrida, a "politics of exodus." A politics of this kind serves "as a political ferment or anxiety, a subversion of fixed assumptions and a privileging of disorder."[1] This is not to suggest that the politics of

---

[1]Jacques Derrida, "Deconstruction and the Other" in *Dialogues with Contemporary Continental Thinkers,* ed. Richard Kearney (Manchester: Manchester University Press, 1984) 120.

exodus advocates wanton anarchy, the sole objective of which is the dissolution of all political institutions and structures. Rather, it encourages us to "preserve a [critical] distance and suspicion with regard to the official political codes governing reality."[2] The politics of exodus, in other words, is not in the business of choosing between the existing order and anarchy, or between absolute homogeneity and absolute heterogeneity; it insists, however, on the ineluctable situatedness of each individual in political formations which are not immune from change and revision, being as they are contingently configured entities. It is precisely in order to accommodate singularity that a totality opens its borders and welcomes the stranger. Of such a politics Derrida says:

> It is a relation in which the other remains absolutely transcendent. I cannot reach the other. I cannot know the other from the inside and so on. That is not an obstacle but the condition of love, of friendship, . . . a condition of the relation to the other.[3]

Love for Derrida, as for Kierkegaard, does not amount to loving oneself (egocentrism), or loving one's own kind to the exclusion of those who are marked by their difference (nationalism, totalitarianism), but takes the form of unconditional responsibility for those who are most foreign and alien, for the exile and the enemy, for those who are outside the system. The love which the politics of exodus endorses expresses itself by way of what Derrida calls "the unconditional law of hospitality."[4] Such a law "invites us" to welcome everyone who comes knocking on the door of the family home or who appeals for asylum at "Immigration," irrespective of nationality, color, creed, or class. Hospitality—unconditional hospitality—urges me to surrender my home (self-possession) to the other, to become his/her hostage.

But how can I be expected to do this? How, that is, can I be expected to give away everything I possess? Surely this is an

---

[2]Derrida, "Deconstruction and the Other," 120

[3]John D. Caputo and Jacques Derrida, *Deconstruction in a Nutshell: A Conversation with Jacques Derrida* (New York: Fordham University Press, 1997) 14.

[4]"Perhaps or Maybe," Jacques Derrida in Conversation with Alexander Garcia Duttmann in *PLI—Warwick Journal of Philosophy* (Department of Philosophy, University of Warwick, England) 8.

impossible demand? For both Derrida and Johannes de Silentio, however, we ought always to "begin by the impossible,"[5] That is, hospitality, *stricto sensu*, should be for *everybody* without exception; indeed, it is only by "praying and weeping"[6] for such an ideal that we can loosen up the limited notion of hospitality that governs our relations with others at any given time. Otherwise expressed, while I know that it is impossible to be unconditionally hospitable, I am nevertheless invited to continually challenge the dominant meaning of this word so as to enlarge its range and scope. Hoping for unconditional hospitality is the way to ensure that conditional hospitality does not become too conditional. Each time I am confronted with a singular appeal for help or generosity I am invited to give more than is expected of me; I am, that is, encouraged to exceed the demand, to push back the limits and to make the Other feel more welcome than convention generally decrees. The singular situation, in other words, is the setting in which I may redefine the nature of hospitality on the basis of an impossible ideal. Derrida explains:

> The otherness of the other who comes to me is singular, he is irreplaceable by any other one, hospitality is offered to an irreplaceable other as a singularity. But the law says to me that you should open your house, your borders, your country, to any other, to anyone. We have the universality of the law, which is its ideal concept, and we have the singularity of the other. Since we cannot practically, pragmatically, or realistically open the door to anyone, since we cannot dream of such a hospitality, which could be perverse if we were simply to open the door, we have to make decisions as to how to respect the unconditional law of hospitality, and at the same time we have to restrict, we have to have a policy of hospitality, public or private. In that case we have to define a policy of absolutely unconditional openness to whoever is coming and, because this is absolutely impossible, we have to produce laws and rules in order to select, in the best possible way, the ones we host, we welcome.[7]

---

[5]Jacques Derrida, *Given Time I: Counterfeit Money*, trans. Peggy Kamuf (Chicago: University of Chicago Press, 1991) 6.

[6]I am playing here on the title of John D. Caputo's *The Prayers and Tears of Jacques Derrida: Religion without Religion* (Bloomington: Indiana University Press, 1997).

[7]Derrida, "Perhaps or Maybe," 8.

We may surmise, therefore, that unconditional hospitality is the most fundamental ideal in a politics of exodus. This requires a continual revision of policy and a constant reassessment of political procedures with the aim of meeting the demands, as far as one can, of this unconditionality. Preparing to welcome the other, preparing to relinquish one's autonomy so as to make room for the outsider, is the *work* of love which the politics of exodus undertakes.

I said at the outset that the type of ethics/politics which I identify in *Works of Love* can act as a viable alternative for those of us facing the ethical and political challenges of a new millennium. This suggests, as my invocation of Derrida will have conveyed, that I take Kierkegaard to be a pivotal figure in late twentieth century "postmodern" thinking. That acknowledged, I do not subscribe to the school of thought which endeavors to reduce Kierkegaard to a mere ironic stylist who seeks to confound the hubris of systematic and totalizing thought through the use of literary strategies alone. Neither do I wish to associate myself with those who summarily dismiss the specifically "religious" dimension of Kierkegaard's writings. For it is precisely in his reflections on religion that the social and political dimension of Kierkegaard's thought is to be located. For me, the postmodern situation is not defined by the dominance of simulacra over so-called "reality," or by political and ethical disintegration, but is, to the contrary, a time when appeals to our hoary truths and idols give way to appeals for justice. Postmodernism, that is, announces a preoccupation with the outcast and marginalized, with the forgotten and the silenced. This is why, much I am sure to the dismay of many of its leading secular exponents, postmodernism on my reading has everything to do with a certain prophetic *religious* spirit or postsecular impulse. As such, it recognizes that the best way to proceed in the ethicopolitical sphere is to have as a guiding criterion, not the deeply secular ideals of formal reason or subjective autonomy, but a quasireligious fidelity to singularity.

I say *prophetic* religious spirit because I wish to avoid giving the impression that I espouse a return to the forms of religious orthodoxy which have served only to stimulate sectarian division and hatred which have plagued our age.[8] "Religion" in this context should be defined as the *work* of challenging the established order in the name of those without a name. Figures like Jesus Christ, Martin Luther King, and Gandhi, sought to upbraid the state for turning a blind eye to the requirements of the impoverished and indigent. Each advocated a religion, as Derrida says, without Religion: a religion which endeavors to roll back the hegemonic tide of established faith so as to tap into the pulse of religion's most fundamental source—hospitality towards the other. I am not, therefore, invoking the usual definition of religion as a strict observance of ecclesiastical rites, but that which determines it as "passion" and "love."

### A Hostage unto Death

It is impossible to speculate on the religious component of postmodern thought without invoking the name of Emmanuel Levinas, a thinker whose entire *raison d'etre* was to define how a certain ethicoreligious spirit could survive the most tumultuous consequences of a postmetaphysical age. Many notable commentators, such as John D. Caputo, Merold Westphal, and Hent de Vries,[9] have sought to make credible comparisons between the work of Levinas and that of Kierkegaard. While these efforts ought to be commended, I ultimately believe such comparisons are ill-founded. By analyzing closely how each thinker deals with the related themes of "love" and "hospitality," it will become apparent

---

[8]The bitter divide between Catholics and Protestants in Northern Ireland is one of many tragic situations one could invoke to drive home this point.

[9]See John D. Caputo, *Against Ethics: Contributions to a Poetics of Obligation with Constant Referernce to Deconstruction* (Bloomington: Indiana University Press, 1993), and "Instants, Secrets, and Singularities: Dealing Death in Kierkegaard and Derrida" in *Kierkegaard in Post/Modernity*, ed. Merold Westphal and Martin J. Matustik (Bloomington: Indiana University Press, 1995) 216-38; Hent de Vries, "Adieu, a dieu, a-Dieu," in *Ethics as First Philosophy: The Significance of Emmanuel Levinas for Philosophy, Literature and Religion*, ed. Adriaan T. Peperzak (New York: Routledge, 1995) 211-20; Merold Westphal, "Levinas's Teleological Suspension of the Religious," in *Ethics as First Philosophy*, 151-60, and "The Transparent Shadow: Kierkegaard and Levinas in Dialogue" in *Kierkegaard in Post/Modernity*, 265-81. See also Mark C. Taylor, "Infinity," in *Altarity* (Chicago: University of Chicago Press, 1987) 185-216.

that Kierkegaard has a more fundamental relationship to Derrida, in that both have a greater sense of what is required for the elimination of social injustice than does Levinas. It is by way of such a confrontation between Kierkegaard and Derrida on the one hand, and Levinas on the other, therefore, that I propose to elucidate the political effectiveness of this quasireligious strain of postmodernism.

In privileging ethics as first philosophy, Levinas strives to demonstrate that responsibility to and for the other ought to override self-preoccupation. In like manner to the portraits of Kierkegaard and Derrida we have thus far painted, Levinas also espouses the virtues of the politics of exodus: justice for the other, hospitality for the stranger, love for the neighbor. Indeed, for this ethicist *par excellence*, it is in and through one's ethical relationship with the other that one's relationship to God is established. "I can only go towards God," says Levinas, "by being ethically concerned by and for the other person."[10] Through the relationship I have with the other "traces of God are to be found"; such a God is not "the Almighty Being of creation, but the persecuted God of the prophets," the biblical God which dismays and disturbs the God of the philosophers.[11] This "biblical perspective" sends tremors and quivers through the "language of intelligibility."[12] The shock of the "jew," that is, traumatizes the Greek philosopher by exposing him to an "absolutely Other" which "perforates the totality of presence" qua ontology.[13]

By insisting that it is through my relationship with the human Other (*autrui*) that traces of God are to be found, Levinas allows the language of ethics *as such*, be infiltrated by the language of religion, a language, that is, of love and hospitality. His primary objective in so doing, is to affirm what lies beyond the purview of philosophical consciousness, to welcome philosophy's stranger, its foreigner and exile. Otherwise expressed, knowledge for Levinas "is the project of an incarnate practice of seizure, appropriation,

---

[10]Emmanuel Levinas, "Ethics of the Infinite," in *Dialogues with Contemporary Continental Thinkers*, ed. Kearney, 59.

[11]Ibid., 67-68.

[12]Ibid., 56.

[13]Ibid., 57.

and satisfaction." The result of such epistemological megalomania is an indefatigable "technological domination" of the world.[14] The principal assimilatory model which Levinas identifies is Hegelianism, in that the object of its dialectical impetus is to make what is other and different subordinate to the same. "The doctrine of absolute knowledge," he states, "promotes a thinking which, in the plenitude of its ambitions, takes no interest in the other qua other."[15] Rationality of this kind sees in "the alterity of things and men" a threat to its own satisfaction, or to the fulfilment of its immanent teleological development.

What is required in order to stem the tide of such systematic intelligibility, according to Levinas, "is a thought which is no longer constructed as a relation of thinking to what is thought about."[16] But how is it possible to think without thinking *of* or *about* something? The response which Levinas purveys is of central significance for an understanding of his thought: he claims that it is indeed an impossible demand to think without having dominance over what is being thought about, unless of course there is something *in us* which evokes thought only to elude it. This something, says Levinas, is "an echo of what Descartes called the idea of the infinite in us—thinking beyond what is capable of being contained in the finitude of the *cogito*."[17] This idea of the infinite is something which thought cannot control or subdue for the very reason that such an idea was not produced by thought. In other words, disturbing the apodictic certainty of the Cogito is an idea which derives from a source other than the Cogito itself.

It must not be concluded from this analysis that Levinas subscribes to a form of Cartesian immanence, where "the revelation of God is a *disclosure* and is achieved in the *adequation of truth*, in the grasp which that which thinks exercises on that which is thought, and thus that meaning or intelligibility would be an economy, in the etymological sense of the term, the economy of a

---

[14]Levinas, "Transcendence and Intelligibility," in *Basic Philosophical Writings*, ed. Adriaan T. Peperzak, Simon Critchley, and Robert Bernasconi, Studies in Continental Thought (Bloomington: Indiana University Press, 1996) 152.

[15]Ibid., 153.

[16]Ibid., 155.

[17]Ibid., 155.

house, of a home, of a certain investment, of a grasping, a possession, a self-satisfaction and an enjoyment."[18] He distances himself, rather, from the purely Cartesian notion of the idea of the infinite by emphasizing that, for Descartes, such a notion "remains a theoretical idea, a contemplation, a knowledge."[19] For Levinas, on the other hand, the relation to the infinite is not one based on knowledge but on "Desire," a Desire which should not, however, be conflated with need. While need can be satisfied, Desire is insatiable. Desire, thus, aims not at totality or unity, but "nourishes itself on its own hungers."[20] As such, it breaks with immanence by reaching out towards the other in whose face one has access to the idea of God; stated differently, the idea of God which confounds thought and which generates Desire is to be found in the social situation, or in the relationship which the "I" has with its neighbor.

In concluding his remarkable essay from 1984, "Transcendence and Intelligibility," Levinas says of this particular form of sociality:

> That the proximity of the Infinite and the sociality that it founds and commands can be better than the *coincidence of unity*; that sociality is an irreducible excellence through its very plurality, even if one cannot say it exuberantly without falling back into the poverty of a proposition; that the relation to or nonindifference toward the other does not consist, for the Other, in being converted into the Same; that religion is not a moment in the "economy" of being; that love is not a demigod—that is certainly also signified by the idea of the infinite in us or by the humanity of man understood as the theology or the intelligibility of the transcendent.[21]

In Levinas's ethicoreligious postmodernism, love of the Other ought to take precedence over self-love to such an extent that I must always be prepared to entertain the shocking possibility that my self-possession has contributed to oppression, starvation, exclusion, and even murder; that is, in being a host, in owning a home, in claiming a "place in the sun" as my own, am I not in

---

[18]Ibid., 156.
[19]Levinas, "The Face," in *Ethics and Infinity*, trans. Richard A. Cohen (Pittsburgh: Duquesne University Press, 1985) 92.
[20]Ibid., 92.
[21]Levinas, "Transcendence and Intelligibility," 159.

some way contributing to the death of the Other in the sense of dispossessing him/her? To be a host, to have the capacity to offer the Other hospitality, is this not predicated upon my usurpation of what is not "mine" by right, a usurpation, as Levinas says, "of spaces belonging to the other man whom I have already oppressed or starved, or driven out into a third world; are they not acts of repulsing, excluding, exiling, stripping, killing?"[22] The relationship to the Other is founded on a form of love which, as he says in the citation from "Transcendence and Intelligibility" above, "is not a moment in the *economy* of being." For Levinas, rather, I must always tremble before the thought that I have, through ownership and possession, evicted the neighbor and made of her a refugee. Such a thought challenges the very structure of community to the extent that we are forced to ask upon whose grave do we dance when we say "we"? Whose life have we taken when we establish the principle of "private property"?

It is Levinas's most fundamental belief that genuine responsibility to the Other comes in the form of a summons, a summons to jettison, what he calls, "the formulas of generality"; that is, I must be prepared to accept responsibility for having caused the death of the Other. Such responsibility is not that for one's "fellow man," but for "the stranger or sojourner"; it is a responsibility so profound that I ought to become hostage to the Other, in the sense that I should be prepared to surrender my home unconditionally to whoever comes. In short, responsibility to the Other antedates my freedom and autonomy, my selfhood and ego:

> It is through the condition of being a hostage that there can be pity, compassion, pardon, and proximity in the world—even the little there is, even the simple "after you sir." All the transfers of sentiment which theorists of original war and egoism use to explain the birth of generosity . . . could not take root in the ego were it not, in its entire being, or rather its entire nonbeing, subjected not to a category, as in the case of matter, but to an unlimited accusative, that is to say, persecution, self, hostage, already substituted for others.[23]

---

[22]Levinas, "Ethics as First Philosophy," in *The Levinas Reader*, ed. Sean Hand (Oxford: Basil Blackwell, 1989) 82.

[23]Levinas, "Substitution," in *Basic Philosophical Writings*, 91.

To be a hostage, to be a responsible host, demands that I relinquish my sovereignty to the point of substituting myself for the Other. This requires that the welcome which I afford the Other be totally unconditional; it demands that, in the face of the Other's misery, I continually "ask myself if my being is justified," and if my being-there (*Dasein*) "is not already then usurpation of somebody's else's place."[24] Such is hospitality without reserve, a hospitality which takes the form of "love without concupiscence."[25] In this sense, I am responsible for the Other to the point of death, or, as Levinas puts it, "I am responsible for the Other without waiting for reciprocity, were I to die for it."[26] Hence, for unconditional hospitality to occur the reciprocal economy between self and other must give way to a nonsymmetrical bond in which "I am subjection to the Other."[27] In this situation, I play host to the stranger to the point of substituting/sacrificing myself for him/her.

Unconditional hospitality on this reading is, therefore, the manner in which the self manifests the depth of responsibility which he/she has for the neighbor in whose face can be captured the idea of God, the transcendent, or infinity. Indeed, to welcome "the Stranger, the widow, and the orphan" is to affirm the infinite in love. As such, "[t]here can be no 'knowledge' of God separated from the relationship with men"; in the face of the Other "is the manifestation of the height in which God is revealed."[28] To become hostage to the Other to the point of substitution is "the glory of a long desire," a Desire "without restrain or reserve." Hence, I am always already in debt to the stranger in that I am responsible for supplanting his/her place in the sun:

> This growing surplus of the Infinite that we have ventured to call glory is not an abstract quintessence. It has a signification in the response to the summons which comes to me from the face of a neighbor, and which could not be evaded; it is the hyperbolic demand which at once exceeds that response. This comes as a

---

[24]Levinas, "Ethics as First Philosophy," 85.
[25]Ibid.
[26]Levinas, "Responsibility for the Other," in *Ethics and Infinity*, 98.
[27]Ibid.
[28]Levinas, *Totality and Infinity: An Essay on Exteriority*, trans. Alphonso Lingis (Pittsburgh: Duquesne University Press, 1969) 78-79.

surprise for the respondent himself by which, ousted from his inwardness as an ego and a "being with two sides," he is awakened, that is, exposed to the other without restraint or reserve. . . . The openness of the ego exposed to the other is the breakup or turning inside out of inwardness. Sincerity is the name of this extraversion. But what else can this inversion or extraversion mean but a responsibility for others such that I keep nothing for myself? A responsibility such that everything in me is debt and donation and such that my being-there is the ultimate being-there where the creditors find the debtor?[29]

### Levinas's Hyperbole

The question which I now wish to pose is this: Is Levinas's notion of unconditional hospitality as I have outlined it, capable of producing practical political results, or is it merely, to invoke his own terminology, a "hyperbolic demand" devoid of political effectiveness? It is surely correct to say, that in the midst of some of the more excessive postmodern gestures of the past thirty years, the thought of Emmanuel Levinas stands apart for its sublimity, sensibility and sheer beauty. Its efficacy should not, however, be judged on this basis alone, for the true measure of any thinker's ideas, I believe, must lie in their ability to respond effectively to the most pressing demands of the age. It is my contention that Levinas's insights do merit serious appraisal by those of us wishing to locate in philosophy a liberating impulse. I am not convinced, however, that such ethicoreligious sensitivity is by itself sufficient to produce significant ramifications in the sociopolitical sphere. That is, I have a number of quite acute reservations concerning the potential of Levinas's paradigm to respond pragmatically to those whose needs warrant immediate practical attention. As such, I am unable to recognize in his thought the spirit of exodus in the most profound sense.

Although Levinas's "protoethics"[30] is founded on the type of selfless love I have identified in the work of Kierkegaard and

---

[29]Levinas, "God and Philosophy," in *The Levinas Reader*, 182-83.

[30]For an argument that runs counter to the one I am advancing here, see Simon Critchley, *The Ethics of Deconstruction: Derrida and Levinas* (Oxford: Blackwell, 1992).

Derrida, I consider his construal of unconditional hospitality too unremitting. As we have seen above, for both Kierkegaard and Derrida the law of unconditional hospitality is impossible to realize, "[s]ince we cannot practically, pragmatically or realistically open the door to anyone."[31] For Levinas, however, the self is ordained to give up everything he/she owns in the name of the Other. Being a host implies becoming a hostage to anyone who knocks at my door and says: "Here I am!" (*Me voici!*). For "the subject who says 'Here I am!' *testifies* to the Infinite." Moreover, "[i]t is through this testimony that the very glory of the Infinite glorifies *itself*."[32] For me, such a demand is hyperbolic in the extreme; what it asks of us is far too much. This is why, I wish to argue, Levinas has difficulty in translating his ethics into a credible politics.

While David Tracy has convincingly contended that Levinas's invocation of Exodus has powerfully helped "political and Christian liberation theology, and perhaps also philosophy, to clarify the human situation as one of exodus and wandering,"[33] I am still not persuaded that Levinas's reading of Exodus possesses the right ingredients for a "*politics* of exodus." For example, all he can say in response to a group of "Latin American students, well versed in the terminology of Marxist liberation and terribly concerned by the suffering and unhappiness of their people in Argentina," when they ask him if he has "ever actually witnessed the utopian rapport with the other" which his ethical philosophy speaks of, is: "Yes, indeed, here in this room."[34] What we may deduce from this is that unconditional hospitality of the Levinasian sort denies us any practical and concrete means to redress the most appalling social inequalities which are endemic to so many cultures and communities today. Surely any politics of liberation or exodus demands more than a mere observance of social protocol? Indeed, even the most perfidious dictators will adhere to the basic demands of etiquette. Hence, Levinas's rejoinder to those Marxist

---

[31]Derrida, "Perhaps or Maybe," 8.

[32]Levinas, "The Glory of Testimony" in *Ethics and Infinity*, 106-107.

[33]See David Tracy, "Response to Adriaan Peperzak on Transcendence," in *Ethics as First Philosophy*, 194-96.

[34]Levinas, "Ethics of the Infinite," 68.

students is, I suggest, indicative of a certain political naivety, a naivety which ultimately renders his work at best idealistic.

## Hospitable Narcissism

If, as I have argued, Levinas's thought is insufficiently equipped to respond to the fundamental problems which beset the age, the work of both Kierkegaard and Derrida is more sensitive to this demand. While there are strong Levinasian resonances running through their respective writings, both thinkers are nevertheless committed to a politics of exodus which has as its most fundamental objective the diminution of social injustice and inequality. Both Kierkegaard and Derrida, that is, espouse a religion of love which, while Levinasian in tone, distinguishes itself by identifying as a foremost political responsibility the need to respond to the singular Other. Deconstruction, despite what some of its most intransigent and trenchant detractors have proclaimed, has always been preoccupied with hospitality as generosity or love towards the other. Such reflections, as I have argued above, bear witness to Derrida's "religion without [established] religion," or his passion and commitment to singular appeals for justice. This is true also of Kierkegaard, who shows that it is only by affirming difference through acts of grace and mercy that true love can be experienced. In both cases, hospitality comes in the form of a "gift" which seeks no return on its investment. In a similar manner to Levinas, both Derrida and Kierkegaard consider it necessary to divest the self of any drive to reduce otherness to sameness, or to welcome the other on the condition that there be compensation in kind. As such, the love and generosity which hospitality on this reading engenders takes the form of a certain *Gelassenheit*, a letting go in which difference is affirmed without condition.

In response to the suggestion that his work contains traces of *Gelassenheit* as developed by Meister Eckhart and later taken up by Heidegger, Derrida says:

> I have no objection to this hypothesis. As you describe this *Gelassenheit*, you are very careful not to talk about love. . . . But why not recognize there love itself, that is, this infinite renunciation which somehow surrenders to the impossible [*se rend a l'impossible*]? To surrender to the other, and this is the impossible, would amount to giving oneself over in going toward the other,

to coming toward the other but without crossing the threshold, and to respecting, to loving even the invisibility that keeps the other inaccessible. To surrendering one's weapons [*rendre les armes*].[35]

Love, for Derrida, is a way of surrendering to the other "but without crossing the threshold"; while loving demands that we lay down our arms and welcome the stranger, we are nevertheless precluded from becoming one with her to the point of substitution. This is so because the other is irreducibly singular, has a unique perspective on the world, has lived a life which no one else has lived. In Kierkegaardian terms, the other is marked off from the self by a certain "residual incommensurability." The other is other, that is, by virtue of the fact that I cannot attain to her "immediately and originally, silently, in communion with the other's own experience";[36] for if I could become one with the other to the extent that my life could be substituted for his/her's, "the other would cease to be other."[37] The upshot of Derrida's analysis here is that it is only upon recognizing sameness that we can affirm otherness, or, I can only affirm the stranger after I have recognized him/her as being somewhat different from myself. Alternatively expressed, it is only through recognition of the other from the point of view of the same that the other can be affirmed as other.

This "invisibility that keeps the other inaccessible," ensures that I can never become a hostage in the Levinasian sense. To love, to welcome the other, necessitates that I retain a sense of belonging and a degree of separation from the neighbor. In other words, how could I be a host if I did not possess a home? Surrendering one's weapons and abandoning oneself to the other is, as Derrida argues, "impossible" by virtue of the fact that I can never totally negate this sense of self. But just because something is impossible does not mean that it cannot be desired and longed for; in fact, it is dreaming the impossible dream which inspires me to deal out more than the average dose of hospitality to the other. The dream

---

[35]Derrida, *On the Name*, trans. Thomas Dutoit (Stanford: Stanford University Press, 1995) 74.

[36]Derrida, "Violence and Metaphysics" in *Writing and Difference*, trans. Alan Bass (London: Routledge, 1978) 124.

[37]Ibid.

is that there be "a policy of absolutely unconditional openness to whoever is coming and because this is absolutely impossible, we have to produce laws and rules in order to select, in the best possible way, the one's we host, we welcome."[38]

For Derrida, thus, I am always before the law, always already coimplicated with others in totalizing relationships, institutions, and communities. The ethical imperative is not to try and escape one's totality/community in the name of Infinity, but to ensure that it remains flexible and open to the incoming of the other. To exhibit generosity or hospitality demands that one keep a vigilant eye on the borders which demarcate the same from the other with the objective of guaranteeing that they do not pose an insurmountable blockade to the stranger.

Derrida crystallizes most poignantly his reflections on hospitality in the following remarkable passage:

> There is not narcissism and nonnarcissism; there are narcissisms that are more or less comprehensive, generous, open, extended. What is called nonnarcissism is in general but the economy of a much more welcoming, hospitable narcissism, one that is much more open to the experience of the other as other. I believe that without a movement of narcissistic reappropriation, the relation to the other would be absolutely destroyed, it would be destroyed in advance. The relation to the other—even if it remains asymmetrical, open, without possible appropriation—must trace a movement of reappropriation in the image of oneself for love to be possible, for example.[39]

For hospitality and love to be possible there has to be a sense of self, of economy, of domesticity. Without narcissism the Otherness of the Other would simply dissolve.

It is my contention that Kierkegaard intended to convey something similar through his powerful invocation of the story of sacrifice in *Fear and Trembling*. When Abraham responds to the appeal of the singular Other, he does so by attempting an act of nonnarcissism in which he strives to make the economy (law [*nomos*] of home [*oikos*]) less restricted and more welcoming. For Kierke-

---

[38]Derrida, "Perhaps or Maybe," 8.
[39]Derrida, *Points . . . : Interviews, 1974–1994*, ed. Elisabeth Weber, trans. Peggy Kamuf et al. (Stanford CA: Stanford University Press, 1995) 199.

gaard, that is, the sacrifice of Isaac metaphorically illustrates that for hospitality to be hospitality, the law of the home must be suspended in the name of the stranger. The family, in other words, undergoes a "spiritual trial" which requires that it give up its arms, or its values, so as to allow the other feel at home.

But for Levinas, on the other hand, Kierkegaard concerned himself little with the demands of hospitality and love. In fact, his was "a subjectivity that was shamelessly exhibitionistic."[40] On this reading, Kierkegaard is a violent thinker whose style, "reckless of scandal and destruction,"[41] inspired a "total rejection of everything."[42] Most disturbingly, however, is Levinas's contention that Kierkegaard's style anticipated and paved the way for the "verbal violences" of National Socialism and its related discourses. If, for Derrida, Kierkegaard is the great thinker of singularity, for Levinas he is little more than a dangerous and whimsical subjectivist who inspired some of the most poisonous and pernicious ideology of our time.

The fundamental problem with Kierkegaard on Levinas's telling, is that he transcended the ethical; in being so concerned with his own subjective inwardeness and salvation, Kierkegaard considered the ethical a threat to a self which sought to remain splendidly isolated from all others and immune from any normative constraints or requirements. Through his invocation of the Genesis story of Abraham, Kierkegaard exhibits a form of religious fanaticism in which his one-on-one with God is privileged over and above his responsibility to his fellow citizens. The sacrifice of the ethical as portrayed here is interpreted by Levinas as a violent act, one which prioritizes death above life, terror over generosity of heart. Consequently, Kierkegaard is profoundly ignorant of how being-with-Others in the ethical context can engender genuine social relations founded upon responsibility and "total altruism."[43]

As argued above, for Levinas, "[b]eing a Self means not being able to hide from responsibility," the responsibility of generating

---

[40]Levinas, "Existence and Ethics," in *Kierkegaard: A Critical Reader*, ed. Jonathan Ree and Jane Chamberlain (Oxford: Blackwell, 1998) 34.

[41]Ibid.

[42]Ibid.

[43]Ibid., 32.

"unique solidarity with Others."[44] In the moment when such responsibility is assumed "the Self is emptied of all imperialism and egoism," is called, that is, into question.[45] Such comments are reminiscent of those cited earlier, in which Levinas instructs that we must, if we desire to be responsible, become hostages of the Other to the point of substitution. His contention that the call of the Other is sufficient to elicit from us "the most radical commitment conceivable: total altruism," is once more predicated upon his dubious belief that we have a natural propensity to respond unselfishly, or to surrender ourselves without reserve to those who summon us. Moreover, this process of being called into question does not demand a shift in attitude or a cultivation of sensitivity towards Others different from ourselves. For Levinas, we require nothing more than the simple etiquette of the social space (the ethical) to ensure the realization of infinite responsibility, and not, as is Kierkegaard's recommendation, a *temporary* suspension of the ethical.

By advocating a suspension of the ethical in this way, Kierkegaard is, for Levinas, responsible in no small measure for the Heideggerian attempt to privilege ontology over ethics as first philosophy; through his surreptitious appropriation of some pivotal Kierkegaardian concepts, Heidegger perceived the ethical as a sphere of "average everydayness" in which inauthenticity flourished. Being-with-others (*Mitsein*) was sacrificed, thus, in favour of Dasein's being-for-itself. Consequently, Heidegger cared more for tools and things than he did for his fellowman, being as the latter was a constant threat to the authentic thinker's project of personal salvation. The Judeo-Christian spirit of his pre-*Being and Time* work was replaced by a Greco-German impulse which was devoid of any ethical substance. Biblical sensitivity, in other words, gave way to teutonic bombast. It was this obsession with Heideggerian ontology and its dubious rapprochement with National Socialism which led Levinas to contend that Kierkegaard's suspension of the ethical amounted to "a kind of justification for violence and terror," and was "the origin of the relegation of

---

[44]Ibid.
[45]Ibid.

ethical phenomena to secondary status and the contempt for the ethical foundation of being."[46]

What is most curious about this appraisal of Kierkegaard by Levinas is that it fails to make reference to the specifically Christian dimension of the former's thought. It neglects, that is, the powerful Kierkegaardian invocation of the *God-man* as unconditioned ethical goal and criterion, and the entire Christian ethic of love (hospitality) which underlies this move. What fundamentally separates Kierkegaard from Heidegger is precisely the former's emphasis on love as a means of challenging the sovereignty of the ego/self. Indeed, far from being a thinker who urged his reader to recoil into some interior space to agonize over his/her own redemption, Kierkegaard considered an openness to Others a prerequisite for genuine selfhood. Such *proto*ethical sensitivity is what earned Kierkegaard the Heideggerian epithet of "ontic thinker"— that is, one who is more concerned with being-with-Others in average everydayness than carving oneself off from the rest of mankind so as to ponder the profundity and luminosity of Being.

To suspend the ethical for Kierkegaard, is not equivalent to abandoning one's time-honored values and mores in the name of anarchic libertinism. If this is what his appropriation of the Abraham story was intended to provoke then Levinas's vitriolic condemnation is in order. But Kierkegaard never sought or advocated anything of the sort. What he did call for was a "*teleological* suspension of the ethical," or a temporary easing of the weight of the universal order—the order of right (*Recht*) and law— from the shoulders of the singular individual. Kierkegaard's analysis in *Fear and Trembling* amounts to a dramatization of what is required if a genuine response to the needs of singularity is to be purveyed; that is, Abraham temporarilly sacrifices the order of law (embodied, as Johannes de Silentio informs us, in Isaac) so as to answer the call of one (God in the Genesis narrative) whose welfare is not safeguarded by the law or the system. Kierkegaard is reacting in this context to the theory of *Sittlichkeit* (social ethics) as developed in Hegel's *Philosophy of Right*. On this telling, singularity is reduced to universality as a consequence of Hegel's

---

[46]Ibid., 31.

insistence that any form of dissension from the "divine" state ought to be considered evil. But for Kierkegaard such privileging of the ethical or the state runs the risk of deifying or divinizing the prevailing order. Unless the order of law (the universal) is sensitive to the requirements of singularity it will simply become dogmatic and oppressive. This is why Kierkegaard is committed to the belief that the single individual is higher than the universal.

On this reading, the reason Kierkegaard calls for a suspension of the ethical is not because he is, as Levinas contends, a religious fundamentalist or fanatic, but because he considers an uncritical devotion to the state as a danger best avoided. This is not to suggest, as I argued earlier, that he advocates a complete renunciation of all civic obligations and duties. On the contrary, what he is urging is that we keep the law flexible enough so as to ensure that it guarantees justice for everyone who comes before it no matter how lowly they may be.

A *teleological* suspension of the ethical (as distinct from a simple *suspension* of the ethical) demands that the ethical and the law be moderated by, what Kierkegaard calls, a religious scruple. While the latter finds Hegel's fusion of God and the state objectionable in the extreme, he nevertheless wishes to keep a certain religious spirit alive. This is so because, in the first instance, Kierkegaard considers a fully secularized state as dangerous as one which believes that its laws have a divine imprimatur; the secular religions of fascism and communism, in other words, far surpassed in violence and brutality the crimes committed "in the name of God" by any of the established religions throughout history. But secondly, and most importantly, Kierkegaard sees in Christianity, as distinct from Christendom, immense resources for keeping the state sensitive to its own contingent foundations and, by implication, to the voice of those singular Others who collapse beneath the weight of its laws. Such a religious impulse, one which privileges the Christ-figure as unconditioned ethical goal and criterion, prevents the established order (the ethical) from ever inoculating itself against the claims which are made upon it by those whose only hope is for a little mercy, generosity, and hospitality. For is it not the case that this figure sought to suspend the law of the Sabbath long enough for the man with the withered hand to be healed? He sought, in other words, to teleologically suspend the

ethical in the name of love and justice. In so doing, he affirmed
singularity above universality, love of the different and Other
above love of the same. This is not to say that a teleological
suspension of the ethical demands that one deny love to one's
own. It is simply to say that the real test in love is to extend that
love to those who are different—"hospitable narcissism."

To choose the Christ-figure as ethical paradigm and prototype,
or to imitate Christ (*imitatio Christi*), is thus a means of keeping the
liberating impulses of religion alive. It serves to transform the
ethical from a sphere in which right and law unremittingly hold
sway, to one in which the needs of singularity are used as a
yardstick to determine if the judicial structures of the state value
legal clarity above justice. If observed from this perspective, it is
easy to see why Derrida takes a contrary view to that held by
Levinas regarding the Kierkegaardian teleological suspension of
the ethical. He says:

> Let us add, in order to do him *justice*, that Kierkegaard had a
> sense of the relationship to the irreducibility of the totally-other,
> not in the egoistic and esthetic here and now, but in the religious
> beyond of the concept, in the direction of a certain Abraham.
> And did he not, in turn—for we must let the other speak—see in
> Ethics, as a moment of Category and Law, the forgetting, in
> anonymity, of the subjectivity of religion? From this point of
> view, the ethical moment is Hegelianism itself, and he says so
> explicitly. Which does not prevent him from reaffirming ethics in
> repetition, and from reproaching Hegel for not having constituted
> a morality.[47]

The fact that Kierkegaard considers it essential that the
emigrant from the sphere of the universal return to the ethical is,
I suggest, what fundamentally distinguishes the latter from
Levinas. For Levinas, as I have repeatedly argued, genuine hospitality is a matter of divesting the ego of all sovereignty so as to
become hostage to the Other, a process he refers to as "total altruism." But for both Kierkegaard and Derrida, there must always be
"a movement of reappropriation in the image of oneself for love
to be possible."[48] There must always be, that is, a sense of self, of

---

[47]Derrida, *Writing and Difference*, 111.
[48]Derrida, *Points . . .*, 199.

home, and of belonging if alterity (Otherness) is to be affirmed, or if the Other is to be recognized as Other. For both these thinkers, the self is ineluctably enmeshed with others in a sociolinguistic matrix, or, stated differently, the self is always already before the law. Affirming singularity, therefore, is not a matter of razing the law to the ground. It is rather a matter of being sensitive to the fact that laws are contingently configured and, as such, have the potential to be rewritten when they become tools of oppression and discrimination.

While it would be incorrect of me to assume that Derrida would follow Kierkegaard in appropriating the Christian God-man as ethical goal and criterion, I am nevertheless convinced that Kierkegaard's Christianity, founded as it is upon the *life* of Christ, sits well with Derrida's appeal on behalf of victims of suffering and injustice. While both thinkers are committed to the belief that love of the Other is predicated upon love of the self, they are no less committed to ensuring that such love be as open and as welcoming as is possible. This implies that for both the Christian Kierkegaard and the prophetic Derrida, the real challenge for the host is to ensure that the home not be open solely to one's own but also to those who are least like "us." In suspending the law of the home long enough to allow the Other access, the spell of narcissism is shattered by an "economy of a much more welcoming, hospitable narcissism."[49] Hospitable narcissism mediates the extremes of totality and infinity, of egomania and total altruism, of xenophobia and unconditional hospitality.

In a discussion of "the neighbor" in *Works of Love*, Kierkegaard deftly encapsulates what is at issue here:

> *Who, then, is the neighbor* [*Næste*]? The word is obviously derived from "nearest" [*Nærmeste*]; thus the neighbor is the person who is nearer to you than anyone else, yet not in the sense of preferential love, since to love someone who in the sense of preferential love is nearer than anyone else is self-love—"do not the pagans do the same?" The neighbor, then, is nearer to you than anyone else. But is he also nearer to you than you are to yourself? No, that he is not, but he is just as near, or he ought to be just as near to you. The concept "neighbor" is actually the redoubling of your

---

[49]Ibid.

> own self; "the neighbor" is what thinkers call "the other," that by
> which the selfishness in self-love is to be tested. (WL, 21)

According to Kierkegaard, there is no great achievement in loving one's own, for even those with the hardest of hearts do that. To love the neighbor, however, demands that I retain my sense of self while concomitantly setting a place at the "family" table for the visitor, the stranger, the Other. By allowing difference to unsettle sameness in this way, "the selfishness in self-love" is put to the test. Kierkegaard, thus, wants to give "economy [the law of the home] its chance." He recognizes (pace Levinas), in other words, that while love of the neighbor requires a superabundance of hospitality, it is simply not the case that it involves becoming a hostage unto death. Self-love, on this telling, is a precondition for love of the Other. This is why the Other in this context is termed a *near*-dweller—"near" in the sense of being a challenge rather than a threat to one's self-sovereignty. Indeed, Kierkegaard insists that until we reach a point where we can cultivate a love for ourselves it will be simply impossible to extend love to the Other, to the singular Other who comes to disturb the security of the same, qua universal order.

The teleological suspension of the ethical, therefore, is precisely that—a *teleological* suspension. The objective of such a lifting of the burden of the law is not to engender "a cult of Passion and Fury," which "brings irresponsibility in its wake and a ferment of disintegration."[50] It is, quite to the contrary, a means of ensuring that the law of the home becomes more flexible, that it does not become a barrier to the Other, to the neighbor who comes in search of asylum. On this reading, the teleological suspension is an act of love for the one who challenges the selfishness of self-love. Indeed, it is, as Kierkegaard insists, a "fulfilling of the law":

> The Law starves out, as it were; with its help one never reaches
> fulfilling, since its purpose is to take away, to require, to exact to
> the utmost, and in the continually remaining indefiniteness in the
> multiplicity of all its provisions is the inexorable exaction of the
> requirements. With every provision the Law requires something,
> and yet there is no limit to the provisions. The Law is therefore

---

[50]Levinas, "Existence and Ethics," 30.

the very opposite of life, but life is the fulfilling. The Law is like death. But I wonder if life and death do not actually know one and the same thing. . . . In a certain sense, then, there is no conflict between the Law and love with regard to knowledge; but love gives, the Law takes, or . . . the Law requires, love gives. There is not one of the Law's provisions, not a single one, that love wants to have removed; on the contrary, love gives them all complete fullness and definiteness for the first time; in love all the Law's provisions are much more definite than they are in the Law. (WL, 105-106)

The love which Kierkegaard commends is that which serves to keep the law honest. The law, by its very nature, is founded on an economy of exchange or on a balance of payments (that is, the law likes to get even). As such, its task is to take with one hand what it purveys with the other. Being retributive, calculating, and cold, the law is insensitive to the needs of those who have long since fallen beneath its weight. "A human being," says Kierkegaard, "groans under the Law. Wherever he looks, he sees only require- ment but never the boundary, alas, like someone who looks out over the ocean and sees wave after wave but never the boundary" (WL, 105). But love and hospitality are the means by which the law takes on a human face; in the moment of love, the law of the home is suspended long enough to allow the neighbor to take his/her place at the table. In this moment, the circle of reappropri- ation and retribution is broken, the economy of regulated exchange collapses, and the gentle hand of love brings the law to fulfillment.

Lest it be forgotten, both Kierkegaard and Derrida have high regard for the ethical, the law, and the universal. But they are deeply cognizant of the fact that the law can only be genuinely lawful when it is balanced by the claims of singularity. To let the Other come, to put the selfishness in self-love to the test, to open one's home to the single individual, is not to destroy the law but to make definite and real the law's provisions.

In love and hospitality the possessive pronouns *mine* and *yours* are put under strain; that is, the borders between myself and the Other tremble in the instant when the law is fulfilled. No longer is the Other determined simply as a moment in the self's quest to reinforce sameness—as when the colonizer sees the Other as an image of himself, a means of expanding the self's horizon—but is affirmed on the basis of what is unique, different, and unassimilable in the Other. Johannes de Silentio, to recall, refers to such difference as *residual incommensurability*, while Derrida favors what we have been calling, *singualrity*. In *Works of Love*, Kierkegaard considers "true love" an affirmation of the "distinctiveness" of Others. In a passage so reminiscent of Lacan's critique of Hegel's notion of the dialectic of consciousness, as a process in which the self feeds off difference in an attempt to surmount alienation, Kierkegaard proffers the following salient observation:

> *The rigid, the domineering person* lacks flexibility, lacks the pliability to comprehend others; he demands his own from everyone, wants everyone to be transformed in his image, to be trimmed according to his pattern for human beings. . . . Whether the rigid and domineering person is assigned a large sphere of activity or a small one, whether he is a tyrant in an empire or a domestic tyrant in a little attic room esentially makes no difference; the nature is the same: domineeringly refusing to go out of oneself, domineeringly wanting to crush the other person's disitnctiveness or torment it to death. (WL, 270-71)

While hospitality towards the Other requires some self-appropriation, some narcissism, it endeavors to keep such narcissism as open and as flexible as is possible. The rigid and domineering person, on the other hand, makes self-love the only order of the day; for him, there is no appreciation of the fact that the Other is unique by virtue of the fact that he/she has lived a distinct life, a life which is irreplaceable. Again, *pace* Levinas, because each life is irreplaceable substitution for the Other is impossible.

Hospitable narcissism does not "seek its own." It does not strive, that is, to reduce the Other to the image of the self, or to put the Other in one's debt. Quite to the contrary, it seeks to be as benevolent and as munificent, as magnanimous and as generous *as is possible*. Love of this kind gives for its own sake, and not for temporal or heavenly rewards. Of course, the self *desires* to give in this way, he or she *wants* to love the Other in a way which does not yield any payback. So such love should not be confused with the "total altrusim" of which Levinas speaks. It is, rather, an act of generosity in which the self loosens up the circle of reappropriation by making it seem, as Kierkegaard instructs, "that the gift looks as if it were the recipient's property" (WL, 274).

To give mercy and compassion is such a gift beyond exchange. This is so simply because, by its very nature, an appeal for mercy is made usually by those who are unable to reciprocate, by those who make a claim on us in the knowledge that they have nothing to give in return. Mercy and compassion, that is, are acts which are not driven by an impulse to bind the other up in debt to the self. To show compassion is to teleologically suspend the ethical, the order of good bookkeeping, with the aim of being excessive rather than reserved or restrained. Genuine compassion and mercy cannot be bought for they amount to acts of munificence which require an act of selflessness on behalf of the donor. Moreover, mercy and compassion are gifts which are not simply the preserve of those who have, for those who have not can also give mercy. Indeed, for Kierkegaard, it is not what form mercy and compassion take, but how they are administered which counts:

> Is it mercifulness when someone who is able to do every-
> thing does everything for the wretched? No. Is it mercifulness if
> someone who is able to do what amounts to nothing does this
> nothing for the wretched? No. Mercifulness is *how* this everything
> and this nothing are done. But then I can indeed just as well see
> mercifulness in this everything and in this nothing; and if this is
> so, then I can actually see it best in this nothing, because being
> able to do everything is a glittering externality that has an acci-
> dental kind of significance that powerfully affects the sensate in
> me, easily draws attention to itself, and disturbs me in seeing
> mercifulness. (WL, 327-28)

Mercy and compassion, in other words, test the selfishness in self-love and should not, therefore, be administered in such a way that they feed the ego's need to be acclaimed. True compassion is a gift which appears as the recipient's own property.

Such is the task of generous and hospitable narcissism: To ensure that the law of one's home does not block the passage to the neighbor, the Other, but that it remains sufficiently malleable and alterable so that when a stranger shows up with only knap-sack and sandals, we will afford him shelter. Such is the essence of Kierkegaard's Christian philosophy and of Derrida's so-called "religion without religion." To be a host in this way does not, let me repeat, imply that one must become a hostage to the Other unto death; it simply demands that we moderate the laws of the home and the land in accordance with the claims of singularity. Responding to appeals for love, compassion, mercy, or justice, obliges us to pay attention to the details and the specifics of the situation which presents itself. Each situation of this type requires a singular response, one which is not based on formal or universal criteria, but one which endeavors to implement whatever is necessary at the political level in order to lessen the pain and hardship of the emigrant. Responding in this way is a gift, something which we give without hope of reward; it is unconditional, selfless love, "love," as John D. Caputo has recently argued, "without measure." For love, as we have suggested above, is the means by which we surrender to the Other without crossing the threshold, or without reducing the distinctiveness of the Other to the point of substitution. While the law calculates and controls, love and justice are excessive and exorbitant gestures. The law is "rigorousness" while love is "gentleness." Love, as the fulfilling of the law, is the "greatest benefaction" (WL, 275) to the emigrant and the stranger whose only wish is for a room, no matter how modest, at the inn.

# 8

# Mutual Responsiveness in Relation: The Challenge of the Ninth Deliberation

## M. J. Ferreira

One of the central disagreements between prominent contemporary characterizations of selfhood and the relationship of the self to an other is rooted in opposing accounts of the character of responsiveness within relation. What is at stake is not only one's response *to* the other, but also the response *from* the other, as well as a significant correlation (in kind and degree) between those responses. One of the deliberations in *Works of Love*, the ninth deliberation of the second series, entitled "The Work of Love in Recollecting One Who Is Dead," has often been singled out as a text in which Kierkegaard makes normative a total disregard of mutual responsiveness in human relationships.

In 1939 T. W. Adorno's general critique of *Works of Love* as an "abstract" and "callous" ethic focused attention on this deliberation's discussion of love of the dead, suggesting that "perhaps one may most accurately summarize Kierkegaard's doctrine of love by saying that he demands that love behave toward all men as if they were dead."[1] For Adorno, this "death-like aspect of Kierkegaard's love," found in perhaps "one of the most important pieces he [Kierkegaard] ever wrote," has a "bad side [which] is obvious", namely, "love of the dead is the one which most rigidly excludes the reciprocity of love."[2] In other words, he charges Kierkegaard with making normative a one-sided relation in which the response *of* the other is irrelevant—hence our "response" to the other is not a genuine response and there is no genuine relation.

---

[1]T. W. Adorno, "On Kierkegaard's Doctrine of Love," *Studies in Philosophy and Social Science* 8 (1939): 413-29; quotations from 416, 421, and 417.

[2]Ibid., 417, 427.

Since such a charge continues to be made today, it is important to reconsider the claims in *Works of Love* that have motivated readers time and again to wonder whether Kierkegaard's account of relation implies the irrelevance of mutuality or reciprocity.[3] In this essay I want to explore this provocative ninth deliberation in detail, and then put it in the context of other parts of *Works of Love* which can illuminate and qualify it. We need to reconsider how Kierkegaard opens himself to this criticism, what is at stake that pressures Kierkegaard into taking a potentially dangerous position on responsiveness, and whether the implication of his challenge to "reciprocity" is finally the annihilation of a responsiveness we intuitively know is essential to human relationships. I shall argue that while a certain kind of "reciprocity" is condemned by Kierkegaard, he leaves room for and even requires significant dimensions of mutual responsiveness within relationship, without which responsibility for the other would be emptied of meaning. My hope is that by contributing to a clarification of what is at stake for Kierkegaard in this regard, I will raise the questions that ought to be put to any account which either endorses or challenges the requirement of reciprocity within relation.

### 1. Love of the Dead: Its Glory and Its Limits

The deliberation on "The Work of Love in Recollecting One Who Is Dead" explores in great detail ways in which love is to be unselfish, free, and faithful. It opens with the suggestion that the

---

[3]The terms "reciprocity" and "mutuality" are often used to point to the same state or condition, and "reciprocity" is itself defined in terms of mutuality. According to *Merriam Webster's Collegiate Dictionary* (10th ed., 1993), *reciprocity* means "mutual dependence, action, or influence." To *reciprocate* is "to give and take mutually" or "to return in kind or degree"; and to reciprocate "implies a mutual or equivalent exchange or a paying back of what one has received." *Mutual* means "directed by each toward the other . . . having the same feelings one for the other . . . shared in common . . . characterized by intimacy." There is, however, an important way in which they differ, namely, since reciprocity can also involve an "inverse relationship" (e.g., returning kindness with contempt) not all cases of reciprocity will involve the *common or shared* element of mutuality. Since what is called reciprocity in the relevant discussions is reciprocity as mutual dependence, action, or influence, I will simply use the two words interchangeably.

relation to one who is dead reveals "a test of what love really is" (WL, 346-47). It concludes with this advice:

> The work of love in recollecting one who is dead is thus a work of the most unselfish, the freest, the most faithful love. Therefore go out and practice it; recollect the one who is dead and just in this way learn to love the living unselfishly, freely, faithfully. In the relationship to one who is dead, you have the criterion by which you can test yourself. (WL, 358)

The question this raises is whether Kierkegaard's reiterated claim that love of the dead provides a "test" or "criterion" of love amounts to what Adorno charges is the demand that "love behave toward all men as if they were dead"? In other words, is this deliberation meant by Kierkegaard to serve the purpose of recommending such an asymmetrical relationship as the highest kind of love?

In order to begin to answer this question, we need to note that in the text we can find two important qualifications. These add to the qualification which follows from Kierkegaard's crucial distinction between what is required in the realm of "justice" (where reciprocity is an appropriate standard) and what is required in the realm of love as such (WL, 265). The first qualification concerns the object of love and the second concerns the purpose of a test.

a. *The Object of Love.* Kierkegaard admittedly sets a stark stage for his account of love of the dead. He suggests that "when a person relates himself to one who is dead, there is only one in this relationship, inasmuch as one who is dead is no actuality"; "one who is dead is no actual object," he continues, because one who is dead "has not the slightest influence, neither disturbing nor accommodating, on the one living who relates himself to him" (WL, 347). He says repeatedly that the dead one "is no *actual* object," but is rather "only the occasion that continually discloses what resides in the one living who relates himself to him or that helps to make manifest the nature of the one living who does not relate himself to him" (WL, 355, 347). In other words, in relation to one who is dead, the (dead) other is only the occasion for a one-sided revelation of the living one. Taken literally as a model of a loving relationship, this deliberation would make normative a radical asymmetry, a total lack of mutuality, which would be troubling; the irrelevance of the response of the other might, in effect, entail an irrelevance of the other.

Kierkegaard, however, does not make the mistake of confusing the dead with the living. In this ninth deliberation, he clearly contrasts cases of loving the dead with cases of loving the living—that is, he contrasts cases "when one actual person relates himself to another actual person" with cases "when a person relates himself to one who is dead." This, at the very least, leaves room for the inference that the claim that the dead one is not an actual being is not meant to recommend that we treat a living neighbor as dead, a nonactual being. Indeed, Kierkegaard assumes the need of an actual other for a relationship with anyone not dead. He writes explicitly that "when one actual person relates himself to another actual person, the result is two, the relationship is constituted" (WL, 347).

Moreover, the same affirmation of the relevance of an actual other is found in the earlier deliberation entitled "Love Does Not Seek Its Own." Kierkegaard writes: "the more profound the revolution [of love], the more completely the distinction '*mine* and *yours*' disappears" (WL, 266). Hence, the following paradoxical picture of relationship results: "Wonderful! There are a *you* and an *I*, and there is no *mine* and *yours*!" But note well the presupposition Kierkegaard puts in place; he insists that "without a *you* and an *I*, there is no love" (even though "with *mine* and *yours*, there is no love") (WL, 266).

Kierkegaard reminds us in the ninth deliberation that when there is such a relationship between two actual beings, "observation of the one person is made difficult" because the second person can cover something of the first, and "the second person can have so much influence that the first one appears different from what he is." On the contrary, "when a person relates himself to one who is dead, there is only one in this relationship" (WL, 347). The latter situation (relation to the dead) is, therefore, one in which it is easier to determine where the initiative comes from and to determine whether it is self-interested or compelled. That is, love of the dead provides a less complicated situation for consideration, one in which certain dynamics are easier to isolate. But that does not of itself entail that Kierkegaard's ideal is to have the kind of relationship in which "there is only one."

b. *Test or Criterion.* Once we recognize the heuristic function of a nonactual other, it can be plausibly argued that for Kierkegaard these traits (unselfishness, faithfulness, and freedom) are natural expectations of our ordinary instances of loving the living,[4] and that the point of the deliberation is to highlight their extreme versions for instructional purposes, rather than to present it as a model to be emulated. Thus, Kierkegaard's claim that the work of love in remembering one who is dead provides a "test" or "criterion" of love does not amount to what Adorno says is the demand that "love behave toward all men as if they were dead."

When one heuristically simplifies the picture of relation with an other, one can see one's own motives more easily. Kierkegaard's appeal to this strategy is shown in his *converse* example: "if, in conversation with someone, you understand the art of making yourself *no one*, you get to know best what resides in this person" (WL, 347). But we can see that in the case of a conversation with one living, one cannot truly become "no one," and such an extreme is not the goal. Kierkegaard is right to suggest that one should listen, rather than talk, if one wants to "get to know best what resides" in the other—and this is precisely in order to cultivate the relationship and to further the dialogue. This methodological advice, with which we would probably all agree, is, however, distorted unduly if we take it to imply Kierkegaard's recommendation that the best conversation for us is the one in which we never speak.

"If, then," he instructs, "you wish to test yourself as to whether you love unselfishly, just pay attention to how you relate yourself to one who is dead" (WL, 350-51); "if you want to test whether you love faithfully, just observe how you relate yourself to one who is dead" (WL, 355). In other words, we do in fact from this work "learn to love the living" (WL, 358), but not by learning to love them as if they were dead. What serves the purposes of testing one's love need not be regarded as the model to be uncriti-

---

[4]See WL, 353, where he writes: "There is so much talk in the world about the necessity for love to be free, that one cannot love as soon as there is the slightest compulsion, that with regard to love there must be no constraint at all. Well, let us see, when it gets down to brass tacks, how it stands with this free love—how the dead are recollected in love, since one who is dead in no way compels anyone."

cally imitated. The relation in which faithfulness or unselfishness can best be isolated and tested because of the radical unresponsiveness of the beloved is not necessarily put forward as the model of relation we should strive to bring about. In what follows I want to examine some other discussions in *Works of Love* which affirm mutual responsiveness; these provide textual support for reading the work of love in recollecting the dead in terms of "criterion" or "test" rather than in terms of a paradigm to be fostered or uncritically imitated.[5]

## 2. The Affirmation of Mutual Responsiveness

Let me indicate briefly some discussions in *Works of Love* where the topic of responsiveness or mutuality is indirectly addressed. I suggest that they help us to appreciate the kind of mutuality which Kierkegaard allows to stand, even encourages.

a. *Recommendations of Responsiveness.* Throughout *Works of Love*, Kierkegaard valorizes responsiveness as constitutive of love. Two instances stand out and can suffice here. One instance consists in the kind of example he relies on as illustration of loving the neighbor—for example, the responsiveness of the Good Samaritan (WL, 22). It is clear that the response to the other is both concrete and practical, and is directed precisely to the other's material needs. A second instance is found in his deliberation on "Our Duty to Love the People We See." Included in this deliberation, which I consider a decisive turning point in *Works of Love*,[6] is a lengthy and detailed consideration of the duty to love people "just as they are," rather than as we would like them to be. We find, then, throughout the text recommendations of compassionate responses to what the neighbor needs—not simply one-sided initiatives

---

[5]It should be noted that the traits which are said to characterize love (unselfishness, faithfulness, and freedom) are drawn directly from the example of the loving "work of recollecting the dead." The deliberation is describing *the loving work of remembering the dead*; it is not, as such, a model which could be uncritically imitated in loving the living, since the strict parallel for the former would be the loving work of *remembering* the living.

[6]See my "Equality, Impartiality, and Moral Blindness in Kierkegaard's *Works of Love*," *Journal of Religious Ethics* 25 (Spring 1997) for a detailed discussion of abstraction and concreteness in this ethic.

which ignore the concrete situation or response of the other. These support the kind of concrete attention to the other's distinctive character and needs which can flesh out the "tender" union of two people which, he says, constitutes neighbor love (WL, 58).

b. *Mutuality as the Implication of the Attack on Self-love.* Works of Love as a whole, it could be argued, constitutes a sustained critique of what Kierkegaard terms "self-love, selfishness, self-seeking, or whatever other names the unloving disposition has" (WL, 264). The deliberation entitled "You Shall Love *the Neighbor*" (II. B.) offers a concentrated version of the bitter attack on "self-love" in its many disguises. The model of nonmutuality, of radical asymmetry, which Adorno attributes to Kierkegaard would, however, come uncomfortably close to the "self-love" which Kierkegaard repeatedly attacks. That is, one-sided initiatives which ignore the other in his/her concrete actuality constitute a form of pernicious self-love. It is just such egocentric initiative that Kierkegaard seems to condemn when he urges us to take care "lest it become more important to you that you are looked upon as loving them than that you love them" (WL, 129).

c. *Mutuality of Claim and Need.* Finally, the first deliberation, "Love's Hidden Life and Its Recognizability by Its Fruits," makes a claim which surely bears strongly on any reading of what loving relationship means for Kierkegaard. He writes, in a passage which deserves close attention, that although words and gestures may deceive, still, to hold back genuine emotion and words "can be the unloving committing of a wrong, just like withholding from someone what you owe him" (WL, 12). He continues, "Your friend, your beloved, your child, or whoever is an object of your love has a claim upon an expression of it also in words if it actually moves you inwardly. The emotion is not your possession but belongs to the other; the expression is your debt to him, since in the emotion you indeed belong to him."

Similarly, Kierkegaard writes in several contexts about "need" in ways which imply mutuality. Though it may come as a surprise, he insists in the deliberation "*You* Shall Love the Neighbor" (II. C.) that "love in a human being is a need, is the expression of riches," and "the greater the need, the greater the riches" (WL, 67). When the need is for more than the "one single particular person," "the need is a wealth." In a striking passage, he repeats: "Love is a need, the deepest need, in the person in whom there is love for the neighbor; he does not need people just to have someone to love, but he needs to love people."

Kierkegaard's approval of the need to love people might seem to sidestep the issue of a *need to be loved*. But he affirms the latter as well in an earlier deliberation, entitled "You *Shall* Love" (II. A.). When he announces there that "a life without loving is not worth living" and claims that "the expression of the greatest riches is to have a need" (WL, 38), the need in question is a need to *be* loved. This is shown first in his approving reference to the "one who feels totally dependent, so that he would lose everything by losing the beloved." He insists, however, that one must distinguish clearly between such love and the need to "possess" the other: the need to "possess" is precisely a "corruptible," "earthly," and "temporal" dependence (WL, 38). He affirms the need *to be loved* most clearly when he condemns the kind of "proud independence that thinks it has no need to feel loved" but rather only "needs other people— not in order to be loved by them but in order to love them, in order to have someone to love" (WL, 39). His judgment is immediate and severe: "How false this independence is! It feels no *need* to be loved and yet *needs* someone to love; therefore it needs another person—in order to gratify its proud self-esteem." His important qualification that one can nonetheless "do without it [the love of the other], while it still continues to love" (WL, 38), expresses Kierkegaard's vehement insistence that what it means to need the other does not preclude a willingness to be hated by the other, should love for the other require it. In the end, the issue of "need" is complicated, because Kierkegaard wants, on the one hand, to appreciate the agent's needs, while he wants, on the other hand, to avoid approving of the kind of need which renders the other instrumental to the agent's satisfaction.

### 3. Justifications

We have now attended to some textual support which leads us to expect that Kierkegaard would not recommend we treat the living as if they were dead. Why then does he deliberately court the dangers of being misunderstood when he says that the loving work of remembering the dead is one from which we can "learn to love the living unselfishly, freely, faithfully"? What is at stake for him in stressing so vehemently in the ninth deliberation the relevance of the one-sided initiative in place when we remember the dead? In what follows I want to reconstruct what I take to be Kierkegaard's two rationales for emphasizing the ways in which a loving relation can be illuminated by focusing on one-sided initiative. I am arguing that both are rationales for such asymmetry precisely as a means of guaranteeing a genuinely loving relationship between two actual beings.

a. *Independence as Guarantee of Fidelity.* The work of remembering one who is dead is, he says, a work "of the most *faithful* love" (WL, 355). It is plausible to assume that the best "test" for faithfulness would be found in a situation in which is removed any possibility of response from the person to be loved which could help the lover to be faithful. Thus, it is useful to highlight such a situation in teaching us to. love the living faithfully. But it is not a model to emulate precisely because in loving the living we are loving one who, in contrast to the dead, *is* an "actual object." How then does the lack of responsiveness in the test case illuminate the way in which we are to love the living?

In his remarks on "change" at the end of the deliberation on the work of love in recollecting the dead, we begin to see what is at stake in Kierkegaard's discussion of independent one-sided initiative. Here we can see how the heuristic notion of lack of an *actual* other, a nonresponsive other, plays its role in an effort to guarantee faithfulness to a living, responsive person. He describes a dialogue in which one person accounts for his own change by blaming the other:

> "It was not I who changed; it was he who changed." Well. What happened then? Did you remain unchanged? "No, of course it was natural and a necessary consequence that I changed too." (WL, 355)

He comments: "At this point we shall not explain how meaningingless this presumably necessary consequence is, whereby it necessarily follows that I change *because* another changes" (WL, 355). The specific point he makes here is that in the case of a relation to one dead, one cannot excuse one's lack of faithfulness by blaming the other for changing—the dead one cannot change so one is unable to maintain the illusion that one's change was caused by another. In this way looking at the relation to the dead is a measuring rod for testing the genuineness of our love. The more general message is that it is meaningless to speak of love which goes up and down with variations or changes in the other. This is what is at stake in the emphasis on nonmutuality—in this sense love is nonmutual. Such faithfulness is not conditional on the love or faithfulness of the other in such a way that there is an automatic corresponding increase or decrease in the faithfulness of the lover.

This understanding of love's faithfulness, its abidingness, is remarkably similar to that found in the early chapter on "duty," "You SHALL Love" (II. A.). He writes there at length of the freedom of love in terms of its "blessed independence" (WL, 37). Kierkegaard emphasizes how duty can make one free: "Duty, however, makes a person dependent and at the same moment eternally independent" (WL, 38). Duty "makes love free in blessed independence" because "such a love stands and does not fall with the contingency of its object" (WL, 39). This is all that nonmutuality need mean.

He insists that "unchangingness is the true independence" in a dialogue reminiscent of the one I noted above:

> If when another person says, "I cannot love you any longer" one proudly answers, "Then I can also stop loving you"—is this independence? Alas, it is dependence, because whether he will continue to love or not depends upon whether the other will love. But the person who answers, "In that case I *shall* still continue to love you"—that person's love is made eternally free in blessed independence. (WL, 39-40)

"Love is not love which alters when it alteration finds"—what is ruled out is the conditionality of a response to the other which varies directly with variations in the beloved. Duty is what allows independence and guarantees fidelity precisely by *disregarding this kind of mutuality*. A mutuality which involves such dependence is rejected.

Such a cautious and prudential approach to love is also condemned in the deliberation, "Love is the Fulfilling of the Law" (III. A). His claim that the "merely human view of love can never go beyond mutuality: the lover is the beloved, and the beloved is the lover" (WL, 121) might seem to be a denigration of mutuality as such. The kind of mutuality he is rejecting is explained, however, a few pages later when he writes: "The world is no better than this; the highest that it acknowledges and loves is, at best, to love the good and humanity, yet in such a way that one also looks to one's own earthly advantage and that of a few others" (WL, 123). To love "in such a way that one also looks out for" is to love in a cautious, prudential way, embodying the kind of mutuality he regards as inadequate.

b. *Infinite Debt.* Another of Kierkegaard's characterizations of love which is relevant to our attempt to determine what role reciprocity or mutuality play in his understanding of relationship is found in the fifth deliberation of the first series, "Our Duty to Remain in Love's Debt to One Another." The leitmotif of that deliberation is that "Love's element is infinitude, inexhaustibility, immeasurability" (WL, 180). He expresses the counterintuitive notion of a duty to remain in debt as follows: "Therefore we can say that *this is the distinctive characteristic of love: that the one who loves by giving, infinitely, runs into infinite debt*" (WL, 177). He explains:

> Ordinarily we say that a person who is loved runs into debt by being loved. . . . And this is indeed true. But such talk is all too reminiscent of an actual bookkeeping arrangement: a debt is incurred and it must be paid off in installments. . . . We are not, however, speaking about that, about *running into debt by receiving.* No, the one who loves runs into debt. . . . To give a person one's love is, as has been said, the highest a person can give—and yet by giving it he runs into an infinite debt. . . . [I]t [love] is even ashamed to become conscious of its deed as a part payment on the debt. (WL, 176-77)

In other words, "love is perhaps more correctly described as an infinite debt; when a person is gripped by love, he feels that this is like being in an infinite debt" (WL, 176).

What is at stake in this radical notion of infinite debt? I suggest that we pay close attention to his examples, for they can usefully clarify the irrelevance of reciprocity to something "infinite." He illustrates as follows: "an actual bookkeeping arrangement is inconceivable, is the greatest abomination to love," and yet this is precisely what occurs when one gives to another with the unspoken addition "See, now I have paid my debt" (WL, 178). "The one who loves needs no calculation and therefore does not waste a moment calculating" (WL, 181); indeed, it is clear to Kierkegaard that "one who loves cannot calculate. . . . To calculate with an infinite quantity is impossible, because to calculate is to make finite." Thus, "for his own sake the lover wishes to remain in debt; he does not wish exemption from any sacrifice, far from it" (WL, 178). The suggestion that we are not always in debt—that is, that our debt to another is not infinite—implies that there is some way of paying off or at least lessening the debt. But love is not about calculation or bookkeeping exchange, nor debts which can be paid off or lessened.[7] "Exchange," he says repeatedly later in the text, is not a symbol of love.[8]

That what is rejected is the economic model of reciprocity as exchange has, in Kierkegaard's mind, already been clarified by the time he considers the asymmetry in love of the dead; this is, I think, obvious, not only when one looks closely at the deliberation on infinite debt to another, but also when one reconsiders the message of the second deliberation in the second series, the deliberation on how "Love Believes All Things—and Yet is Never Deceived." Referring to a "lower view of love, therefore a lower love that has no view of love in itself," he says this view "regards loving as a demand (reciprocal love is the demand) and being loved (reciprocal love) as an earthly good, as temporal—and yet, alas, as the highest bliss" (WL, 237). He continues:

> Yes, when this is the case, the deception is certainly able to play the master, just as in the commercial world. A person pays out money in order to purchase some convenience; he has paid out the money, but he did not get the convenience—well, then he has been duped. He makes a love deal; he barters his love, but he did not receive reciprocal love in exchange—well, then he has been deceived. (WL, 237)

He continues:

---

[7]See also WL, 132: "As soon as you believe that you have done enough in your love or have loved long enough and now must claim something from the other, you discover that your love is in the process of becoming a requirement, as if, however self-sacrificing and devoted your love is, there were still a boundary where it must show itself to be fundamentally a requirement."

[8]WL, 266, 267, 269.

the one who truly loves regards demanding reciprocal love simply as a defilement, a degradation, and regards loving without the reward of reciprocal love as the highest blessedness. . . . To love is indeed the highest good, but in that case only the love that demands reciprocal love, that is, the false love, can be deceived by remaining ignorant of the unworthiness of the object. (WL, 241)[9]

The Danish word translated as "reciprocity" in each of the above instances is *Gjenkjerlighed* or *repayment love*. The only reciprocity being condemned is, therefore, that of *repayment love*.

It is noteworthy that in the one instance in which we find a positive evaluation of what is translated in English as reciprocity, a different Danish word is in place. Kierkegaard concedes the importance of a kind of reciprocity when he writes:

> But to be and to remain in an infinite debt is an expression of the infinitude of love; thus by remaining in debt it remains in its element. There is a reciprocal relationship [*Vexel-Forhold*] here, but infinite from both sides. In the one case, it is the beloved, who in every manifestation of the lover's love lovingly apprehends the immeasurability; in the other, it is the lover, who feels the immeasurability because he acknowledges the debt to be infinite. . . . What marvelous like for like in this infinitude!" (WL, 181-82)

This "reciprocal relationship [*Vexel-Forhold*] . . . [is] infinite from both sides" (WL, 181). This "Vexel-Forhold," this "like for like," is recommended although reciprocity as repayment-love [*Gjenkjerlighed*], as an economic tit for tat, is ruled out.

In sum, we have seen Kierkegaard's general contrast between love of the dead and love of the living found in the controversial ninth deliberation itself, as well as the way in which he in many places uses a narrow technical meaning of reciprocity (as economic exchange, payment-love). Moreover, we have seen him hint at the "marvelous like for like," infinite from both sides, which does

---

[9]Note, however, the danger of arrogance incurred in such a view: "Just by unconditionally not requiring the slightest reciprocal love, the one who truly loves has taken an unassailable position; he can no more be deceived out of his love than a man can be tricked out of the money he tenders as a gift and gives to someone" (WL, 242).

enhance a loving relationship. Kierkegaard illuminates the discussion by proposing a number of important distinctions within the category of responsiveness. He distinguishes between two attitudes toward response *to* the other: the goal is to love the people we see, "just as they are," yet the other's change cannot carry in its train an automatic change in us. He distinguishes between two attitudes toward response *by* the other: the goal is to be independent enough (the relation asymmetrical enough) to preclude love's going up and down with variations in the other, yet dependent enough to admit our need of the other and the claim of the other on us for our expression of love. He distinguishes between two kinds of dependence: he rejects a certain kind of dependence on the other's response, yet allows that we genuinely need the other.

### 4. Objections Revisited

Let's reconsider now how the ninth deliberation looks against this background. What in Kierkegaard's characterizations of *the work of love in recollecting one who is dead* seems most problematical in terms of what we can learn from it about loving the living? The first—namely, that the expression of love in remembering the dead is *"a work of the most unselfish love"*—is not itself surprising. Loving the living unselfishly seems an appropriate thing to recommend. Kierkegaard's way of describing such unselfishness, however, may seem extreme: unselfishness lies in the way such recollecting excludes "every possibility of repayment," including "the repayment of reciprocal love" (WL, 349). A critic could argue that this entails that *any positive response* on the part of the other invalidates our love for him or her; this means that any hope for or expectation of the other's love is considered selfish and hence excluded from love. The work of remembering the dead could appropriately be described as one in which there is no possibility of any response—the dead one is not an "actual object." In this test situation love cannot be reciprocated, so we are clearly able to determine what is motivating our work of remembering the dead. But it is important to note that what we should learn from that about loving the living is couched in terms of "repayment," not "response." What Kierkegaard is excluding is "every possibility of repayment [*Gjengeld*]," including "the repayment of reciprocal love" [*Gjenkjerlighedens Gjengjeld*]. Here the notion of "repayment" can be read as characterizing a particular kind of attitude to the other—namely, one in which "repayment," even the repayment of "repayment love," is seen as the motive for my love, that on which I make my love conditional. But not every response from the other is ruled out as irrelevant because not every response is "repayment" in that technical sense. If every positive response were ruled out as vitiating love, we could not make any sense of his strong affirmation of our need for others, our need to be loved.

We saw earlier Kierkegaard's rationale for emphasizing the independence or freedom of love in order to guarantee fidelity. It seems unproblematic to claim as he does that love must be freely given, and that "the stronger the compelling, the less free is the love" (WL, 351). Kierkegaard's illustrations of such freedom raise questions, however, about whether love of the living is supposed to preclude any *influence* by the other, any response which could influence us. Probably the harshest claim in this chapter is the one implied in the suggestion that

> What can extort from one a work of love can be extremely varied and thus cannot be enumerated. The child cries, the pauper begs, the widow pesters, deference constrains, misery compels, etc. But any love in work that is extorted in this way is not free. (WL, 351)

A critic could object that Kierkegaard seems to rule out the relevance of anything *needed or demanded by* the other; this makes it impossible to consider that anything is ever lovingly given to an other, that the other can ever be lovingly responded to. It must be admitted that compulsion, for Kierkegaard, is found everywhere along a remarkably broad spectrum of conditions: the infant "that lies there in all its helplessness" illustrates helplessness "in its most compelling form" (WL, 351), and compulsion precludes love. Moreover, even "daily sight and habit" are "coercive" and make it difficult to determine whether love is free (WL, 354). It is easy enough to agree with him that compulsion precludes love since love cannot be extracted against our will. The question is whether influence of any kind counts as compulsion, whether anything which could claim our response or call forth a response from us militates against the freedom of our love.[10]

Any account of what Kierkegaard rules out of a genuine loving relation must take into account his recognition, noted above, of the legitimacy of the claim of the other on us. He cannot, therefore, be recommending a relation in which no response of the other can be responded to. His notion of "responsibility" for the other is not empty as long as it is seen in this broader context, which includes the example of the Good Samaritan as well as his acknowledgment of the less obvious claims of the other on us.

If the extreme scenario of unresponding love of the unresponsive other were the goal toward which we should strive, Kierkegaard's entire ethic of love would be put in jeopardy—as puritan, at best, and hateful, at worst. Extreme nonresponsiveness *of the other to us* would be the most effective way of guaranteeing nonresponsiveness *to the other* as a concrete being. Such irrelevance of the other evacuates all responsiveness, and hence responsibility, from the agent's side. If nothing about the other were allowed to affect our response to him/her, it would not be genuine response *to* the other. The heuristic excessiveness of Kierkegaard's tests, however, need not be read as if he were proposing that we treat the living as if they were dead. I suggest that we read his extreme sensitivity to what counts as "repayment" as well as his extreme sensitivity to what counts as "compulsion" in the light of what Kierkegaard repeatedly affirms about our need to love and be loved, the claim of the other on us, the activeness of compassion, and our responsibility to take care of others. The reminders I have collected together suggest that we can read Kierkegaard's claims in the deliberation on recollecting the dead as presenting a model of relationship (with the dead) which communicates the kind of mutuality we should avoid—namely, forms of bartering, tit for tat repayment, economic exchange, compelled response and self-

---

[10]This question recalls his earlier claim that genuine love is not determined by its object, as is the case in erotic love, for the object of genuine love "is without any of the more precise specifications of dissimilarity, which means that this love is recognizable only by love" (WL, 66).

serving response.[11] What we are being urged by Kierkegaard to practice is presented indirectly, in contrast to this *unloving kind of mutuality*. The ninth deliberation shows us *only* that some forms of mutuality are disguised versions of self-love. Warning against making our love conditional on an expected or actual response by the other does not amount to claiming that the response of the other is irrelevant. I hope to have shown that significant modes of mutuality remain in place in Kierkegaard's account of loving relationship—as we would expect, given his lovely reminder that "what you can have only for yourself alone is never the highest" (WL, 27).

---

[11]Adorno himself recognized that within the very doctrine he so harshly attacked for failing to appreciate reciprocity, a deep ethical insight was present: Kierkegaard describes, he says, "love absolutely void of any barter, of any 'requital,' and, therefore, the only unmutilated love permitted by our society" (WL, 427). Adorno's assessment is particularly interesting in its ambivalence, seeing not only "the worst" but also "the best" of Kierkegaard in his discussion of such love. I have suggested that the best becomes the worst when a test is taken for a condition to be achieved.

# 9

# Loving "No One," Loving Everyone: The Work of Love in Recollecting One Dead in Kierkegaard's Works of Love

Louise Carroll Keeley

Charges abound against Kierkegaard, both implied and direct, that his philosophy is essentially acosmic. On this view, Kierkegaard attends to the single individual alone before God and the inward maneuverings of that subject, beyond the reach of partnership, community, or world. Kierkegaard's dialectical probings, though deep, are circumscribed: only the individual, as if unattached, provides a fit subject for analysis.

Although most will agree that this is certainly not Kierkegaard's position in *Works of Love* where neighbor love is featured most prominently, one section gives pause. In the penultimate chapter of *Works of Love*, Kierkegaard praises a singularly disturbing kind of work—the work of love in recollecting one dead. It disturbs by finding in the *dead* the occasion for its work and turning there for edification. In so turning, it seems to lend credibility to the thesis that one's human associates—alive, worldly, and involved in communal ventures—are not the proper beneficiaries of one's works of love.

Apart from its seemingly problematic content, one must reckon with its placement within the volume as a whole. In positioning this work so prominently at the text's closing Kierkegaard implies some privileged status for it that begins to echo retroactively throughout the text. The oddity is so compelling that one might even anticipate the jest: Kierkegaard exceeds the Socratic requirement that philosophers be half-dead by demanding that his associates be completely so!

I will argue in what follows that the real significance of this chapter is frequently missed and that the objections posed against

Kierkegaard are typically rooted in a common misunderstanding. This misunderstanding, in its succinct expression, involves a simple omission: the category of the neighbor is left out. But the absence of the neighbor is a serious exclusion if it is here that Kierkegaard's most decisive expression of neighbor love is to be found.

I note, first, that this decisiveness emerges from within a context where the inexhaustibility of love's work is affirmed. Kierkegaard nowhere claims to provide a complete account of neighbor love but only to present it in its most vividly memorable form. Second, I will argue that this chapter's thesis is decisive in terms of the organizing plan of the entire book. It provides a *summary* of the whole, a *test* to assess the progress of the learner, and an incentive to undertake the *task* which remains with confidence in the sustaining love of God.

As summary, test, and task, "The Work of Love in Recollecting One Who is Dead" answers its chief critics: despite its apparent preoccupation with the dead, its real focus rests on life and love's essential requirements for the living.

### Being Dead Wrong: Misunderstanding Neighbor Love

The mistaken objections begin with a misunderstanding of what Kierkegaard means by neighbor love. Theodor Adorno's article "On Kierkegaard's Doctrine of Love," originally published in 1940, pays special attention to the chapter on recollection of the dead and typifies one misunderstanding of neighbor love. Adorno asserts that "perhaps one may most accurately summarize Kierkegaard's doctrine of love by saying that he demands that love behave towards all men as if they were dead."[1] His observation is succinct in its critical view: all, "as if . . . dead." But analysis reveals that not only is Adorno's interpretation of Kierkegaard mistaken—it is, if one will pardon the expression—*dead* wrong.

Adorno distinguishes between the pseudonymous philosophical writings and what he calls Kierkegaard's "religious sermons," which in this view include *Works of Love*, despite the fact that Kier-

---

[1]Theodor W. Adorno, "On Kierkegaard's Doctrine of Love," in *Modern Critical Views*, ed. Harold Bloom (New York: Chelsea House, 1989) 22-23.

kegaard claims to speak "without authority" (WL, 47).[2] According to him these "sermons" produce a "tiresome and unpleasant reading" that "affect a sort of preaching naiveté" which "threatens to slip into loquacious boredom at any moment."[3] They feature "the verbosity of an interminable monologue," complains Adorno: "If the philosophical writings wish to 'cheat' the reader into truth, the theological ones, in turn, wish to make it as difficult, as uninteresting, as insipid . . . as possible."[4]

But Adorno does appreciate the significance of Kierkegaard's thought in "The Work of Love in Recollecting One Who is Dead": "There is good reason to regard this speech as one of the most important pieces he ever wrote. I should like to emphasize . . . that the death-like aspect of Kierkegaard's love comprises the best and the worst of his philosophy."[5] He adds later: "The bad side is obvious: love for the dead is the one which most rigidly excludes the reciprocity of love that necessarily takes the beloved one as living himself."[6] At its worst, Adorno charges, this leads to a "reified and fetish" kind of love.[7] He chides Kierkegaard for the callousness with which he "sets out to expel nature with a pitchfork."[8] Still, Adorno does not minimize what can be praised: "But, at the same time, it is love absolutely void of any barter, of any 'requital', and, therefore, the only unmutilated love permitted by our society. The paradox that the only true love is love for the dead is the perfect expression of our situation."[9]

Adorno misunderstands Kierkegaard on a number of counts. The first misunderstanding is the most serious and far-reaching: according to Adorno, Kierkegaard "regards love as a matter of pure inwardness."[10] He goes further: "In love, the other person becomes a mere 'stumbling block' to subjective inwardness."[11] But

---

[2] Ibid., 19.
[3] Ibid., 20-21.
[4] Ibid., 21.
[5] Ibid., 23.
[6] Ibid., 32.
[7] Ibid., 32.
[8] Ibid., 23.
[9] Ibid., 32.
[10] Ibid., 21.
[11] Ibid., 21.

the achievement of a potentiated inwardness is not the goal of love
per se, as if the neighbor simply provided another occasion for
self-development. In *Works of Love*, every deepening of love's
subjective side entails a comparable movement in the outward
direction: "What love does, that it is; what it is, that it does—at
one and the same moment. At the same moment it goes out of
itself (the outward direction), it is in itself (the inward direction);
and at the same moment it is in itself, it goes out of itself in such
a way that this outward going and this returning, this returning
and this outward going are simultaneously one and the same"
(WL, 280). Love's being and love's doing are inseparably connected; a strengthening of love in one direction signals a commensu-
rate strengthening of love in the opposite direction.[12]

Second, Adorno protests that Christian love, in Kierkegaard's
view, is not sufficiently concrete; indeed, it is so abstract that it is
essentially "objectless" or, at any rate, "the object of love is, in a
way, irrelevant."[13] At this point Adorno's disagreement with Kierkegaard is most telling. For Kierkegaard, the object of love is the
neighbor (*Næste*) and "The word is obviously derived from 'nearest
[*Nærmeste*]'; thus the neighbor is the person who is nearer to you
than anyone else, yet not in the sense of preferential love" (WL,
21). Here Adorno is purposefully contrary: "The concept of the
neighbor which Kierkegaard makes the measure of love is, in a
certain sense, that of the farthest."[14] He argues further that "the
neighbor is reduced to the general principle of the otherness or of
the universal human" and that love for such a neighbor is callous,
unnatural, absurd, and decidedly dangerous.[15]

Before attending to the dangers that Adorno warns against, it
is important to make clear that this is not Kierkegaard's understanding of neighbor at all. "Love for the neighbor is spirit's love"
(WL, 56), according to Kierkegaard; the neighbor is not universal

---

[12]See Louise Carroll Keeley, "Subjectivity and World in *Works of Love*," in
*Foundations of Kierkegaard's Vision of Community: Religion, Ethics, and Politics in Kier-
kegaard*, ed. George B. Connell and C. Stephen Evans (Atlantic Highlands NJ:
Humanities Press, 1992) 96-108.

[13]Adorno, "On Kierkegaard's Doctrine of Love," 21.

[14]Ibid., 22.

[15]Ibid., 25.

humanity in the abstract, but "the other you" (WL, 53). But "the other you" is not in the least abstract: every concrete, existing individuality qualifies. In Kierkegaard's text the neighbor is insistently concrete: "To be sure, 'neighbor' in itself is a multiplicity, since 'the neighbor' means 'all people,' and yet in another sense one person is enough" (WL, 21).

Whereas erotic love designates its object as body-psyche-spirit and the friend is configured as merely psyche-spirit, the neighbor's status as pure spirit is most simple and inclusive of all. But Adorno repeatedly confuses these categories. In charging Kierkegaard with neglecting the reciprocity of love, Adorno has the *beloved* in mind, a category of preferential love. Preferential love's beloved is not the neighbor—or, more accurately, he too is the neighbor, as *all* are, but the neighbor need not be the beloved. The neighbor need not, and often does not reciprocate.

But Kierkegaard does not rescind the imperative to love one's neighbor because the neighbor fails to respond in kind. Quite the opposite: if anything, the requirement is renewed, with increased vigor and urgency. When Adorno goes on to criticize Kierkegaard for his refusal to employ "any real, nonsymbolical, nonmetaphorical case of human love in order to apply his doctrine to it" the consistency of his confusion becomes apparent.[16] It is Kierkegaard's relationship to Regina that Adorno disqualifies by virtue of its metaphorical and poetic quality.[17]

Adorno denounces Kierkegaard for what he calls "Kierkegaard's reckless spiritualization of love."[18] This is the core of his social critique: fueled by a "spiteful orthodoxy," *Works of Love* neglects "social insight."[19] Indeed, Adorno charges that it promotes the maintenance of the status quo, conformism, inequality, mis-

---

[16]Ibid., 24.

[17]But surely this is nonsense, on two counts. First, their relationship is not merely metaphorical; to claim that it is requires that existence be factored out. Second, Kierkegaard's relationship to Regina is an example of preferential rather than neighbor love. Adorno's selection of this relationship as an example of a failed case at hand underscores his own failure to discriminate neighbor adequately. Nor does Kierkegaard's summons to love the neighbor entail the expulsion of nature, as Adorno suggests, but rather openness to grace.

[18]Adorno, "On Kierkegaard's Doctrine of Love," 23.

[19]Ibid., 27.

anthropy, and domination. His succinct judgment of Kierkegaard's doctrine of love? "Its content is oppression."[20]

This is a stunning charge but it is fundamentally wrong. It assumes, as noted earlier, the thoroughgoing inwardness of Kierkegaard's love, bereft of any outgoing principle. But Kierkegaard's focus is on *works* of love. Although it is true that these works need not achieve a worldly result in order to be a work of love (as mercifulness, even when impotent, attests), their direction is outgoing. This is true even in the work of love in recollecting one dead, which might seem to be destined to accomplish nothing worldly at all. But even here, in the most unlikely of works, the beneficiaries are one's living contemporaries.

The social may be the highest reality for Adorno, but it is not for Kierkegaard. It does not follow from this that Kierkegaard is not interested in the social at all. But it is true that Kierkegaard does not believe that the achievement of worldly equality, even if possible, would constitute the highest task or realize our highest humanity. Instead, Kierkegaard emphasizes the equality of the eternal and the human being's spiritual reality. Because the spiritual has eternal decisiveness whereas the social claims only a temporal one, Kierkegaard champions spiritual renewal not social reform.

Adorno's neglect of the neighbor issues from his Marxism. The strained isolationist piety of Perry D. LeFevre—an "Adorno for the pious"[21]—produces a similar neglect of the neighbor in his writings. LeFevre regards social dependencies of any sort as impediments to the deepening of one's prayer life, and he recommends solitude and the detachment from social ties as the proper course for those who take their relationship with God seriously. In LeFevre's view, "prayer is a relation which isolates from others" such that "God can become the individual's unique confidante . . . only in solitude."[22] But where does this leave the neighbor, except excluded? The Good Samaritan is effectively edged out.

---

[20]Ibid., 28.

[21]The characterization is from Robert L. Perkins in a private communication.

[22]Perry D. LeFevre, *The Prayers of Kierkegaard* (Chicago: University of Chicago Press, 1956) 207.

*Beyond Solitude: The Inexhaustibility of Love's Works*

Kierkegaard not only multiplies the opportunities for the Good Samaritan to act, he infinitizes them. Every occasion is a suitable occasion to love. But Kierkegaard does not profess to account for every work of love—or, for that matter, for *any* work—in all of its depth. In his brief Preface to the lengthy deliberations of *Works of Love*, Kierkegaard cautions the reader to refrain from assuming that any particular work of love has been adequately described, let alone the totality of love's works:

> They are *Christian deliberations*, therefore not about *love* but about *works of love*.
> They are about *works of love*, not as if hereby all its works were now added up and described, oh, far from it. . . . Something that in its total richness is *essentially* inexhaustible is also in its smallest work *essentially* indescribable just because essentially it is totally present everywhere and *essentially* cannot be described. (WL, 3)

These cautionary observations concerning the inexhaustibility of love's works and the resistance to description of each single work of love are reminders that the deliberations which follow are not complete. Each mark points to a prior and a subsequent depth which the analysis must affirm but cannot exhaust. In his book on Kierkegaard's *Works of Love*—published in memoriam as "a work of love . . . in remembering him," Paul Müller analyzes the difficulty:

> That love's works in their innermost sense are indescribable is implied by two closely connected considerations. The first is that it is in principle impossible to enumerate all the works which belong to love; because of its utter richness love is essentially inexhaustible. "Christian love is eternal," and inexhaustibility is precisely a characteristic of eternity. The second consideration, which follows from the first, is that it is in principle impossible to describe even a single one of love's works exhaustively once and for all. Love's essence, which is inexhaustible, eternal, and rich is completely and fully posited in each of love's

works. Precisely in virtue of its infinity, love itself remains hidden in its finite expressions.[23]

But if Kierkegaard is quite explicit in his denial that love's works can be totalled up and reckoned, what sense does it make to call one work of love more decisive than another? Clearly, any presumed decisiveness cannot be attributed to its being more readily fathomed. In its ground, too, it must be infinite. But in the work under consideration, love's requirement is posed with the severe simplicity of love itself: to love all alike, unselfishly, freely, faithfully. The work of love in recollecting one dead functions as a paradigm for love's intended outcome: spare in its teachings, uncompromising in its demands, but decisive in its insistence on both.

The book itself functions as a personal "recollection" for Kierkegaard. In their historical introduction to their translation of *Works of Love*, Howard and Edna Hong contend that Kierkegaard "certainly" intended "The Work of Love in Recollecting One Who is Dead" to be "an act of love in filial piety" toward his parents (WL, xiv).[24] If he recollects them in love in and through the writing of this chapter, Kierkegaard performs the work of love he writes about (though since inwardness is the domain for such recollecting, our preliminary "if" applies). But this work is not merely a private memorial to Kierkegaard's parents. Nor can it end with

---

[23]Paul Müller, *Kierkegaard's "Works of Love": Christian Ethics and the Maieutic Ideal*, trans. and ed. by C. Stephen Evans and Jan Evans (Copenhagen: C. A. Reitzel, 1993) 6-7.

[24]It has often been observed that Kierkegaard's deep respect for paternal love (evidenced especially in his relationship with his own father) has no exact equivalent in his writing with respect to maternal love. Though Hong and Hong claim that *Works of Love* is intended as a loving recollection of both parents, references to his mother are, to the best of my knowledge, decidedly absent from his authorship. Moreover, there is no mention whatsoever of his mother's death in the journal entries of 1834, the year Ane Sørensdatter Lund died. The editors of Kierkegaard's *Journals and Papers* take note of this omission but add that "H. L. Martensen states that the young student took his mother's death very hard" and that "Martensen's mother said she had never seen a person so grieved over a death" (JP, 5:472-73n.109). In the *Journals and Papers* there is a separate listing for "Father (S.K.)" plus numerous additional references for a total of more than seventy entries.

them and remain love: it requires something further. In Kierkegaard's view, there is plentiful grace to be found at the grave but
it is a grace which must eventually turn back to the living and find
in them its highest expression. In loving recollection of the dead,
the pull of contemporaneity's tether is not eased but rather
tightened and strained:

> I do not know to whom I am speaking about this, whether
> anyone is concerned about such things; but this I know, that such
> people have lived. . . . And for them I can write, comforting
> myself with the beautiful words: "Write!" "For whom?" "For the
> dead, for those whom you have loved in some past"—and in
> loving them I shall indeed also meet the dearest among the
> contemporaries. (WL, 362)

In "The Work of Love in Recollecting One Who is Dead," the
summary, the test, and the task are laid out and the reader is
invited to study, to learn, and to act. But it is only in the situation
of contemporaneity that the invitation can be answered at all.

### "Recollecting One Who Is Dead" as Summary of Works of Love: Structure, Method, and Content

The penultimate chapter of Works of Love functions as a
summary in three ways—in its structure, its method, and in its
thematic content.

First, in the context of the book's *structure* as a whole, it offers
a summary perspective. This chapter abbreviates what Kierkegaard's other chapters elongate but it does so with fidelity to that
longer account. The sheer lengthiness of the book documents the
difficulties of love's way, but once one has resolved upon love's
course, this chapter summarizes *how*: unselfishly, freely, faithfully.

Second, the *method* which Kierkegaard both practices and urges
is *recollection*, a kind of methodological summary where ideality
itself is retrieved. In this respect it differs essentially from memory,
which makes no claim to abbreviate at all, but instead prefers to
accumulate details.

The thematic *content* of this chapter acts as a summary in a
third and final way. Although death and the "no one" who is
deceased are its focus, the chapter examines them in such a way
as to highlight life and the neighbor. Life achieves its most brief

expression in death, and neighbor finds in "no one" its own most abbreviated account. How structure, method, and content all contribute to the chapter's status as summary will be examined by considering each aspect in turn.

*Structure as Summary.* Kierkegaard observes in the very first words of the chapter that "if in one way or another a person is afraid of being unable to maintain an overview of something that is multifarious and prolix, he tries to make or acquire a brief summary of the whole for the sake of a full view" (WL, 345). Although the context makes clear that Kierkegaard has death in mind as "the briefest summary" (WL, 345) of all, his words carry the weight of an announcement. Surely the deliberations which preceded this one might qualify as "multifarious and prolix" in detail, and lengthy in development. Might not this chapter punctuate those long deliberations by providing a manageable summary of the whole?

The evidence is not conclusive, but it is suggestive. What is certain is that what Kierkegaard teaches in this chapter is unselfish, free, and faithful love. Just as all of the commandments can be summed up in two—to love God and to love one's neighbor—so too might Kierkegaard's lengthy enumerations of love's works find their apt summation in such a love. In what follows it will be shown that these three are the essential criteria for determining "what love really is" and their presence or absence constitute *Works of Love's* test. If so, whoever masters these three (though who can so claim?) can expect to have competency in the others, too.[25]

*Method as Summary: Recollection.* The method which Kierkegaard advises to achieve these results is recollection—itself another summary. To understand why Kierkegaard advocates the work of love in recollecting one dead, and why recollection is itself a kind

---

[25]But it should be noted that Kierkegaard provides this summary in a context where the inexhaustibility of love's works has already been decisively affirmed. Thus it is a summary that is preceded by a concession that its undertaking can never entirely succeed. Yet this is precisely the point: if the summary could provide a full accounting it could do so only by a radical finitizing of love in its every expression. But this is completely contrary to Kierkegaard's deeply held conviction that love is always grounded in the infinitely bountiful love of God.

of summary, requires a differentiation between recollection and memory as Kierkegaard understands them. He highlights these differences most sharply in *Stages on Life's Way*.

Kierkegaard notes three major differences. First, recollection seeks to ascertain what is essential to any past—not as a mere situation with carefully crafted edges, but in terms of an overall ideality: "Recollection wants to maintain for a person the eternal continuity in life and assure him that his earthly existence remains *uno tenore* (uninterrupted), one breath, and expressible in one breath" (SLW, 10). Because recollection recollects what is eternal, it is both "strenuous and conscientious in a way completely different from indiscriminate memory" (SLW, 10), which is always tied to temporality and its ledger. Recollection provides an "impression of the whole" whereas memory "has to do with the concrete, isolated fact, an individual event"; hence "memory remembers sporadically and lets forgetting come in between the particulars" whereas "recollection recollects the continuity in the individual's life."[26] Memory's details are accidental and inessential: any scrap will suffice. As the mound of detail mounts, it can discourage genuine recollection, which seeks to grasp the meaning of the whole.[27] The whole is not found beneath the load of randomly

---

[26]See K. Nordentoft, "Recollection" in *Bibliotheca Kierkegaardiana: Kierkegaard and Human Values*, vol. 7, ed. Niels Thulstrup and Marie Mikulová Thulstrup (Copenhagen: C. A. Reitzels Boghandel, 1980) 76-78.

[27]Recollection as philosophical method is first demonstrated by Plato in the *Meno* and later employed to good effect in the *Symposium* where *eros* is the topic under discussion. Kierkegaard does not use the term with the same precision that Plato did. In Plato's understanding, truth is immanent: the seeker strives to overcome forgetfulness in order to make explicit what one always already knows. Kierkegaard makes it clear—especially in *Philosophical Fragments*—that he does not subscribe to this doctrine of recollection: for Kierkegaard, the truth is eternal and transcendent, and the path to truth, paradoxically, goes through the Teacher. But both Plato and Kierkegaard find in recollection a sort of prompting toward ideality and both confound that process by beginning with an overwhelming mass of detail. The *Symposium* begins with a complicated system of narration: Apollodorus, who got his information from Aristodemus (who did not claim to reproduce the speeches verbatim) now tells an unnamed friend what two days ago he told to Glaucon. Since the banquet took place when Apollodorus was still "in the nursery" (*Symposium* 173.a), he cannot claim direct knowledge of these events, but he does claim that "something like this" (*Symposium* 174.a) happened

assembled memories or even in the contours of the ever-accumu-
lating pile. The essential ideality which recollection strains to grasp
is so distinct from the accumulation of remembered details that it
must forego memory's project in order to undertake its own. Kierkegaard does not advise us to remember the dead as one does
when one fixes upon mere details or facts. Instead, recollection
focuses on the eternal, the essential, its continuity, and its ideality.
In this respect it achieves the wholeness of a summary by expressing what is essential.

The second point of difference between the two is this: memory
operates in the context of immediacy whereas recollection requires

---

many years earlier. If one asks why the narrative structure is so complex, the
answer seems to be that it evokes recollection. By virtue of this intentional dis-
tancing, the whole project is cloaked in a certain ideality. The superfluous details
which memory surrenders contribute to but are distinct from the more ideal
climate which recollection seeks to realize. To do this it must backtrack through
the sludge of detail but it does so for the sake of apprehending something deeper
and more essential. One must trudge backwards beneath the heap of actuality,
time, and ever new impressions which work to erase recollection in order to discover what all possess in common (WL, 354).

Kierkegaard uses a similar strategy in *Stages On Life's Way*. Its subtitle
announces that these are "Studies by Various Persons," thereby suggesting that
some confusion might be likely. Hilarius Bookbinder compiles, forwards to the
press, and publishes the papers of a certain literatus that he finds in his
possession, at the urging of a philosophy student in his employ. These papers
turn out to consist of several books by several authors. The first concerns us especially. "In Vino Veritas," related by William Afham, is billed as "A Recollection."
In recollecting the structure of the *Symposium*, it features five preliminary
speeches by Johannes the Seducer, Victor Eremita, Constantine Constantius, the
young man, and the fashion designer. "But who, then, am I?" we hear at the end
of the section, a question posed by an anonymous thief who steals papers from
Victor Eremita who in turn had stolen them from Judge William (SLW, 86). This
plurality of speakers and personae seems intentionally bewildering unless it is designed to prompt recollection by urging a retreat from this cacophony of voices.
It is significant that Hilarius Bookbinder begins his account by counseling that
"there ought to be honesty in everything" (SLW, 3) whereas in William Afham's
preface to "In Vino Veritas," we are reminded that it is "a splendid occupation
to prepare a secret for oneself" (SLW, 9). The secret is communicated within the
domain of truth: it is a secret veritas. And in the context of *Stages on Life's Way*,
it is recollection which yields up the secret. See Plato, *The Collected Dialogues of
Plato*, ed. Edith Hamilton and Huntington Cairns (Princeton NJ: Princeton
University Press, 1961).

reflection. The opening words of *Works of Love* attest to the nature of the undertaking and the requirement to do likewise: "These Christian deliberations, which are the fruit of much deliberation, will be understood slowly but then also easily" (WL, 3). What is remembered can just as easily be forgotten, but either way it transpires in the present tense. Memory's bookkeeping is exact and unambiguous: either remembered or forgotten, but not in both columns at once, and always computed in immediacy. By contrast, recollection is a difficult art: "To conjure up the past for oneself is not as difficult as to conjure away the present for the sake of recollection. This is the essential art of recollection and is reflection to the second power" (SLW, 13). In "The Work of Love in Recollecting One Who is Dead," reflection weans one (for a time!) from absorption in one's own present and gives significance to someone else's status as eternal. But this is only the beginning. Face to face with another's death, one soon inquires about oneself. The one dead functions as an occasion for the other to reflect upon his own eternal validity. Recollection foreshortens everything; reflection puts one in mind of one's *own* prospects and task. Müller makes the point succinctly: "The reflection over remembering one dead is especially important for Kierkegaard because it is by this remembrance that the individual is brought to the place where he is completely alone with himself in a maieutic situation where no self deception is possible, and where the rememberer is therefore unconditionally forced to make the necessary admissions which exclusively concern himself."[28] Recollection works against the tendency toward disparateness and division; it unifies by accenting the essential.

Finally, camaraderie in memory aids in the accumulation of detail whereas "a fellowship of recollection does not exist" (SLW, 14). The plurality of voices in Plato's *Symposium*, for example, do not recollect together what love is. Instead, through their instrumentality, the reader's understanding is elicited or drawn forth, maieutically assisted by them. If one's memory tires or fails someone else might reinvigorate it by contributing his memories to the pool of remembered events. One memory—even if it is not

---

[28]Müller, *Kierkegaard's "Works of Love,"* 52-53.

one's own—might occasion another and that memory in turn might evoke a subsequent one. But partnership in recollection— where the contributions of both partners to the undertaking are equal—cannot exist.

Instead, one can be assisted in the work of recollection by someone who acts maieutically, as Socrates does for the slave boy in the *Meno*. But this maieutic intervention can work only because it is assumed that the slave is already in possession of these truths and consequently needs only to make that possession explicit. The assistant evokes, incites, prompts, and entices forth what he understands to be already laid down. In "The Work of Love In Recollecting One Who is Dead" the deceased "acts" as the maieutic assistant in occasioning recollection of his—and one's own—eternal significance. In recollection, as in most summaries, nothing extraneous is welcome.

But something is required in advance. Paul Müller reminds us that *Works of Love* presupposes that a similar ground in *love* has already been laid down by God:

> God has placed love in man. Love is therefore not something the person himself produces out of nothing, neither by himself nor with others; rather it must be assumed as being "fundamental" (*i Grunden*). Therefore, one person can really only bring to fruition love in another, that is to say, maieutically entice it forth or foster it. Love's presence as God-given dowry is itself the fundamental thought in Kierkegaard's anthropology.[29]

If Müller is correct, one can neither plant nor eradicate love as the foundation in another: to love another person is to help that person love God, to be loved by another person is to be helped to love God, but in neither case does love originate in the self (WL, 107).

*Content as Summary.* In "The Work of Love in Recollecting One Who Is Dead," Kierkegaard's themes are death and the deceased "no one." Just as the structure of the chapter provides an apt summation of the book's teaching and recollection proves a suitable method to achieve a "brief summary" of the essential

---

[29]Ibid., 14.

view, so too do these themes point to and summarize something beyond themselves.

In Kierkegaard's view, "death is the briefest summary of life, or life traced back to its briefest form" (WL, 345). Death "abbreviates the prolixity of all the complicated relationships" (WL, 346) by erasing the comparisons which dissimilarities evoke. Death confers an equivalence upon all by declaring that all alike must die. "If, then, you are bewildered as you consider the multiple paths of life, then go out to the dead, 'where all paths meet'—then a full view is easy" (WL, 345).

Moreover, recollection as method and death as its occasioning thought work in tandem throughout the chapter. Death itself is eminently suitable to evoke recollection. Death's presence foreshortens recollection's movement. Death jolts recollection forth, casting the essential into the foreground. In doing so it reveals that the mounds of personal detail which had preoccupied memory or occasioned forgetfulness are inessential. Death facilitates recollection by giving a vividness to the eternal which the details of life tend to obfuscate. In so doing death replicates what it asks of recollection—*it gives the essential the prominence of the essential, the eternal the status of the eternal.* Though anything might prompt recollection, death has a unique power to do so.

Kierkegaard's designation of the dead one as "no one" also serves to provides a summary: "when a person relates himself to one who is dead, there is only one in this relationship, inasmuch as one who is dead is no actuality; no one, no one can make himself *no one* as well as one who is dead, because he is *no one*" (WL, 347). Contrary to ordinary expectation, this "no one" enables us to gain some insight into what Kierkegaard means in *Works of Love* by neighbor.

How can this be so? The neighbor, according to Kierkegaard, is unmistakable: "Christianity has made it eternally impossible to mistake him . . . since the neighbor, to be sure, is *all people*" (WL, 51-52; emphasis added). But if the dead one is *no one* and the neighbor includes *all*, how can any linkage be established between them?

Both the *no one* who has died and the neighbor's *"other you"* (WL, 53) are both designated under the aspect of *eternal equality*. In death, what is distinctive about a person—on the basis of which one had preferred them to someone else—has been stripped away and discarded: before God, all are eternally equal in their essential humanity. The earthly neighbor is positioned similarly: no distinguishing characteristics matter in the determination of who counts as one's neighbor precisely because everyone already counts—not by virtue of what distinguishes them, but by virtue of what they have in common.

In "The Work of Love in Recollecting One Who is Dead" who is the "one dead"? Kierkegaard answers "no one". For most mourners, this is an exceedingly curious and even cruel observation: the one they are grieving is very decisively not "no one"; he is instead a very definite *this one and no other*. Though all have death in common, each death is a particular event, undergone by one alone. Similarly, it seems to the mourner that death strikes with particular force when *this one who is beloved* is taken. It seems this way because the dead one *is* beloved.

In the context of *Works of Love*, bereavement becomes a predicament. One does not ordinarily recollect the one dead whom one does not know.[30] If one does, it is usually because they represent some ideal one upholds or shares—not because one has an affective relationship toward the person in whom the ideal had been incarnated. Accordingly, recollection in this context might seem more formal and ceremonial than personal: one respects the ideal and hence mourns the passing of the person who embodied it, either inwardly or by designation. In the former case one might mourn the passing of a much admired humanitarian; in the latter case, one might pay one's respects at the tomb of the unknown soldier.

More typically, the loved one recollected is one who in life had been loved with a preferential love: parent, spouse, child, sibling, friend—these are the persons who come to mind. But preferential love is not Kierkegaard's focus in *Works of Love*. Quite the opposite: his theme is Christian love of the neighbor, which shows no partiality either by preference or aversion. How, then, can "The Work of Love in Recollecting One Who is Dead" be properly

---

[30]I have said that one does not ordinarily do this, but I think there is at least one prominent exception to this rule that makes a decisive claim upon us, not only as individuals but also in terms of a community of memory. This claim will be addressed later.

designated as an act of neighbor-love, let alone as a kind of summary of the whole?[31]

In this work of recollecting, the one for whom one had a preference is now designated more fundamentally under the aspect of the equality of the eternal. But this is the category of the neighbor. Kierkegaard has insisted throughout *Works of Love* that those for whom we have a partiality must never be excluded from the requirement to love all alike as neighbors. In this context of recollecting one dead, the beloved supplies the most vivid example to illustrate how this is done.[32] More exactly, Kierkegaard shows

---

[31]Müller takes the position that simply being dead is the single criterion that qualifies one ("no one"?) for being lovingly recollected by another, and of course this is certainly true. For Müller, the identity of the dead person is indifferent: "he is purely and simply one who is dead—and that is sufficient, when the remembrance of him is not identical with simply deepening oneself in the past with its reminders, but is, on the contrary, to be used for guidance in one's relations with those still living" (Müller, *Kierkegaard's "Works of Love,"* 52). Since Kierkegaard is "indifferent" to who the dead person is, and one dead person is as qualified as another, it follows that one who had been beloved as lover or friend would qualify equally well—though Müller might think that the work of recollection here is more arduous and prone to relapse into memory than in other cases. I have argued, on the other hand, that, as a matter of fact, it is the beloved who is recollected most frequently, but that to the degree that one achieves recollection in the Kierkegaardian sense the beloved is necessarily recollected under the category of eternity, as neighbor. In this sense, as in Müller's, everyone qualifies and no one comes better equipped than anyone else.

[32]Daniel Day Williams offers the interesting observation—in a context partially critical of Kierkegaard—that "affection may be the first school of *agape*." He writes of Kierkegaard: "what he fails to see clearly is that earthly loves may themselves come into the service of God." Williams sees this relation as operative in two directions. Impoverished familial love can be the source of a failure to love one's neighbor; conversely, family love must be revitalized by an ongoing attention to one's neighbor: "Failure to love the neighbor may be born in the failure of love in the family. If Kierkegaard sees this he does not make it a part of his reconciliation of *agape* and the earthly loves. The point may be put in another way. The sexual relationship and the family loves can be blocked and corroded when there is no outgoing love toward the neighbor. . . . *It is not only self-abnegation but also fulfillment which the outgoing love of agape offers to love as affection, and affection may be the first school of agape*" (emphasis added). In our present context, the dying of one beloved, for whom one had a special affection, can occasion a deepened love of the neighbor since one can see vividly how death makes neighbors of everyone by removing finite distinctions and allowing the equality of the eternal to be the

how even the most preferential kinds of love must be recast within the light of eternity. This transition from preferential love to unconditional, Christian love represents an advance but it is progress with a cost: although the dissimilarity (which preference relies upon) is a disguise, "in the end death must use force to tear it from him" in order to reveal the similarity "which is common to all, the eternal resemblance, the likeness" (WL, 88). The distinctions of the temporal are equalized in the eternal; reciprocity gives way to renunciation; self-love is replaced by self-sacrifice.[33] In this way the love of no one shows how love is completely dependent upon the lover, not the object of love. Thus it previews the unconditional (and nonpreferential) love of God for us, which we too should strive to express: "When you love the neighbor, then you are like God. Therefore go and do likewise" (WL, 63).

Death extracts what most are reluctant to give: the beloved acquires the new designation "no one". But is this "no one," perhaps, the ultimate expression for nonpreferential love? When all earthly distinctions are erased and the silence of eternity is imposed, all alike are "no one". But the "no one" of death puts one in mind of one's neighbor: "Death . . . abolishes all dissimilarities, but preference is always related to dissimilarities; yet the way to life and to the eternal goes through death and through the abolition of dissimilarities—therefore only love for the neighbor truly leads to life" (WL, 62). The neighbor is a category for which everyone qualifies and from which no one is excluded:

---

focus. Similarly, the work of love in recollecting one dead, understood as an act of neighbor-love, ought to revitalize and give new tonality to one's preferential loves. See Daniel Day Williams, *The Spirit and the Forms of Love* (New York: University Press of America, 1981) 200-201.

[33]See Arnold B. Come, *Kierkegaard as Humanist: Discovering My Self* (Montreal: McGill-Queen's University Press, 1995) 324-97, and David Gouwens, *Kierkegaard as Religious Thinker* (Cambridge: Cambridge University Press, 1996) 190-208. Müller observes that Kierkegaard's major concern is "to effect a radical humanizing of love. . . . Kierkegaard therefore does not really discuss human love versus Christian love, which really would be unnatural in the deepest sense. On the contrary, he has left this debate behind him, simply because love, when its task is being realized in this life on earth, must show forth the genuinely human *and* display the condition for its realization. Seen Christianly, this condition is salvation and reconciliation in Christ." See Müller, *Kierkegaard's "Works of Love,"* 11.

With the destruction of partiality as the law for love the neighbor is purely spiritually determined; everyone is the neighbor. And furthermore, the neighbor concept is a spiritual determinant of every person; by it the fundamental equality among all persons which is the condition for neighbor love is posited. "The neighbor is every person; for on the basis of distinctions he is not your neighbor, nor on the basis of likeness to you as being different from other people. He is your neighbor on the basis of equality with you before God; but this equality absolutely every person has, and he has it absolutely."[34]

Hence love of the neighbor means eternal equality in loving and the banishment of all preference or inclination. No special authentication is needed: comparisons, preferences, aversions, partialities, attractiveness—all are irrelevant in determining who one's neighbor is. Death effects a similar result: it, too, confers an equivalence upon all so that the equality within the common situation is affirmed. Early on in *Works of Love*, Kierkegaard had cautioned the reader to remember that "it is very important for a person in all his relationships, and with regard to every task, that undivided attention be concentrated immediately upon the essential and the decisive" (WL, 95). In "The Work of Love in Recollecting One Who Is Dead," this is exactly where one's attention is directed.

In his pseudonymous literature Kierkegaard had frequently suggested that some forms of communication require the suppression of oneself—a sort of becoming "no one"—so as to emancipate the recipient of the communication. In the present context, Kierkegaard reminds us of something similar: "And if, in conversation with someone, you understand the art of making yourself *no one*, you get to know best what resides in this person" (WL, 347). Certainly, Kierkegaard's own mastery of this art cannot be questioned.[35] Even in the context of "The Work of Love in Praising

---

[34]Müller, *Kierkegaard's "Works of Love,"* 25.

[35]Müller observes that "the nature of the subject which is being communicated ought to determine the communication's form and method. Now Kierkegaard does not explicitly touch on the problems concerning the dialectic of communication here in *Works of Love*, nevertheless, the issue can be glimpsed in a couple of places. . . . The overriding thought in both of them is that the method of communication in ethics must build on the idea implicit in the "maieutical method," which is that the way for an author to stimulate self-actualization is to

Love"—a work for which Kierkegaard's writing of *Works of Love* would seem to qualify him—he takes pains to suppress himself. This reiterates an authorial decision evident throughout *Works of Love* to communicate love's works by suppressing the self with its propensity to interrupt and to disturb. But in our present context it is the dead who are designated as "no one": "no one can make himself *no one* as well as one who is dead, because he is *no one*" (WL, 347). In the presence of the "no one" of death—the one, that is, who is thoroughly suppressed—might not the living one be essentially disclosed? Just as one can suppress oneself outwardly and make oneself into nothing in one's relationship to others, so in death the other is already "suppressed" and this provides an occasion to learn about oneself and one's relationship to God: "The one who is living is disclosed; here he must show himself exactly as he is, because one who is dead . . . is no actual object; he is only the occasion that continually discloses what resides in the one living" (WL, 347). Although the disclosure is never complete until one earns death's designation "no one," Kierkegaard proposes a test for the one still living to measure love's degree and kind.

### "Recollecting One Who Is Dead" as Test: Unselfish, Free, and Faithful Love

In addition to functioning as a summary of *Works of Love* this chapter also serves as a *test*:[36] "in writing about love, how then could I leave unused this occasion to make a test of what love really is? Truly, if you want to ascertain what love there is in you or in another person, then pay attention to how he relates himself to one who is dead" (WL, 346-47). Appropriately, it comes at the end of the volume where one's first period of instruction seems over and one's lessons might be expected to take hold. But this test will not promote self-congratulation or easy confidence. The examined undertakes a self-assessment where the criteria are infinite and can never be completely met: one fails. The test is included for the sake of a task which directs one to one's living

---

withdraw from the scene." See Müller, *Kierkegaard's "Works of Love,"* 3-4.

[36]"The main question in the examination existence gives to men is this: Do you have love? We shall now proceed to find out, says Christianity." JP, 3:2449.

contemporaries and the manifold opportunities for works of love which they provide. "It has always been very important to those who truly think about human life to test again and again, with the help of the brief summary, what they have understood about life" (WL, 345). Müller's formulation seems intentionally provocative in its dismissal of living contemporaries, but he does so in order to accent the test's effectiveness as a measure: "If the individual wants to test love's actual implications, and get clear about the extent to which love actually dwells in him, he does not need his living contemporaries. To the contrary, his relationship to someone dead provides a more accurate measuring rod."[37]

Even though death provides a strong incentive for self-deception[38], this work of love provides a powerful incentive against it. The disclosure of the self effected by the recollection of one dead is the test's work. When the test is undertaken with the intention of disclosing the self it requires an examination of conscience. But to the extent that this disclosure is constantly deepened and never finalized, one's conscience must be examined continually, with increasing resolve. In Kierkegaard's view, the highlighting of our sins and failures ought to lead us to repentance, but it also situates us to learn to love the living. Because "every human relation between person and person (is) a relation of conscience" (WL, 135) what is disclosed and acknowledged in repentance is not merely some personal failure with consequences only for the self but also sin in relationship to other human beings. Hence genuine repentance will always turn one toward the living and the works of love which love requires. Moreover, the test simultaneously discloses our failures and God's love, but the focus rests upon the latter. As Kierkegaard tells us elsewhere: God's love is greater than the heart which condemns itself.

Throughout the chapter, Kierkegaard outlines "a test of what love really is" (WL, 346-47). He contends that the presence or

---

[37]Müller, Kierkegaard's "Works of Love," 51-52.

[38]"Who wants to brace up fully to the creatures we are, clawing and gasping for breath in a universe beyond our ken? I think such events illustrate the meaning of Pascal's chilling reflection: 'Men are so necessarily mad that not to be mad would amount to another form of madness.'" See Ernest Becker, The Denial of Death (New York: The Free Press, 1973) 27.

absence of three essential criteria of love—unselfishness, freedom, and faithfulness—are most readily observable in the context of this work of love and hence function as "a measuring rod . . . which disclose the meaning of self-renunciation."[39]Here the sorting out of the intertwinings of love and self-love can be managed most successfully: "Truly, if you want to ascertain what love there is in you or in another person, then pay attention to how he relates himself to one who is dead" (WL, 347).

These criteria are not posed here for the first time. In keeping with our thesis that this chapter functions as an overview of the whole, it is worth recalling that they have been articulated early on and implied throughout:

> "You shall love." *Only when it is a duty to love, only then is love eternally secured against every change, eternally made free in blessed independence, eternally and happily secured against despair.* (WL, 29)

But in the present context one is able to dispense with the "double accounting" (WL, 347) since the one dead (as "no one") has already been silenced.[40] In this silence Kierkegaard anticipates a

---

[39]Müller, *Kierkegaard's "Works of Love,"* 54.

[40]Outka points out that Kierkegaard's position is sharply critiqued by the defenders of mutuality in love who "have maintained that apart from it (mutuality), the criterion for agapeistic actions appears to be only what exemplifies or expresses something resident in the agent." If so, "one might conclude then that the neighbor is little more than an *occasion* for disclosing the state of the agent." Outka concedes that "perhaps Kierkegaard comes uncomfortably close at times to such a conclusion. He does insist rather stridently on the complete indifference to any kind of response." Outka notes in a footnote that "the classic illustration is his discussion of 'the work of love in remembering one dead.' One who is dead is not an actual object; he is only the occasion which continually reveals what resides in the one living who relates himself to him or which helps to make clear how it is with one living who does not relate himself to him." But Outka makes two further observations which are relevant. The first is that he does not believe that these competing positions are accurately represented by their opponents' most extreme accounting: "Thus the only alternatives are not, as is often suggested by the disputants, either an interest in a response which is actually an interest in self-aggrandizement, or a confinement to the agent's inner states so that, for example a recluse may love as fully and appropriately as a parent or statesman." Secondly, Outka questions whether the claim that in Kierkegaard's philosophy the neighbor is reducible to an occasion to disclose the state of the agent "applies to most of his treatment of neighbor-

startling result: every alteration must be assigned to oneself; any dependency must originate in oneself; any despair must be acknowledged as one's own. This is an upheaval of the profoundest sort in that it makes manifest what one might most wish to conceal and in the process tells the truth about oneself. On the other hand, the same practice might yield a glimpse into a human heart where the unselfishness, freedom, and faithfulness of love shine forth. If it does, it will catch love in one of its purest and most beautiful expressions.[41]

Kierkegaard makes three calculations about love's purity. To the degree that one succeeds in lovingly recollecting the dead, one shows one's love to be unselfish, free, and faithful. But this is one instance where a simple pass/fail will not do; besides, the examination is never really over until one joins the ones one recollects in death. While one is not usually either absolutely selfish or thoroughly selfless, these measurements can be made with sufficient clarity to orient one toward the specific task. No matter the degree of unselfishness, freedom or fidelity, in every case these measurements affirm that love is dependent upon the lover, not the object of love.

The work of love in recollecting one dead is an example of the most unselfish love because any repayment is impossible. Worldly love expects repayment: "in one way or another there must be a

---

love." At the very least, this can be"legitimately questioned." I argue in what follows that the agapeistic event goes into the future by opening up to one's living contemporaries. See Gene Outka, *Agape: An Ethical Analysis* (New Haven CT: Yale University Press, 1972) 279-82.

[41]Müller explains Kierkegaard's argument this way: "isolation with one dead is precisely the perfect situation from the viewpoint of the maieutic. . . . In an ordinary observation-situation the relationship is complex; the observer and the object of observation affect each other mutually, so that 'a double calculation' is necessary. But in relationship to one dead only the observer is present, since a dead person is not an actuality. 'No one, absolutely no one, can make himself *nobody* as one dead can, for he is *nobody.*' Because the observation cannot be disturbed by any reciprocal action, it is the observer alone who reveals himself. A dead person is not an actual object and therefore cannot intervene in any way; he is merely the occasion for the one living to reveal himself and what is present within him. As far as the dead person himself is concerned, he has done what he can to bring himself into oblivion." See Müller, *Kierkegaard's "Works of Love,"* 53-54.

little profit involved with love" (WL, 483). One who disdains it might be reproached as Christ was who chose "tax collectors and sinners . . . unable to reciprocate" (WL, 482) as the ones whom he loved best. Ordinarily, repayment occurs in one of two ways: in exchange for love one reciprocates (but not with love), or else one reciprocates by repaying love for love. That the first is modeled on a business transaction is easy to see, but Kierkegaard targets the second kind, esteemed in the world as love, as equally selfish. Outka maintains that "the intractableness of suspicion is one of the psychological indications Kierkegaard cites to illustrate what is finally dominant in preferential relations: instead of regarding the other for his own sake, the self is moved by a secretly controlling interest in receiving affection in return, in acquiring some private benefit."[42] Even if repayment is delayed such that one's love is rewarded only by the prospect of a return in the future (as Kierkegaard claims is the case in parents' love for their children),[43] in his view this prospect obscures the difference between love and self-love. Instead, Kierkegaard proposes a standard which forgoes repayment entirely—in fact, one wherein repayment is made impossible: "If, then, you wish to test yourself as to whether you love unselfishly, just pay attention to how you relate yourself to one who is dead" (WL, 350-51).

Kierkegaard acknowledges "a similarity between lovingly recollecting one who is dead and parents' love for their children" (WL, 349).[44] But in one of his customary reversals from the ordinary way of thinking, loving recollection of one dead is esteemed as higher: "the two greatest good works are these: to give a human being life and to recollect one who is dead; yet the first work of love has a repayment" (WL, 349).

---

[42]Outka, *Agape: An Ethical Analysis*, 18.

[43]I do not think most parents are motivated mainly by the prospect of a future return; instead, the return is made on a daily basis in the affection our children show us, and in the joy our relationship to them brings. Of course, Kierkegaard would say that this substantiates his point that a return is either made or expected.

[44]Adorno observes that "Kierkegaard realizes the enigmatic interweaving of death and childhood." See Adorno, "On Kierkegaard's Doctrine of Love," 33.

In attributing self-love to parental love Kierkegaard does not mean to denigrate it—after all, he has just identified parental love as the closest correlate to the work of love in recollecting one dead. Instead, his point seems to be that even here—where *selflessness* might be most likely to be found—*selfishness* persists.[45] If so, the work of love in recollecting one who is dead acquires a deeper and more profound significance as the remaining instance of unselfish love.[46]

In the test's second moment, the examination probes the degree of freedom in one's love. This criterion, too, has been presumed throughout *Works of Love*: "As soon as love, in its relation to its object, does not in that relation relate itself just as much to itself . . . it is dependent in a false sense, it has the law of its existence outside itself" (WL, 38). Kierkegaard acknowledges that human relationships can be more or less free, often shifting in their various dependencies, but in the work of love in recollecting one dead, no compulsion exists. Just as this work of love did not merely forbid or discourage repayment but made it entirely

---

[45]In the supplemental writings appended by the editors to *Works of Love*, Kierkegaard underscores what he takes to be the residual selfishness toward which maternal love in particular is prone: "maternal love as such is simply self-love raised to a higher power. . . . In the Scriptures it is never maternal love as such that is compared with God's love for a human being; the comparison is only with the strength of maternal love" (WL, 483).

[46]It is interesting to observe that throughout the chapter Kierkegaard insists upon the pairing of birth and death, natality and mortality. Birth and human natality contribute the initial frame of reference, the first parenthesis which orients one in the forward-looking direction. Death and human mortality provide, humanly speaking, the last glimpse into life as it recedes and passes. In death, the parenthesis is closed. In this way the chapter establishes both a prospective and a retrospective love; in the first, parental love goes into the future with joyful expectation; in the second, one living no more is recalled in loving recollection. What seemed an eccentric and perhaps disturbing focus for love—namely, the one dead—now turns out to presuppose in a very explicit way that there be an "unbreakable circle." Though natality and mortality demarcate the beginning and the end of human life, all human life is bound within the wider history of God's prior love. Hence human love has both a prior and a subsequent history: "the heart bound infinitely to God has a prior history . . . [and] just as surely as you do not become nothing, it does not end at a grave" (WL, 149-50). See Müller, *Kierkegaard's "Works of Love,"* 71.

impossible, so too the dead can extort nothing whatsoever from the one still living. If one recollects the dead in love, one does so on one's own initiative, freely, without constraint.[47] The conclusion is the same again: "if you want to test whether you love freely, just watch how over a period of time you relate yourself to one who is dead" (WL, 353).

The work of love in recollecting one dead tests whether or not a person's love is faithful by removing any extrinsic aids and incentives to fidelity. To the extent that the one dead is "no one," that is "no actual object" at all, no assistance whatsoever is forthcoming from him. Throughout, he remains unchanged, unmoved, incapable of alliance, and a nagging reminder that any alteration in the love must originate from somewhere else for he persists utterly the same: "here it is out of the question that it was the one dead who changed. If a change occurs in this relationship, I must be the one who has changed. Therefore, if you want to test whether you love faithfully, just observe how you relate yourself to one who is dead" (WL, 355).

In relationship to one dead, unselfishness, freedom, and faithfulness together provide the criterion for assessing love's progress: "the one who uses this criterion will easily be able to . . . loathe the whole mass of excuses that actuality usually has promptly at hand to explain that it is the other one who is selfish, the other one who is to blame for his being forgotten because he does not call attention to himself, the other one who is faithless" (WL, 358). Employing the criterion enables one to recognize the pervasiveness of one's own failures in love. It shifts one's attention away from the evasions of comparison and fixes one's gaze firmly on oneself. The test's results are sure and unmistakable: no one can pass muster! One's own selfishness, compulsions, and faithlessness become obvious, and they do so in a context which forbids mitigating in-

---

[47]It is significant that Kierkegaard mentions the infant as one thought ill-equipped to compel, and hence as one who might potentially rival the one dead in terms of his ability to measure freedom in love. But Kierkegaard insists that this perspective is mistaken because the cry of the infant, which he uses to bring attention to his helplessness, *does* compel. Because some parents need this compulsion to act, parental love does not provide the same degree of accuracy in its assessment of love's freedom.

terpretation.[48] Hence, at the end of his analysis of selected works of love—(the end, save the work of love in praising love which follows like a hymn)—Kierkegaard pauses on a note of repentance. This work of love is a recollection which must detour into repentance if its summons to practice love is to take hold. The labors of repentance are preceded by the decision to lovingly recollect one dead (which one then fails to do to love's specifications). To become aware of one's failures within the wider context that love draws is the first step toward repentance and toward grace.

The love which emerges in the recollection of one dead and accomplishes the turn toward repentance conforms to Sylvia Walsh's description of Kierkegaard's Christian love. She argues that "spiritual or Christian love is characterized by Kierkegaard as a transcendent, transforming, inclusive, edifying, abiding, and spontaneous love . . . "[49] and the correspondences are clear. The work of love in recollecting one dead is transcendent because it is grounded in divine love: "All human love thus has a transcendent matrix in the eternal, whether that is acknowledged or not, but Christian love is distinguished by the fact that it is love that has become *consciously* grounded upon the eternal or God."[50]

Second, this work of love has undergone the transformation of the eternal "so as to eradicate the element of selfishness";[51] in fact, Kierkegaard singles out this work as the *best* indicator of the selflessness of one's love, since all repayment is made impossible.

Third, I have argued that despite appearances to the contrary, this work of love is inclusive: it is not reserved for the objects of

---

[48]Perhaps it is an extension of our "duty to love the people we see" to include ourselves precisely when our weaknesses are most glaring. But it does not follow that we are authorized to allow the most lenient interpretation of our own sinfulness, since to do so would forestall repentance. In our own case what is called for is a ready admission of sin.

[49]Sylvia I. Walsh, "Forming the Heart: The Role of Love in Kierkegaard's Thought," in *The Grammar of the Heart*, ed. Richard H. Bell (San Francisco: Harper & Row, 1988) 236.

[50]Ibid., 236. See also Timothy Houston Polk, *The Biblical Kierkegaard: Reading by the Rule of Faith* (Macon GA: Mercer University Press, 1997) 40. Polk, too, employs Walsh's categories, writing of transcendence that "We are not its author. Rather love authors us."

[51]Walsh, "Forming the Heart," 237.

preferential love, despite that fact that it is the beloved or friend who most likely occasions this work of love. But in loving recollection of the "no one" of death, even the beloved takes on the designation "neighbor": eternity's common mark, our eternal likeness and absolute equality before God is the focus. Granted that "the friend or beloved should be loved first and foremost, like others, as a neighbor. The Christian view, Kierkegaard claims, is that 'what is eternally basic must also be the basis of every expression of what is special.' Thus, while we certainly love persons in our special relations differently from the way we love others, this difference is not essential, since we love them fundamentally as we love others, that is, as a neighbor."[52] In the work of love in recollecting one who is dead, this "first and foremost" is reiterated once again *at the end*: death confers an equivalence upon all, thereby reminding us in the most vivid way of our common humanity.

Fourth, this work of love, like the others analyzed in the second half of Kierkegaard's volume, is edifying or upbuilding, though it qualifies as edifying in an unusual way. Death sees to it that the one recollected is not built up, but life allows that others might be. First of all, the one who recollects is edified by undertaking this work of love: he tests himself to assess the degree to which his love is selfless, free, and faithful. Moreover, to the extent that he assumes a practice, his love proves edifying to others. It is at this point that his living contemporaries become the beneficiaries of this practice and are themselves built up.

Fifth, to say that this work of love abides is to say that it is not transient, perishable, or prone to change. Once again, this work of love can claim a special prerogative here. It teaches fidelity by fixing the lover's attention on the degree to which he remains unchanged, since the one recollected has already achieved the changelessness mandated by death.

Finally, this love remains spontaneous despite Christianity's insistence that love be understood as duty. The perplexing tension between the spontaneity and freedom of love and its status as commanded notwithstanding, Walsh argues that the contradiction

---

[52]Ibid., 241.

is merely apparent: "in Kierkegaard's view, duty and inclination, law and love coincide in Christian love in such a way as to enable us to preserve or to regain the spontaneity of love and keep it from becoming subject to 'the lukewarmness and indifference of habit.'"[53]

"*Recollecting One Who Is Dead*" as Task:
*Guidance, Blessing, and Prayer*

Kierkegaard ends by exhorting one to undertake this work of love as a kind of preliminary instruction that must eventually return to the present and to the practice of love which is the focus throughout the book. Whoever commits himself to this task will be guided aright through life, and the recipient of this work's special blessing. The practice of this work will make of his life a prayer. Kierkegaard writes:

> The work of love in recollecting one who is dead is thus a work of the most unselfish, the freest, the most faithful love. Therefore go out and practice it; recollect the one who is dead and just in this way *learn to love the living unselfishly, freely, faithfully.* . . . Recollect the one who is dead; then in addition to the *blessing* that is inseparable from this work of love you will also have the best *guidance* for rightly understanding life: that it is our duty to love the people we do not see *but also those we do see.* The duty to love the people we see cannot cease because death separates them from us, because the duty is eternal; but accordingly *neither can the duty to those who are dead separate the living from us in such a way that they do not become the objects of our love.* (WL, 358; emphasis added)

How the work of love in recollecting one dead provides the best guidance for those who would understand life has been argued throughout. Certainly this work of love is a kind of spiritual exercise: its practice develops selflessness, independence, and fidelity in proportion to one's expertise in love. These qualities in turn then act as expert guides as one navigates one's way through time. Moreover, these are guides whose intelligibility is not suspect and whose meanings are not ambiguous. Whatever

---

[53]Ibid., 244.

develops unselfish, free, and faithful love is affirmed; whatever tears it down is not. The difficulty is not so much in the discernment as in the doing: the signposts guide aright, but our hearts are not always disposed to be so guided.

Where lies the blessing that Kierkegaard deems inseparable from this work of love? It lies in a paradox. To the extent that selfishness, false dependencies, and faithlessness persist, one is moored to repentance. But for Kierkegaard, repentance is a great blessing. In genuine repentance one reverses one's direction and recovers the path from which one had departed. Thus repentance repositions one to be guided further aright.

But perhaps the greatest blessing that this work of love carries is the opportunity to gain some insight into God's love—pure abundance in giving, unconditional, ever faithful. What human love strives to achieve, God is. God's love displays toward us, the living, the same characteristics that we struggle to acquire in the work of love in recollecting one dead—but God's expression of Love is absolute. We can muster a momentary unselfishness, against the odds; God's love is always so. On occasion we can love without coercion; the love of God is always freely given. Fidelity in love is something that we strain to express; God's love persists the same yesterday, today, and tomorrow. The halting and tentative efforts that we manage are subsumed within the larger frame where God's love becomes most prominent. In the display of our failures what Love achieves is revealed. Hence this is an extraordinary blessing because it offers us a personal experience of the very love that we are instructed to practice on others.

To be the beneficiary of God's faithful love and to become aware of this most unmistakably precisely when one's own shortcomings in love are most vivid requires that we assume the status of one dead—not literally, to be sure, but by way of a kind of consent which acknowledges our utter reliance upon God. When this is done, though it is never completely done, our experience of being loved assumes prominence. In our own case, we understand very clearly that love is dependent upon the Lover and not any presumed perfections in the object of love. It is not our worthiness that evokes God's Love but God's Love which might evoke in us a more holy love of others.

Just as children learn to love as they have been loved by human parents, so too are we instructed to love as we have been loved by God. Our duty to those who are dead does not separate the living from us but rather refocuses and intensifies our duty to love them as God has so abundantly loved us.[54] Müller is insistent upon this point: "One must make use of love; it is supposed to be employed, not in loving the invisible, but that brother we see in the real world. The duty to love wins actuality and truth exclusively *by finding and remaining in the actual world, as the task assigned to one.*"[55]

Though Kierkegaard ends the chapter with a reminder of the claim that the living make upon us, this has really been his focus throughout: "Go out to the dead . . . in order *there* to take an aim at life" (WL, 345). It is the living who exact the most powerful claim upon one's attention. In a book about the concrete works of love it would be surprising if this were not the case. Surely it cannot end with the "no one" of death—as if love originated in its Hidden Source only to narrow, dry up, and terminate in death. Besides, if the one dead is "no one," who is benefitted or affected by this work of love? Even if nothing is accomplished by the world's standards which remain totally incommensurable with love's, (and this might well be the case, as it is shown to be in "mercifulness, a work of love even if it can give nothing and is able to do nothing") still, to the degree that it is a work of love it must transform.[56] But who is transformed? Since the "no one" of death cannot be, it must be the case that the one who performs the work is changed as are the living beneficiaries of one's practice.

But holy practices are always connected to prayer for Kierkegaard. This practice, too, when fully developed, must originate in,

---

[54]Müller affirms a similar triangulation when he writes: "That which is invoked, is *the Spirit of Love*. . . . The witness which the Spirit will bring about in the believer by making Christ's offering contemporary to him is that he should love God as he himself is loved, and love his neighbor as he loves himself. With that love wherein the individual loves God, he shall love his neighbor because his life is grounded in God's love. The precondition and requirement for practicing works of love is therefore the mutual love between God and the individual." See Müller, *Kierkegaard's "Works of Love,"* 8-9.

[55]Ibid., 27.

[56]Walsh, "Forming the Heart," 237-40.

be sustained by, and terminate in prayer. It is noteworthy that *Works of Love* is preceded by a carefully crafted prayer, which appears only once even though the preface which immediately precedes it is repeated verbatim in Part II.[57] Surely this omission, obviously purposeful, is intended to remind us that the prayer oversees the whole—not just for Kierkegaard who undertook the labor of writing about love's works, but for those who labor mightily to love.

Müller insists on this point: "without prayer there is no possibility of practicing the works of love."[58] Prayer makes explicit that all works of love are rooted in God's love as Source. But our question pertains more precisely to the work of love in recollecting one dead. In what way does it presume prayer? After all, it is certainly the case that the practice of recollecting the dead is undertaken by everyone, worldwide, including those with no professed religious faith. Surely for these, and perhaps for many others, there is no explicit presumption of prayer. It seems, instead, a human undertaking of the most ordinary sort—an attempt to recover—to import, out of sequence—some thought of the deceased to give meaning to one's present. In recollecting one dead, one looks to the past to revivify the present—the very present which owes its present diminution to the death of the one mourned.

But this undertaking cannot succeed—that is, cannot secure the hope desired by the mourner—if it never ventures beyond the

---

[57]Müller attends carefully to the significance of the opening prayer: "the prayer and the conclusion do not merely formally constitute the book's frame, but also lay down the objective perspective in which the whole of its contents should be seen." He observes that Kierkegaard makes a linguistic distinction between acts of charity (*Kjerlighedsgjerninger*) and works of love (*Kjerlighedens Gjerninger*). Müller argues that Kierkegaard intended to challenge the prevailing assumption that only certain acts can be authenticated as works of love and that these qualify necessarily solely by virtue of what they do—feeding the hungry, clothing the naked, etc. Certainly, acts of charity can qualify as works of love if performed lovingly, but works of love cannot be identified with or reduced to any specifiable acts exhibiting certain external criteria. In effect Kierkegaard makes the summons to love more strenuous and demanding by multiplying opportunities: every occasion provides an opportunity to realize love's work. See Müller, *Kierkegaard's "Works of Love,"* 7-12.

[58]Ibid., 8.

categories of time to touch the eternal through prayer. Seen within the limited frame that time plots out, the past is always slippage, and always increasingly so. Granted, temporality authorizes a brief respite in its allowance of recollection in the ordinary, or nonphilosophical sense, but the thought of the beloved dead can only comfort momentarily before it, too, suffers the fate of becoming past. This is a perfect instance of forgetting to knot the thread: the activity might well be ongoing but the labor produces nothing that lasts.

In this scheme the dead one suffers a *double vanquishing*—first, and most decisively through his own death, but subsequently through the eventual, yet certain, deaths of the ones who had remembered him. With their deaths all memory of him is obliterated, as if he never existed. If no one exists to keep one's memory alive, no trace of one's existence, so insistent and so precious while alive, can persist. In the *Symposium* Plato spoke about a vicarious or metaphorical "immortality in time": one can live on through the production of human children, via fame and power, or through one's soul-progeny of *phronesis* and *arete*.[59] In the present context what is attempted is something different—a vicarious *mortality*, initiated through the agency or instrumentality of the one still living, is what is sought for the deceased. In the Platonic version, one's consolation is one's expectation that one will live on through one's children. In the present version, one's children (or their substitutes in memory) attempt to retain or recoup some aspect of the dead one's mortality, though even this cannot be retained for long. Just as Plato's promise of vicarious immortality does not satisfy our deepest desires for genuine or literal immortality, so too must this attempt to achieve vicarious mortality for another fail. What is missing from both of them is the category of the eternal.

In "The Work of Love in Recollecting One Who is Dead," Kierkegaard presupposes the reality of the eternal. All love has its hidden source in God's eternal love and all love rejoins Love when enacted in the world as work. Hence all works of love, when undertaken with Love in mind, are prayers. Though the deceased has suffered the vanquishing of death, the mourner does not

---

[59]Plato, *Symposium* 208a-209e.

concede death's triumph as final. Instead, prayerful recollection of the dead commends the deceased to the unconditional love of God and finds consolation in the prospect that "what is decisive is that with God everything is possible" (SUD, 38). Certainly Kierkegaard was familiar with and practiced this sort of intercessory prayer for the dead. In a prayer entered in his journal the year after his father's death Kierkegaard writes: "Even if you seem at times to withdraw your hand from us, we nevertheless know that you are only closing it to hide the more abundant blessing in it, that you close it only to open it again and satisfy all that lives with blessing."[60] In commending another to the love of God through Christ it is blessing that one ultimately expects. But one must never forget what this entails for oneself—a readiness to undertake, unceasingly, these prayerful of works of love. Once again, the work of love which began by attending to the one dead now fixes its focus upon the one still living. In recollecting the dead we recall our own assignment in all of its difficult simplicity: to love God and to love one's neighbor, both seen and unseen.

*The Response to Adorno and LeFevre:*
*The Recovery of Neighbor Love*

As noted earlier, Adorno argues that Kierkegaard's works of love fail to address the most fundamental and bitter social inequalities. Given Adorno's insistence upon the preeminence of the social, such an omission seems to him intolerably neglectful. LeFevre, for his part, advocates a theology of isolationist prayer, with the social effectively trumped. One burden of my argument has been to suggest how little either appreciates the seriousness and care with which Kierkegaard understands the neighbor and the implications that this has for love and its works. Loving "no one" entails loving everyone, the neighbor who is ever present. In concluding, I want to probe this with reference to the Holocaust. For something of what Kierkegaard *does* mean can be found in the most unlikely way: in the Holocaust, *the inverse of Kierkegaard's neighbor* is represented most compellingly. Hence free and faithful remembrance of these many dead reminds us both of the enormity

---

[60]JP, 3:3381.

of human evil *and* the need to renounce it by keeping the neighbor always in view.

Much has been written in the last fifty years[61] about the necessity for remembering the millions who died in the Holocaust, whose execution led to the charging of their murderers with the commission of "crimes against humanity." Hannah Arendt found this crime so profoundly inhumane—in Adolf Eichmann's case, for example—that she doubted any one would want to share the earth with him.[62] But the more pressing point concerns the need to remember the victims of this horror in order to ensure against its repetition.

For those of us who have no first hand experience of this evil, and hence have no personal memory to recover, the route to remembrance runs through the testimony of survivors. These testimonies—in whatever form they appear, including literature—are essential. They help to make the past a part of our communal memory—a piece of human history that is acknowledged, communicated, and memorialized as evil—to make explicit that the enormity of this evil must never be allowed to happen again. Johann Baptist Metz speaks of "a solidarity in memory with the dead which breaks the grip of history as a history of triumph and conquest."[63] Though Kierkegaard's discussion of the work of love in recollecting one dead is the work of *one* recollecting *one* deceased, it seems to me that his work invites us to include the work of the human community in remembering these many dead.

---

[61]Simone Weil described a heartrending pain at the thought of the sufferings of others *centuries earlier*, whose affliction and death she could not possibly know firsthand: "There is only one time when I really know nothing of this certitude any longer. It is when I am in contact with the affliction of other people, those who are indifferent or unknown to me as much as the others, perhaps even more, including those of the most remote ages of antiquity. This contact causes me such atrocious pain and so utterly rends my soul that as a result the love of God becomes almost impossible for me for a while. It would take very little more to make me say impossible." See Simone Weil, *Waiting for God*, trans. Emma Crafurd (New York: Harper & Row, 1951) 91.

[62]Hannah Arendt, *Eichmann in Jerusalem* (New York: Penguin Books, 1963) 279.

[63]Johann Baptist Metz, *Faith in History and Society: Toward a Practical Fundamental Theology*, trans. David Smith (New York: Seabury Press, 1980) 184.

How this might be an authentic work of love comes through in Primo Levi's memoir *Survival at Auschwitz: The Nazi Assault on Humanity*. His text is not only a personal refusal to let oblivion take its natural course, or even a memorial to those whose testimonies can no longer be solicited or heard. It also speaks with great authority to those who have no personal memory of these events and might be tempted for that reason to take insufficient note.[64] It does this by implying that we can all see ourselves here if we attend with sufficient humanity, and if we do not so attend we are to be held accountable:

> Many people—many nations—can find themselves holding, more or less wittingly, that "every stranger is an enemy." For the most part this conviction lies deep down like some latent infection; it betrays itself only in random, disconnected acts, and does not lie at the base of a system of reason. But when this does come about, when the unspoken dogma becomes the major premise in a syllogism, then, at the end of the chain, there is the Lager.[65]

If the Lager is to be rejected, only one way is recommended: "Meditate that this came about: I commend these words to you. Carve them in your hearts . . . repeat them to your children. . . ."[66]

The Nazis at Auschwitz and elsewhere set one elemental plan in operation: to deprive their victims of their humanity. Levi recounts their "funereal science"[67] from arrest through deportation, enslavement, and forced labor. The murderers attempted to obliterate all worldly distinctions and to force their victims to renounce all significant relationships. In so doing they conferred an enforced equivalence: everything personal and humane was excised and the human being was reduced to a beast or a thing.[68]

---

[64]"The need to tell our story to 'the rest,' to make 'the rest' participate in it, had taken on for us, before our liberation and after, the character of an immediate and violent impulse, to the point of competing with our other elementary needs. The book has been written to satisfy this need." See Primo Levi, *Survival in Auschwitz: The Nazi Assault on Humanity*, trans. Stuart Woolf (New York: Simon & Schuster, 1996) 9.

[65]Ibid., 9.

[66]Ibid., 11.

[67]Ibid., 28.

[68]Levi describes this phenomenon repeatedly: the "Lager was a great machine to reduce us to beasts"; "every one was aware that only a man is worthy of a

In this setting, every brutality conspired to reduce human life to its lowest and most animal expression. Levi describes this as being "on the bottom":

> When we finish, everyone remains in his own corner and we do not dare lift our eyes to look at one another. There is nowhere to look in a mirror, but our appearance stands in front of us, reflected in a hundred livid faces, in a hundred miserable and sordid puppets. We are transformed into the phantoms glimpsed yesterday evening. Then for the first time we became aware that our language lacks words to express this offense, the demolition of a man. In a moment, with almost prophetic intuition, the reality was revealed to us: we had reached the bottom. It is not possible to sink lower than this; no human condition is more miserable than this, not could it conceivably be so. Nothing belongs to us any more; they have taken away our clothes, our shoes, even our hair; if we speak, they will not listen to us, and if they listen, they will not understand. They will even take away our name: and if we want to keep it, we will have to find ourselves the strength to do so, to manage somehow so that behind the name something of us, of us as we were, still remains.[69]

This being "on the bottom" is the demonic inversion of Kierkegaard's concept of the neighbor. In both, earthly distinctions are erased, but one proceeds by reducing the human being to the level of the beast, whereas the other envisions the equality of the eternal as spirit.

Adorno had posed this question: "For what can loving one's neighbor mean, if one can neither help him nor interfere with a setting of the world which makes such help impossible?"[70] Primo

---

name, and that Null Achtzehn (018) is no longer a man"; the murderers were resolved "to annihilate us first as men in order to kill us more slowly afterwards"; "everything, like us!, named by numbers and letters"; "we are the slaves of the slaves, whom all can give orders to and our name is the number which we carry"; "without hair, without honor and without names, beaten every day, more abject every day, and they never see in our eyes a light of rebellion, or of peace, or of faith. They know us as thieves and untrustworthy, muddy, ragged and starving, and mistaking the effect for the cause, they judge us worthy of our abasement. Who could tell one of our faces from the other? For them we are 'Kazett', a singular neuter word". See ibid., 41-42, 51, 72, and 121.

[69]Ibid., 26-27.

[70]Adorno, "On Kierkegaard's Doctrine of Love," 26.

Levi answers this question when he remembers how "in this world shaken every day more deeply by the omens of its nearing end, amidst new terrors and hopes . . . I happened to meet Lorenzo." Lorenzo was an Italian civilian who could not meet Adorno's second requirement for assistance: Auschwitz as "a setting of the world" remained, for the moment, invulnerable. In fact, he could barely manage the bit of material help that Adorno mentions: "In concrete terms it amounts to little: an Italian civilian worker brought me a piece of bread and the remainder of his ration every day for six months; he gave me a vest of his, full of patches; he wrote a postcard on my behalf to Italy and brought me the reply. For all this he neither asked not accepted any reward, because he was good and simple and did not think that one did good for a reward."[71] But it is not primarily for his material assistance that Levi recollects Lorenzo:

> I believe that it was really due to Lorenzo that I am alive today; and not so much for his material aid, as for his having constantly reminded me by his presence, by his natural and plain manner of being good, that there still existed a just world outside our own, something and someone still pure and whole, not corrupt, not savage, extraneous to hatred and terror; something difficult to define, a remote possibility of good, but for which it was worth surviving. The personages in these pages are not men. Their humanity is buried, or they themselves have buried it, under an offence received or inflicted on someone else. The evil and insane SS men, the Kapos, the politicals, the criminals, the prominents, great and small, down to the indifferent slave Häftlinge, all the grades of the mad hierarchy created by the Germans paradoxically fraternized in a uniform internal desolation. But Lorenzo was a man; his humanity was pure and uncontaminated, he was outside this world of negation. Thanks to Lorenzo, I managed not to forget that I myself was a man.[72]

What Lorenzo managed and Levi praised was love of the neighbor. In so doing he answers Adorno's query by *living otherwise*. Kierkegaard, too, ever mindful of love's double danger (WL, 194-96), reminds us that love's task must be realized in action and in recollection of these many dead.

---

[71]Levi, *Survival in Auschwitz*, 119.
[72]Ibid., 121-22.

# 10

## Four Narratives on the Interhuman:
## Kierkegaard, Buber, Rosenzweig, and Levinas

### Michael Oppenheim

At the heart of Søren Kierkegaard's *Works of Love* is a powerful and incisive narrative about the nature of the interhuman, that is, the importance, possibilities, and limits of relationships between humans. I believe that one way of elucidating the significance of this text is to explore it in the context of philosophic narratives of the interhuman that arise out of another religious tradition. Franz Rosenzweig (1886–1929), Martin Buber (1878–1965) and Emmanuel Levinas (1906–1995) are three twentieth century Jewish philosophers whose insights into the interaction between humans have both provided a foundation for a major stream of modern Jewish philosophy and left profound imprints on the works of other philosophers and religious thinkers. As with Kierkegaard, they combine an abiding concern for the interhuman with the conviction that the relationship to God is essential for authentic relations between persons.

The project of examining four philosophers in one essay, especially four philosophers as complex as these, is more than a little overwhelming. However, I believe that it is manageable and fruitful if the proper parameters are respected. First, the analysis will be restricted to a text or a few central texts in the case of each thinker.[1] For Kierkegaard this is, obviously, the *Works of Love*. For

---

[1]Although I will not discuss it here, there is a primary literature of critique by some of these thinkers of one another. A number of Buber's criticisms of Kierkegaard's views are examined by Robert L. Perkins in his "Buber and Kierkegaard: A Philosophic Encounter," in *Martin Buber: A Centenary Volume*, ed. Haim Gordon and Jochanan Bloch (Israel: American Associates of Ben Gurion University, 1984). There is also a discussion of Levinas's criticisms of Buber's thought in Robert

Buber it is *I and Thou*,[2] with Rosenzweig it is *The Star of Redemption*,[3] and with Levinas, *Totality and Infinity*[4] and *Otherwise than Being, or, Beyond Essence*.[5] Second, this comparative effort will confine itself to the narratives of the interhuman that the four provide. Third, this is only an initial inquiry. It will diagram important and distinctive elements in each portrayal, but some of the subtlety and detail cannot be included in this project, such as, for example, the early genesis of the individual.

In this article, I will explore these philosophers' discussions of the relationships between humans and the role that the God-relationship plays in these by lifting, reworking, and constructing four stories from the texts. I have broken the narratives into three segments, each with a particular focus. The first part will explore the ways that the authors characterize the "natural state" of relations between persons. Each author provides an explicit portrait of the individual and a detailed discussion of what relationships to others in the everyday world are like. The second segment looks at the individual's God-relationship. It will examine the way that the relationship with the divine emerges, the basic dynamics or movements that constitute this interaction, and the

---

Bernasconi, " 'Failure of Communication' as a Surplus: Dialogue and Lack of Dialogue Between Buber and Levinas," in *The Provocation of Levinas*, ed. Robert Bernasconi and David Wood (New York: Routledge, 1988). On the other hand, Perkins argues that Buber and Kierkegaard share views about politics and society, in "The Politics of Existence: Buber and Kierkegaard," in *Kierkegaard in Post/Modernity*, ed. Martin J. Matustik and Merold Westphal (Bloomington: Indiana University Press, 1995) 167-81.

[2]Martin Buber, *I and Thou*, trans. Walter Kaufmann (New York: Charles Scribner's Sons, 1970). Hereafter I shall use the sigla IT.

[3]Fran Rosenzweig, *The Star of Redemption*, trans. William W. Hallo (Boston: Beacon Press, 1972). Hereafter I shall use the sigla SR.

[4]Emmanuel Levinas, *Totality and Infinity: An Essay on Exteriority*, trans. Alphonso Lingis (Pittsburgh: Duquesne University Press, 1988) and Emmanuel Levinas, *Otherwise than Being, or, beyond Essence*, trans. Alphonso Lingis (The Hague: Martinus Nijhoff Publishers, 1981). Hereafter I use the sigla TI and OTB.

[5]There are important differences between these two works of Levinas, which will not be apparent from this treatment. See Alphonso Lingis's "Translator's Introduction" to *Otherwise than Being*, xv-xvi. This issue is also addressed in Richard A. Cohen's *Elevations: The Height of the Good in Rosenzweig and Levinas* (Chicago: University of Chicago Press, 1994) 145.

nature of the transformation that the individual has undergone. The third section examines the character of the transformed interhuman that follows in the wake of the relationship to God.

A more explicit comparative discussion will come at both the beginning and conclusion. At the beginning I will present three views that tie together their presentations and at the end I will briefly explore some of the intriguing similarities between the narratives.

*Works of Love* provides a fruitful ground for constructing this specific narrative by Kierkegaard. While many of his writings, including the early pseudonymous ones, examine different life-stages which treat the life with others, *Works of Love* is authored in his own name and presents what he saw as the most accurate standpoint—the Christian—concerning the interhuman. It explores human relationships in terms of the fundamental opposition between human love and Christian love. Additionally, it carefully and meticulously conducts this exploration in terms of a plethora of examples from everyday life. At one point, Kierkegaard offered a précis of his text which highlights this aspect: "The deliberation seeks, with the help of thought and a little knowledge of human nature, only to penetrate the illusions [about love] or to understand those apostolic words within the daily situation of life, precisely where the illusions are at home" (WL, 124).

### For the Sake of Comparison

In order for this comparison to be more than a juxtaposition of positions, the objects of analysis must share a common core of views. This shared foundation allows the differences to have significance as competing or complementary options concerning a particular subject. In such a case, differences may be subtle, but they chart meaningful alternatives. The narratives of the inter-human offered by Kierkegaard, Buber, Rosenzweig, and Levinas diagram meaningful alternatives, because they reveal a number of common, underlying themes in their storylines. Three of these are that relationships to other persons are the sine qua non of human living, the quest for authenticity ultimately points to a relationship to the divine, and the relationship to God requires the individual to turn to the neighbor.

The first view testifies to the absolute importance of relationships between persons in any examination of the nature and meaning of human existence. All of these philosophers reject the model of the autonomous self that has been preeminent at least since the time of Descartes, one that gives primacy to self-consciousness, self-reliance, and self-direction.[6] The second theme underscores their shared understanding that human life points beyond itself and is grounded in a relationship to the transcendent. The last position unequivocally finds that the God-relationship is expressed and verified through the treatment of the neighbor. Together, these themes fuse together stories of the relationship to other persons with the discourse about the relationship to God.

Kierkegaard's admonition about the importance of relationship to others in any story about the self is unambiguous: "The commandment is that you *shall* love, but ah, if you will understand yourself and life, then it seems that it should not need to be commanded, because to love people is the only thing worth living for, and without this love you are not really living" (WL, 375). Thus, for Kierkegaard in *Works of Love*, the question will not be whether an essential relationship to another is important—as it is "the only thing worth living for"—but, about the nature of genuine love.

Buber phrases the matter of the pivotal place others have in the story of a life in different, but clearly parallel, terms. In *I and Thou* he is insistent that it is impossible to speak of a person in isolation. Early in the text he writes that "there is no I as such" (IT, 54). Further, he affirms that to become an authentic self, an "I" or "person," one must enter into significant relations to others: "Man becomes an I through a You" (IT, 80),[7] and "Persons appear by entering into relation to other persons" (IT, 112).

---

[6]The importance of this model for Western thought is explored in Suzanne R. Kirschner's *The Religious and Romantic Origins of Psychoanalysis* (Cambridge: Cambridge University Press, 1996) 33-62.

[7]Walter Kaufmann, the translator of the version of *I and Thou* I am using here, prefers the word "You" to the word "Thou." He finds the latter word too affected and remote (IT, 14-18). I continue to use the word "Thou" for Buber's German word "Du," except when quoting from Kaufmann's translation, precisely because the I-Thou attitude is not the customary way people turn to one another.

In poetic language, Rosenzweig indicates that the quintessential relationship to another, the love for the neighbor, both brings the development of the self to fruition and directs it in the world. He claims that with the commandment to "love the neighbor," the "soul is declared of age . . . and sets forth into the world" (SR, 205).

It is diagnostic of Levinas that the relationship to the other that Kierkegaard and Rosenzweig see by way of the religious commandment to love the neighbor and that Buber portrays as the relationship to a Thou, he describes in terms of ethics. For Levinas, one comes to be, one is born, through "serving" the other. In *Totality and Infinity* he writes: "The accomplishing of the I qua I and morality constitute one sole and same process in being . . . [coming] to birth . . . [in] serving the poor, the stranger, the widow, and the orphan" (TI, 245).

A second proposition that lies at the foundation of each of the four stories is the idea that the God-relationship is essential to the development of a self. However, this statement, this presupposition, is more implicit than explicit in the narratives. A major goal of all four authors is to demonstrate that the God-relationship is not an end in itself or something that can be vital if lived in seclusion. As a consequence of this paramount interest, the discussion of the importance of the God-relationship itself is usually somewhat subdued. The following examples will illuminate both this presupposition and its decentered place.

Kierkegaard holds that it is only through the relationship to God that a person acquires both substance and distinctiveness. The first idea is put as: "essentially every human being indeed stands by himself—through God's help" (WL, 278). He expresses the second element: "the source and origin of all distinctiveness" is "to be oneself" "*before God*" (WL, 271).

Buber discusses the essential nature of the God-relationship by indicating that it fulfills all other truly defining relationships, that is, the whole realm of the I-Thou. He writes that the inner power in each person to turn toward another, that is, "the innate You," "attains perfection solely in the immediate relationship to the You [God] that in accordance with its nature cannot become an It" (IT, 123). Elliptically Buber also expresses the notion that the relationship to the divine sustains and provides meaning: "You need God in order to be, and God needs you—for that which is the meaning of your life" (IT, 130).

Rosenzweig also affirms that to be able to move beyond oneself and thus to become fully human, God must first transform the self. He writes that it is "only by virtue of the fact that he [God] loves us and awakens our dead Self" that the person emerges to that status of "beloved and requiting soul" (SR, 381).

Likewise, Levinas expresses in many contexts the integral role of the God-relationship in the constitution of the self. The self is upheld or confirmed by standing before God's judgment in the context of the relation of the self to the other. In his terms: "To place oneself under the judgment of God is to exalt [one's] subjectivity. . . . The judgment of God that judges me at the same time confirms me" (TI, 246).

A third theme that pervades the four narratives is the connection between the God-relationship and the neighbor. Unlike the second theme just discussed, there is an abundance of explicit examples that illustrate this message. Here are two, among many other ways, that Kierkegaard puts it: "In the Christian sense, to love people is to love God, and to love God is to love people" (WL, 384), and, that a person "actually loves the unseen [God] will be known by his loving the brother he sees" (WL, 160).

Buber underscored the tie between the interhuman and the relationship to God in his "Afterword" to *I and Thou*, written three and one-half decades earlier, where he states: "the close association of the relation to God with the relation to one's fellow men . . . is my most essential concern" (IT, 171).

Rosenzweig virtually reiterates Kierkegaard's point and language through an assertion that almost conflates the two relationships: "The love for God is to express itself in love for one's neighbor" (SR, 214).

Levinas again utilizes the vocabulary of ethics to discuss the juncture of the self's relationship to the divine and to other humans. The austerity of the terminology does not eclipse the depth of expression, as he writes: "God rises to his supreme and ultimate presence as correlate to the justice rendered unto men" (TI, 78).

### The Self as Obstacle

The point of departure for the four narratives is the portrait of the life of the individual with others, a life that has not yet established what one might call a personal relationship to the divine. This first stage will profoundly color all the succeeding characterizations and have important ramifications particularly in terms of what the God-relationship provides to the interhuman. The key question here is whether persons are so constituted that they have it in their own power to form meaningful human relationships or whether the self is itself an obstacle to establishing and maintaining these. Put in another way, in beginning the story of the self, is the interhuman an arena of authenticity or of alienation? We will see that while there are distinctive elements in each position, there are also a number of overlapping features.

Kierkegaard argues throughout *Works of Love* that the individual is alienated from others until his or her life has undergone the radical transformation of the Christian God-relationship. This alienation is described in terms of self-love. For him, all human relationships are pervaded (WL, 369) and perverted by a self-love that neither cares for the other nor even breaks through to the other. The diametrical opposite of this is Christian love, the definition of which Kierkegaard takes from the apostle Paul's statement in 1 Corinthians 13:5: Love "never seeks its own" (WL, 212).

Kierkegaard demonstrates the omnipresence of self-love through a philosophical/psychological analysis that explores concrete human relations, especially those that most would regard as the highest, that is, erotic love—"life's most beautiful happiness," and friendship—"the greatest temporal good" (WL, 267). He characterizes erotic love and friendship as being, among other things: passionate—dependent on the self's own desires and wants, preferential—looking for that "other I," adoring—desiring an intimate relationship to someone special, calculating—ever alert to whether the other's response at a minimum meets one's expenditures, and blind to the true nature of the other, that is, seeing only the self in the other.

While erotic love in particular is often praised for its passionate selflessness and spontaneity, Kierkegaard is deeply suspicious of this "play of feelings, drives, inclinations, and passions" (WL, 25). The partiality or preference that pervades both erotic love and friendship reveal the self's quest for itself. Kierkegaard writes:

> Just as self-love selfishly embraces this one and only *self* that makes it self-love, so also erotic love's passionate preference selfishly encircles this one and only beloved, and friendship's passionate preference encircles this one and only friend. For this reason the beloved and the friend are called, remarkably and profoundly, to be sure, the *other self*, the *other I*. (WL, 53)

Similarly, Kierkegaard reveals that the passion of adoration turns back upon the self when he writes: "Well, now, to admire another person is certainly not self-love; but to be loved by the one and only admired one, would not this relation turn back in a selfish way into the *I* who loves—his other *I*" (WL, 54)?

For Kierkegaard, the praise of love's mutuality actually hides the demand for "reciprocal love" (WL, 237). Human love reveals a calculus, where "the lover is the beloved, and the beloved is the lover" (WL, 121), rather than a free giving. Additionally, love ends with a type of expanded self, composed of "the joined, the exchanged *yours* and *mine*" (WL, 267). Given all of this, it is not surprising that Kierkegaard not only argues that human love cannot escape the prison of the self, but questions whether the beloved or friend is actually seen in her or his own terms at all (WL, 270).

Martin Buber's *I and Thou* presents a very different portrait of what it means to be human. For him, the interhuman is characterized by *two* types of relationship or modes of interaction. There is "the I of the basic word I-You and the I of the basic word I-It" (IT, 54). Buber is saying that persons have two potential ways of relating—to other persons, nature, God, etc.—and that these ways indicate and express the two-fold nature of the I. His use of the terminology "basic word" suggests that language is a key to both understanding this two-fold nature and to its living expression.

The basic word "I-It" refers to an approach or attitude of experiencing something or someone as a static thing.[8] It is an

---

[8]The element of time plays an important part in Buber's presentation of the two basic attitudes (IT, 63-64). By turning the other into a thing, both the self and the object live in the past. Buber means by this that the individual enters the I-It

instrumental or functional way of attending to a world "of nothing but objects" (IT, 64). In this realm the I or self determines what is important in the other. Relationships are ruled by "goal directed verbs" (IT, 54), that is, by the self's feelings, needs, and goals. The other person is just an extension of the self and the relationship follows from what the subject wishes to do "with the things that he experiences and uses" (IT, 63). Much of the description of this attitude is reminiscent of Kierkegaard's portrait of human interactions, particularly Buber's characterization of the I-It in terms of the "false drive for self-affirmation" with its correlate of "the having of things" (IT, 126). Overall, Buber maintains that the I-It attitude is not bad, it only becomes evil when it dominates and overwhelms the possibility of a second type of relation (IT, 97).

The "I-Thou" attitude that Buber portrays has no parallel in Kierkegaard's discussion of natural human relations in *Works of Love*, nor in the presentations of Rosenzweig or Levinas. The I-Thou attitude is one of standing in a true or "direct" relation (IT, 62). The self speaks as "a deed of my whole being . . . my essential deed" (IT, 62), and the other is affirmed on its own terms or in its entirety (IT, 58). Correspondingly, the self's preoccupation with itself is lost as the other holds the self in what Buber describes as the "power of exclusiveness" (IT, 58). The relationship is also characterized by an authentic mutuality and reciprocity of the one side of the relation for the other (IT, 67).

According to Buber, since the other is not an object and cannot be sought, the I-Thou relation emerges out of "sacrifice and grace" (IT, 110). He means by this that the self and its interests must be put aside or sacrificed and, even beyond this, that the relationship requires more than just a willingness or design of the self. Buber also describes this in terms of love, however, this is obviously not the love that arises out of desire or need but a love which is "responsibility of an I for a You" (IT, 66).

---

relationship having already decided what the meaning and possibilities of the relationship are. The individual is not open, that is, will not see or chooses to ignore, responses by the other that go outside the fixed parameters set beforehand. On the other hand, the I-Thou relationship lives in the present, because the individual listens to the other without deciding in advance what will be said.

Although Buber holds that both relations are integral to being a full person, the priority of one over the other is essential to his presentation. The I-Thou relation is in some sense both onto-genetically and phylogenetically, that is pertaining to the develop-ment of the individual and the species, anterior to the I-It relation. He writes: "In the beginning is the [I-Thou] relation—as the category of being, as readiness, as a form that reaches out to be filled, as a model of the soul; the *a priori* of relation; *the innate You*" (IT, 78). Following the "natural association" (IT, 76) of the prenatal infant with the mother and of the infant with the world, the child slowly develops an independent sense of self and then of objects distinct from him or her. The I-It relation, and a more developed I-Thou relation, follow from these first developments.

Buber recognizes a parallel between the life of the individual and that of human history in terms of the "progressive increase of the It-world" (IT, 88). Thus, while the I-Thou relation is the first relation and also that which makes the individual a human in the fullest sense, the I-It relation—with its tendency toward alienating the person from others and the world—has become the norm or customary mode of the everyday.

It is important to note that Buber finds that there are three "spheres" (IT, 56) or areas of relations that are addressed by the two basic types of attitude, as well as an additional sphere (the relationship to the divine) which is exclusive to the I-Thou attitude. The three are the relations to the world of nature, to humans, and to the cultural products of humans or the realm of art (IT, 56-57). I-Thou and I-It relations are possible in each of these spheres. Despite this, the model for the I-Thou attitude is the life with persons (IT, 112), for it is primarily with persons that this relation is fulfilled. Finally, the relation to God or what Buber calls the "eternal Thou" is only possible in terms of the dialogue of "I" and "thou." God is hidden from every approach that attempts to treat Him or Her as an "it" or object.

Rosenzweig's portrayal of the natural state of humans in the *Star of Redemption* is very much in narrative form. There are phylo-genetic and ontogenetic dimensions, although this is complicated and not a single history. Rosenzweig holds that the individual is not born a self. One is born as just another member of the human species, a creature or "piece of the world" (SR, 71). The distinctiveness of what one means by a self erupts. At a certain point in its maturation, the self wills itself in its particularity, out of the combination of "defiance and character," or, alternately, of "hubris and *daimon*" (SR, 167). With the self's emergence, the individual is an utterly autonomous entity; one who is "solitary man in the hardest sense of the word" (71).[9] Formed in this way, it is not surprising that relationship, speech, trust and love are foreign to the self. The life of solitariness, one's being alone facing death, fully characterizes the cage of life for the individual. This cage will only be opened by the relationship to God.

Rosenzweig looks to the tragic hero of Greek drama to illustrate the basic nature of the human untouched by the divine. This is a tale of fundamental alienation from the other. The hero of tragedy lives a life of isolation and self-containment which culminates in his or her self-destruction. This figure, driven by a distinctive character, remains unrelated in any significant way to anyone else. Living essentially speechless, the hero is able to trust only in himself or herself. The central and defining event of that life is the encounter with death: "Death, his own death, has become the sovereign event of his life" (SR, 76-77).

Emmanuel Levinas presents a story about the nature of the human that has two layers. On the one hand, he characterizes the I as being fundamentally turned back upon itself or being self-absorbed. He writes in *Totality and Infinity* that: "To be an I is . . . to have identity as one's content" (TI, 36). Put in another way, the human is a "being whose existing consists in identifying itself, in recovering its identity throughout all that happens to it" (TI, 36). Some features of this identification are explored by the author in terms of the body, labor, possession, and economy (TI, 38). Levinas calls this state the "concreteness of egoism" (TI, 38), and depicts its freedom as "egoist spontaneity" (TI, 43).

This mode of existence is not innocent. Other persons are encountered, but only as objects, subject to my power and freedom (TI, 84). The other is something to be dominated, possessed or dis-

---

[9]Rosenzweig depicts the development of men and women differently. Isolation is not as intense for women, even in the natural state. He believes that the central event for women is the encounter with *eros*, and not with *thantatos* (SR, 156).

carded; to be incorporated, surmounted, enveloped by my world—the same—or to be wiped out. Here freedom is arbitrary and unjustified, and beneath it lurks a self murderous and violent (TI, 84). This is the I of egoism, which Levinas does not hesitate to characterize from the point of view of ethics as "detestable" (TI, 88).

Still, Levinas sees the constitution of the self as more complex than this basic egoism. The self is not a single whole. While it is ruled by its own enjoyment, egoism, and happiness, it also is pulled by a metaphysical desire for what is beyond the self (TI, 34). In Levinas's *Otherwise than Being, or, Beyond Essence* this dimension is discussed in terms of the way that subjectivity is an openness to the other that, while initiated by that other, is structured by one's very body (skin), language (the saying), and thought. He writes that: "Subjectivity . . . obligated with regard to the neighbor, is the breaking point where essence is exceeded by the infinite" (OTB, 12).

Thus, subjectivity, existing as a self, is both enjoyment (utilizing what is outside of the self), and expulsion, that is, being assigned and compelled by the other (OTB, 101). This later feature, which results in the self split, forced, or hostaged, can also be expressed in terms of responsibility. For Levinas, the call of the other is not some later event that occurs in one's life; it demarcates or constitutes the very nature of being human from the first. Levinas writes: "Responsibility for another is not an accident that happens to a subject, but precedes essence in it" (OTB, 114). Further, responsibility implies or implicates more than just another human; it is tied to Levinas's understanding of God.

Finally, although Levinas's treatment is somewhat reminiscent of Buber's depiction of humans' twofold attitude, there are significant differences.[10] Most importantly, Buber sees the I-Thou relationship as being a primary ingredient or expression of living as a person, while Levinas insists that what is dominant is the egoism that entraps the individual; an egoism that must be

---

[10]Levinas has written many articles that critique Buber's presentation. On the whole, his more pessimistic philosophical anthropology makes him deeply suspicious that the mutuality of I and Thou is just another expression of egoism. See n. 1, above.

ruptured by something from the outside, something transcendent, that is, by the Other.[11]

## The Relationship to God

The second stage to be examined in the four narratives concerns the initiation and genesis of the relationship to God. This relationship eventually either overcomes the alienation of the interhuman in the cases of Kierkegaard, Rosenzweig and Levinas, or fulfills the integrity of the interhuman, as is in the instance of Buber's story. Three dimensions of the divine-human relationship will be explored, which are the sequence, the dynamics, and the nature of the transformation that the individual undergoes. As will become apparent in the following, while I have noted these three different dimensions, they are actually blended together in distinctive ways by each of the four philosophers.

First, there is the question of sequence, that is, whether an authentic relationship with other persons precedes or follows the divine-human relationship. The relationship to the divine must take precedence, if humans are inextricably entangled in self-love, solitude, or egoism. Alternately, if the potentiality for healthy relationships is innate, a rescue from the outside is unnecessary and the God-relationship can *follow* upon the establishment of the interhuman.

Second, the nature and dynamics of the relationship with God will be described. We will look at the way that the relation is initiated and also at the expression of its evolution or unfolding. Finally, the manner in which the individual is transformed by the encounter with God will be explored. How does an incursion from the transcendent change the situation of the individual? What is the nature of the new powers bestowed upon humans?

Within Kierkegaard's presentation the matter of sequence, that is, whether meaningful human relations precede or come after the God-relationship, is absolutely clear. Given that in their natural

---

[11]Levinas often capitalizes the term "Other." This signifies the transcendence of the other beyond the self. This Other may be either a person or the divine. Alphonso Lingis, the distinguished translator of many of Levinas's works, briefly discusses the capitalization of this term (TI, 24-25).

state humans are egocentric and radically alienated from others, it follows that for a change in that situation to occur something from the outside must be introduced. This something from the outside is the God-relationship: "The matter is quite simple. A person should begin with loving the unseen, God, because then he himself will learn what it is to love" (WL, 160). Kierkegaard puts this theo-centrically, when he writes that one "belongs first and foremost to God before he belongs to any other relationship" (WL, 140).

The basic argument is that genuine love is neither innate to the individual nor can it be learned from another person. God is the only suitable, the only possible, teacher. As Kierkegaard expressed it: "Therefore it is not the wife who is to teach the husband how he is to love her, or the husband the wife . . . but it is God who is to teach each individual how he is to love" (WL, 113).

There is no explicit discussion in *Works of Love* of exactly how the relationship to God begins or is initiated. It appears that the condition for its emergence is the individual's honest recognition of his or her "inner state" (WL, 361), in this case, the inability out of human powers alone to overcome self-love and to authentically love the other. With this thought the self testifies to its own failure and in self-denial accepts God's power. Kierkegaard's view is that "only in self-denial can one hold fast to God" (WL, 364).

The transformation takes hold with the individual's acceptance of God's command to love the neighbor. In Kierkegaard's terminology, one becomes God's Thou or "You" by accepting the command to love (WL, 90). When the command directs life, then love becomes a duty rather than the result of the individual's desires. Thus, in *Works of Love*, the God-relationship is fundamentally one based on self-denial and duty.

The way God's love is *internalized* by the individual is also not explicitly revealed in Kierkegaard's text. He indicates that a discussion of this is not in harmony with the goal of his book, which is to describe the nature of authentic human relationships, those *outward acts*, those "works of love" (WL, 282; 301). Still, a sense is given of that serene bliss that comes from being in a relationship to God. He says that in attending to, obeying and ultimately appropriating the commandment to love the neighbor, one goes with God (WL, 77), breathes and has one's sustenance in God (WL, 244). Kierkegaard also portrays the person directed by the commandment as God's "instrument" (WL, 363) and as having God as a "coworker" (WL, 362).

For Kierkegaard's portrayal, how is the individual transformed when the commandment and duty are taken up? With the commandment, passion and spontaneity are overridden by the eternal, by a direction that neither changes nor allows evasion (WL, 29). Whatever the self sees, desires, and decides is uprooted or overturned, because the eternal law of loving the neighbor has become the only guidance, the only desire. Kierkegaard puts all of this bluntly: the new self, the Christian, has "no *mine* at all" (WL, 268).

This change in the self is put in other ways, for example, as the shift from despair to hope (WL, 246-63) or faith (WL, 295). Despair is adrift in perceived changes and defects in the other, while hope is undeterred by the outward and continually sees the possibility of the good. Hope is thus beyond the purely human; it is a power of the reconstituted self. As stated in *Works of Love*: "*Only when it is a duty to love, only then is love eternally secured against every change, eternally made free in blessed independence, eternally and happily secured against despair*" (WL, 29).

It is important to note that self-denial does not destroy the uniqueness and meaning of the individual's life. Rather, Kierkegaard explicitly equates the overcoming of the self and establishment of the God-relationship with true individuality or "distinctiveness" (WL, 271). Distinctiveness is not based on the accidental outward characteristics of a person, but on being "oneself" or a self "before God" (WL, 271). One lives out her or his individuality through the unique role that is bestowed by the grace of God's governance, or as God's instrument for others.

Buber's discussion of sequence differs dramatically from what is given in Kierkegaard's *Works of Love*. For him the I-Thou relationship between persons precedes or has priority over the divine-human encounter. As we saw earlier, humans have the power to actualize two types of relationships, and one of these, the I-Thou relationship, is the highest human expression. Buber is not hesitant to designate this relationship as one of "love" in terms of the interhuman realm. For him, life with other persons, that mutuality and reciprocity of the I-Thou realm, is the necessary training or preparation for the latter relationship to God. In his words: "When one has achieved steadfastness in this state [of relating to the world], one is able to venture forth toward the supreme encounter" with God (IT, 125).

There are two additional, and somewhat mitigating, aspects of the priority of the human over the God-relationship in Buber's presentation. First, the I-Thou turning toward the world and others is not seen as fully autonomous or separate from the meeting with God. Buber holds that the relationship to God is the natural, the inevitable step following the meeting with others, or, alternatively, that the God-relationship is a dimension of every true encounter in the world. He writes: "Through every single You the basic word addresses the eternal You" (IT, 123), and that: "In every sphere, through everything that becomes present to us, we gaze toward the train of the eternal You" (IT, 57).

Second, it is in some sense accurate to say that a prior relationship to God grounds the I-Thou relationship to others. This point is not a major one in Buber's text, but it is implied. A prior relationship to God, at least in terms of the human as created, provides the initial potentiality of humans to turn towards others and address them as "thou." He puts this as: "The mediatorship of the You of all beings accounts for the fullness of our relationships to them" (IT, 123). However, since existing as a created being or a creature is what characterizes the natural condition of persons, it is still proper to declare that for Buber humans are so constituted that they can relate meaningfully to others and that these relationships must precede the turning toward God.

Buber provides a careful description of the dynamics or essential features that make up the relationship to God, at least to the extent that this can be put into words (IT, 158). He speaks of three interrelated movements (IT, 157-60). The recipient of revelation, first, has a sense that someone is present and concerned. Second, the individual finds that his or her life, in fact, that all life has meaning. Words cannot articulate what the meaning is, but one feels it and this feeling is never completely lost. Third, the individual is thrust back into the world. The God-relationship requires that one puts its truth "to the proof in action" in the world with others (IT, 160). According to Buber, in fulfilling God's word or mission as it is given, one "always has God before him" (IT, 164).

Although Buber unhesitatingly affirms the importance of the relationship to God, the nature of the transformation that the God-relationship brings to the self is rather discrete. As we saw, the relationship to other humans and the world is a training of the self and the God-relationship is a completion. The "innate You," that is, the individual's innate power to call upon others, achieves "perfection solely in the immediate relationship to" the eternal Thou (IT, 123). The person sees the world in a new way: "the world becomes wholly present to him for the first time in the fullness of the presence, illuminated by eternity" (IT, 157). In addition, the individual now recognizes the meaningfulness of her or his life and of life overall to the extent that the question of the life's meaningfulness is no longer pressing (IT, 158-59). While the insecurity, challenge, and openness of the realm of the I-Thou must always remain (IT, 83; 126), following the encounter with God the self has a firmer direction.

Rosenzweig's position concerning the question of sequence, similarly to his view of humans' original situation, is reminiscent of Kierkegaard. Since humans on their own are closed in upon themselves and fixated by the threat of death, they require a catalyst to overcome this predicament. Consequently, the God-relationship necessarily precedes authentic human meetings: "It is only . . . in the love of God that the flower of the soul begins to grow out of the rock of the self. Previously man had been a senseless and speechless introvert; only now is he—beloved soul" (SR, 169).

The dynamics of the relationship to God is depicted by Rosenzweig in the *Star of Redemption* as a love scene between two lovers (SR, 156-204). God is the initiating lover and the individual or soul is the beloved. God first gives love to the soul, by commanding that the soul love Him. The initial reaction of the soul, however, is shame, for not having loved before. Eventually the soul acknowledges God and accepts His love in trust, faithfulness, and peace (SR, 170-71). Thus, for Rosenzweig, the authentic I emerges in response to God's presence as an I.

However, the exchange between the two partners necessitates another step. God's momentary revelation must be both made everlasting and expressed in the world. For Rosenzweig, this cannot be achieved in the isolation of the I and Thou between God and the soul. Only in the world, through the individual's turning in love to the neighbor, is permanence or redemption achieved. Rosenzweig writes about this as: "He whom God's love has chosen hears God's command . . . and sets out for the land that God will show him. . . . the realm of redemption" (SR, 251).

How does the God-relationship transform the individual in Rosenzweig's narrative? As we have seen, the *Star of Redemption* outlines the becoming of a person as the movement from being an enclosed self to living as a speaking and loving soul. The shift of terminology from self to soul underscores this transformation. The fear of death that was the self's overriding concern, a concern that halted a real life with others, is no longer allowed to be the cap-stone to life. It has been replaced by the soul's trust; trust in the Creator and patience and hope to wait for the Redeemer (SR, 382).

Revelation, which is God's liberating love, elicits both speech and love from the individual. For Rosenzweig, the two are synonymous. Both require that the self open to the other. Both speech and love are the currencies in the mutuality of relationship. The other can be of concern, because the fear of one's own death has been lifted: "The living soul, loved by God, triumphs over all that is mortal, and that is all that can be objectively stated about it" (SR, 202).

Another way of describing what is given to the individual is to examine Rosenzweig's concept of orientation. Revelation teaches that neither the individual's life nor the world are ruled by blind fate. There is providence, that is, purpose. The world has been created and is pointed toward redemption. The transformed individual feels that she or he has been assigned a particular time and place and must respond to that assignment by way of her or his life (SR, 392). Just as Buber, Rosenzweig is convinced that the individual's everyday life is permeated by a sense of mission and a recognition that God's command in the world must be verified, that is to say, answered (SR, 393).

With Levinas, it appears that the relationship to the other pre-cedes the encounter with the divine in the context of the story of the development of the self.[12] However, it can also be argued that

---

[12]In Merold Westphal's view, Levinas affirms that the relationship to the neighbor precedes the relationship to God. He sees this priority as one of the fundamental features that distinguishes Levinas's position from that of Kierke-gaard. See Westphal's "The Transparent Shadow: Kierkegaard and Levinas in Dialogue," in *Kierkegaard in Post/Modernity*, ed. Martin J. Matustik and Merold

since the two relationships are so intimately bound together, there is no real priority. On the one hand, Levinas explicitly rules out the priority of the God-relationship, because he contends that there is no direct relationship to God. The relationship to God is *always* mediated by the relationship to one's neighbor (TI, 78-79). Yet, on the other hand, there is a trace of the presence of the divine in the authentic relationship to the neighbor. More concretely, a trace of God is revealed when one looks into the face the other. As Levinas states it: "The Other is not the incarnation of God, but precisely by his face, in which he is disincarnate, is the manifestation of the height in which God is revealed" (TI, 79).[13]

Levinas displays great austerity in speaking of God or the God-relationship. Still, a suggestive breach to this appears in the final footnote to *Otherwise than Being*. He alludes to the rabbinic commentary about Moses' death through the kiss of God (Deut. 34:5), and ties this mysterious closeness to God with the "passivity and obedience, in the inspiration by the other for the other" (OTB, 200).

In terms of Levinas's depiction of the transformed individual, the quality, as it were, of Levinas's story is reminiscent of that of Kierkegaard. For the former, since the egoism of the self is so entrenched, the shattering of the individual's natural attitude must

---

Westphal (Bloomington: Indiana University Press, 1995) 273-74. However, there is a problem with another difference that Westphal finds between the two philosophers. He is correct that Levinas rejects "the specifically Christian 'salvation drama' of Kierkegaard," 277, but I believe it is inaccurate to state that Levinas does not envision "a fundamental alteration of experience as we now endure it," 277, or that he "has a philosophy of sin without salvation," 278. Although Westphal at one point refers to Levinas's short essay "Loving the Torah More than God," 280, he overlooks some subtle aspects of it. For Levinas the distinctive Jewish understanding is that God's presence is manifested in this world through Torah and the individual's conscience. Additionally, the fullness of this presence *is* awaited in the future when, finally, "justice and power must join." Emmanuel Levinas, *Difficult Freedom: Essays on Judaism*, tran. Sean Hand (Baltimore: John Hopkins University Press, 1990) 145.

[13]It might appear that the face has priority over the relationship to the divine, but Levinas's presentation is not unambiguous on this point. Robert Gibbs has found that "For Levinas there is no gap between the encounter with the other and the self-sanctification before God; the two moments are entwined in the experience of the face of the other," *Correlations in Rosenzweig and Levinas* (Princeton NJ: Princeton University Press, 1992) 187.

be radical. The language utilized by Levinas is nothing less than violent.[14] To achieve authentic subjectivity the individual must become hollowed out, inverted, extroverted, denucleated, even persecuted. In his words: "The subjectivity of the subject is persecution and martyrdom" (OTB, 146). The individual is made nothing less than a substitute, a hostage to the other (OTB, 146).

Again, it is the face of the poor and the stranger that overturns the individual, that overcomes every defense that the person might erect (TI, 213). The other forces the individual to justify himself or herself, recognizing that the other has a right over the self (TI, 40). Alternatively, the spontaneity of egoism is brought into question through ethics (TI, 40). Ultimately, the face-to-face relationship causes shame, "where, qua I, I am not innocent spontaneity but usurper and murderer" (TI, 84).

Levinas also has a more positive way of seeing the results of this rupture of the self. The encounter with the other teaches the self what it could not find on its own; it provides meaning which is beyond the grasp of the ego. Following upon a theme of Rosenzweig's, Levinas sees the face-to-face relation as answering even the threat of one's death. The other does not eliminate death, but allows a "forgetting of death" (OTB, 141), or provides a meaning that even death cannot wipe away. Levinas writes: "No one is so hypocritical as to claim that he has taken from death its sting. . . . But we can have responsibilities and attachments through which death takes on a meaning" (OTB, 129).

For Levinas, even language is not that autonomous medium that many postmodernists see, but something founded on the face-to-face. As he puts it: "Meaning is the face of the Other, and all recourse to words takes place already within the primordial face-to-face of language" (TI, 206).

---

[14]There is a comparison of Rosenzweig's view that the self must be put aside in order to meet the other and Levinas's language of the necessity for the self to be ruptured or torn, in my *Speaking/Writing of God: Jewish Philosophical Reflections on the Life with Others* (Albany: State University of New York Press, 1997) 17-18.

*The Transformed Interhuman*

The last stage that will be explored in the four narratives is the exposition concerning the way that the interhuman has been remade by the encounter with the divine. This includes a description of both what has changed in terms of the relationship to others and how the new interhuman is lived out. Since all of the philosophers insist that the fruits—in Kierkegaard's terms—of the God-relationship must be expressed among others, this is a necessary part, in fact, the highlight, of their overall stories.

How has the relationship to God changed the possibilities for human interaction, according to Kierkegaard? Fundamentally, Christian love is the result of the God-relationship, through the command to love the neighbor, mediating all human relations. The interhuman is no longer constituted simply by persons or directly between them. At several points, Kierkegaard speaks of God as being the necessary "middle term" of the interhuman realm (WL, 107; 113; 339).

Obviously, in discussing the nature of this new interhuman, the contrast between human love and Christian love continues to animate Kierkegaard's *Works of Love*. Earlier we saw that human love is preferential, in terms of the other's perceived advantages (for the self), calculating or dependent upon the other's response, transient, blind to the true nature of the other—seeing only the self in the other, and, ultimately, for the sake of the self. Alternatively, that love that has been refined or purged by God is toward everyone, without distinctions, independent of the other's response, constant, aware of the distinctiveness of the other, and, finally, for the sake of the other.

Since Christian love is in response to an inescapable demand or command from God to love the neighbor, it extends to everyone. Whoever one encounters is the neighbor, or as Kierkegaard puts it " 'the neighbor' means 'all people' " (WL, 21). At the same time, relating to the other in the presence of God wipes away differences or distinctions that would elicit the self's preferences. Before God, even the seemingly most important human differences evaporate or are leveled (WL, 342). Additionally, because the command is unceasing, Christian love has continuity (WL, 32) having gone through "the change of eternity" for *only when it is a duty to love, only then is love eternally secured"* (WL, 32).

As a reflection of the relationship to the divine, Christian love is, thus, independent of all outward circumstances—which includes even the possible responses of the one that must be loved (WL, 39). In this vein, Kierkegaard speaks of Christian love in terms of conscience, rather than of calculation. The relation to the divine "transforms every relationship between person and person into a relationship of conscience" (WL, 137). The other's love is not demanded and the other's possible hostility does not override the duty that must be fulfilled.

As a result of self-denial and God's becoming the mediator of the interhuman, the other no longer exists in the shadow of the self. Christian love penetrates through the earlier blindness to truly see the neighbor. Through the God-relationship the individual "loves every human being according to his distinctiveness . . . he loves what is the other's own" (WL, 269). In Kierkegaard's treatment this means that the other is seen in terms of what is most important and distinct about him or her, the uniqueness of that particular person's relationship to God.

Further, while there are other features of this love, perhaps its most important characteristic is that it is honestly for the sake of the neighbor. In Kierkegaard's understanding this is equated with what is for the highest benefit for the other, which is, again, the other's God-relationship. These overall features of the transformed interhuman are summarized by Kierkegaard in terms of a new mutuality: *"to help another person to love God is to love another person; to be helped by another person to love God is to be loved"* (WL, 107).

The first stage of the examination of Buber's narrative in *I and Thou* indicated that humans have the ability to authentically turn to one another, in some sense prior to and outside of the God-relation. In light of this, it is much more difficult to see what the encounter with the divine directly adds to this realm of the "between." The change will be a matter of degree, rather than exhibiting some dramatic transformation.

One possible way of eliciting what might be changed is to explore the third feature of Buber's description of the nature of (all) revelation. We saw that the meeting with the eternal Thou must be verified or put "to the proof in action" in the world (IT,

159). In this way there might be an additional depth to all human relations, because they are not just a matter of persons either singly or in communities entering into I-Thou relations. Such relations are verifications or extensions of the encounter with the divine.

Thus, God's presence and direction continually accompany I-Thou relations. Again, what might be meant by this? In the afterword to *I and Thou* Buber elaborates the notion of how God's presence is felt: "God's address to man penetrates the events in all our lives and all the events in the world around us . . . and turns it into instruction, into demands for you and me" (IT, 182). Although this statement is reminiscent of Kierkegaard's position that the interhuman must be directed by God's demands or commands, it is more clearly tied to Buber's view, which we have seen before, that each person has a unique place in the world or a mission given by God.

The treatment of the transformed interhuman is also not fully developed in Rosenzweig's *Star of Redemption*, which moves from the portrayal of the encounter with God to a discussion of religious community. Further, the change in the possibilities of human relationships are expressed in poetic language and only through clues. Still, some elaboration is possible based upon Rosenzweig's discussion of revelation, which he saw as a model for the exchange of "I" and "Thou" between persons (SR, 199), and redemption.

If the command to love God signals the commencement of the personal experience of God's presence, the way leads out of the personal and private experience of God by the second command, to love the neighbor (SR, 214). The individual's life in the world is henceforth guided by this obligation. Who is the neighbor according to Rosenzweig? The neighbor is everyone and concretely, the one who stands closest to one, the nighest (*das Nebenmensch*) (SR, 218). This means that one consequence of the encounter with God is that the individual has an obligation to every person that is met in the unfolding of the hourly and daily rhythms of life.

Loving the neighbor adds a new dynamic to the interhuman and even to the divine processes of creation, revelation, and redemption. Turning to the other begins again that process—for the neighbor—of hearing the divine word, feeling the divine presence, and then turning to the next person. Through love of the neighbor, the other ceases to be an "it," simply another part of creation. She or he becomes a soul, as did the original beloved of God. As Rosenzweig put it: "Rather he [the neighbor] is like You, like your You, a You like You, an I—soul" (SR, 240). This ensouling of the other and eventually of the world constitutes the course of redemption.

Rosenzweig indicates that a trace of the divine animates and remains present throughout the transformed interhuman. In fact, turning toward other persons is portrayed in the *Star of Redemption* as walking in the presence of God (SR, 422-24). The human face reflects God's truth; the face of the neighbor radiates God's countenance. Rosenzweig writes that God's truth has "become countenance which glances at me and out of which I glance" (SR, 423).

Perhaps it is in speech between persons—and for Rosenzweig the dynamics of love and speech are similar—that the results of the divine encounter are clearest. Just as God's love brought the individual out of her or his isolating fear of death and mute existence, the love of neighbor opens up the neighbor to the possibilities of the I and Thou of speech for the first time. In turning to the neighbor the other is acknowledged as something separate from the self, as something "independent and freely confronting" (SR, 175). Speech exhibits a mutuality, where the acknowledgment of the other can be exchanged between the partners.

Finally, Rosenzweig holds that there is a significant communal dimension to the new possibilities of human relationships. The end of isolation allows persons to form together into a "we." This we grows out of the dual of I and Thou and continually increases. Although limited and recognizing that there are others that stand outside, its goal is to eventually include everyone (SR, 236-37). Starting with the nighest, the "we" builds to an "all." In Rosenzweig's words: "The effect of the love of 'neighbor' is that 'Anyone' and 'all the world' thus belong together" (SR, 236).

Thus, although the details of the new relation to others are not fully worked out in the *Star of Redemption*, there is a significant difference between human existence before and after God's revelation. The self is not limited to its initial isolation and muteness. For Rosenzweig, radical transformation of the self through the love of God and love of neighbor is a reality, for "love [and thus also speech] is man's momentary self-transformation, his self-denial" (SR, 163).

For Levinas, the face-to-face relation, with the concomitant divine command not to kill, fundamentally transforms the possibilities of human interaction. The other is no longer just an object to the self, something to be mastered, usurped or even murdered. The other stands in her or his height above the self and through this the egoism of the self is overwhelmed. As Levinas expressed it: "To recognize the Other is to give. But it is to give to the master, to the lord, to him whom one approaches as 'You' in a dimension of height" (TI, 75). In other words, the face-to-face establishes for the first time an authentic interhuman, the realm of ethics.

Perhaps the most pervasive characteristic of the altered interhuman is responsibility. The self which turns upon itself and is delegitimated in its own eyes becomes subsequently a responsible self. The individual comes to recognize—to be obsessed with (OTB, 87)—an unrelenting responsibility, where one must answer with a "*here I am* . . . for everything and for everyone" (OTB, 114). More importantly, not only is the self made responsible, but it is granted the powers to fulfill that which it is called upon to give (TI, 215).

Many of the features of the authentic interhuman, of a fraternity of equality and command (TI, 214), are discussed by Levinas in terms of language. Language unveils the separation of the partners, the dependence of the self on the other, and even the priority of the other (TI, 73). Communication between persons reveals a discourse where welcoming is possible (TI, 178). Such communication is more than a repeat of the same; it is creative. The new is allowed to appear, because the other represents something outside of mere being, something of transcendence (OTB, 182). Further, through communication meaning is created (TI, 66) and truth can be legitimately sought. Finally, language or discourse is even tied to love. In Levinas's words: "The metaphysical event of transcendence—the welcome of the Other, hospitality—Desire and language—is not accomplished as love. But the transcendence of discourse is bound to love" (TI, 254).

*Conclusion. Of the Self, the Interpersonal, and Transcendence*

The narratives of Kierkegaard, Buber, Rosenzweig and Levinas present distinct yet overlapping portraits of what it means to be a human with others. In this conclusion I want to recapitulate and extend the treatment by examining the understanding of the fundamental social nature of the self, the depiction of the types of alienation from others, the view that a transcendent opening from this alienation is both possible and necessary, and finally, the role of the metaphor of God as person in the narratives. While these are only a few of the areas that appear in the above presentation, I believe that they are some of the more diagnostic ones. These foci will illuminate what the narratives share rather than what separates or clearly differentiates them.

All of these portrayals are built upon the insight that, in Buber's words, "There is no I as such." Individuals cannot be understood or examined in isolation from others. These philosophers' expositions of the nature of the human converge on the social character of existence. Thus it is such features as erotic love, friendship, speaking, and being responsible which are taken as quintessential. More pointedly, it is only in relation to other persons and to God that life gains direction and meaning. Meaning is not self-engendered. Life becomes meaningful when the self is put aside and a concern for the other takes precedence.

Yet, these treatments of the social character of human life do not conclude with some view that, ultimately, the individual self is not real. The discourse about authenticity does not abandon the vocabulary of the individual self by arguing that the highest is a losing the self or a merging the self with either other persons or the divine. The uniqueness of each life is upheld through relationship.

Individuality is achieved when the self accepts the directive of God to turn to and help other persons. Kierkegaard discusses this in terms of being God's Thou or instrument. He speaks of being directed by Governance to a life dedicated to loving the neighbor. Additionally for Kierkegaard, the dynamic of becoming a full individual is tied to recognizing the concrete reality of the other. For him, self-love prevented the individual from seeing the other except as an extension or in the shadow of the self. When the transformed individual sees the other in that person's particular terms, the individual subject also finally exists in his or her own. In Kierkegaard's words, as quoted previously: "To have distinctiveness is to believe in the distinctiveness of everyone else, because distinctiveness is not mine but is God's gift" (WL, 271).

For Buber, Rosenzweig, and Levinas the matter is essentially similar. The individuality of the self or the uniqueness of one's life results from accepting the call in the midst of the interaction with the particular persons one comes up against. As Buber expresses this: "The meaning we receive [from revelation] can be put to the proof in action only by each person in the uniqueness of his being and in the uniqueness of his life" (IT, 159). Rosenzweig explores the unique place each person is given in God's plan or in terms of "mission": "The personal is verified as eternal truth: birth and rebirth, station and mission, located Here and decisive Now of life" (SR, 394). Finally, Levinas extends this view of the way that relationship to the other establishes distinctiveness or individuality. He affirms something that, I believe, is an element in the other thinkers as well, that is, that specific others draw out the self one is to be. He writes: "Exposedness ["exposure to the other"] is the one-in-responsibility [the self], and thus the one in its uniqueness" (OTB, 56).

The four narratives probe in an intense, unrelenting manner the types of alienation or sickness that haunt relationships between persons. Actually, it is in terms of this subject that one might expect a chasm between the portrait offered by Kierkegaard, a Christian, and those of the Jewish philosophers, Buber, Rosenzweig and Levinas. However, it does not appear that the Christian doctrine of original sin, which has no corresponding notion in the Jewish tradition, radically differentiates Kierkegaard's view of alienation from the Jewish ones.[15]

As we have seen, Kierkegaard's diagnosis centers on self-love. He uncovers the overriding concern for the self behind all relations. Forming exclusive relationships, that is, selecting an "extraordinary" person as lover or friend, can be seen "through" as an effort of the self to maintain itself as something exceptional. Demanding mutuality in relations is a subtle type of calculus that looks out for what the self receives back. In all, the omnipresent reach of the self does not allow the other to be understood or

---

[15]Of course, there are areas where Kierkegaard's treatment is distinctive. His discussions of erotic love and marriage that portray these as problematic in terms of the God-relationship have no clear parallel in the works of the other authors. See WL, 137-45.

cared for in his or her own terms. For Kierkegaard, there is no *human* escape from the self's passion to aggrandize itself and, consequently, to erase the other.

Buber's portrayal of the dynamics of the interhuman provides more hope about the possibilities for authentic mutuality, but it is by no means a naive narrative. The I-Thou encounter momentarily and, at best, briefly, sporadically punctuates the everyday. It must redeem those other relations that are the preponderant ones. These, of the I-It realm, always tie the other to the self's desires and plans. The other is objectified, a passive piece, moved not by concern for but by the self's designs upon. Further, because the objectifying *modus vivendi* of the I-It is set by the self before the other is encountered, no word or protest can be heard in the midst of the relationship. In the I-It realm there is no present; there is no speech or listening, no real interchange.

Rosenzweig's self is also blind to the other. However, rather than self-interest, Rosenzweig finds that fear prevents true relation. Limited by his or her own powers, the individual sees no meaning in life and is conscious of being cast upon the road to death. Haunted by this, there is no speech, no love. The self is closed upon itself, not by choice, but through, as it were, fate. This conclusion is embodied in the figure of the tragic hero.

For Levinas, egoism does not allow the other to be seen, to be faced. The other, once more, is an object. At best "it" is used, abused, moved for the sake of the individual's comfort or happiness. More ominously, the self seeks to either incorporate or eradicate. It wants to build up more of the self-same, and is violent toward that which cannot be made over into its image.

Each of these portraits of sickness add perspectives upon the customary failures of the interhuman realm. More important, however, is the shared idea that sickness has a remedy. For all four philosophers, the self has the possibility of transcending this usual condition. They hold that, freedom, spontaneity *in relationships*, more importantly, love and responsibility are not illusions. These features of human experience may not be easy to achieve and may not be dominant in the normal run of things, but they are not totally outside of human existence. Recognizing, through another relationship, this time to the divine, the alienation that pervades the usual brings a freedom for new possibilities of existence.

The divine teaches of the category of the neighbor, that one is responsible to each of one's others. In addition, the divine provides the powers to realize this responsibility. Thus, we learn from the philosophical narratives that transcendence of the self is not part of the self's own story. Transcendence of one's normal condition is reached through relationship and this transcendence is the basis for further relationships. As the narratives relate: the transformed self must continually "bear fruits" or be put to the "proof in action" in terms of the neighbor.

A final area of inquiry concerns the omnipresence and role of the metaphor of God as person in the four narratives. There is a profusion of examples of the metaphor of God as person in Kierkegaard's narrative. God is educator, colaborer, one's Thou, the presence of the third in any relation. As sometimes is the case in terms of another person, the presence of God evokes "modesty" from the individual (WL, 341-42). Crucial to Kierkegaard's argument is the view that authentic love, that is a concern for the other—for the sake of the other—can only be learned from the encounter with the divine.

Buber's use of the metaphor of God as person is equally transparent. God is a Thou, in fact, the only Thou that cannot be transformed into an it. The I-Thou relationship, of mutuality, reciprocity, love, and responsibility, becomes in Buber's discourse equally as true in terms of the encounter with the divine as it is in the interhuman realm, for "the relation to a human being is the proper metaphor for relation to God" (IT, 151). In the "Afterword" he adds that for him: "The designation of God as a person is indispensable" (IT, 180), and "It is as *absolute person* that God enters into direct relationship to us" (IT, 181-82).

For Rosenzweig, the relation of lovers which he draws from the erotic poem *The Song of Songs*, drives the whole *Star of Redemption*. For the book's centerpiece is the relationship between God/the lover and the soul/the beloved, which explores the nature of revelation. The power and poetry of this section is dazzling. Rosenzweig expresses the response of the individual to God's command to love God with all one's heart and soul: "The beloved's admission of love responds to the lover's demand of love" (SR, 178). He depicts faithfulness as possession: "And because the soul holds on to him, therefore God allows himself to be held by it" (SR, 170).

Finally, Rosenzweig introduces a dramatic maternal metaphor to characterize the serenity of God's love: "The soul is at peace in the love of God, like a child in the arms of its mother" (SR, 171).

While Levinas is more austere than probably all of the other philosophers, anthropomorphic metaphors are also vitally important for his story. There is no direct relationship to God, but in the face-to-face relation God appears to call, command, and judge. One, in turn, bears witness to God by being accountable for the other. In his words: "the 'here I am' signifies me in the name of God, at the service of men" (OTB, 149).

Why is the metaphor of God as person a significant feature of each of the four stories of the interhuman? The importance of the interhuman is reinforced through the understanding that God is to be experienced not as void, principle, or inner power but in the same manner as persons, as the neighbor. If God were nothingness or void, the parallel ultimate notions of the self and the other would be void or nothingness. If a vocabulary of God as principle dominated, then the realm of thought might overcome the importance of what can be done and experienced in the everyday through and in the passions. Finally, if the divine were an inner power, then the theme about the self as obstacle would not be possible. When the divine is narrated as person, and the encounter as a dialogue or love relationship, then the ultimate value of the neighbor as separate and as one who is met in the everyday is confirmed.

# 11

# The Child and Kierkegaard's "One Who Loves": The Agapic Flip Side of Peter Pan

## Eric Ziolkowski

While Kierkegaard scholars routinely discuss the crucial bearing of his unusual childhood, and especially his early relationship with his father, upon his later development as a thinker and writer,[1] surprisingly little attention is devoted to the significance of the child as a type in his published works, both pseudonymous and nonpseudonymous, as well as in his journals. The import of this subject is hinted at in the brief note to the eight entries on childhood and children, dating from 1837 to 1849, compiled in the Hong edition of the *Journals*: "In connection with his illumination of the various steps in the development of the individual, Kierkegaard considers the period of childhood in some detail. Through his own experience in childhood he knew how important this portion of life is for a person's later development" (JP, 1:509).

That Kierkegaard was, in the Hongs' words, "a keen observer of children" (JP, 1, p. 510), is already apparent in a journal entry of 1837 where, reacting to a recent essay by Poul M. Møller on telling stories to children,[2] he elaborates thoughts of his own about childhood and about the sort of storytelling he deems appropriate for children (JP, 1:265). In an entry twelve years later on Galatians

---

[1]In the standard biographies such discussions often involve declarations to the effect that "if ever the child was father of the man, it was in this instance" (Walter Lowrie, *A Short Life of Kierkegaard* [Princeton NJ: Princeton University Press, 1965] 54); or that his childhood relationship with his father, "above all, made him the man he later became; the shadow of Michael Pedersen Kierkegaard was cast across the whole path of his life" (Josiah Thompson, *Kierkegaard* [New York: Alfred A. Knopf, 1973] 33).

[2]"Om at fortaelle Børn Eventyr" (1836–1837), in Poul M. Møller, *Efterladte Skrifter*, 3 vols. (Copenhagen: Reitzel, 1839–1843) 3:322-25.

4:1-7, Kierkegaard invokes the child to illustrate the God-relationship. After observing our progression from first being "slaves under the law," to then becoming "children," then finally "children who cry Abba, Father, and co-heirs of Christ," he concludes that

> there is an increasing openness in relation to God. But it is not like the relationship between adults and children, in which the openness comes after the child has grown up; here it is the reverse—one does not begin as a child but as a slave, and the openness increases as one becomes more and more a child. (JP, 1:272)

Singled out by the Hongs as representative of the many allusions to the child that are found in Kierkegaard's writings, these two journal entries would furnish helpful starting points for a deeper investigation of the use of children by him and his pseudonyms. Although differently nuanced insights into children are arrived at in each of his works, my ultimate aim in what follows will be to examine the specific use of the child figure in *Works of Love*, whose appearance in 1847 fell between the years of the two entries above. As we shall see, the perspective conveyed by *Works of Love* toward childhood, like those expressed in Kierkegaard's other writings, displays a distinctive dialectical oscillation between positive and negative attitudes, thus befitting the maieutic aim peculiar to his entire corpus.

However, as the conception of childhood as a stage *sui generis* in a human being's life appears to be a relatively recent development in Western intellectual and cultural history, the extensive usage of the child as a type throughout Kierkegaard's oeuvre crystallizes what was in his time still a relatively new, developing Christian tendency of perceiving children as creatures endowed with a psychology distinct from that of adults, and hence with minds that will respond differently from adult minds to the central doctrines and images of Christian faith. For this reason, before we examine the employment of the child as a type in *Works of Love*, it will be beneficial first, briefly, to consider the general history of reflection on the child in the Christian West, concentrating on the views of Jesus, St. Paul, St. Augustine, and Rousseau as chief points of reference; and then, again briefly, to locate Kierkegaard and his pseudonyms in their relationship to that history.

### Bipolar Western Views of Childhood

Today, notwithstanding the not-so-rare news stories of terrible crimes committed by children, such as the 1993 abduction and slaying of two-year-old James Bulger by a pair of ten-year-old boys in Liverpool, England, or the more recent proliferation of fatal shootings in American high schools by students sixteen years old and younger, the conventional notion of childhood still approximates the one summed up by the entry on "Child" in *The Herder Dictionary of Symbols*:

> A symbol of spontaneity and innocence, qualities alluded to in the New Testament ("Except ye be converted and become as little children, ye shall not enter into the kingdom of heaven." Matt. 18:3).[3]

This declaration by Christ (cf. Mark 10:15; Luke 18:17), together with his teaching that the kingdom of heaven "belongs" to "such" as children (Matt. 19:14; Mark 10:14; Luke 18:16), might seem to dissociate them from Adam's guilt and to defy Aristotle's idea of the child as an "imperfect" being whose "excellence is not relative to himself alone, but to the perfect man and to his teacher."[4] To be sure, while he praises children for their humbleness, Jesus himself never characterizes them as perfect or innocent; if he privileges them in the order of salvation, he does not explicitly do so because of any inherent spiritual qualities or dispositions.[5] Yet these facts have mattered little, as Jesus has often been mistaken as the source of the clichéd Romantic notion of children as little innocents.

Directly related to the popular misunderstanding of Jesus' exaltation of children is the common assumption that the traditional Christian view of them has always been identical with his view. In actuality, although Jesus' association of children with humility

---

[3]*The Herder Dictionary of Symbols: Symbols from Art, Archaeology, Mythology, Literature, and Religion* (Wilmette IL: Chiron Publications, 1986) 37.

[4]Aristotle, *Politics*, trans B. Jowett, 2.1260a.31-33, in *The Complete Works of Aristotle*, 2 vols., ed. Jonathan Barnes (Princeton NJ: Princeton University Press, 1984) 2:2000.

[5]As noted by S. Légasse, *Jésus et l'enfant: "Enfants," "petits" et "simples" dans la tradition synoptique* (Paris: J. Gabalda, 1969) 340.

and salvation is supported by 1 Peter 2:2 ("Like newborn babes, long for the pure spiritual milk, that by it you may grow up to salvation"), his positive assessment of them finds stiff opposition elsewhere in the New Testament, particularly in the famous analogy invoked by St. Paul to illustrate his own religious conversion: "When I was a child, I spoke like a child, I thought like a child, I reasoned like a child; when I became a man, I gave up childish ways" (1 Cor. 13:11). For Paul, abandoning "childish ways" connotes recognizing that knowledge and the capacity to convey it prophetically or in tongues are faulty, and hence are less valuable gifts than faith, hope, and love. Seeming to assume the Aristotelian notion of the child as an imperfect being whose "excellence" is relative to the perfect man, he has already submitted that "when the perfect comes, the imperfect will pass away" (1 Cor. 13:10). Here "the perfect" means spiritual maturity, or becoming "a man," while "the imperfect" means spiritual infancy, or "childish ways." Paul is essentially urging his readers to grow up, and to stop thinking like little children (see 1 Cor. 14:20).

Paul's promotion of the spiritual superiority of adulthood over childhood corresponds to his figural understanding of the first man, Adam, through whose transgression humankind inherited sin, condemnation, and death, as the "type" of Christ, the second Adam who acquits, justifies, and restores humankind to life (Rom. 5:12-21; 1 Cor. 15:22, 45-49). Of all stages of life, infancy and childhood would seem the ones most closely linked to original sin, as every infant born is an heir of Adam's fallenness and can only hope to be redeemed by converting later in life to faith in Christ, as Paul himself was converted on the road to Damascus.

If the views expressed by Jesus and Paul established two main, opposed poles of opinion between which subsequent Christian attitudes toward children could develop, it was Paul's perspective, not Jesus', that conditioned Christian thinking about children for well over the next millennium and a half. However, not Paul, but Augustine was chiefly responsible for this legacy. It is in Augustine's writings, most notably the opening books of his *Confessions*, that the implicit Pauline linkage of infancy and childhood with Adamic sin first achieves full and explicit expression. An astute ponderer of babies, he believed that the earliest evidence of sin is detectable in their behavior, and consequently that all unbaptized

children, even if born of the faithful, perish *(pereunt)*.[6] Having seen
that an infant, even when fully fed, would become angry and
jealous at seeing another infant at its mother's breast, he concluded
that "it is not the mind of infants that is 'innocent,' but the
weakness of its infantile members."[7] In other words, infants would
sin if only they could physically do so.

Augustine's rejection of the notion of infantile "innocence"
carried over to his view of older children, whom he saw as
existing within the fallen condition bequeathed by Adam,[8] much
as Paul had recalled having lived as a lawless child (Rom. 7:9). In
associating children with Adamic guilt rather than the heavenly
humility that Jesus ascribed to them, Augustine could only strain
to square the latter view with the memory of his own peccadillos
as a boy: lying, theft, cheating, and indulgence in frivolity.
Addressing God he asked:

> Is this boyish innocence [*innocentia puerilis*]? It is not, Lord. It is
> not. . . . For these are the same things, the very same things,
> which, as we depart from teachers and masters, from nuts and
> balls and pet birds, proceeding to kings, gold, estates, and slaves,
> continue on as more years pass in succession, just as greater
> punishments succeed the ferule. Therefore, our King, it was
> [only] a symbol of humility which you praised in the [diminu-
> tive] stature of childhood, saying: To such belongs the kingdom
> of heaven.[9]

Thus precluding any literalistic interpretation of Jesus' expressed favoritism for children, the Augustinian view of the child
as innately sinful predominated throughout the Middle Ages in the
Christian West. Consequently, as suggested by medieval art,
children were valued mainly as adults-to-be. The rare pictures in
which they appear tend to portray them as diminutive men;
according to Philippe Ariès, this absence of lifelike representations

---

[6]E.g., Augustine, Sermon 294.19.18, delivered at Carthage, in *Patrologia cursus
completus. Series latina*, 221 vols., ed. J.-P. Migne (Paris, 1844–1866) 38:1347.

[7]Augustine, *Confessions* 1.7.11; my translation. All references to this work are
to *Sancti Aureli Augustini Confessionum, libri tredecim*, ed. Pius Knöll, *Corpus
Scriptorum Ecclesiasticorum Latinorum* 33.

[8]E.g., Augustine, *Confessions* 1.9.14; *City of God* 22.22.34.

[9]Augustine, *Confessions* 1.19.30; my translation.

of children shows that "there was no place for childhood in the medieval world."[10] Only during the thirteenth century did actual child morphology begin to be depicted in art, which anticipated what Ariès chronicles as the gradual "discovery" of childhood as a period of life separate and distinct from adulthood, and the modern idea of childish innocence. This idea, by Ariès' account, emerged in the moral and pedagogical literature of the late sixteenth century and the seventeenth century, and was exemplified by the frequency with which painters and engravers of that period portrayed the Gospel scene of Jesus' blessing of the children, a scene which hitherto had been rarely portrayed.[11]

An irony which Ariès does not adequately account for is that these developments followed the age of the Protestant reformers, whose dominant theologies had reemphasized the doctrine of original sin and hence the notion that children are inherently depraved. Heightening this irony, the tendency of thought away from the medieval negativism toward children culminated only a couple of centuries after the Reformation in Rousseau's treatise on education, *Émile* (1762), which opens with the assertion: "Everything is good as it leaves the hands of the Author of things; everything degenerates in the hands of man."[12]

Here we arrive at an attitude toward children that is the very antithesis of the centuries-old Augustinian wariness toward them. For Rousseau, not only is nothing wrong with childhood; on the contrary, children are meant by Nature "to be children before being men. . . . Childhood has its ways of seeing, thinking, and feeling which are proper to it. Nothing is less sensible than to want to substitute ours for theirs."[13] His position on the educative value of punishing children is thus the opposite of Augustine's. The

---

[10]Philippe Ariès, *Centuries of Childhood: A Social History of Family Life*, trans. Robert Baldick (New York: Vintage, 1962) 33.

[11]See ibid., 100-27. On the rarity of medieval depictions of Jesus' blessing of the children, and the frequency of late-sixteenth-century and seventeenth-century portrayals of that scene, see *Lexikon der christlichen Ikonographie*, 8 vols, ed. Engelbert Kirschbaum with Günter Bandmann et al. (Rome: Herder, 1968–1976) 2:513-14, s.v. "Kindersegnung Jesu."

[12]Jean-Jacques Rousseau, *Émile, or, On Education*, trans., intro., and notes by Allan Bloom (New York: Basic Books, 1979) 37.

[13]Ibid., 90.

latter, citing the paternal advice of Ecclesiasticus (Sirach) 30:12, could suggest that the harsh corporal punishments employed in Roman schools were necessary for counteracting children's natural inclination toward sloth, indolence, and other vices, and were but a natural consequence of the perverted, fallen nature with which every child is endowed at birth.[14] Rousseau, in contrast, contends that because the child's actions are devoid of morality, "he can do nothing which is morally bad and which merits either punishment or reprimand."[15]

It is to Rousseau, Ariès notes, that the modern association of childhood with primitivism and irrationalism may be traced, although Hegel, as noted by another scholar, is right to observe that Jesus anteceded Rousseau in exalting the child as norm.[16] The later hallowing of childhood by Romantic poets and theorists, most notably Blake, Wordsworth, and Coleridge in England, and Schiller and Novalis in Germany, is well documented. Anticipated by Jesus and Rousseau, as well as by the seventeenth-century English religious poets Thomas Traherne and Henry Vaughan, who saw the child as viewing the world through prelapsarian eyes, the Romantics equated childhood with Adam's condition in Eden and exalted the child's "freshness of sensation" (Coleridge) as a norm for adult artistic experience.[17]

This brings us to Kierkegaard, whose birth in 1813 coincided with the major period of German Romanticism, the so-called *Jüngere Romantik* or *Hochromantik* which encompassed the years of the Napoleonic wars (1805–ca. 1815). As a student for eleven years at the University of Copenhagen, he would be initially allured but eventually disenchanted by the literature, aesthetics, and philosophy of that movement. Reflecting the conflicting but lasting impacts of both his youthful immersion in Romanticism, and his

---

[14]Augustine, *City of God* 22.22.34.

[15]Rousseau, *Émile*, 92.

[16]See Ariès, *Centuries of Childhood*, 119; M. H. Abrams, *Natural Supernaturalism: Tradition and Revolution in Romantic Literature* (New York: W. W. Norton, 1973) 382.

[17]See, e.g., Peter Coveney, *The Image of Childhood: The Individual and Society: A Study of the Theme in English Literature*, rev. ed. (Baltimore: Penguin Books, 1967) esp. 37-90; Abrams, *Natural Supernaturalism*, esp. 377-483.

earlier, austerely pietistic upbringing by his father, Kierkegaard's writings convey attitudes toward the child that fluctuate remarkably between Pauline, Augustinian wariness, and the favoritism expressed by Jesus, Rousseau, as well as the Romantics.

## "A Sinner without the Consciousness of Sin"

In a journal entry of February 1836, midway through his career as a university student, Kierkegaard wrote: "The irony of life must of necessity be most intrinsic to childhood, to the age of imagination; . . . this is why it is present in the romantic school" (JP, 2:1669; repr. in CI, 425). This comment seems innocuous enough; the association drawn between childhood and the Romantic school does not imply anything unfavorable about either the child or Romanticism, both of which are in turn associated with the imagination, that human capacity the Romantics extolled above all others. If neither of these associations was original, what is noteworthy about this entry is that it shows him already contemplating childhood as a distinct stage of life. His reflections on childhood thereafter would not always prove so neutral.

In his aforecited journal entry of the next year, Kierkegaard asks, "*what significance* does childhood really have? Is it a stage with significance only because it conditions, in a way, the following stages—or does it have independent value?" (JP, 1:265). Both these positions strike him as laughably flawed. Adherents to the first position essentially kill time, as though all would be well "if children could be shut up in the dark and force-fed on an accelerated schedule like chickens" (JP, 1:265). Adherents to the second position come to regard childhood as "fundamentally the highest level attainable by human beings," beyond which everything is "progressive degeneration" (JP, 1:265). Both views are misleading because both "must presuppose the emptiness of childhood" (JP, 1:265).

While not constituting criticisms of childhood per se, these observations call attention to the conceptual pitfalls of regarding childhood in either of two wrong ways. Although he never defines childhood here, he does distinguish it by stressing that storytelling, instruction, and upbringing should be conducted in a special Socratic mode "to allow the child *to bring forth the life within him in*

*all stillness*" (JP, 1:265). By the same token, as Kierkegaard elsewhere made clear during the same year this entry was written, if
stories told *to* children must be conveyed only in a certain way,
then it is also imperative for stories *about* childhood to offer a
faithful portrayal of the child's mind. In his scathing 1838 review
of Hans Christian Andersen's *Kun en Spillemand* (1837, *Only a
Fiddler*), a novel whose first six chapters portray its protagonist's
childhood, Kierkegaard contends that the author there fails to
depict "a completely childlike consciousness":

> Instead, it often becomes either childishness, undigested reminis-
> cences from a specific, concrete period of childhood, or, what we
> particularly have in view here, one speaks as an adult about the
> impression made by life and then adds at appropriate intervals
> that one must remember childhood, the great creative power of
> childhood imagination. (EPW, 86)

As these comments reveal, a significant change has occurred in
Kierkegaard's thinking since he called childhood "the age of
imagination" in his aforecited 1836 journal entry. There, he used
that phrase earnestly in associating childhood with Romanticism.
Here, with undisguised sarcasm he draws the phrase "childhood
imagination" directly from the pages of *Kun en Spillemand* to deride
what he views as Andersen's unsuccessful attempt to depict a
fictional child through a clichéd, adult, romanticized notion of
childhood.[18]

This change of attitude toward childhood as "the age of
imagination," and hence toward the association of childhood with
Romanticism, would come to a head four years later in a passage
toward the end of Kierkegaard's dissertation (1841) on Socratic and
Romantic irony. Making reference to a criticism leveled by
Heinrich Heine specifically against the poet and dramatist Ludwig
Tieck, but also, by extension, against the whole school of Romantic

---

[18]Julia Watkin supplies the following two examples from H. C. Andersen, *Kun
en Spillemand*, 3 vols. (Copenhagen: C. A. Reitzel, 1837) 1:15, 18: "But for
childhood imagination a wealth lay in it"; "Childhood imagination needs only to
scratch in the ground with a stick in order to create a castle with halls and
corridors" (EPW, 256n.117; Watkin's trans.).

poets and writers,[19] Kierkegaard sums up his own disenchantment with that school by likening what he now sees as the Romantics' somnambulistic detachment from reality to the mentality of an infant:

> The world is rejuvenated, but as Heine so wittily remarked, it was rejuvenated by romanticism to such a degree that it became a baby again. The tragedy of romanticism is that what it seizes upon is not actuality. Poetry awakens; the powerful longings, the mysterious intimations, the inspiring feelings awaken; nature awakens; the enchanted princess awakens—the romanticist falls asleep. (CI, 304)

As anticipated by this passage, the attitude toward childhood that will tend to underlie references to the infant in Kierkegaard's subsequent writings, both published and unpublished, pseudonymous and nonpseudonymous, is one utterly divorced from the Romantic idealization of children. Having mused as early as 1837 that "[c]hildhood is the paradigmatic part of life; adulthood its syntax" (JP, 1:266), he realized that anything "paradigmatic" must share the essence of whatever it is the paradigm for, and therefore that the child cannot be dissociated from the sinfulness of the adult human condition. Accordingly, while sarcastically stating his preference "to talk with children, for one may still dare to hope they may become rational beings," the aesthete "A" of *Either/Or* notes—no less sarcastically—that when a baby is asked what it wants, it babbles *da-da*, an utterance which in Danish also connotes "spanking": "And with such observations life begins, and yet we deny hereditary sin" (EO, 1:19; see 606n.8; cf. JP, 5:5184; repr. EO, 1:467). The ethicist Judge William, though referring only once explicitly to "hereditary sin" (EO, 2:190), stresses: "[T]hat a child is born in sin is the most profound expression of its highest worth, that it is precisely a transfiguration of human life that everything related to it is assigned to the category of sin" (92). And Johannes Climacus similarly affirms that Christianity rejects "the sentimental view of the child's innocence"; as the idea of humankind as fallen

---

[19]*The Romantic School*, bk. 1, trans. Helen Mustard, in Heinrich Heine, *The Romantic School and Other Essays*, ed. Jost Hermand and Robert C. Holub (New York: Continuum, 1985) 18.

assumes the notion of "the child as sinner," Christianity "cannot provide the period of childhood with any advantage" (CUP, 1:592). The child, its consciousness qualified as "immediate" and hence indeterminate and excluding doubt (see JC, 167), can therefore be defined as "a sinner without the consciousness of sin" (CUP, 1:592).

We might pause here to locate this insight in relation to Augustine and Rousseau, our two nonbiblical reference points in Western thinking regarding the child. While Rousseau and the Romantics would easily concur that the child by nature is "without the consciousness of sin," the idea of the child as "a sinner" is antithetical to their view. On the other hand, the whole idea of the child as "a sinner without the consciousness of sin" seems borne out by a comment that surfaces during one of Augustine's painful listings of his own boyhood flaws and misdeeds: "For I did not see the whirlpool of filthiness into which I had plunged from [the sight of] your eyes [*non enim uidebam uoraginem turpitudinis, in quam proiectus eram ab oculis tuis*]."[20] However, if Augustine can recall his own life as a puerile "sinner without the consciousness of sin," it is his obsession with recollecting his own various types of boyhood transgressions and distinguishing them as symptoms of sin that distinguishes his view of childhood from those of Kierkegaard, Climacus, and Kierkegaard's other pseudonyms.

Perhaps reflecting in part his experience of having been regularly mocked by boys in the streets during the period of the Corsair Affair,[21] passing allusions to naughty children do crop up in Kierkegaard's writings (e.g., WL, 203-204). Nonetheless, he and his pseudonyms depict the sinfulness of children no less than the sinfulness of adults as "something quite other than a series of transgressions; it is a spiritual attitude that is at the same time psychological and metaphysical."[22] Hereditary sin is certainly discussed in his writings, particularly *The Concept of Anxiety* and *The Sickness Unto Death*; yet Kierkegaard and his pseudonyms display nothing approaching the Augustinian preoccupation with

---

[20]Augustine, *Confessions* 1.19.30; my translation.
[21]See JP, 5:5887 (repr. in COR, 212); 5:5894 (repr. in COR, 217); 5:5937; 5:5998 (repr. in COR, 220); 6:6160 (repr. in COR, 227).
[22]Henri Rondet, *Original Sin: The Patristic and Theological Background*, trans. Cajetan Finegan (Staten Island NY: Alba House, 1972) 206.

it.[23] For Vigilius Haufniensis, what is anticipatory (if not yet explicitly symptomatic) of sin in the child is "[t]he anxiety that is posited in innocence" (CA, 42), while the closest that Anti-Climacus comes to associating children with original sin is in finding them marked by the same "imperfection" as the unchristian "natural man," namely, "not to recognize the horrifying, and then, implicit in this, to shrink from what is not horrifying" (SUD, 8). In identifying sin with the despair which adults feel in the face of the eternal, Anti-Climacus observes that "only bad temper, not despair, is associated with children," since we can only assume "that the eternal is present in the child κατὰ δύναμιν [potentially]" (SUD, 49n.).

Located somewhere between the opposed attitudes of Augustine and Rousseau, Climacus's view of childhood, like Kierkegaard's own, shows no sign of having been directly influenced by either of those two thinkers.[24] The closest precursor to Kierkegaard's ambivalent perspective on children, I believe, is the poet-philosopher William Blake. Although a celebrant of childhood's innocence, Blake was also, like Kierkegaard, a sober acknowledger of how that innocence is inevitably tempered by experience; hence the child as a type figures prominently in both his *Songs of Innocence* (1789) and *Songs of Experience* (1794), which, when published together, bore the subtitle: "Shewing the Two Contrary States of the Human Soul."[25] Anticipating Kierkegaard's notion of

---

[23]See Johannes Hohlenberg, *Sören Kierkegaard*, trans. T. H. Croxall (New York: Pantheon, 1954) 131; cited by Rondet, *Original Sin*, 206.

[24]Kierkegaard expressed mixed reactions to Augustine and Rousseau. Although his examination of the stages of existence was presumably influenced by Augustine's notion that "man" must develop through "three stages" (JP, 1:29), he saw Augustine as having "done incalculable harm" by "confus[ing] the concept of faith" (JP, 1:180). And while he could consider a statement by the vicar in book 4 of *Émile* "splendid" (JP, 3:3824), he viewed Rousseau himself as "totally ignorant of Christianity," particularly with regard to the matter of suffering (JP, 3:3827), and therefore ranked him among "muddleheads" (JP, 6:6794). (Cf. the Hongs' comments on Kierkegaard's journal entries on these two figures [JP, 1, p. 504; 3, pp. 924-25].) Nowhere, however, does Kierkegaard comment specifically on either Augustine's or Rousseau's attitude toward the child.

[25]As Northrop Frye points out, "real children are not symbols of innocence: the *Songs of Innocence* would be intolerably sentimental if they were. One finds a great deal more than innocence in any child: there is the childish as well as the childlike; the jealousy and vanity that all humans naturally have" (*Fearful Symme-*

childhood as "the paradigmatic part of life," Blake saw it—in Alfred Kazin's words—"as the nucleus of the whole human story."[26] For example, "The Little Boy Lost," the eighth poem of *Songs of Innocence*, expresses an intense form of childish anxiety through the same image of lostness that Haufniensis employs to characterize innocence "brought to its uttermost": "Innocence is not guilty, yet there is anxiety as though it were lost" (CA, 45).[27]

Yet Kierkegaard knew nothing of Blake. The two chief sources of influence upon Kierkegaard's attitude toward the child are clearly Jesus and Paul, neither of whose own assessments of children he entirely or straightforwardly accepted.

True to the irrepressibly dialectical tendency of his thinking, Kierkegaard was keenly aware of the opposition we noted earlier between Jesus and Paul's views of childhood, both of which views are invoked in sermons of 1844, and later in Anti-Climacus's *Practice in Christianity*.[28] In 1849, the year before *Practice* appeared, Kierkegaard suggested in his journal that the way someone assesses his or her childhood in the light of the Christic and Pauline views will provide a key to that person's personality. After quoting 1 Corinthians 13:11 he wrote: "One could speak on the theme: *what judgment do you make on your childhood and your youth? Do you judge that it was foolishness and fancies?*"—in accordance with the Pauline passage. "Or do you judge that you were at that time closest to the Most High?"—in consistency with Christ's claim about heaven belonging to "such" as children. "Just tell me how you judge your childhood and your youth, and I will tell you who you are" (JP, 1:271).

Although Kierkegaard's notion that one's "openness" in relation to God "increases as one becomes more and more a child"

---

try: *A Study of William Blake* [Princeton NJ: Princeton University Press, 1947] 235).

[26]Alfred Kazin, introduction to his edition of *The Portable Blake* (New York: Viking, 1946; repr. Harmondsworth, Middlesex, England: Penguin, 1986) 39.

[27]This particular analogy between Blake and Haufniensis is drawn by Lorraine Clark, *Blake, Kierkegaard, and the Spectre of Dialectic* (Cambridge: Cambridge University Press, 1991) 57.

[28]See EUD, 240 (on Matt. 18:3), 399 (on 1 Cor. 13.11); PC, 191 (on Matt. 18:3), 198 (for an apparent allusion to 1 Cor. 13.12, the verse that immediately follows the Pauline verse in question).

accords with Jesus' idea of heaven's belonging to "such" as children, and although he had once enunciated a warning consonant with the one issued by Jesus about the fate that awaits corrupters of children (Matt. 18:6; cf. JP, 1:91; repr. in CA, 169), he apparently held little sympathy for the conventional reading of Jesus' consecration of children. Anticipating several critiques which Kierkegaard will elaborate in 1854 of the literal interpretation of Matthew 19:13-15 and Luke 18:15-17 (see JP, 1:370; 1:548; 1:549), Climacus observes that a "childish," "sentimental" understanding of Jesus' blessing of children makes Christianity ridiculous. For if it were literally true that the child will face none of the difficulties that an adult must face to enter heaven, then it would seem "best to die as a child" (CUP, 1:593).

Despite the lack here of any explicit citation of 1 Corinthians 13:11, we can hardly miss Climacus's implicit affirmation of the truth behind Paul's testimony to the need for giving up "childish ways" and becoming "a man." However, this verse itself can be misleading; as Kierkegaard elsewhere urges in reference to it, "let us never forget that even the more mature person always retains some of the child's lack of judgment" (EUD, 399). Likewise Climacus asserted earlier that "it is a mediocre existence when the adult cuts away all communication with childhood" (CUP, 348). This view squares with two other crucial ideas articulated by Kierkegaard and his pseudonyms, ideas that might seem upon first consideration to suggest that Christianity involves a kind of recovery of childhood innocence and simplicity. One of these ideas, which has an unacknowledged Rousseauistic resonance, is that from God's perspective the definitive, most desirable quality of the single individual is "primitivity." As explained by the Hongs, this term for Kierkegaard "does not have the slightly disparaging ring of the undeveloped that it has in modern Danish"; rather, it is used in his various writings to denote the human being's "original and uncorrupted capacity to receive an impression without being influenced by 'the others' . . . or by current views."[29]

---

[29]JP, 3, p. 887. For Kierkegaard's own discussions of this notion in entries dating from the years 1849–1854, see JP, 3, pp. 3558-61. A number of allusions to "primitivity" in the pseudonymous writings are cited by the Hongs, JP, 3:887-88.

The notion of primitivity is clearly related to the other idea, which is first developed by Johannes de Silentio in his reaction to the Hegelian valuation of the outer (*das Äussere*) or externalization (*die Entäusserung*), as symbolized by the adult, over the inner (*das Innere*), as symbolized by the child. The paradox of faith, according to Silentio, is that it elevates interiority above exteriority. However, as he further suggests, this does *not* mean that faith brings about a return to a childlike state. For just as the single individual's "primitivity" must finally not be equated with the condition of childhood, so this higher interiority is one "that is not identical, please note, with the first but is a new interiority" (FT, 69). Phrased otherwise, "Faith is not the first immediacy," that is, the aesthetic immediacy of the child, "but a later immediacy" (FT, 82)—a conclusion reiterated not only by Kierkegaard in a journal entry of 1848 (JP, 2:1123) but by Frater Taciturnus (SLW, 399) and Johannes Climacus (CUP, 1:347, 347n.).

Ultimately, regardless how much Climacus's implicit agreement with 1 Corinthians 13:11 must be qualified by notions of primitivity and of faith as a second immediacy, Paul's talk of giving up "childish ways" and becoming "a man" itself begs the question. As the rest of his verse indicates, the mature, true Christian is someone who is no longer a child, and who, like the converted Paul, no longer speaks, thinks, or reasons "like a child." Yet the whole passage in which this verse occurs revolves around the theme of love, which Paul sets above faith and hope as a spiritual gift (1 Cor. 13.4-13). So what is the relation of the child to Christian love?

On September 29, 1847, nineteen months after the publication of the book in which Climacus made his observations above, *Works of Love* appeared under Kierkegaard's own name. In this book, as we might suspect from its title, answers are provided to the question just posed, and we shall find proof that the same thing might be said of Kierkegaard that has been said of Blake: "His faith in the creative richness of love has the same source as his feeling for the secret richness of childhood."[30]

---

[30]Kazin, introduction to *The Portable Blake*, 39.

## The Child's Significance in Works of Love

References to the child abound in *Works of Love*, particularly in the second of the book's two series of discourses. Yet from the first of these references on, the views reflected display the same pendulum-like oscillation which we have observed elsewhere in Kierkegaard between the opposed attitudes expressed by Christ and Paul toward children. The initial allusions occur toward the end of the second discourse of the first series, where the child is associated with "the simplest person" and "the wisest" insofar as all three types exist "at the distance of a quiet hour of life's confusion," and understand "with almost equal ease, what every person should do," namely, to love one's neighbor (WL, 78, 79). Just as the association with simplicity calls to mind Jesus' emphasis on children's humility, so the association with wisdom contradicts Paul's view of the child as spiritually and epistemologically imperfect.

However, lest we be deceived that Kierkegaard has forsaken his own dialectical perspective on the matter, he presently closes this discourse by making a pointedly Pauline allusion to "childishness" as representing the very lowest of the ascending stages of maturation through which a person must progress in order to become fully receptive to the divine imperative, "*you* shall." Harking back to the ironic homology implied by *Either/Or's* "A" between the infant's utterance of *da-da* and the spankings which children provoke as a result of hereditary sin (EO, 1:19), Kierkegaard perceives the inherent self-centeredness of children as a condition which any individual must outgrow in order to enter into a relationship of obeisance to the eternal:

> It is a mark of childishness to say: *Me wants, me—me;* a mark of adolescence to say: *I—and I—and I;* the sign of maturity and the devotion of the eternal is to will to understand that this *I* has no significance unless it becomes the *you* to whom eternity incessantly speaks and says: *You* shall, *you* shall, *you* shall. (WL, 90)

This last passage does not exhaust Kierkegaard's usage of the child in the first series of discourses in *Works of Love*. Having invoked the child as typifying in and of itself a pair of positive virtues (simplicity, wisdom) as well as a pair of venial flaws (self-centeredness, immaturity), he also refers to the child as a symbol of, or an analogue to, specific aspects of adult human existence. Early in the third discourse, to illustrate the ease with which a person will backslide from a promise to fulfill the law, he likens such a promise to a changeling. At the moment of birth,

> when the mother's joy is greatest because her suffering is over, . . . then come, so thinks superstition, the hostile powers and place a changeling in place of the child. In the great but therefore also dangerous moment of beginning, when one is supposed to begin, the hostile powers come and slip in a changeling promise and prevent one from making the actual beginning. (WL, 95)

Noteworthy here is not only the focus on the relationship of mother to child (a relationship which receives closer scrutiny in the second series of discourses) but the appeal to "superstition" regarding this matter. Near the end of this discourse, whether wittingly or not, Kierkegaard likewise introduces with regard to the human "spirit" an analogy that recalls the stock usage of the child figure in medieval art as a symbolic representation of the human soul.[31] That "a child must learn to spell before it can learn to read" is likened to the fact that a person's spiritual advancement must begin not at "the great moment of the resolution, the intention, the promise," but rather, in "struggl[ing] with oneself in self-denial" (WL, 133).

The use of the child to symbolize aspects of adult existence reaches its first point of culmination in the fifth and final discourse of the book's first series, where a simile is established between a certain disposition of well-raised children and a certain hallmark of Christian love. Even when away from home and among strangers, according to Kierkegaard, the well-raised child will behave as it has been brought up, because it "never forgets that the judgment is at home, where the parents do the judging" (WL, 189). Likewise it is God who cultivates a person's Christian love. Yet just as a child is earnestly brought up not in order to remain at home with parents but in order to go out into the world, so God cultivates a person's Christian love so as "to send love out into the world" (WL, 190). Like the well-raised child among strangers, such love "never for a moment forgets where it is to be judged" (WL,

---

[31]On this symbol see, e.g., Ariès, *Centuries of Childhood*, 36, 124.

190). A similar idea is further evoked to distinguish the Christian from the surrounding world, and thereby to explain God's invisibility and inaudibility in the world.

> When a strictly brought-up child is together with naughty or less well behaved children and is unwilling to join them in their misbehavior, which they themselves, for the most part, do not regard as misbehavior—the naughty children know of no other explanation for this than that the child must be a queer and daft child. They do not see that . . . the strictly brought-up child, wherever it is, is continually accompanied by its parents' criterion for what it may and may not do. (WL, 203)

This scenario furnishes a metaphor for the difference between the Christian and the world. As long as the parents (=God) of the well-raised child (=the Christian) remain invisible, this child's naughty peers (=the world) will mistakenly assume that it simply does not like their kind of fun and is "queer and daft," or that it likes their fun but is afraid to join in. Like the world in its own bafflement at the Christian who does not share its passions and desires, the naughty children "think well of their misbehavior, and therefore they want [the strictly brought-up child] to join them and be a plucky boy—just like the others" (WL, 204).

In drawing to a close the first series of discourses in *Works of Love*, this use of the child to explain the distinctness of the Christian's God-relationship prepares for the use of the child in the second series, which will likewise end with a reference to "the well-disciplined child," whose "unforgettable impression of rigorousness" is complemented by the "unforgettable fear and trembling" experienced by "the person who relates himself to God's love" in an earnest manner (WL, 385-86). In the second series, not only does the child continue to be associated with "simplicity" (WL, 346) and mentioned as a symbol of spiritual qualities, but increasingly the child's relationship with parents, and especially with the mother, will be analyzed as a metaphor for the agapic relationship between the Christian and God.

One reason why Kierkegaard can so readily appeal to the child as a metaphor for certain spiritual qualities is that, as we noted earlier, he, like Blake, does not allow the distinct aspects of childhood to obscure the child's "paradigmatic" nature. This point becomes all the more clear in the third discourse of the second series, where he considers the association of the child with hope. The child and the youth are easily associated with hope, as they themselves are both "still a possibility" (WL, 250), and as the child, the antithesis of the dead person, "thrive[s] and grow[s] toward the future" (WL, 350). Nonetheless, Kierkegaard scoffs at the conventional tendency to call the initial period of a person's life "the age of hope or of possibility" (WL, 251). Hope is oriented toward the possibility of good, whose own possibility is dependent upon the eternal, which extends over a person's entire life, not just over a single age. To illustrate how anyone who fails to see that "the whole of one's life should be the time of hope" must be in despair, Kierkegaard again draws upon his own insight into child psychology. To assist a child with a very large task, he observes, one does not present the task all at once; to do so would cause the child to despair. Instead,

> One assigns a small part at a time, but always enough so that the child at no point stops as if it were finished, but not so much that the child cannot manage it. This is the pious fraud in upbringing; it actually suppresses something. If the child is deceived, this is because the instructor is a human being who cannot vouch for the next moment. (WL, 252)

Here, in stressing a pedagogic method that allows the child to fulfill tasks on its own, Kierkegaard's advice reflects his own maieutic strategy as author. However, in functioning as midwife in the Socratic sense, the ideal educator in his view also does something in relation to children that is analogous to what God does in relation to human beings. The ideal educator, in bringing up many children at once, "takes the individual child's eyes away from him—that is, in everything he makes the child look at him" (WL, 377). The same thing is done by God: through his glance into every human being's conscience, God requires each person to look back at him, and thereby governs the entire world and brings up innumerable human beings. "But," like the adult who mistakes his or her worldly dealings for actuality, but is led by God to grasp that these are only being employed for his or her upbringing, "the child who is being brought up readily imagines that his relationship to his comrades, the little world that they form, is actuality, whereas the educator teaches him with his glance that all this is being used to bring up the child" (WL, 377). Through this analogy, it is as if Kierkegaard were retelling Plato's myth of the cave, inserting God as the educator who frees the prisoners and enables them to discern the unreality of the shadows which they mistook for real.

The child's earliest upbringing is a task assigned by nature not to an "educator" but to the child's parents, and initially to the mother in particular. Unlike Augustine, who practically deified his mother in his *Confessions* to reveal the role of providential agent which he believed she had played in his childhood, youth, and early adulthood,[32] Kierkegaard famously makes no mention ever of his own mother. Nonetheless, he shares with his ancient predecessor a fixation with the image of the mother breast-feeding her infant as a metaphor for the demonstration of God's love for the human being. Just as Augustine could suggest that he himself in adulthood was like an infant being suckled by God (*sugens lac tuum*), or that converted sinners are those who cast themselves upon God's breast (*in sinu tuo*), or that God's Word was made flesh in order that God's wisdom might suckle our infancy (*ut infantiae nostrae lactesceret sapientia tua*),[33] so Kierkegaard finds God's encompassing love reflected in the "upbuilding sight" of a mother lovingly holding a sleeping baby at her breast (WL, 214).

Still, as forewarned by the "Exordium" of *Fear and Trembling*, where Johannes de Silentio contemplates the deception and concealment through which, and the sorrow with which, the mother must ultimately wean the child from her breast (FT, 11-14; cf. JP, 5:5640; repr. WL, 398; see also FT, 246), Kierkegaard is well aware of more painful implications of the breast-feeding image. Consistent with his ambivalence toward the child, which will lead him still in the book's "Conclusion" to lament the ease with which God's love is sentimentalized and softened into "a fabulous and childish conception" (WL, 376), Kierkegaard never succumbs to conventional, sentimental assumptions about the spectacle of the mother with child. For him, the moment the mother's love ceases to be visible in her expression, the sight of her with her child

---

[32]See Eric J. Ziolkowski, "St. Augustine: Monica's Boy, Antitype of Aeneas," in *Journal of Literature and Theology* 9 (1995): 1-23.

[33]Augustine, *Confessions* 4.1.1; 5.2.2; 7.18.24.

ceases to be edifying (see WL, 214). Likewise he confides in his journal his suspicion that "maternal love as such is simply self-love raised to a higher power," though it is still "a beautiful figure" (JP, 3:2425; repr. WL, 483). Accordingly, in the first discourse of the second series in *Works of Love*, when deliberating upon Paul's claim that "love builds up" (1 Cor. 8:1), he clarifies what is meant by the saying that the mother tolerates "all her child's naughtiness" (WL, 221). The saying means not that such a mother forbearingly endures evil but that "as a mother she is continually remembering that this is a child and thus is continually presupposing that the child still loves her and that this will surely show itself" (WL, 221). In other words, presupposed by the mother is the economic logic which underlies another proverb cited much earlier, namely, "that children are in love's debt to their parents because they have loved them first, so that the children's love is only a part-payment on the debt or a repayment" (WL, 176).

This factor of "repayment" makes possible the cynical distinction which Kierkegaard draws between "the two greatest works" of love, giving a human being life and recollecting one who has died: unlike the latter work, the former involves repayment. Were it not for this factor, he speculates, there would be many fathers and mothers "whose love would grow cold" (WL, 349). Indeed, were the otherwise helpless infant incapable of crying and thus of "extort[ing]" works of love from its parents, numerous parents would probably "forget the child" (WL, 351, 352).

Conveyed in the ninth and penultimate discourse of the second series, these cynical speculations about a frequent contingency of parental love merely present the opposite side of the picture which this series' second discourse painted of the child who tries to deceive the parents. Once again evoking the analogy between the parent-child and God-human relationships, Kierkegaard there asserted that it is just as impossible for a child to deceive its parents as for an adult human to deceive God, and that both the child and the adult in such cases deceive themselves, since the parent and God are superior to them, and "true superiority can never be deceived if it remains faithful to itself" (WL, 236).

In the fifth discourse of the book's second series, that is, about halfway between the second and ninth discourses with their discussions of self-deceptive children and parents whose love for their children "would grow cold," we encounter the most poignantly positive image of the child in the entire book, an image that would reinforce Climacus's notion of the child as a creature "without the consciousness of sin" while doing nothing to support the accompanying idea of the child as "a sinner." In discoursing upon the phrase "love covers a multitude of sins," from 1 Peter 4:8, Kierkegaard relates this text to 1 Corinthians 14:20, suggesting that the life of the person who loves expresses the Pauline command to be a babe in evil (see WL, 285). The world, he observes, reveres knowledge of evil as wisdom, though wisdom is knowledge of the good. On the assumption that "the one who loves" neither has nor wants knowledge of evil, Kierkegaard asserts that "in this regard he is and remains, he wants to be and wants to remain, a child" (WL, 285). Having made this assertion, which remarkably defies Paul's testimony about the need to give up "childish ways" to become "a man," Kierkegaard introduces a thought experiment involving a child—an experiment comparable to the one elaborated elsewhere by Anti-Climacus to imagine how a child might react when first shown a picture of, and told about, the Crucifixion (see PC, 174-78; cf. JP, 1:270; WA, 55).[34] "Put a child in a den of thieves," Kierkegaard now tells us,

> (but the child must not remain there so long that it is corrupted itself); that is, let it remain there only for a very brief time. Then let it come home and tell everything it has experienced. You will note that the child, who is a good observer and has an excellent memory (as does every child), will tell everything in the greatest detail, yet in such a way that in a certain sense the most important is omitted. (WL, 285)

What is missing from the child's story, Kierkegaard points out to us, is something the child never discovered: the evil. Yet, as he further insists, the child's account of what it saw and heard is completely accurate. What the child lacks, and what "so often makes a child's story the most profound mockery of the adults," is "knowledge of evil" (WL, 286). The child knows nothing of evil,

---

[34]For discussion see Eric J. Ziolkowski, "A Picture Not Worth a Thousand Words: Kierkegaard, Christ, and the Child," in *Religious Studies and Theology* 17/2 (January 1999).

nor even feels any inclination to desire knowledge of evil, and it is in this respect that "the one who loves is like the child" (WL, 286). That "the one who loves" will fail to discover the "multitude of sins" of which the author of 1 Peter spoke reminds Kierkegaard of a child's game, as when we play that we do not see the child standing right before us, or the child plays that it does not see us: "The childlikeness, then, is that, as in a game, the one who loves with his eyes open cannot see what is taking place right in front of him; the solemnity is that it is the evil that he cannot see" (WL, 287).

With this analogy, the pendulum of Kierkegaardian attitude toward children swings closer than in any other place in his writings to Jesus' injunction to the disciples that they should "become like children." Yet even here, in Kierkegaard's hypothetical experiment with the child who is to be placed in a thieves' den, there is a dialectical implication that subtly reminds us of how tenuous the child's ascribed "innocence" must be. Just as Jesus followed up his own injunction with the warning about the awful drowning that awaits "whoever causes one of these little ones . . . to sin" (Matt. 18:6), so the success of Kierkegaard's experiment in establishing the analogy between the child and "the one who loves" depends on the parenthetical qualification that the child must not remain among the thieves "so long that it is corrupted itself."

This qualification, together with Kierkegaard's portrait of "the one who loves," may mark the distance between the author of *Works of Love* and readers today in their perceptions of children.

## Conclusion

Although there is ample documentation of what Leslie Fiedler called "the profanation of the child" in twentieth century literature,[35] one need think only of Peter Pan, the character created by J. M. Barrie during the early decades of the century, and Richard

---

[35]See Leslie Fiedler, "The Eye of Innocence," *The Collected Essays of Leslie Fiedler*, 2 vols. (New York: Stein and Day, 1971) 502-11. For more recent cogitations on the same phenomenon see, e.g., Joyce Carol Oates, "Killer Kids," *The New York Review* (11 November 1997): 16-20.

Hughes's 1929 novel *The Innocent Voyage*, later republished under the title *A High Wind in Jamaica*, to gauge two crucial differences between us and Kierkegaard in our attitude toward the child. Barrie, whose depiction of children as "gay and innocent and heartless"[36] aptly sums up the sentimental Victorian view of children, bequeathed to Western culture what has become one of our most popular myths of childhood, the story of "the boy who would not grow up."[37] This epithet may seem suggestively close to Kierkegaard's description of "the one who loves" as someone who "is and remains," "wants to be and wants to remain a child." Yet the pagan personality, not to mention the pagan name, of Barrie's hero is a far cry from Kierkegaard's ideal Christian—as is also the common "syndrome" of arrested social development among contemporary adult males that has been named after Peter Pan.[38] Indeed, though they both remain not grown up in certain senses, Peter Pan and Kierkegaard's "one who loves" would seem to be ethically and religiously opposed flip sides of each other.

As for Kierkegaard's imagining what a child would or would not observe "in a den of thieves," *A High Wind in Jamaica* attests to our own century's loss of even a pretended restraint about trying to preserve any false sense of the child as an uncorrupted type. Whereas Kierkegaard wanted his imaginary child removed from amongst the thieves before it was "corrupted itself," Hughes's novel, whose publication is said to have delivered the death blow to the Victorian cult of childhood, tells of a group of children captured by pirates, among whom one, a ten-year-old girl, becomes a remorseless killer. In subsequent novels such as William Golding's *Lord of the Flies* and William March's *The Bad Seed*, both of which appeared in 1954, it does not take the company of pirates to prompt equally wicked behavior among children.

---

[36]The closing phrase of the novel *Peter and Wendy* (1911), in J. M. Barrie, *Peter Pan in Kensington Gardens. Peter and Wendy*, ed. Peter Hollindale (Oxford: Oxford University Press, 1991) 226.

[37]The subtitle of the play *Peter Pan* (premiere 1904), in *The Plays of J. M. Barrie* (New York: Charles Scribner's Sons, 1929) 1-94.

[38]See Dan Kiley, *The Peter Pan Syndrome: Men Who Have Never Grown Up* (New York: Dodd, Mead, and Co., 1983).

From the vantage of our own prodigious, millennial consciousness of sin and evil, we can only speculate over the fear and
trembling with which Kierkegaard might have pondered the consequences of *not* removing the child from among the thieves—before
it was too late.

# 12

## Rhetoric in *Kierkegaard's* Works of Love or *No Sooner Said than Done**

### Begonya Saez Tajafuerce

*Litera gesta docet, quid credas Allegoria*
*Moralis quid agas, quo tendas Anagogia.* (Pap. X 2 A 540; 1850)

But if an author has his own distinctive conception of communication, if all his distinctiveness and the reality of his historical significance are perhaps focused precisely in this, well, then it will be a long drawn out affair—O, school of patience. (JP, 1:645)

According to a journal entry, from around the time when *Works of Love* was partly nothing but a draft, Søren Kierkegaard was becoming more and more interested in giving "a series of twelve lectures on the dialectic of communication. After that, twelve lectures on erotic love (*Elskov*), friendship (*Venskab*), and love (*Kjerlighed*)" (JP, 5:5996). Given this, it would seem clear that the connection between the first and the second series of lectures is merely a chronological one; once the first series is finished, the next one will follow. Hence, temporally speaking, both series are two equally significant contiguous items on a planning list.

However, after having reflected on the consequences that such a public, open, "outer" undertaking (namely, actual lecturing) would imply, Kierkegaard confesses, "I have put the lectures away and have taken up my interrupted work (the first part of which I finished): 'Works of Love.' The dialectic of communication must be done as a book" (JP, 5:6005).

---

*This work has been made possible by a generous postdoctoral grant (F.P.U.) from the Ministerio de Educación y Cultura (Spain), and was written at the Søren Kierkegaard Research Centre in Copenhagen, which is supported by the Danish National Research Foundation.

Now, suddenly, the mere chronological interrelatedness of both series seems insufficient to describe the relationship between them. This is not simply because of the banal reason that Kierkegaard has clearly been working on both projects at the same time, but also, and especially, because Kierkegaard has "put the lectures away." He certainly did not do so in the sense that he completely rejected them as a project, but, rather, in the sense that he reconceived them, so that he would now be able to abandon the systematic and instructive approach they required and, once more, put them into practice. The "dialectic of communication" will now conform to a new shape, namely, the shape of a new "book," even if not a book on the "dialectic of communication" as such, but an unfinished book, *Works of Love*, which they will configurate.

If this reading holds, then it could be stated that *Works of Love* might be understood as one exemplary expression of the dialectic of communication. Hence, it could likewise be stressed, firstly, that the issue of the book has an *ethical-religious* character, as it is well known that the dialectic of communication applies for "ethical and ethical-religious" matters (JP, 5:6004 and 1:648-57), and, secondly, the text, in spite of Kierkegaard's "own" signature, does have an analogous *indirect textual character* to the so called pseudonymous works, where, as it is well known, the communication of "ethical and ethical-religious" matters is "indirect" (JP, 1:648-75).

Both assumptions, concerning the thematic and the discursive coordinates of *Works of Love* respectively, will be at the basis of the present reading. Likewise, I will presuppose a double conception of language. On the one hand I assume a *pragmatic* conception, according to which certain uses of language might perform certain acts within the discourse, and, on the other, a *rhetorical* conception, according to which certain uses of language in specific pragmatic situations might adopt specific shapes in order to obtain a specific effect. Thus I will not explicitly pay attention to love from a phenomenological perspective, but, on the contrary, I will focus the divine commandment of love: "Thou shalt love your neighbor" (*Du skal elske din Næste*), to seek the specificity of the discourse by the agency of which love is brought into sight, and, concretely, into ethical-religious sight, that is, both as *demand* and as *paradox*.

*Language in Use. A Pragmatic Reading of* Works of Love

The general question of the use of language will refer to the
two major hermeneutic keys provided by contemporary philosophy of language, namely the Wittgensteinian notion of *language
game* and the Austinian theory of *speech-acts*. Employing the first
notion, I will address the question concerning the kind of language
game Kierkegaard is playing, when he qualifies *Works of Love*, as
a text, with the subtitle: "Some Christian Deliberations (*Overveiel-
ser*) in the form of Discourses (*i Talers Form*)." Employing the
notion of speech-act, I will address the question concerning the
sort of "performance," or linguistic action, if any, the text conceals.

(1) *Kierkegaardian Language Game.* Given the assumption that
*Works of Love* not only deals with the ethical-religious, but communicates it to the reader, from the point of view of linguistic pragmatics it is possible to state that language is primarily conceived
of as *discourse*. However, why should Kierkegaard fall into the contradiction of *writing* a *talk*, a discourse? There are probably several
reasons which could explain this not insignificant oxymoron.[1]

---

[1]Eberhard Harbsmeier considers this oxymoronic explanation which reads
very close to the "Diary of the Secucer" as follows: "Das geschriebene Wort ist
verfürerischer als das gesprochene, weil der Leser mit ihm allein ist" (301). In his
reading, the accent falls clearly upon the scriptural or grammatical aspect of the
oxymoron. See "Das Erbaulich als Kunst des Gesprächs. Reflexionen über die
homiletischen Perspektiven in Kierkegaards erbaulichen Reden" in *Kierkegaard
Studies. Yearbook 1996*, ed. Niels Jørgen Cappelørn and Hermann Deuser (Berlin,
New York: Walter de Gruyter, 1996) 293-313. The article includes (294n.3) a large
bibliographical account of secondary literature on the issue, edification, in Kierkegaard's works and thought. Initially (chap. 1), Harbsmeier's reflections are briefly
devoted to edification "als *literarische* . . . Kategorie," and later (chap. 2), entirely
devoted to "Die erbauliche Rede als geschriebener Text."
    However, an explanation of the oxymoronic array that will underline its oral
or verbal aspect, indeed, its discursive character, should probably be understood
according to Rodney Kennedy's remarks about Plato's conception of "good"
rhetoric, namely, that "oral rhetoric is to be preferred to the art of writing" among
other things, because the written word would "defeat the dynamic that only
orality can bring to discourse." Rodney Kennedy, *The Creative Power of Metaphor.
A Rhetorical Homiletics* (Lanham, New York, London: University Press of America,
1993) 20.

For instance, one could, as is often done, suggest that in spite of their doctrinal character Kierkegaard will not call the texts signed under "his own" name and addressed to a faithful hearer *senso stricto* "sermons," as he did not have the "(divine) authority" to do so, since he was not ordained. Similarly, and on the basis of the journal entry about the two series of lectures, quoted at the beginning, one could also assume that *Works of Love* indeed was conceived as a text for ethical-religious "instruction," in the very same sense in which Kierkegaard understands ("second" or "last") "instruction" in several entries of his journals (JP, 1:939). Even Climacus, in full agreement with Kierkegaard also in journals (JP, 1:1060), conceives "existence-communication" in the *Postcript* (CUP, 1:357)[2] in terms of "instruction." According to such a reading, *Works of Love* will not only be addressed to a devotional public, as in the case of a "sermon," but to a public in general, an audience constituted of singular hearers/readers.

In either of these cases, two considerations apply: (1) to begin with, to write a discourse, that is, to conceive a written text as a spoken text, and, therewith, to apply the rules of a spoken text to a written text, implies interaction as a formal premise. In this case, a reaction from the hearer/reader is expected, precisely as it is also within an explicit conversational frame; that is, an answer is awaited, although, in principle, not established. Already in the prefaces to both "series" (WL, 3-4, 207), Kierkegaard, as a "theorist of reception," openly addresses the reader, namely, "the singular individual" (*Hiin Enkelte*) and reflects upon how the text should be received, by both giving advice and warning against an inconvenient reading. Hence to write a discourse indicates only a verbal contradiction, which vanishes as soon as the written text is conceived *as* a discourse, that is, as playing according to the language rules of communication.

At the same time, (2) "to write a discourse" needs some further consideration, at least as far as the category of "discourse" within

---

[2]It is interesting that Climacus considers the question of "existence-communication" precisely in the paragraphs where he considers "the subjective *thinker's form*," and that he asserts that "the form of his communication is his *style*" (CUP, 1:357), sharing the presuppostion of a parallel move to the one intended in this article.

the Kierkegaardian framework is concerned, and inasmuch as there is more than one sort of discourse, hence more than one sort of language-game, being played. In this sense, a two-level schema could be established. Firstly, as is stated in the rough draft for the "lectures," there are two general kinds of communication (hence of discourse): a "scientific" (*Videnskab*) and an "artistic" (*Kunst*) one (JP, 6004, 1:648-57). This can be taken as indicating a distinction between an informative, doctrinare language game, and an emotive, suggestive language game. Also, secondly (and as a specification of the so-called "artistic" discourse), at least four sorts of discourse require our attention according to Kierkegaard, namely, the devotional (*gudelig*), edifying (*opbyggelig*), Christian (*christelig*), and religious (*religiøs*), each of which will require its own respective and specific language game. I shall examine this more precisely in the section "Language in form." However, it can be pointed out, in the context of *Works of Love*, that the differentiation of the "Christian" and the "edifying" discourse from a pragmatic point of view will be emphasized, and that, despite its opening words, *Works of Love* should not be read regarding either the language game of the Christian discourse or that of the edifying discourse, as if these were incommensurable, but, on the contrary, a simultaneous reading will be required. The following approach to the text, now in terms of linguistic performance, will hopefully serve partially to make good on this hypothesis.

(2) *Kierkegaardian Linguistic Performance.* By now, reference has been made to the configuration of the discourse in *Works of Love* in terms of language games, and it has been shown that from this perspective Kierkegaard has in mind the rules of verbal communication, and also that he likewise practices the rules of "Christian" and "edifying" discourse, according to his own considerations as found in the "Lectures" and, more generally, in his journals.

From the point of view of linguistic pragmatics, language performs certain acts that have an effect on the audience or reader,and this is also true in *Works of Love*.[3] The following

---

[3]It should be clarified that in the following the statement "language performs" presupposes and refers to Austin's theory of linguistic "speech-acts," and, specifically, to what he calls "perlocution," that is, to the "performance of an act ( . . . ) which will produce certain consequential effects upon the feelings,

paragraph from the journals, a quotation which eventually was reformulated for the final text of *Works of Love* (Lecture X, "The Work of Love in Praising Love"), evinces that Kierkegaard himself shares this pragmatic standpoint:

> This w. of love (*Kjerlighedens G.*) to praise love
>
> ———
>
> Intr.
> "To say is no art, but to do." It is also true, of course, when one excepts the cases where to say is the art (Poetry-Eloquence). However (*Dog*), for love it holds good to the highest degree that to do is the major issue. And yet (*Men dog*), to praise love is a work. (Pap. VIII 2 B 58,1)

In spite of the fact that Kierkegaard surely could not be defended as an exemplary exponent of the "pragmatic (linguistic) turn," the last quotation seems to be significant in the present discussion, because it subtly, that is, with reservations (*dog*), undermines the traditional opposition between language and action,[4]

———

thoughts, or actions of the audience, or of the speaker, or of other persons." J. L. Austin, *How to Do Things with Words* (repr.: Cambridge MA: Harvard University Press, 1975; orig. 1962) 101.

Jakob Bøggild has also discussed the question of linguistic performance in *Works of Love* in relation to a rhetorical reading of the text: " 'Playing Stranger': *Works of Love* caught in the Act," in *Kierkegaard Studies. Yearbook 1998*, ed. Niels Jørgen Cappelørn and Jon Stewart (Berlin, New York: Walter de Gruyter, 1998) 158-73. However, his approach is not based on the conceptual framework of the philosophy of language, but on the one of deconstruction. Bøggild's reading of performativity in *Works of Love* refers back to the aesthetical notion of the sublime, and concludes that *Works of Love* brings the reader into a position of "strangeness," not only in front of the text (and its author), but also in front of himself/herself, and therefore, forces him/her into an ethical reestablishment of a self-relationship.

[4]This is in my view the crucial issue to which one must pay attention in order to carry a discussion about Kierkegaard's works discursively considered from an ethical perspective. To reject the opposition between language and action (between Kierkegaardian aesthetics and ethics, is the departure point, the absolute methodological a priori of any pragmatic-rhetorical reading, such as I present in this article. This is the same opposition to which Judge Wilhelm in *Either/Or*, part 2, subscribes, and on which he founds his critique of A as being indifferent not only to the established normativity that rules all activity, but to activity in general. Linguistic action is no action in Judge Wilhelm's conception, because his

according to which, language belongs in principle to the realm of ideality, and is thereby excluded from the realm of actuality to which action belongs. Per contra, "to praise love," that is, the linguistic (poetic) and exalted undertaking of admiring, approving, and above all, commending love, *is a work*, that is, an action, and so it belongs at some level to the realm of actuality.

Still, in another text in his journals that "should not be used," Kierkegaard dares "to call this text a work of love (*en Kjerlighedens Gjerning*)," and he indeed explains that he has been "honestly working to render love (*gjøre Kjerligheden*) as beautiful as it truly is, and it is our desire that the one who reads it should be won for love (*maatte vindes for Kjerligheden*)," and he adds: "This is our work" (Pap. VIII2 B 73). It is not only Kierkegaard's work, but also the work of the text as a text, the work that *Works of Love* issues (see also Pap. VIII2 B 58,11).

---

is an extremely restricted, codified, and finally conventional conception of (ethical) praxis in general. Much closer to A's literary praxis, and to current literary criticism, Kierkegaard conceives of language pragmatically and rhetorically at once as interaction of two general kinds, either "scientific," i.e., informative, or "artistic," i.e., engaging, encouraging, demanding, etc. Paraphrasing Northrop Frye, Kierkegaard's opposition refers both to a use of language that "faithfully reflects or informs about states of affairs," and to another use where language itself is "affected by personal agendas and wishes and, therefore, colors and distorts the facts that it intends to reflect." Northrop Frye, *Anatomy of Criticism* (Princeton NJ: Princeton University Press, 1990) 262.

Indeed, the second use of language reveals language as the medium through which facts are not only made transparent, as it were, but they are literally *made*. In this view, facts are thus coconstituted by and in language, and language is not merely understood as a medium but, rather, as an activity *senso stricto*.

By contrast, the ethically relevant opposition that should be defended in the context of *Works of Love*, and in Kierkegaard's works in general is not the one between language and action but rather the one between epistemology or theory (i.e., knowledge) and ethics or praxis (i.e., action).

In this new light, language's primary ethical task is not to convey knowledge on ethical matters, for which reason its primary addressee is not the Socratic individual who does not know the good, the ethically ignorant, as much as the Aristotelian *akratés*, that is, the individual that, in spite of knowing the good, does not actualize it. Hence only when the discussion about the ethical in Kierkegaard's works is based on the opposition between knowledge and action, as opposed to the one between language and action, is it possible that it moves away from Judge Wilhelm's ethical conventionalism.

Hence, if the notion of language game seemed useful for un-
masking the apparently oxymoronic character of a "written talk/
discourse," the notion of linguistic performance has allowed us to
unmask a second apparent oxymoron, namely, the conception of
a text, that is, of a linguistic entity, and simultaneously as an act,
that is, as an action. In both cases, it has been shown that the
apparently nonsensical relationship instead depicted a well
cemented categorial and formal unity. Interestingly, these are not
the sole oxymorons to be unmasked in *Works of Love*.

As a matter of fact, the praise *(anprise)* of love that Kierkegaard
claims to be the work of love in *Works of Love*, serves to commend
*(anbefale)* love. Now, ethical-religiously speaking, the praise of love
serves to command *(befale;* "Essentially the commandment is . . .
commanding": *Budet er . . . befalende,* WL, 41) love. This means that,
in being praised, love is indirectly brought into sight as a demand
*(Fordring)*. It seems clear that, as a praise of love, *Works of Love* is
a work of love that demands a work of love from its readers. And
it serves to remind us that this is not one demand among others
within the moral order, but it is the foundational demand of the
moral order or ethos.[5]

Yet why should love, which, according to *Works of Love* is presupposed (WL, 16), and by definition is an instinct *(Trang,* WL, 10),
need to be demanded at all or, even more strongly, commanded,
and thereby become a duty *(Pligt)*? Is not this conception of love
fundamentally counterintuitive? Or, in other words, does it not
constitute a new oxymoron? The following quotation, however,
seems to undermine the former presumption: "*You* **shall** *love,*
because this is the very mark of Christian love and its distinctive
characteristic—that it contains this *apparent contradiction*: to love is
a duty" (WL, 24; emphasis added).

Ergo, once again, the oxymoron was only a *fata morgana* after
all. However, not an innocuous one, because, he writes

---

[5]The foundational character of the love commandment has its theological and
biblical parallel in Paul (Romans 13:9c) and in the gospel written by Matthew
(22:37-40), according to which all the commandments are grounded on the
commandment of love: "Thou shalt love your neighbor."

take a pagan [or a reader] who is not spoiled by having learned thoughtlessly to patter Christianity by rote or has not been spoiled by the delusion of being a Christian—and this commandment "You *shall* love," will not only surprise him but will disturb him, will be an offense to him. For this very reason that which is the mark of Christianity—"Everything has become new"—again fits the commandment of love. (WL, 25)

In this respect, the oxymoron does not have a casual character; on the contrary, it is precisely by force of both its oxymoronic character and configuration that the commandment leaves the pagan— and the reader—everything but indifferent. Now, what difference does it make to approach the divine commandment, "Thou shalt love your neighbor," as a *commandment*? The answer to this question is twofold, corresponding to the ethical-religious perspective I have been referring to since the beginning of this paper.

Considered from the ethical perspective, the commandment makes a difference insofar as it leads the reader to Christian love, which has to be actualized. In this perspective, *Works of Love* issues an originary demand (*Fordring*), the fulfillment of which implies a qualification of every action, given its eternal validity (cf. WL, 41), by virtue of which the commandment implies a qualification of love as duty, that is, as originary and fundamental duty, that requires absolute observance. It seems to me that both notions, demand and duty, allow for a reading where the ethical cannot simply be considered as the general (in the sense of the Danish *det Almene*) as a once and for all given metaphysical moral condition, but as a fundamental *task*, the task of tasks, so to speak.[6]

---

[6]Hence from this standpoint, *Works of Love* becomes relevant for the discussion of Kierkegaard's conception of the ethical, especially if we agree that the ethical in *Works of Love* is conceived of in relation to the same conceptual framework as it is conceived of by Vigilius Haufniensis in his preface to *The Concept of Anxiety*, where he writes:

So the new science begins with dogmatics in the same sense that immanental science begins with metaphysics. Here ethics finds its place as the science that has as a task for actuality, the dogmatic consciousness of actuality. This ethics does not ignore sin, and it does not have its ideality in making ideal demands; rather, it has its ideality in the penetrating consciousness of actuality, of the actuality of sin, but note carefully, not with metaphysical light-mindedness or with psychological con-

Concomitantly, in the religious perspective, the commandment makes a difference in the sense that, in spite of the *"essentially inexhaustible* [and] *undescribable"* (WL, 3, 207) character of Christian love, it brings love to sight *as* Christian love. Properly speaking, one should state that, through the commandment, and considered as a work of love, thus as the fulfilling of the demand of love and as the strict and absolute observance of the duty to love, *Works of Love* is the paradoxical *revelation* of Christian love. Thus, in *Works of Love,* not only is love made manifest as a demand and a duty, but love as the love of God, and God himself, also becomes "totally present everywhere," that is, actual (WL, 3, 207).

As a specific re-creation of love, *Works of Love* is the topos for the creation of love. As a con-figuration of love, *Works of Love* allows the trans-figuration of love, parallel to the transfiguration of Christ described by Kierkegaard as follows:

> Christ was the fulfilling of the Law. How this thought is to be understood we are to learn from him, because he was *the explanation,* and only when the explanation *is* what it explains, when the explainer *is* what is explained, when the explanation (*Forklaringen*) is the transfiguration (*Forklarelsen*), only then is the relation the right one. (WL, 101)

Thus, the performance of the commandment of love implies both a demand related to an absolute duty and a revelation related to an absolute paradox. From a rhetorical point of view, this double performance requires the forms of both an edifying and a Christian discourse. And this will be the twofold rhetorical frame from which I shall approach *Works of Love* in what follows.

First, however, let me share in a brief interlude an examination of the notion of *authority,* which I take to be the key notion that not only lies at the background of the present discussion, but also, at

---

cupiscence. . . . The new ethics presupposes dogmatics, and by means of hereditary sin it explains the sin of the single individual, while at the same time it sets ideality as a task, not by a movement from above and downward but from below and upward. (CA, 20)

Furthermore, "ethics is never observing but always accusing, judging, and acting. . . . Ethics never allows itself to be fooled and does not waste time on such deliberations" (CA, 22-23).

the basis of any discussion about Kierkegaard's own discursive praxis.

## (Dis)Authorization of Language

The notion of authority has a qualitative relevance in Kierkegaard's works and thought. But here I call attention only to its significance for the configuration of the discourse of *Works of Love*. On the one hand, the point of departure is the conviction that "What the world needs most of all right now is this *You shall*, pronounced with authority. This is the only thing that can give impetus" (JP, 4:4893). However, on the other hand, it is made clear also in the lectures on the dialectics of communication that there is a fundamental (Kierkegaardian) limiting premise related to the "pronunciation" of this "You shall" or "You must," that should not be overlooked. It is, that "in regard to the ethical, one person cannot have authority in relation to another because, ethically, God is the master teacher and every man is an apprentice " (JP, 1:649, 16). In the context of an ethical religious discourse based indeed on a fundamental "You shall," the author is deprived of ethical-religious authority, that is, precisely the required authority, and must confess to the reader: "I have nothing to say to you, at the most, I can tell what eternity has told me, while I am certain that eternity says the same to you and to everyone that will listen" (Pap. VIII 2 B 31, 26). Basically, this assumption implies that the author remains silent; at most, the author can speak only secretly between the lines.[7]

---

[7]The question of silence deserves a longer and deeper discussion than I can develop here. However, I would like to insist that both from an ethical and a rhetorical perspective, silence is an unavoidable question as far as Kierkegaard's ethical-religious communication is concerned. In this twofold context, where both ethics and rhetoric are involved, it is relevant that silence and action are equally considered as opposed to knowledge. Hence silence is not the opposite of language or discourse, but, on the contrary, it is at once (1) the thematical a priori of the discourse, as far as its matter or object is the paradox, i.e., not only the unthinkable, but also and specifically the unsayable, and (2) the formal a priori of discourse, indeed, its *modus operandi*, literally speaking, that is, the way in which and by force of which language operates and thereby acts. In this sense, I agree with Joakim Garff, that in *Fear and Trembling*, "in order to maintain Abraham as

But this assumption brings two other consequences in its train:
(1) it implies that certain language games and/or performances
lose not only their operativity but their authority, and (2) it also
causes a displacement of authority within the discourse, thus
turning the whole dynamics of communication upside down. Let
us examine these two consequences.

(1) In the lectures, Kierkegaard clearly *dis*authorizes the
"scientific" language game and/or performance as opposed to the
"artistic" one, because by its force the reader is expected to get
acquainted with the object being communicated, and thus, he/she
is expected to establish a mere epistemological relationship with it,
he/she is expected to merely know the communicated object. This
kind of linguistic undertaking is not inadequate just because it
overlooks the (ethical-religious) distinctiveness of the message to
be communicated, and turns the "You shall," into a state of affairs,
denying its essentially prescriptive character. The "scientific"
discourse is also illegitimate because it displays an unjustified and
illicit authority, namely an "immanental authority, not the
paradoxical conception of authority" (JP, 1:183). To this extent, the
"scientific" language game and/or performance is disauthorized.

In the light of rhetoric and from the point of view of modern
linguistics, the Kierkegaardian disauthorization of "scientific"
discourse implies, first, a limitation of the *descriptive* function of
language, as is made clear in regards to Christian love and its
works in the introductions to both series in *Works of Love*, and,
second, a restriction of the *expressive* function of language because

the representative of the paradox. . . . He [*de silentio*] writes not only *from* silence,
but also *about* silence." Joakim Garff, "Johannes de silentio: Rhetorician of
Silence," in *Kierkegaard Studies. Yearbook 1996*, ed. Niels Jørgen Cappelørn and
Hermann Deuser (Berlin, New York: Walter de Gruyter, 1996) 186-210.

Furthermore, Oliva Blanchette, Robert L. Perkins, and Gene Fendt have also
considered the notion of silence specifically related to *Fear and Trembling* in their
articles included in *International Kierkegaard Commentary: Fear and Trembling*
(Macon GA: Mercer University Press, 1993): "The Silencing of Philosophy" (29-65);
"Abraham's Silence Aesthetically Considered" (155-76); and "Whose Fear and
Trembling" (177-91), respectively. Oliva Blanchette's remarks about the requirement that faith issues for the philosophical discourse, which "cannot reconcile the
contradiction" (29) that faith implies, are not only relevant, but also illuminating
for the present discussion.

Christian love becomes thereby nothing but "an explanation [of love] in riddles" (WL, 30). Hence within the discursive context of *Works of Love*, both the *descriptive* and the *poetic* linguistic functions are objects of disapprobation, because they do not and cannot take into account the major discursive fact that

> The divine authority of the Gospel does not speak to one person about another, does not speak to you, my listener, about me, or to me about you—no, when the Gospel speaks, it speaks to the single individual. It does not speak *about* us human beings, you and me, but speaks *to* us human beings, to you and me. (WL, 14)

Instead, it seems clear that Kierkegaard explicitly defends the conative function of language as the only one being both appropriate and licit, and he therefore highlights the urge for appellation, for an "engaging, striking, interesting—in short, . . . enthralling" (JP, 1:643) use of language. We should keep this in mind, as it will be the crucial cipher of what Kierkegaard calls "artistic" communication and, eventually, "existential communication" (*Existens-Meddelese*).

(2) According to this view, a displacement of authority takes place. However, given that authority *in toto* is far from erased or rejected, the interesting question is now, where in the discourse then does the authority lie? As the matter of fact, the previous quotation from *Works of Love* anticipates the twofold answer to that question.

Having been displaced from the author, who no longer speaks, or, at the most, only in a secret manner, and from the descriptive and expressive functions of language, which cannot convey the message in its distinctiveness, authority is now to be found in its divine and indeed "paradoxical" force and shape in "the Gospel," which "speaks *to* us human beings, to you and me" (WL, 14). In *Works of Love*, as in every ethical-religious discourse, "eternity commands 'You shall love' " (WL, 42); indeed "the love commandment is of divine origin" (WL, 42), because, as Kierkegaard asks, "Who would have this courage [to command] except eternity; who has the right to say this *shall* except eternity . . . where can this command have its home except in eternity?" (WL, 41)[8]

---

[8]Indeed, as indicated in a journal entry about some of his Christian discourses:

Obviously, such a fundamental displacement or reassignment of authority affects the complete dynamics of the discourse and of the communicative process. And Kierkegaard has studied the changes that the process undergoes with extreme and insightful meticulousness in his lectures about the dialectics of the ethical-religious communication. The point here is that the whole set of expectations regarding the elements of the discourse is turned upside down.

As we have just seen, as far as the author or the narrator is concerned, he remains silent, that is, only accidentally and obliquely acting within the discourse of *Works of Love*. Instead, he loans his voice to a radically silent entity, namely "the Gospels," which now speak and, thereby, as already remarked, "exceptionally become *"wholly present"* in the text (JP, 1:761). But the author or narrator is not the sole element within the discourse that is subjected to this fundamental redefinition.

Similarly and crucially, the message, the divine commandment "You shall love," far from being a determinate one, that is, a perfectly defined cognitive unity, established through a stable and univocal medium or code, becomes an ethical-religious *desideratum*. In this view,

> Love is the fulfilling of the Law. *Despite all its many provisions* [or determinations, *Bestemmelser*], *the Law is still somewhat indefinite.* . . . the Law is taken up into love, it is the shadow of what is to come . . . there is only one sketch that is completely definite, and that is the work itself. . . . Thus the Law is a sketch and love the fulfilling and the entirely definite; in love the Law is the entirely definite. (WL, 104)

Since the only definite determination of the law is its fulfillment, which must in fact be extralinguistic, language remains indeterminate *ex actio*, as it were, and this equally implies that "the law has no capability of providing the power which results in life, even though it is life it has in view."[9] The fundamental ambiguity

---

"What is essentially Christian . . . is specifically that the authority of the Bible is affirmed, that it is not something one has thought out but something commanded, something with authority" (JP, 1:207).

[9]In Paul Müller's words in *Kristendom, etik og majeutik i Søren Kierkegaard's "Kjerlighedens Gjerninger"* (Copenhagen: Københavns Universitets Institut for

that the divine commandment performs simultaneously both a *demand* and a *revelation*, as shown above, forces the medium, language itself and its basic structures—logic and grammar—to collapse and open up for a new word which is, above all, a new world. These are the parameters of the "change of eternity" or its transfiguration *via* language, the parameters where "everything has become new" (WL, 25).

Indeed, once its roots have been undermined, language can no longer be a medium to convey *"what this [or that] word signifies (betegner) in ordinary speech"* (WL, 120). Thus language is used in a fundamentally different way, although the same words are being used. Kierkegaard has a sharp understanding of this linguistic (and, indeed, edifying) dynamic in the opening paragraphs of the first discourse in the second series, "Love Builds up," which begins, "All human speech, even the divine speech of Holy Scripture, about the spiritual is essentially metaphorical [*overført*, carried over] speech" (WL, 209), and where a clear distinction is made between "the spiritual person and the sensate-physical person" who "say the same thing; yet there is an infinite difference. . . . There is a *world* of difference between the two; the one has made the transition [*Overgang*] or let himself be *carried over* [*føre over*] to the other side, while the other remains on this side; yet they have the connection that both are using the same words" (WL, 209; emphasis added).

The two relevant consequences for our present discussion are, on the one hand, that, given its indeterminate character, the law has, linguistically speaking no power by itself to guarantee its fulfilling; on the other hand, given the "metaphorical" character of language, the message might only be understood by those who already have been "carried over," and have reached the "other side," that is, by those "who have ears to hear" (WL, 210).

Interestingly, in both cases, the authority of the discourse is eventually given to the audience and/or reader who indeed has the ears, that is, the ability to understand the message from the

---

Religionshistorie, 1983) 38: "Loven formår slet ikke at frembringe den magt, som fører til livet, selv om det virkelig er livet, den har for øje." In English trans. by C. Stephen Evans and Jan Evans, in *Kierkegaard's "Works of Love." Christian Ethics and the Maieutic Ideal* (Copenhagen: C. A. Reitzel, 1993) 29.

"other side," that is, as a *revelation* and as a *demand*, and, consequently, has the power to determine the law, to fulfill its message
by actualizing it. However, still one problem remains: what
happens to those who do not "have ears to hear" either the
revelation or the demand? As we saw, Kierkegaard considers the
fact that these might be appalled, offended, but, still, how are they
"carried over" from a false oxymoron to understanding? In other
words, how is the "deaf" audience and/or reader "carried over"
to Christian love? And in Kierkegaard's own words:

> What courage it takes to say for the first time, "You *shall* love,"
> or, more correctly, what divine authority it takes to turn the
> natural man's conceptions and ideas upside down with this
> phrase! There at the boundary where human language halts and
> courage fails, there revelation breaks forth with divine origination
> and proclaims what is not difficult to understand in the sense of
> profundity or human parallels but which did not arise in any
> human being's heart. (WL, 24-25)

Once it has been admitted that ethical-religious authority lies
in divine "proclamation"[10] and, indeed, in the response of the audience and/or the reader, the restructuring of the dynamics of communication has been fulfilled. Consequently, the discourse has undergone a radical modification, and now responds to what Kierkegaard himself calls "inverted dialectics," which he described as a

> special kind of dialectic, a dialectic of quality. The most likely
> way to think of it is that the predecessor (John the Baptist) certi-
> fies that Jesus is the expected one. But this, dialectically, is im-

---

[10]As already mentioned, it is solely the authority of the Bible that counts, and
this implies a disauthorization of the author and of certain uses of language.
However, a further step could be taken, by virtue of which the biblical text again
should be rhetorically considered as a metaphor of the only acceptable authority
according to Kierkegaard, a nonimmanent authority and thus beyond rhetorical
matters. This is the authority on which the success of the communicative
undertaking, also in *Works of Love*, depends, as far as both the revelation and the
demand of Christian love "depend entirely on the extent to which God allows
[us] to listen." George A. Kennedy, *Classical Rhetoric and its Christian and Secular
Tradition from Ancient to Modern Times* (Chapel Hill: University of North Carolina
Press, 1981) 122. The success of ethical-religious communication thus, seems to
depend as well on an extrarhetorical feature, on transcendental authority *senso
stricto*, namely grace.

proper subordination, because in order to certify, the certifier must be superior. Therefore it is John the Baptist who sends disciples to Christ to ask him whether he is the expected one— and then it is Christ who, after having answered the disciples, concludes by certifying John the Baptist as the legitimate forerunner. It is not Christ who props himself up with the authority of the predecessor (which is a paralogism)—no, it is he who draws the predecessor within his authority and by virtue of his authority certifies him to be the legitimate predecessor. Now for the first time the predecessor's words to the believers that Christ is the expected one really have authority, now when Christ has certified that the predecesor really is the predecessor. This seems to be a circle, but it is as far as possible from that; it is the one and only consistency within the dialectic of authority. (JP, 1:764)

Having established the dialectic of authority as the new dialectic of discourse, let us now approach *Works of Love* and see what consequences this dialectic has for its configuration.

### *Language in Form. A Rhetorical Reading of* Works of Love

The following considerations entail a rhetorical reading of *Works of Love* based on the preceeding discussion of authority and the (dis)authorization of certain uses of language. However, my chief aim is not so much to relocate authority in the discourse as such, but rather to examine its configuration and shape.

Having assumed the consequences of the displacement of authority in the "artistic" discourse, the main linguistic problem that Kierkegaard has to cope with in *Works of Love* is how to say the unsayable. Taking into account that *Works of Love* might be considered respectively as a "Christian" or as an "edifying" discourse, the problem is twofold, namely: how might *Works of Love* issue both a revelation and a demand. What does it take to *say love as the Christian law* and what to *say love as the Christian duty*, respectively? In other words, the main question here is how love, at once both the fundamental paradox and the fundamental task, not only can be but must be said. The main problem will then be which means supply the text with the force that is needed to reveal and to demand Christian love. Hence after showing the discursive role that Kierkegaard gives rhetoric, seen as the appropriate and licit means to communicate the ethical-religious, I shall suggest to what genre *Works of Love* might be adscribed to from a rhetorical perspective.

Both the journal entries and the loose papers from 1845 make clear that Kierkegaard became increasingly interested in rhetoric, not only as *ars oratoria* (which he will eventually criticize and dismiss as sheer stylistic eloquence and a cheap means for speculation and persuasion), but, rather, as *ars argumentativa*, as he finds it in Aristotle, where rhetoric provides the means "to awaken faith" (JP, 1:627). Moreover, Kierkegaard suggests that "a new science must be introduced: the Christian rhetoric art of speaking (or rhetoric, *Talekunst*), to be constructed *admodum* Aristotle's *Rhetoric*. Dogmatics as a whole is a misunderstanding, especially as it now has been developed" (JP, 1:627).[11]

I believe there is a significant coincidence between Kierkegaard's complaints about the "misunderstanding" that affects "the whole dogmatic" and the one that affects "the ethical-religious," in that both founder on "the delusion and confusion of the modern age . . . that the ethical is communicated as scholarship and science," because "art is understood only aesthetically as fine art" (JP, 1:649, 1, 5). What does it mean, that dogmatic, the ethical-religious, and the works of love, should be communicated as an art as opposed to a science? Or, in other words, which are the characteristics of an "artistic" discourse as opposed to a "scientific" discourse? The answer to this question is the first step toward the discussion of the genre to which *Works of Love* should be adscribed.

The "artistic" is much a broader concept in Kierkegaard's conceptual landscape than "fine art," so the expression "artistic discourse" need not mean an exclusively aesthetic discourse. That is, the purpose of the discourse is not solely evocative or, in generic terms, an aesthetic performance, designed merely to please the reader emotionally, and, in the best case, bring the reader closer to a knowledge of the message. The predicate "artistic" here can by no means refer to a beautiful, nice, enjoyable or even emotive discourse exclusively, that is, to affection. Rather, "artistic" designates

---

[11]Kierkegaard had even thought of the author of this Christian Rhetoric, and it should by now be no surprise that the elected candidate was none other than Johannes de silentio (JP, 5:5786).

a very precise use of language, a strategy, by force of which the audience and/or reader "begins immediately to do it," that is, to do what they are told, to actualize the message, to give to the law and love, as far as *Works of Love* is concerned (JP, 1:653, 3), the determination they are lacking, so that the message "achieves actuality," and communication becomes "an existential situation" where that which is revealed and demanded, "the ethical and again the Christian are made actual" (JP, 1:653, 18).

Hopefully, it is clear by now that, from a rhetorical perspective, *Works of Love* is an example of "artistic" discourse. However, Kierkegaard himself provides some other rhetorical tools, indeed categories, to take a second step in order to adscribe a genre to his work. Thus, he speaks in his journals of, at least four sorts of discourse: devotional (*gudelig*), edifying (*opbyggelig*), Christian (*christelig*), and religious (*religøs*).[12] Kierkegaard has been fairly clear about *Works of Love*, in that he classifies it as "Christian deliberations" (WL, 3, 207).

Precisely in this respect, Kierkegaard introduces a rather systematic and valid distinction "between an Upbuilding Discourse and reflections," which relies upon his conviction that

> [r]eflections do not presuppose the qualifying concepts as given and understood; therefore they must not so much move, mollify, reassure, persuade, as *awaken* and provoke men and sharpen thought. The time for reflections is indeed before action, and their purpose therefore is to rightly relate all the elements into the proper motion. Reflections ought to be a "gadfly"; therefore their tone ought to be quite different from that of upbuilding [*opbyggelige*] or edifying discourse, which rests in mood, but reflections ought in the good sense to be impatient. (JP, 1:641)

---

[12]Kierkegaard has nowhere given any systematic stylistic instructions as far as the four sorts of discourse are concerned. However, he keeps in mind a basic differentiation, a basic golden rule, as it were, which should be followed in order to avoid both "speculative" and "historizing" discourses, as opposed to ethical-religious discourses. In this respect, Kierkegaard, in perfect consistency with Climacus's comments on the same issue in *Philosophical Fragments* and in *Postscript*, offers a stylistic approximation to what a discourse should *not* be like, if the ethical-religious message is to be respected. He then depicts *via negativa* what might be a twofold rhetorical countermodel for ethical-religious communication (JP, 1:625-26).

Certainly, *Works of Love* issues, as we have seen, a Christian revelation, as far as it conveys love as a duty, embodied in the formulation of a law, thus, in the sense that it conveys a fundamental oxymoron, or, from the Christian point of view, a fundamental paradox, which forces the "qualification of concepts" that "*awakens*" the reader, affecting his/her reception of the text, and also the configuration of its meaning.

But Kierkegaard continues: "An upbuilding discourse about love presupposes that men know essentially what love is and seeks to win them to it, to move them. But this is in fact not the case. Therefore the 'reflections' must first fetch them up out to the cellar, call to them, turn their comfortable way of thinking topsy-turvy with the dialectic of truth" (JP, 1:641).

Now, given the performative force that any "Christian" discourse conceals, according to Kierkegaard, it seems plausible that such a "Christian reflection" might very well be read in the light of Kierkegaardian "ethical-religious communication, namely, Christian" communication. Due to the fact that Christian communication "is direct-indirect" (JP, 1:657), writes Kierkegaard, "a knowledge about Christianity must certainly be communicated in advance. But this is only a preliminary" (JP, 1:653, 29). And would it not be defensible, that in regards to the present reading of *Works of Love* as an ethical-religious discourse, this "preliminary" (before action) corresponds to "Christian reflection," hence to the Christian revelation or proclamation of the law "You shall love"?

If we assent to the above, and in spite of Kierkegaard's univocal and clear adscription of *Works of Love* to the genre shared by all "Christian" discourses, a further adscription seems to follow the preliminary one. Let us risk the generic qualification of *Works of Love* now as *edifying* discourse.

Two major reasons, which have already been partially examined, corroborate this rhetorical characterization. The first refers back to the assumption for which I have argued that, from the point of view of linguistic pragmatics, *Works of Love* endeavours to "praise" Christian love and, to this extent, it is a "work of love." Now, this assumption cannot only be strongly argued in Kierkegaards own terms, but it can also be substantially supported within the frame of classical rhetoric, according to which discursive "praise" belongs to the *epideictic genre*. According to all manuals of classic rhetoric, the epideictic genre, the most excellent example of which is the *encomium*, stands for a ceremonial or formal expression of praise of honour and virtue, which partly entails a heuristic performance, but which likewise provides counseling for a course of action. For which reason, the epideictic discourse not only facilitates the future action of the audience but it also encourages it. Therefore, as an appraisal of love, or, rather, as an *encomium* of Christian virtues and deeds, *Works of Love* is an edifying discourse.

The second reason why *Works of Love* might be adscribed to the genre of edification, is that, once the law has been proclaimed, once love has been "Christianly reflected" on, and once the reader has been "awakened" to this fundamental duty to love, once love has been "qualified" as a demand, its fulfillment is still a *desideratum*. In other words, solely conceived of as a "Christian" discourse, *Works of Love* only manages to bring the law into sight, to make it manifest, but, as we have seen, it encompasses the enactment of the law with difficulties. If neither this fundamental demand that has to be fulfilled nor the ethical aspect of Christian communication are to be neglected, then, *Works of Love* must necessarily be understood as an edifying discourse which, Kierkegaard *dixit*: "presupposes that men know essentially what love is and seeks to win them to it, to move them" (JP 1:641).

And yet, the question still remains as to how the reader of *Works of Love* eventually happens to "dive into" the waters of Christian love and to stay, float, and even swim comfortably in them (JP, 1:653, 17). I shall try to answer this question in what I take to be at once the third step of the present undertaking to adscribe a genre to *Works of Love*. This certainly compels a stylistic pirouette, in that, in order to advocate *Works of Love* both as a Christian and as an edifying discourse, I will have to operate respectively with two kinds of rhetorical tools: those of a structural kind, which basically subvert the logical (and grammatical) configuration of the discourse, and those of a figurative kind or tropes, which basically subvert the semantical configuration of the discourse.

Literally, to inquire about the form of *Works of Love* as a "Christian" discourse or as an "edifying" discourse implies inquiring respectively about the rhetorical means for bringing

Christian love into sight (that is, for the Christian revelation and the fundamental Christian demand to take place), to take shape, within the discourse.

However, a preliminary and crucial remark should be made, if only to avoid an arbitrary stylistic reading of *Works of Love*. Once it has been agreed that *Works of Love* is an example of Kierkegaardian "ethical-religious communication," and that this circumstance determines the configuration of the text, as far as its form, that is, its style is concerned, a rhetorical reading of *Works of Love* seems to be permissible. And yet, not every rhetorical reading is permissible. There are at least two reasons for such a limitation, and I would dare to affirm that they apply not only to *Works of Love*, but to the whole Kierkegaardian corpus in general. The first reason for being cautious while proceeding rhetorically is text-immanent. To be more precise, it is based on a very specific rhetorical unity located at the very beginning of the text, namely, the "Prayer." By force of this "prayer," the reader is literally moved to a very exclusive order of things; the reader is literally, by means of the text, transported outside the text, not in the sense that he/she is shown the "signified," or the "object of reference" of the discourse, but, rather, in the sense that he/she is shown the *source of meaning* of the discourse. The "prayer" in *Works of Love* is the necessary rhetorical key to open the text rhetorically. Why is this so? To begin with, the prayer designates a very specific context of signification with which the author identifies. This is the context of a religious community, a community of believers, thus, faith being the cementing principle. A rhetorical reading of *Works of Love* will have to keep this context of signification in mind, to stress the figures through which this context is highlighted, if only to avoid becoming a banal reading, that is, an arbitrary stylistic reading which would only pay attention to whatever rhetorical figures might be found within the text, conceived of as a fragmentary and not necessarily coherent significative unity. But the prayer also designates a unique addressee, who is at the same time evoked and invoked as follows:

> How could one speak properly about love if you were forgotten,
> . . . you who revealed what love is, you our Savior and Redeemer, who gave yourself in order to save all. . . . O Eternal Love, you who are everywhere present and never without witness

where you are called upon, be not without witness in what will
be said here about love or about works of love. (WL, 3-4)

Indeed, insofar as this unique addressee, "our Saviour and
Redeemer," is what He says, that is, insofar as He does what He
says, namely, "eternal love," all discourse about works of love
should evoke Him, that is remember Him, and invoke Him, that
is ask for His assistance. By being the paradigmatic figure both of
the revelation of the Law and of the fulfillment of its demand,
Christ is the paradigm to be followed in *Works of Love*; not least the
rhetorical paradigm.[13]

I will return to this statement and its consequences; but first,
let me explain the second reason that will confirm the need to limit
the rhetorical perspective for reading *Works of Love*, one that points
outside the text.

Kierkegaard remarks in his journals: "Aristotle places the art
of speaking and the media for awakening faith in relationship to
probability, so that it is concerned (in contrast to knowledge) with
what can be relevant in another way" (JP, 1:628). So far, so good.
This reflection upon the capabilities of language as regards faith,
not (only) with an epistemological interest ("in contrast to
knowledge"), seems to keep Aristotle and Kierkegaard close to
each other. However, Kierkegaard inmediately adds: "Christian
eloquence will be distinguished from the Greek in that it is
concerned only with *improbability*, with showing that it is improba-

---

[13]In his rhetorical analysis of the biblical texts, Wayne A. Meeks suggests a
stylistic qualification, which to a certain extent could be useful for the present
discussion. Indeed, Meeks speaks of "a cruciform style" when he refers to the fact
that it was in "the prose of letters, by Paul and his imitators, that the polarities
of Christ's career were made into a model for the Christian life": *The Origins of
Christian Morality* (New Haven CT and London: Yale University Press, 1993) 87.

In this sense, it would be possible to defend Christ rhetorically as an
example, given that Christ brings into sight the will of God, not in the sense that
he is a *descriptor* of Christian life, and, as such, exclusively considered in his
human shape as the one who provides a list of virtues to which Christian life has
to adjust, but neither in the sense that he is a *prescriptor* of the law, and, as such,
exclusively considered in his divine shape as a Kantian regulative idea, deprived
therefore of all immanent or even subjective connotation. Christ is the paradigm
in the sense that he brings into sight the necessity and possibility of love at once,
because he is the one who requires love by giving it.

ble, in order that one can then *believe* it. Here probability is to be rejected just as much as improbability in the other, but both have in common the distinction from knowledge" (JP, 1:628).

Indeed, we are and remain within a pragmatic paradigm, in so far as what must follow from "eloquence" is primarily "action," works of love, and not "knowledge" or *words* of love. "Action" is the object, that is, the *telos*, of both Christian and Greek eloquence. By contrast, the differentiation that Kierkegaard is sharpening here, is bound to the matter of Christian eloquence or "*improbability*," as opposed to the object of Greek eloquence or "*probability*." Despite the fact that both pursue the adherence of the audience, that is, its becoming faithfully attached with the message being told and translating it into life-terms, Christian eloquence differs from Greek eloquence in that it does not and must not provide any proofs for that attachment to be made epistemologically secure, where "proof" includes not only logical but also rhetorical syllogisms or enthymemes. Any of these discursive tools, rhetorical or not, might "prevent acting" (JP, 1:631), that is, they might withdraw the demand entailed within the law of Christian love, and thereby, the edifying accent of *Works of Love*. And likewise, they might prevent faith, that is, they might conceal the revelation issued by the law of Christian love, and in this way, they might preclude Christian love itself. In Kierkegaard's own words:

> The first point developed in this discourse was that we must believe in love—otherwise we simply will not notice that it exists; but now the discourse returns to the first point and says, repeating: Believe in love! If we are to know love, this is the first and the last thing to say about it. (WL, 16)

Being belief in what is basically improbable, that is, faith being both the legitimate cause and consequence of Christian eloquence, it seems that it could very well be stated that the object of such eloquence is the *paradox*. Therefore, the relevant rhetorical question in *Works of Love* considered as a "Christian" discourse is: how can and/or shall the paradox be said? At the same time, considering *Works of Love* as an "edifying" discourse, the question embraces a parallel object, namely, the *task*. If the first question takes into account that as a fundamental "improbability," the paradox seems to be unsayable (at least through rational, that is, logical linguistic structures), the second question takes into account "the [equally] essentially Christian, which is not related to knowing but to acting" (WL, 96).

One could mislead oneself both as an author and as a reader by falling into the temptation of believing that poetry would supply a good linguistic (and semantic) basis for the paradox and the task to be said. However, one learns very quickly that Kierkegaard does not seem very keen on a poetical use of language to say the law of love in *Works of Love*, and this is not only because the poet speaks in "riddles," but, specifically, because the nature of Christian love and of poetic language, such as the Christian and the poet as poet, are basically contradictory, incommensurable, incompatible[14]. Hence to express Christian love poetically is a chimera because

> Christian love is eternal. Therefore no one, if he understands himself, would think of saying of Christian love that it blossoms. No poet, if he understands himself, would think of singing its praises. What the poet sings about must have the sadness, which is the riddle of his own life, that it must blossom—and, alas, must perish. But Christian love abides, and for that very reason it *is*. What perishes blossoms, and what blossoms perishes, but something that *is* cannot be sung about—it must be believed and it must be lived. (WL, 8)[15]

On the one hand, this quotation helps us understand that what matters for the Christian discourse of love is not what matters for the poetical discourse of love, because,

> the point of the essentially Christian is that it is presence (*det Nærværende*). For this reason no poet and no speaker can portray it, for they use too much imagination. This again is the very reason (this error) that the poet and speaker themselves come to

---

[14]For a discussion on the limits of a metaphorical and/or poetical use of language in and according to *Works of Love*, see Darío González, "Poetics and the 'Being' of Love," in *Kierkegaard Studies. Yearbook 1998*. ed. Niels Jørgen Cappelørn and Jon Stewart (Berlin, New York: Walter de Gruyter, 1998) 129-46.

[15]In this very sense, Kierkegaard adds that "erotic love and friendship, as the poet understands them, contain no moral task" (WL, 50-51). The poet does not have sense for *duty* but only for *fortune*, so when the time comes for Christian love to be morally said, the poet is lacking the prior and fundamental understanding that "when one *shall* love the neighbor, then the task *is*, the moral task, which in turn is the origin of all tasks" (WL, 51).

be loved and esteemed. For it is *at a distance* that Christianity appears lovable in men's eyes. Only a dialectician can portray Christianity, because by continuously taking away all illusions he drills it, so to speak, into the present. Consequently it will go hard with such a dialectical person, for Christianity which is *wholly present* is hateful and disturbing. (JP, 1:761)

Therefore, to say love poetically inevitably results in a fundamental "confusion" of "*both* poetic *and* Christian love" (WL, 50). From this standpoint Kierkegaard stresses:

The poet and Christianity explain diametrically opposite things, or, more accurately expressed, the poet really explains nothing, because he explains erotic love and friendship—in riddles . . . but Christianity explains love eternally. From this, one again sees that it is an impossibility to live according to both explanations simultaneously, since the greatest possible contrast between the two explanations is surely this, that the one is no explanation and the other is the explanation. (WL, 50)

Indeed, for the one is a promise (WL, 98), the other is the law.

On the other hand, to state that love *is* and that it cannot be sung about, but that it must be "believed and lived," corresponds to the remark that whereas the purpose of Christian eloquence is that the audience accepts the committment the message entails, so that it is "believed" and "lived," poetic eloquence pursues what Kierkegaard repeatedly criticizes later in *Christian Discourses* and in *Practice in Christianity*, namely, the audience's *admiration* (*Beundring*).[16] And admiration, just like proof, will indeed be rejected as constituting a primary obstacle to both action and faith and, consequently, to love.

---

[16]In the *Christian Discourses*, admiration is explicitly opposed to "belief" (CD, 240-46), whereas its counterpart in *Practice in Christianity* is "imitation" (PC 233-57). Also Johannes Climacus, in relation to the subjective thinker and his style and within his discussion of the "actual and ethical subjectivity" in *Postscript*, has considered the convenience and inconvenience, advantages and disadvantages of admiration as opposed to demand and he concludes that "What is great with regard to the universal must therefore not be presented as an object for admiration, but as a *requirement* [or demand, *Fordring*]. In the form of possibility, the presentation becomes a requirement ( . . . ) then whether or not the reader wants to exist in it is placed as close as possible to him" (CUP, 1:358-59).

Thus, neither a logical nor a poetic use of language are capable of embracing the Christian paradox, and the Christian task embodied in Christian love. Where then, are the paradox and the task admitted in language without being either dismantled or distorted? How is language to be used, so that love *is* in it, and it is as "hateful and disturbing" in its presence as Christianity itself, and it is in a way that it awakens the understanding of faith, that will be followed by its fulfillment, by the works of love? Once again, how is love to be said? At this point, this seems indeed to be an impossible undertaking. Not only is there a lack of authority, given that authority suffers a fundamental displacement in the discourse, but there is also a lack of linguistic tools, given that love seems to escape language by nature, by virtue of which, love could possibly and legitimately, be said.

I would like now to return to a statement made earlier in this paper, that Christ, conceived of both as the incarnation of paradox, the sign of contradiction, and also as the deed of eternal love, the spirit of love, grounds the rhetorical pattern of/in *Works of Love*, as reflected in its character of "Christian" and "edifying" discourse respectively. Hence *Works of Love* is, discursively speaking, not only an example of "ethical-religious communication" but, indeed, an example of Christian rhetoric *strictissimo senso*.

Insofar as this rhetorical pattern amounts to establishing *Works of Love* in what Kierkegaard had called the "dialectic of authority," that is, this "special kind of dialectic, a dialectic of quality," wherein Christ "by virtue of his authority certifies" that the word and work not only of John the Baptist, but those of Kierkegaard as well, are legitimate (JP, 1:764), Kierkegaard's word and, consequently, work are, as he himself declares, "*apostolic*" (WL, 106). But, secondly, to regard Christ as a rhetorical pattern also amounts to considering certain rhetorical tools as legitimate means to say love as paradox and as task. In the first case, the required figure will be as subversive to grammar, or the logical structure of language, as the paradox, and its presence in the text as "hateful and disturbing" as the presence of Christ(ianity) is for existence; in the second case, the required figure will subvert the semantic weight of the text, as the love shown by Christ(ianity) does to existence.

In other words, by being love, Christ is at once the oxymoron,[17] that is, an internally contradictory figure, and the icon, that is, an externally exemplary figure, who sets the rhetorical pattern of/in *Works of Love*. In Kierkegaard's words, Christ is the one who relates to the law of love in a way that "fixes an everlasting chasmic abyss between the God-man and every other person," for he is the one "we are to learn from him because, he was *the explanation*" (WL, 101).

Now, supported by the oxymoronic framework of *Works of Love*, love obliquely appears through a multiplicity of contradictory formulations. Certainly, the most obvious oxymoron, considered so by Kierkegaard himself, relates to the negative and basic determination of Christian love as duty (WL, 24). As a matter of fact,

---

[17]Hermann Deuser has insightfully considered the "Christological construction of the Paradox" in Kierkegaard's discourses, in his books *Sören Kierkegaard. Die paradoxe Dialektik des politischen Christen* (München: Chr. Kaiser Verlag, 1974) and *Kierkegaard. Die Philosophie des religiösen Schriftstellers* (Darmstadt: Wissenschaftliche Buchgesellschaft, 1985) esp. chap. 3, "Kierkegaards Sprache: Literatur als Lebensform," where the former quotation originates (158). Deuser defends the argumentative and linguistic role of Christ as archetype within the Christian discourse, there where "die Sprache kann es nicht ausdrücken" (*Sören Kierkegaard. Die Paradoxe Dialektik*, 216-17); that is, according to my presentation of *Works of Love*, as *revelation*. Indeed, the main performance of Christian discourse by force of the figure of Christ is that love is brought into sight, but, as we have also seen, not solely; love is also a *demand*. Thus considered as an archetype, the figure of Christ fulfills as well an edifying performance, in the sense that it constitutes the example to be followed by the reader in order to fulfill the law or the love commandment.

Deuser admits that there is a continuity between the Christian and the edifying discourses, but he does not thematize it. Concomitantly, Deuser reads Christ as the sign of both existential and textual paradox, as it were, in terms of "tautology," underlining thereby that the discourse "cannot be what it demands" (*Sören Kierkegaard. Die Paradoxe Dialektik*, 232), it can only make the demand present, without explaining, without giving good or bad reasons for the reader to fulfill it. To a certain extent, this responds to what I have designated as the transfiguration of Christian love in *Works of Love*, and, as such, as the absolute presence of Christ as love in the text. However, a tautological configuration of the Christian paradox seems to be insufficient, once again, as it remains oblivious to Christ as the sign of contradiction, namely, as the oxymoron, by force of which Christianity is at the same time *"wholly present* [and] is hateful and disturbing" (JP, 1:761).

the titles of the five articles at the first series of *Works of Love* suggest that this is the oxymoronic context, as it were, to which all discourse about love will refer. However, within this oxymoronic context attention is paid to other formulations. Hence love is here (WL, I, 8-16) specifically determined by the law as a demand, at once hidden and recognizable by its fruits, made manifest in its hidden life. Likewise, *"Only when it is a duty to love, only then is love eternally made free in blessed independency"* (WL II. A, 37-40). Next the law demands to love the neighbor as one loves oneself, therefore, love to the neighbor is self-love and "however, is self-denial's love" (WL II. B, 55-60). Also, by demanding love, Christianity "allows the dissimilarities to stand but teaches the equality of eternity" (WL II. C, 72-88). Even the law of love, as we have already seen, suffers from this oxymoronic nature (cf. WL III. A, 104), which *"despite all its many determinations, the Law is still somewhat indeterminate"* (WL, 21; translation slightly modified). No less counterintuitive is love presented (WL III. B, 143 and 147) as *"a matter of conscience and thus is not a matter of drives and inclination, or a matter of feeling"* especially if it is at the same time stated that love *"must therefore be out of a pure heart and out of a sincere faith"*; or to agree that Christian love is a purely spiritual love, and at the same time (WL IV, 173), agree that "the Christian point of view, however, is that to love is to love precisely the person one sees," and that, in doing so, *"the one who loves by giving, infinitely, runs into infinite debt"* (WL V, 177). These are the main, let us say, oxymoronic maxims, through which love is shown in the first series of *Works of Love*; and their oxymoronic nature is what, according to Kierkegaard, is the distinctive characteristic (*Eiendommelighed*) of love. However, and precisely, paradoxically therefore, it is maintained throughout the first series in *Works of Love*, that love has to be believed in.

In the second series, it is also stressed that love has to be lived. Accordingly, *Works of Love* experiences a significative pragmatic turn in the sense that it is not only the revelation of love as a demand, or love being related to this demand, that matters, but the way in which love itself relates to this demand, and fulfills its own demand. Thus, what matters is how love works, "love in its outward direction" (WL, 282). Besides love itself, the works of Christian love will be presented by the force of oxymoronic figures.

The "distinctive" pragmatic point of departure for the second series of *Works of Love* ethically speaking is that "love builds up" or edifies (*opbygger*) (WL, I, 216); edification is love's major work, in which love is at once "the ground" and "the building," for "to build up" is always "to build up love." In and as edification, "love believes all things—and yet, is never deceived" (WL II, 225) "love hopes all things—and yet is never put to shame," (WL III, 246) love, conceived of as sacrifice, did seek its (Christ's) own, so that "love does not seek its own" (WL IV, 264) after it (Him). Also, "love hides a multitude of sins," even if "to discover is indeed something praiseworthy, something admired"; by contrast, *"what it [love] cannot avoid seeing or hearing, it hides by silence, by a mitigating explanation, by forgiveness"* (WL V, 283 and 289). What Kierkegaard considers to be a "very upbuilding thought" is that "Love abides," in spite and because it cannot be waited for or "love is displaced, it ceases . . . it comes to a break. Christianity, however, does not know this use of language, does not understand it, refuses to understand it"; instead, Christianity insists that one *"falls away from love,"* thus, love abides (WL VI, 301-304). The last four chapters in the second series of *Works of Love* refer to four specific works of love, which of course share with love its oxymoronic nature, and make its oxymoronic dynamics manifest.

However, the interesting point towards which my microreading should hopefully lead is that from the point of view to which attention is drawn by the prayer at the beginning of the text, that is, from the point of view of Christianity, this fundamentally oxymoronic framework of *Works of Love* is declared to be merely "apparent." Indeed, what the oxymoronic framework is calling upon is that this 'apparency', this indetermination has to be determined, that is, the law has to be fulfilled. The "edifying" accent of *Works of Love* is now strongest.

In other words, by the rhetorical sign of love's contradictory nature, we still find ourselves at the "preliminary" Kierkegaard was referring to in his journals. For this contradiction to be shown "apparent," an icon or exemplary figure is needed to reveal that "everything has become new" (WL, 25) by the work of love. Insofar as Christ in *Works of Love* is at once the work of love and the working love, he is thereby its icon, the icon of a Christian rhetoric or, in this case, of a Christian tropology.

It is particularly interesting to pay attention to the figures that constitute the semantic "edifying" (over)weight in *Works of Love*. At one and the same time these both teach the reader and move[18] him/her into love; literally, they will help the reader into love, and in doing so, according to *Works of Love*, they will perform as well a work of love.[19] These are the *chreiai*[20] or *sententiae*, phrases

---

[18]Kierkegaard has indeed inherited the Augustinian rhetorical device (found in *De doctrina cristiana*, Liber IV, XII 27), according to which a discourse must "teach, please, and move" (*ut doceat, ut delectat, ut flectat*). In his dissertation "On Christian Rhetoric. The Significance of Søren Kierkegaard's Dialectic of Ethical and Ethical-Religious Communication for Philosophical and Theological Pedagogy" (Ph.D. diss., Princeton Theological Seminary, 1982), Robert Morris Goldstein relates the question of the ethical-religious *kinesis*, as it were, to which he attributes a heuristic power, to the question of the "pathos-filled transition," presented by Climacus in *Postscript*. Goldstein, whose approach to Kierkegaard's rhetorical praxis is grounded on an Aristotelian conceptual framework, reads *kinesis* in this twofold context as *reduplication* (144-59).

[19]In his book *Works of Love?: Reflections on* Works of Love (Baltimore MD: Scripta Humanistica, 1990), Gene Fendt discusses the question of whether *Works of Love* is a work of love or of self-love, and he concludes the latter. In spite of the fact that Fendt's is a discursive reading, it does not enter in any dialogue to philosophy of language or any other theoretical device from which this question might be illuminated, as presented in the first part of this paper, but, instead, and interestingly, it denounces a performative contradiction, which is based on the fact that *Works of Love* is the work of a "self-lover" (17) and, as such, fundamentally contrary to the fundamental work of Christian love, namely, "self-renunciation" (*Selv-fornægtelse*) or "self-denial" (Hong). Fendt founds his accusation on Kierkegaard's own and final words in *Works of Love*, which Fendt, however, has not fully considered. Indeed, Fendt is right in pointing out the aforementioned contradiction, but what he does not explicitly realize is that, once again, we find ourselves in front of an "apparent (self)-contradiction," due to the very nature of love, and, furthermore, to the very task of bringing this "apparently contradictory" nature into sight. Kierkegaard's explanation of his self-contradiction, and, thereby, self-defense, reads:

> To praise self-denial's love and then to want to be oneself the one who loves—that is, . . . a lack of self-denial. If the speaker is not the self-lover, he easily becomes unsure or untruthful; either he will be tempted to gain advantage for himself from the praising, which is to defraud the object, or he will fall into a kind of embarrassment so that he does not even dare to say everything about how glorious this love is, out of fear that someone would think that he is speaking of himself. But if the speaker is a self-lover or, to imagine the ultimate, the most self-loving person among a people whom loving speakers call the people of love—

attributed to Christ in the Gospels, on the one hand, and the parables, stories narrated by Christ to His disciples, on the other. *Works of Love* is generously seeded with them, and it will not only be superfluous, but indeed eccentric, to try to select examples of these exemplary ones. So I shall rather leave it, respectfully, to the reader.

## Closing Remarks

About the same time that Kierkegaard was working on the lectures on the dialectic of communication, and on *Works of Love*, he also wrote the following:

> In a discourse to be read an introduction is important. The readers come to the work with all kinds of heterogeneous impressions, and therefore the introduction must be a kind of striptease in order to get them to come along. Therefore an introduction needs to be engaging, striking, interesting—in short, it should be enthralling (*fangende*). (JP, 1:639)

---

then, yes, then he can freely speak about self-denial's love, happier in having made himself into the most self-loving person than that simple wise man was in being the ugliest. . . .

Thus when the speaker, in order that the true love can be spoken about altogether truly, has had to make himself into the most self-loving of all, and the content of his discourse must be about loving the unlovable object—then every advantage or gain is impossible. (WL, 372, 374)

In the very end, however, the question, such as Fendt presents it, remains unanswered, because "it is possible that it is vanity, pride—in short, something bad, but it is also possible that it is love" (WL, 374).

[20]Meeks (*The Origins of Christian Morality*, 74) reminds us that for the first Christians "both in the completed Gospels and in the older traditions and collections they incorporate, the chreiai attributed to Jesus also exemplify the moral attitudes a follower of Jesus ought to have." Thus the sayings of Jesus give formal shape to the rhetorical ethos which is required in all morally determined discourse, and which provides the authority it demands. Indeed, rhetorically speaking, the sayings of Jesus in *Works of Love*, given in the form of quotation or *exergo*, work as an *argument of authority*, or *argumentum ad verecundiam*, as far as they guarantee, by means of their prestigious and exemplary nature, that the action they re-create, is ethically praisable, as Chaïm Perelman explains in his book, *l'Empire rhétorique. Rhétorique et argumentation* (Paris: Vrin, 1977) 102-26.

Let me bring the present reading of *Works of Love* to an end by confessing that this quotation has been significant here for two reasons. The first one has already been discussed, and it refers back to my consideration of the "prayer" at the beginning of *Works of Love* as the substantial "introduction" of the text, that is, as its fundamental source of meaning, as the "kind of striptease" whereby any rhetorical reading of *Works of Love* both stands and falls. The second reason is my own awareness, that the present reading is nothing but an "introduction." Many rhetorical devices could, and probably should, follow; devices by virtue of which, *Works of Love* will be submitted to even further and narrower degrees of genre adscription, by being read in the light of, for instance, Greek and Jewish rhetoric as it is found in the Gospels, maybe even as it is found in a specific author, and Matthew is explicitly a possible path to be followed, if not Paul; or in the light of a rhetoric of preaching, according to which several sermon forms might be established, among which the homily would certainly be a relevant type.

In the end, a common hermeneutic device to cope with Kierkegaardian "ethical-religious communication" seems to make this diversity of rhetorical perspectives in one way or another literally "enthralling," namely, the impossibility of escaping a Christian standpoint.

# 13

## *Erotic Love in the Religious Existence-Sphere*

### Ronald M. Green and Theresa M. Ellis

*Works of Love* has often been regarded as a religious discourse devoted to the theme of Christian love. Throughout, Kierkegaard draws a contrast between Christian love, which aims at the good of every fellow human being, and the particularized forms of merely human attachments: friendship, erotic love, or marriage. Because of this contrast, it is easy to conclude that Kierkegaard's vision of the religious sphere of existence holds no place for erotic love, with its passionate intensity and particular focus. However, there are repeated suggestions in *Works of Love* that Christian faith transforms but does not replace special love for another human being, just as marriage transforms but does not eliminate erotic attraction to another person. These suggestions are important, because they indicate that *Works of Love* is not just a treatment of Christian love but also, in some ways, the culmination of a comprehensive philosophy of love present in Kierkegaard's writings.

Kierkegaard's attention to the theme of particularized or erotically charged love between persons is one of the more neglected aspects of his work. Insightful discussions of *Works of Love*, such as those by Gene Outka or Gilbert Meilaender, do not usually link this work to Kierkegaard's treatments of erotic love.[1] In turn, scholarly examinations of "love" in Kierkegaard's writings report the views of his pseudonyms on erotic and married love, but few seek to present these as a coherent position or to integrate them with Kierkegaard's discussion of Christian love in *Works of Love*.

---

[1]Gene Outka, *Agape: An Ethical Analysis* (New Haven CT: Yale University Press, 1972) 13-24; Gilbert Meilaender, *Friendship: A Study in Theological Ethics* (Notre Dame IN: University of Notre Dame Press, 1981) 7, 27-28, 35, 42-47, 53, 62-64, 84.

For example, Irving Singer, who includes a discussion of Kierkegaard within his broad philosophical treatment of love, focuses on *Works of Love* in terms of the contrast Kierkegaard draws there between particular attachments, especially erotic or romantic love (*Elskov*) and Christian love (*Kjærlighed*). According to Singer, by the time Kierkegaard reaches *Works of Love*, "all idealizations of romantic love have been discounted. Though hallowed by religious love, marriage no longer functions as a vehicle toward the ideal. The ethical universal [of marriage] has been swallowed up by the love of God. All other values are subsumed under that alone."[2] In reaching this conclusion, Singer mentions Kierkegaard's extensive treatments of erotic love and marital love only in passing. Recently, some writers have begun to link *Works of Love* to Kierkegaard's other treatments of love and male-female relationships generally.[3] But these emergent discussions, often in the context of other interests, have not fully highlighted how important themes of love are for Kierkegaard's authorship as a whole.

This relative neglect is unfortunate. Despite its obvious importance in human life, erotic love between human beings has been little studied by philosophers or theologians. There are a handful of classical treatments, of which Plato's *Symposium* is perhaps best known. In the modern era, a small number of philosophers—

---

[2]Irving Singer, *The Nature of Love*, 3 vols. (Chicago: University of Chicago Press, 1984) 3:47.

[3]See, e.g., the following discussions by Sylvia Walsh: "Forming the Heart: The Role of Love in Kierkegaard's Thought," in *The Grammar of the Heart*, ed. Richard H. Bell (San Francisco: Harper & Row, 1988) 234-56; *Living Poetically: Kierkegaard's Existential Aesthetics* (University Park PA: Pennsylvania State University Press, 1994) esp. 99-109, 181-88, 262-66; "On 'Feminine' and 'Masculine' Forms of Despair," in *Feminist Interpretations of Soren Kierkegaard*, ed. Céline Léon and Sylvia Walsh (University Park PA: Pennsylvania State University Press, 1997) 203-15; and "Kierkegaard's Philosophy of Love," in *The Nature and Pursuit of Love: The Philosophy of Irving Singer*, ed. David Goicoechea (Amherst NY: Prometheus Books, 1995) 167-79. Also M. Jamie Ferreira, "Equality, Impartiality, Moral Blindness in Kierkegaard's *Works of Love*," *Journal of Religious Ethics* 25/1 (1997): 65-85; and Amy Laura Hall, "Poets, Cynics, and Thieves: Vicious Love and Divine Protection in Repetition and *Works of Love*," unpublished paper delivered at the 1996 annual meeting of the American Academy of Religion.

among them Singer, Robert Solomon, and Laurence Thomas[4]—
have sought to analyze the experience of being in love with
another person. Within this relatively meager philosophical tradition, therefore, Kierkegaard's contribution bulks large. He devotes
entire sections of *Either/Or, Fear and Trembling, Repetition, Stages on
Life's Way,* and *Two Ages* to this topic, and he and his pseudonyms
repeatedly discuss the similarities and differences between erotic
love, married love, and Christian love throughout the pseudonymous and devotional writings.

Kierkegaard's treatments of love also provide a major tool for
understanding his thinking as a whole. His writings repeatedly
offer instances of human-to-human love as illustrations of larger
aesthetic, ethical, and religious truths. For example, in *Fear and
Trembling,* Johannes Climacus uses the fate of a star-crossed lover
who finds himself hopelessly in love with a princess to illustrate
the psychological dynamics and decision making of a "Knight of
Infinite Resignation" (FT, 41-44). In *Either/Or,* Judge William's
extensive reflections on his marriage become a means of illustrat-
ing the contrast between the aesthetic and ethical spheres of
existence. Kierkegaard's writings can be said to use human-to-
human love (as St. Paul does in Ephesians 5:31-32) to point readers
toward higher, spiritual truths. Thus, Kierkegaard's philosophy of
love is an important contribution to our thinking about this under-
examined subject. It also furnishes a useful point of entry into his
authorship as a whole.

Fully to develop Kierkegaard's philosophy of love is a separate
task that still awaits doing. Our aim here is much more limited: to
provide a brief sketch of some of the main elements of this philosophy as a way of illuminating the conception of erotic and marital
love developed in *Works of Love*.[5] Superficially regarded, *Works of*

---

[4]Singer, *The Nature of Love*; Robert C. Solomon, *About Love: Reinventing Romance
for Our Times* (Lanham MD: Rowman & Littlefield, 1994); Laurence Thomas,
"Reasons for Loving," in *The Philosophy of (Erotic) Love,* ed. Robert C. Solomon
(Lawrence KS: University Press of Kansas, 1991) 467-76.

[5]Some of the material in this discussion is drawn from Theresa M. Ellis's
Dartmouth College honors dissertation, " 'A Kiss Which Was Something More
than a Peck': Kierkegaard's Embrace of Romantic and Erotic Love in his
Pseudonymous and Religious Writings" (Hanover NH, 1997).

*Love* can be seen as presenting Christian love in dramatic contrast both to friendship and to particularized erotic love for another human being in any of its forms: whether married or unmarried. To fully understand Christian love, therefore, we must at least know the common features of its precursor forms. In a deeper sense, however, we will try to show that in *Works of Love* (and the writings on love that precede it) erotic love for Kierkegaard is less an antitype to Christian love than it is a driving force that leads to it. Propelled from crisis to crisis by its own inherent tensions and contradictions, erotic love moves from tumultuous aesthetic expression, through the challenges of married love, until it ultimately finds rest and peace in the religious sphere of existence. To understand the nature of Christian love and why it ultimately transforms all preliminary forms of love, we must examine what Kierkegaard (or his pseudonyms) has to say about the nature of love in its evolving expressions.

This discussion has three parts. First we propose to identify the features that mark erotic love in all its forms. In fact, these features are present in every form of love, including Christian-religious love, although one feature—exclusivity—may not initially appear to be so. Second, we wish to develop the way by which love serves as a driving force that leads individuals, dialectically, from one sphere of existence to another. Finally, drawing on a series of suggestive comments by Kierkegaard in *Works of Love*, we hope to evidence the ways that erotic love reaches its culmination and fulfillment in the religious sphere of existence.

### Features of Erotic Love

In the corpus of Kierkegaard's writings, we can identify a series of features that he or a pseudonym offers as common to erotic love in its aesthetic expressions and its form as married love. Although Kierkegaard sometimes applies the term erotic love (*Elskov*) only to the more purely aesthetic expressions of love, we will use the term "erotic love" for all the forms of person-to-person, physical-emotional attraction in which these features are found. Used this way, erotic love also refers to "romantic love" (*romantiske Kjærlighed*)[6] and "marriage" (*Ægteskab*), terms that Kierkegaard employs to denote particular varieties of erotically charged male-female relations.[7]

Much could be said about each of the six features we bring to the fore: love's passionate nature; its exclusivity; its nonrationality; its tendency toward equality; its tendency to unite freedom and necessity as well as time and eternity. To some extent the persistent emphasis of these features in Kierkegaard's direct and pseudonymous writings reflects a kind of phenomenological analysis of the experience of love. In other respects, their presence in Kierkegaard's writings betrays the influence of generations of literary explorations of love, the proximate influence of the Romantic movement, and features of Kierkegaard's own complex biography, including his broken engagement to Regine Olsen. A full account of Kierkegaard's thinking about love would have to comprehend the many influences and assumptions that go into it. We put these matters aside in order to provide here a brief overview of the position we find in his writings.

## Love Is a Passion

Within the corpus of Kierkegaard's writings, passion (*Lidenskab*) can be understood as a driving desire that consumes an individual and pushes her or him onwards toward a goal. It can take many forms. In *Philosophical Fragments*, for example, Johannes Climacus tells us that reasoned thought has a passion that involves never being satisfied with a superficial explanation and always seeking to determine the essence of things. This eventually takes the form of driving the understanding "to want to discover something that thought itself cannot think" (PF, 37). Religion, too, is marked by

---

[6]In *Either/Or* Kierkegaard frequently uses this term to refer to the depiction of erotic love and "first love" in the theatrical and poetic literature of his day: see, e.g., EO, 1:250; 2:19-22, 28, 31, 47. Romantic love, therefore, seems to belong to the larger category of erotic love (*Elskov*) and represents its imaginative literary embodiment.

[7]Strictly speaking, nothing in Kierkegaard's conception of person-to-person erotic love necessitates its being heterosexual, but obviously Kierkegaard was very much a child of his time in failing to develop his philosophy of love in other than heterosexual ways.

passion. "Behold, faith is indeed the highest passion of subjectivity," Climacus tells us in the *Postscript* (CUP, 1:132), and later adds, in a memorable definition, "Faith is the contradiction between the infinite passion of inwardness and the objective uncertainty" (CUP, 1:204). Passion, finally, is an omnipresent feature of erotic love in all its forms. "To love without passion is an impossibility," Kierkegaard tells us in *Works of Love* (WL, 50). In *Either/or* the aesthete tells us that erotic love develops quickly, opening for the lovers "with a snap as the passion flower does" (EO, 1:241). Elvira, that consummate example of erotic attachment, stands out for "the staggering intensity of her passion" (EO, 1:191). Despite its potential for abuse and his disclaimer that he has no intention to sanction "every unshaven passion" (JP, 3:3127), Kierkegaard seems largely to regard passion in positive terms. He considered its lack of passion as one of the great shortcomings of his era, what he termed its "tragedy of reason and reflection" (JP, 3:3129). Frater Taciturnus, in *Stages on Life's Way*, remarks that "The same thing that weakened faith in love—the lack of a sense of the infinite—will also weaken faith in the other passions" (SLW, 410). In view of this, we can understand why erotic love should play such an important part in Kierkegaard's thinking and why instances of erotic love abound in his writings as metaphors for religious faith.

### Love Is Exclusive

The whole passion of erotic love is focused on a single individual: "[E]rotic love intensifies in the direction that there is but one and only one beloved" (WL, 49); "Passion always has this unconditional characteristic—that it excludes the third" (WL, 50). True love also is exclusive across time: it permits the love of only one person in a lifetime. To recoil from a failed love affair into a new relationship is not to fall in love for a second time, says Kierkegaard, but to admit that the first love really was no love at all. In erotic love, Kierkegaard tells us,

> there is but one and only one beloved in the whole world, and this one and only one time of erotic love is love, is everything; the second time is nothing. Ordinarily one says proverbially that just one time does not count. Here, in contrast, one time is unconditionally everything and the second time is unconditionally the ruin of everything. (WL, 49)

This is the reason why frustrated but genuine loves, in Kierke-gaard's writings, always culminate in resignation and solitude.

*Love Is Nonrational*

To say that love is a passion is partly to identify its nonrational nature. This does not mean that it is irrational to become erotically or romantically involved with another person, but that loving another often defies rational analysis or explanation. There can be no "why" for a love, no reasons why one particular person be-comes the one you love, no pattern of reasoned thought that leads to the choice of the beloved. Although a person in love can describe in glowing terms the features of the beloved to whom he or she is attracted, these features are usually more a reflection of the attraction than an explanation or justification of it. That "love is blind" and that lovers, up to a point, will overlook features of the beloved that are offensive or odious only reinforces the observation that love is a passionate attraction defying rational explanation.

In *Stages on Life's Way*, the young man, who confesses that he has never been in love, mentions this odd feature of erotic love in order to ridicule it. He finds it "comic" that, while all human beings want to love and all lovers celebrate their love, no one seems able to explain "what it is that they love" (SLW, 34). He continues,

> If erotic love expressed itself in loving the first that comes along, then it would be understandable that one cannot explain oneself more precisely, but since erotic love expresses itself in loving a one and only, a one and only in the whole world, such a prodi-gious act of separation must in itself contain a dialectic of reasons one would have to decline to hear, not so much because it explained nothing as because it would be too long-winded to listen to. But no, the lover cannot explain anything at all. He has seen hundreds and hundreds of women; he may be getting on in years, has felt nothing. Suddenly he sees her, the one and only—Catherine. Is this not comic; is it not comic that what is going to transfigure and embellish all life—erotic love—is not like a mustard seed that grows to a great tree but, even less, is essen-tially nothing at all, for not a single antecedent criterion can be stated, as if, for example, there were a specific age in which the phenomenon made its appearance. And not a single reason can

be stated as to why he chooses her, her alone in the whole world. . . . (SLW, 36)

## Love Equalizes the Lovers

Love demands equality between the lovers. Individuals who are unequal—in social standing, wealth, learning, talents and abilities, or any other attribute—can fall in love. Once they do, however, they are compelled by their erotic passion to regard one another as equals. One cannot look down on one's beloved, and though one can look up, in the experience of awe and devotion, what is esteemed is the beloved qua beloved, not the possessor of status or other worldly goods. In love, the state of being loved and the ability to love are the essential and defining features of personhood, and these exclude all other differentiating criteria.

So powerful is this dynamic of love for Kierkegaard that worldly differences can even become an obstacle to love's expression. In *Philosophical Fragments* we meet a king in love with a humble maiden who, in order to accomplish his desire to win her, must conceal his royal status and come to her in the form of a commoner. After their marriage, Johannes Climacus observes: " Let all be festive while erotic love celebrates its triumph, for erotic love is jubilant when it unites equal and equal and is triumphant when it makes equal in erotic love that which was unequal" (PF, 27). Shortly after reading this erotic example, we learn that it has bearing on the love of God for human beings through Jesus Christ. This illustrates how erotic love for Kierkegaard serves as an instrument for conveying larger religious truths. It also suggests how love in all its forms shares common features.

## Love Unites Freedom and Necessity

Lovers typically believe themselves fated or destined for one another. Their love "has to be" (EO, 2:20). Understood religiously, this sense of fatedness takes the form of viewing the lover not as one's chosen person but as God's gift. Thus, the Married Man, identified as the author of "Some Reflections on Married Life" in *Stages on Life's Way*,[8] remarks that the phrase "to choose" in love does not mean "wanting to set someone up as the beloved" but rather "wanting to accept the beloved" and to "thank the god for the gift" (SLW, 121). Even the seducer, Kierkegaard's renowned aesthete, "lets falling in love stand as something he cannot give himself" (SLW, 148). At the same time, this acceptance of the beloved in no way abrogates freedom. Kierkegaard never suggests that God coerces anyone into loving the beloved. Quite the contrary, a man realizes that he loves a woman, chooses her, and then recognizes that God made her known to him. As Judge William puts it, "in its genius romantic love is free and that precisely . . . is what constitutes its greatness" (EO, 2:21). In *Stages on Life's Way*, the Married Man tells us that "the person who received the gracious gift of immediacy, lets himself be married to it in the resolution—and this is indeed the beautiful meaning of marriage" (SLW, 148). In *Two Ages* Kierkegaard joins love's themes of passion and freedom when he says: "As is the case with all passion, so it is true of erotic love that the one initiated into it stands free in the consecrated moment of falling in love, free on the rash summit of illusion, free and surveying the whole wide world" (TA, 50).

Love thus "unites freedom and necessity" (EO, 2:45). This "unity of contrasts" (EO, 2:60) is not unique to erotic love. As Judge William makes clear in *Either/Or*, freely choosing our given life situation is a defining feature of the ethical sphere of existence. Nevertheless, erotic love serves as a special symbol for all of human life because it so intensely expresses our nature as situated yet free beings. Indeed, Kierkegaard's treatments of erotic love suggest that its importance in human life is at least partly owed to the ways in which it permits us to live out and joyfully express these paradoxes of human existence.

---

[8]The Married Man in *Stages* is identified before his lengthy manuscript as Judge William (SLW, 82-86). However, so as not to confuse these two possibly different expressions of pseudonymous points of view, we here refer to this personage of *Stages* as the Married Man.

## Love Unites Time and Eternity

Mortal, caught up in time, subject to change and decay, humans are also spiritual beings who crave connection with that which endures. Nothing better illustrates the ability of love to express and resolve the paradoxes of human life than the way it brings eternity into time. Poetry and song celebrate the belief that "love is forever." Lovers typically say that they have always loved one another and that their love will never die. For Kierkegaard, these sentiments are not poetic exaggerations: they convey love's most distinctive and impressive feature. Romantic love, Judge William tells us, "is noble by virtue of the consciousness of the eternal that it assimilates, for it is this that distinguishes all love [Kjærlighed] from lust [Vellyst]: that it bears a stamp of eternity" (EO, 2:21). The young man in *Stages on Life's Way* describes the kiss as the confirmation of love because it provides physical expression of the couple's eternal love for one fervent moment in time (SLW, 42). In *Either/Or* Judge William deploys this understanding in his defense of married love. The married man, he explains, is by no means lost in the humdrum of household life. On the contrary, he "has not killed time but has rescued and preserved it in eternity. The married man who does this is truly living poetically; he solves the great riddle, to live in eternity and yet to hear the cabinet clock strike in such a way that its striking does not shorten but lengthens his eternity" (EO, 2:138). These themes continue to resonate throughout Kierkegaard's authored writings. In *Works of Love*, Kierkegaard asks what it is that "connects the temporal and eternity," and answers "what else but love" (WL, 6).

## Love's Dialectic

In Kierkegaard's writings, these features of erotic love are integrated within a dynamic and dialectical understanding of love's trajectory in human life. The delineation of this dialectical trajectory constitutes Kierkegaard's most important philosophical contribution to our understanding of love. Movement forward in love's course is required because the features of love, though present in every existence sphere, are less suitably expressed in some existence spheres than others. As a driving force, therefore, love can either propel individuals into despair or force them to leap forward to a new existence-sphere where love's deepest intentionality finds more adequate expression. Passionate yearning leading to self-development through a crisis that precipitates decision characterizes the whole dialectic of existence for Kierkegaard. That erotic love illustrates this dialectic so well reveals its importance in Kierkegaard's thinking.

### Love in the Aesthetic Existence-Sphere

The aesthetic sphere of existence is marked by the predominance of mood, feeling, and satisfactions or dissatisfactions visited on the individual from without by her or his experiences. Persons whose existence is defined within this sphere find the essence of their being outside themselves. The aesthete in love experiences all the features of love we have mentioned, but because of the aesthete's essential presuppositions, these features become experiences before which the self is a passive agent: one suffers one's love. Understood in this way, erotic love in the aesthetic sphere contradicts itself in many ways. Love can even turn into its opposite. One who is passionately and irrevocably devoted to the lover can also become a helpless victim of the lover's whims. This is exploited by the seducer, who revels in fatally binding another to himself. For the seducer's victim, as is true of Donna Elvira, the timeless devotion of love transmutes itself into an eternal obsession leading to hatred for oneself and one's betrayer (EO, 1:196).

The aesthete savors love's intense joys. The seducer in *Either/Or* confesses that he is dazed by the experience of falling in love and has "gone under in love-rapture" (EO, 1:324). Yet since the constant flow of satisfactions is his life's task, the aesthetically inclined individual simultaneously fears the prospect of attachment to another because it threatens loss of control (EO, 1:297). One response is cynically to ridicule love. The young man in *Stages* does so when he remarks, "It is comic that erotic love's lofty soaring (wanting to belong to each other for all eternity) always ends up . . . in the pantry" (SLW, 42). In *Either/Or*, the aesthete pokes fun at the widower and widow, each with five children, who "combine forces" and "nevertheless assure one another on the wedding day that this love is their first love" (EO, 1:254). Yet this derision is really the deepest despair and self-contradiction since no one knows better than the aesthete does that erotic love brings life's highest satisfactions. In *Either/Or* Judge William underscores this self-contradiction when he tells the young man, "you do not believe in the eternity of first love. . . . It is you who so often set yourself up as its knight, and yet you do not believe in it—indeed, you profane it" (EO, 2:145).

### Love in the Ethical Existence-Sphere

This collision within the aesthetic existence-sphere—that its highest goal cannot be achieved within its own presuppositions—can either drive lovers to despair or propel them onward to the ethical sphere of existence. The challenge before lovers is to actualize love's deepest promise, especially its ability to offer an intense satisfaction resistant to change. This can be accomplished only through ethical resolve. By accepting the imperative of (marital) commitment, "You shall love," lovers become assured of the continuance of their relationship and the triumph of their love, including its aesthetic and erotic dimensions, over all of life's reverses. This in no way excludes an aesthetic-erotic dimension of their love. Marriage "presupposes [erotic love] not as something past but as something present" (EO, 2:36). Beginning in erotic attachment, and then set on a firm basis of mutual commitment, marital love is able to "preserve the aesthetic even in everyday life" (EO, 2:9).

In *Either/Or*, Judge William extensively develops the logic of this position in his letter to the young aesthete. The Judge is aware that, superficially regarded, a duty to love seems to be a self-contradiction: a sign that constraint is necessary because spontaneous affection has vanished or will soon do so. The Judge frames the aesthete's objection: "You say, 'Within itself, marital love is hiding something completely different; it seems so gentle and beautiful and tender, but as soon as the door is shut on the married couple and before one can say Jack Robinson, out comes Master Erik;[9] then the tune is changed to duty' " (EO, 2:145). The aesthete's

---

[9]A decorated birch branch with which children awaken their parents on Shrove Monday. Here, presumably, the birch of discipline.

mistake here is to believe that duty is something external to the couple's love. Instead, it is their deepest wish, and it is freely accepted by them, first in their mutual commitment and then in their marital vows.[10] It also provides the confidence that unending continuance in love can be achieved. Because ought implies can,[11] the lovers' wholehearted acceptance of this duty presupposes their faith that their love can and will abide:

> [M]arital love . . . in the ethical and the religious already has duty within itself, and when duty manifests itself to them it is not a stranger, a shameless outsider, who nevertheless has such an authority that by virtue of the secrecy of love one does not dare to show him the door. No, he comes as an old intimate, as a friend, as a confidant whom the lovers both know in the deepest secrecy of their love. . . . To them it would not be sufficient for duty to say encouragingly, "It can be done, love can be preserved"; but because he says: "It shall be preserved," there is an implicit authority that corresponds to the inwardness of their wish. Love casts out fear, but if love nevertheless fears for itself a moment, for its own salvation, then duty is precisely the divine nourishment love needs, for duty says, "Fear not; you shall [skal] conquer"—says it not just in the future sense, for then it is only a hope, but in the imperative mood, and therein rests a conviction that nothing can shake. (EO, 2:146)

This passage suggests not only that the aesthetic fulfillment of erotic love requires ethical resolve, but also that this resolve contains a religious dimension. Lovers perceive their drive to mutual obligation as a form of divinely given "nourishment" and a guarantee of their love's continuance. Like all ethical resolve, therefore, marital duty rests on religious faith.[12] In *Stages on Life's Way*,

---

[10]Without diminishing the importance of the wedding ceremony, the Judge emphasizes the primacy of each of the lovers' inward commitment to the other, and he affirms that the wedding ceremony "allows what was already in motion to appear in the external world" (EO, 2:93).

[11]For a more extensive discussion of the logic of the Judge's argument and its possible dependence on Kantian presuppositions, see Ronald M. Green, "Kierkegaard's Great Critique: *Either/Or* as a Kantian Transcendental Deduction," in *International Kierkegaard Commentary: Either/Or II*, ed. Robert L. Perkins (Macon GA: Mercer University Press, 1995) 139-53.

[12]For a discussion of Kierkegaard's understanding of the relationship between ethical resolve and religious faith, see Ronald M. Green, *Kierkegaard and Kant: The*

the Married Man exalts these implicit religious dimensions of the ethical component of married love. A person, he observes, "does not dare cling to himself as a singular individual if he is going to venture out with his love. His comfort is precisely that he is just like other human beings and in this common humanity is in relationship with God by faith and by the resolution" (SLW, 164).

### Love in the Christian-Religious Existence-Sphere: One View

Has erotic love a place in the Christian-religious sphere of existence? Despite the natural assumption that love's dialectical development might continue into this sphere, there are several reasons for believing that erotic love reaches its culmination in marriage and does not carry over from the ethical to the specifically Christian religious existence-sphere. Paradoxically, the ethically informed religious dimensions of marital love form one of several obstacles to imagining a particular Christian-religious expression of erotic love. For if erotic love can reach complete fulfillment in marital expression, where it rests gently on faith in God's presence as guarantor of the relationship, what need is there for the dramatic crisis and decision that typically mark the transition from one existence-sphere to another? Christian faith, Kierkegaard and his pseudonyms tell us, always involves a leap beyond the ethical sphere of existence precipitated by the experiences of sin, guilt, and repentance (CUP, 1:257-68; cf. JP, 1:452; 4:4011, 4012). The Judge's vision of marital love evidences nothing like this. Although repentance has its place in the Judge's concept of the formation of the self (EO, 2:216-18, 237-38), he does not typically bring sin, guilt, or repentance into relation to the ethical reality of marriage. Marriage's challenge resides for him primarily in the ethical decision to commit to another person. Hence, in its religious dimensions, marriage is bound up with the joyous choice/receipt of the other that moves erotic love from aesthetic immediacy into marital permanence. As the Judge says, "The religious is not so alien to human nature that there must be a break in order to awaken it" (EO, 2:89).

---

*Hidden Debt* (Albany NY: SUNY Press, 1992) 137-38.

Of course, neither Judge William nor his alter ego, the Married Man, in *Stages on Life's Way* should be taken as representative of Kierkegaard's entire view. Both express, at best, only the earliest expression of the religious (Religiousness A). An alternate view, suggested by *Fear and Trembling*, and seemingly confirmed by some aspects of *Works of Love*, offers a far more discontinuous vision of the fate of erotic love as one moves from the ethical to the Christian-religious sphere of existence. However, this vision also presents obstacles to believing that erotic love has any place in this sphere. Here it is the themes of resignation and self-renunciation that predominate. The lover who chooses God must be prepared to sacrifice any worldly love to the divine command. Abraham evidenced this kind of faith when he offered Isaac up as a sacrifice. This is the faith of all other Knights of Faith who, disagreeing with the claim of the Married Man in *Stages on Life's Way* that marriage is "the highest telos of individual life" (SLW, 101), choose instead to subordinate marital or family obligations to an absolute duty to God (FT, 70; CUP, 1:408-409).

On this understanding, there appears to be no room for erotic love in the Christian-religious sphere of existence. One who lives religiously either retreats to the monastery or chooses, as Kierkegaard did, to remain unmarried.[13] In this way, the transition to the Christian-religious sphere is decidedly a crisis and a leap, but one that leads wholly away from erotic love in any of its forms.

*Works of Love* can be read to support this view. For example, its criticism of the exclusivity of erotic love and its insistence that Christian love is inclusive, taking every neighbor for its object, appear to erase one of the essential presuppositions of erotic love. "Christian love," says Kierkegaard, "teaches us to love all people, unconditionally all. Just as unconditionally and powerfully as erotic love intensifies in the direction that there is but one and only

---

[13]Kierkegaard's writings contain statements of respect for monasticism's religious intensity—its "passion and respect for the absolute telos" (CUP, 1:414) along with criticisms of its effort to leave the world and establish outward signs of what must properly be expressed as religious inwardness within the world: "The Middle Ages wanted a little cubbyhole in order to be able to occupy itself properly with the absolute; but it was precisely by this that the absolute was lost, because it still became something outward" (CUP, 1:408).

one beloved, just as unconditionally and powerfully does Christian love intensify in the opposite direction" (WL, 49). The insistence that true love is selfless and the repeated assertion that beneath a veneer of passionate selflessness, all erotic and marital love is merely secret, enhanced and augmented self-love, also seems to eliminate any foothold for particular relationships. "Erotic love and friendship are preferential love and the passion of preferential love; Christian love is self-denial's love" (WL, 52). In view of these rejections of the essential presuppositions of erotic love, it would seem that anyone committed to the kind of Christian love extolled in *Works of Love* must be prepared to avoid marriage, or, if married, must await its eschatological dissolution. "In the resurrection, they neither marry nor are given in marriage" (Mathew 22:30; Luke 20:35).

## An Alternate View

As compelling as this negative picture of erotic love's continuance in the Christian-religious sphere might be, however, there are statements throughout *Works of Love* that call it into question and hold out a possibility of Christian love united with ongoing romantic-erotic attachment to another person. To use an image borrowed from *Either/Or*, this view sees religious love not as eccentric to erotic love, but concentric with it (EO, 2:30). For example, after urging the reader to "take away the distinction of preferential love so that you can love the neighbor," Kierkegaard continues:

> But you are not to cease loving the beloved because of this—far from it. If in order to love the neighbor you would have to begin by giving up loving those for whom you have preference, the word "neighbor" would be the greatest deception ever conceived. Moreover, it would even be a contradiction, since inasmuch as the neighbor is all people surely no one can be excluded—should we now say, least of all the beloved? (WL, 61)

Again:

> No, love the beloved faithfully and tenderly, but let love for the neighbor be the sanctifying element in your union's covenant with God. (WL, 62)

And again:

Christianity . . . knows only one kind of love, the spirit's love, but this can lie at the base of and be present in every other expression of love. (WL, 146)

In keeping with this conception, religious love does not put an end to worldly attachments, including intense erotic-romantic love for another person or marital devotion. Christians are no more required to renounce a loving, committed relationship with another person than they are to give up food or drink (WL, 47, 52). Indeed, "the doctrine about love for the neighbor" is specifically intended "for transforming erotic love and friendship" and is meant to "permeate everything" (WL, 112). "Christianity does not want to make changes in externals; neither does it want to abolish drives and inclination—it wants only to make infinity's change in the inner being" (WL, 139). Sylvia Walsh succinctly captures the spirit of this alternate view of love in the religious existence sphere when she remarks that "the intent of the dialectic points beyond mere differentiation and opposition to an eventual or ultimate union of the natural and spiritual, the temporal and the eternal, the human and the Christian through the transforming power of self-renouncing love."[14]

### Features of Religious Erotic Love

What, then, is this transformation? What form does erotic love take in the religious existence-sphere? What changes does it undergo that distinguish it from the ethical expression of love in marriage, as depicted by Judge William or the Married Man? In seeking the answers to these questions we can be guided by an understanding of the basic dialectic that governs all movement from existence-sphere to existence-sphere in Kierkegaard's thought. Thus, the transition from the ethical to the religious stage of erotic love will be abrupt: a leap rather than an evolution. It will be precipitated by a collision or crisis: something within its earlier presuppositions that threatens to drive it to the edge of despair or that undermines its highest aspirations. It will pass through choice and resolve and emerge to rest on essentially different premises than

---

[14]"Kierkegaard's Philosophy of Love," 173.

the forms of love that preceded it. Yet, it will be in continuity with these previous forms and a completion of them. Just as the ethical stage of love, marriage, seeks always to retain the aesthetic-erotic dimension of love and even intensifies it by adding duration and continuity to the erotic's passion, so might erotic love in the religious existence-sphere continue and intensify love's erotic and ethical elements. It will be, as Sylvia Walsh says, drawing on Judge William's suggestive phrasings, a passionate but deeply reflective "second immediacy."[15]

Against this background, we can directly approach the question of erotic love in the Christian-religious existence-sphere by asking what could possibly upset the kind of resolved marital love sketched by defenders like Judge William and the Married Man? A variety of answers present themselves and all involve causes that erode or challenge the basis of marriage's mutual commitment. Most obvious among these is infidelity on the part of either partner, a breach that assaults the other's pride and sense of justice and that inevitably saps his or her resolve to remain in the relationship. Related to this, and equally painful, is the sense that the beloved has become hostile or alienated. Another threat are changes in the beloved (or the self) that are extensive enough to raise the question of whether either is any longer really the same person. Although the importance of certain qualities in the beloved at the start of an erotic relationship may be more a reflection of the love than an explanation for it, fundamental changes in the beloved's most attractive features (or their conversion into their opposite) can shatter resolve by raising the question of whether the lover really is the same person to whom one has pledged eternal devotion. Similarly, deep changes in one can undermine the foundations of one's love for the other. Finally, either partner's freedom can threaten the resolve to faithfulness. Although mutual freedom, as we have seen, is the premise of all erotic love, freedom and independence also are a deep threat to love because, in freedom,

---

[15]Sylvia Walsh, "Forming the Heart: The Role of Love in Kierkegaard's Thought," 244. George Connell critiques the Judge's position here, arguing that his vision of marriage as protecting and sustaining immediate erotic love "makes demands altogether exceeding human capacity." See his *To Be One Thing. Personal Unity in Kierkegaard's Thought* (Macon GA: Mercer University Press, 1985) 179.

the lover or the beloved can change nature, rebel against, and even reject the love relationship.

How, then, can love survive such assaults? How can erotic love's deep inner intentionality toward continuity be preserved before this host of troubling transformations in oneself and the object of one's love? In *Either/Or* Judge William seems to be unaware of these problems. He and his wife live in untroubled unity. They hold no secrets from one another and even confess to one another breaches of fidelity (EO, 2:117, 119, 179). Against this too simple vision, *Works of Love* can be read as dealing with the real stresses that threaten marital continuity and offering a response to them with a vision of religious love that penetrates and transforms, but does not necessarily abolish, erotic attachment. We can see this by looking closely at some of the distinguishing features of the neighbor-regarding love Kierkegaard describes in order to see how it addresses the assaults that threaten even the most devoted and passionate love relationship.

### It Is Not Based on Preference

One distinctive feature of the religious love that Kierkegaard depicts is that it is not focused on what distinguishes the beloved, on what Kierkegaard calls "passionate preference," but on the beloved's essentially human qualities. Kierkegaard terms this "the eternal equality in loving" (WL, 58). "In being king, beggar, rich man, poor man, male, female, etc., we are not like each other— therein we are indeed different. But in being the neighbor we are all unconditionally like each other" (WL, 89). This essential perception of likeness rather than difference, Kierkegaard insists, applies also to the marital relationship:

> Your wife must first and foremost be to you the neighbor; that she is your wife is then a more precise specification of your particular relationship to each other. But what is the eternal foundation must also be the foundation of every expression of the particular. (WL, 141)

Superficially regarded, this placement of the beloved on a plane of equality with others would seem to be a demotion in status. For how can being seen to be like others be superior to being the extolled object of erotic love and preference? Yet, when we consider that one of the greatest threats to erotic love is precisely the perception by one party to a relationship that the other has changed or lost those features that cemented preference in the first place, we see the importance for love's continuance in what Kierkegaard is saying here. "[T]he task," Kierkegaard reminds us, "is to find the once given and chosen object—lovable, and to continue to find him lovable no matter how he has changed" (WL, 159). We do this by loving the (actual) person we see, by accepting her or him as they are and not as we would have them be, and by recognizing that they are an imperfect creature like ourselves and all other human beings. In these ways love is strengthened against all the deceptions and disappointments that preference can undergo. In this way, as well, love achieves the unconditional acceptance of the other to which marriage aspires but which its basis in preference sometimes threatens. Many statements in *Works of Love* reinforce this point:

> To be able to love a person despite his weaknesses and defects and imperfections is still not perfect love, but rather this, to be able to find him lovable despite and with his weaknesses and defects and imperfections. (WL, 157-58)

> When it is a duty in loving to love the people we see, *then in loving the actual individual person it is important that one does not substitute an imaginary idea of how we think or could wish that this person should be.* (WL, 164)

> The Christian point of view, however, is that to love is to love precisely the person one sees. The emphasis is not on loving the perfections one sees in a person, but the emphasis is on loving the person one sees, whether one sees perfections or imperfections in the person, yes, however distressingly this person has changed, inasmuch as he has not ceased to be the same person. He who loves the perfections he sees in a person does not see the person and therefore ceases to love if the perfections cease, when the change begins, although this change, even the most distressing, still does not mean that the person ceases to exist. (WL, 173)

Of course, all erotic love purports to love the real person who is the beloved. Marital love trumpets its acceptance of the beloved "for better or for worse" and cherishes its knowledge of the other's most intimate and embarrassing secrets and vulnerabilities. Yet, what Kierkegaard is suggesting here, is that erotic love's greatest fear is precisely the simple humanity of the beloved: his or her likeness to others and possession of real human (as opposed to enchanting) imperfections. By placing this shared humanity to the fore and by resolving to love the beloved for this shared humanness more than for all the features that elicit passion, Christian love therefore fulfills what erotic love promises. It does so, however, in a way that must initially shock the lover's sensibilities and that is arrived at, not through a natural evolution of love, but through a religiously empowered resolve to continue loving despite the stresses to which preference is subject.

It may be objected that Christian love, by seeing the common humanity—the neighbor—in the beloved removes one of the essential features of erotic love: its exclusiveness. Yet Kierkegaard is quick to state that even when seen as a human being, as one neighbor among others, the beloved remains fully the beloved, fully the special and chosen one. Religiously informed erotic love is at once intensely universal and intensely particular. Indeed, to distinguish these two aspects of the beloved, to see the beloved first as the chosen one and then as just another human being, or in some respects as the beloved and in other respects as the neighbor, is to artificially separate elements that must completely commingle in a single, multidimensional perception:

> The beloved, the friend, is of course a human being also in the more ordinary sense and exists as such for the rest of us, but for you he should exist essentially only as the beloved if you are to fulfill the duty of loving the person you see. If there is a duality in your relationship so that to you he is just partly just this individual human being in the more ordinary sense, partly the beloved in particular, then you do not love the person you see. Instead it is as if you had two ears in the sense that you do not, as is normal, hear one thing with both ears but hear one thing with one and something else with the other. (WL, 165)

Kierkegaard continues by observing that any such separation in one's perception of the beloved amounts to a critical self-withholding that is incompatible with love. Somehow, we are to avoid this dichotomy of consciousness: while recognizing that the beloved is a human being like all the others we are called to love, we must also never forget that this is our special one, one person's special one. Particularity and universality, exclusivity and openness, are not opposites but are mutually reinforcing. Just as we should love the beloved with the honest and penetrating regard that accompanies our love for every human being, so we should blindly love "every human being as the lover loves the beloved" (WL, 69).

An illustration from popular culture may help make this difficult point clearer. In the film *Gone with the Wind* there is an episode where Melanie Wilkes and Scarlett O'Hara are shown serving long hours as volunteers in a Confederate military hospital. Near the end of the day, Melanie makes one more effort to comfort a wounded soldier. When Scarlett asks Melanie how she can summon up the strength to do this, Melanie replies, "This might be Ashley." Melanie is the film's most obviously saintly figure. Her remark illustrates the intimate union of universal and erotic love that Kierkegaard suggests. For Melanie, the wounded solider/ neighbor is the beloved: his countenance elicits from her the passionate regard she feels for Ashley Wilkes. Her hope is that another woman elsewhere may similarly care for Ashley if he is wounded. From this moment forward, Ashley himself will evoke for Melanie all the wounded soldiers she has comforted. Erotic love's exclusivity has been simultaneously intensified and transcended.

Finally, we might add that to see the beloved as he or she is, with all the defects of a human being (including, presumably the propensity toward sin), does not mean that we must accept those defects without struggling to change them. As M. Jamie Ferreira points out, "Love is not only accepting; it is also challenging."[16] Kierkegaard tells us that "The relationship itself will with integrated power fight against the imperfection, overcome the defect. . . . The two are to hold together all the more firmly and inwardly in order to remove the weakness" (WL, 166-67). Thus, erotic love in the religious stage evidences another paradox: unconditional acceptance of the beloved conjoined with a moral will toward the beloved's betterment. In this sense, erotic love provides a profound

---

[16]Ferreira, "Equality, Impartiality, Moral Blindness in Kierkegaard's *Works of Love*," 82.

illustration of a repeated theme in Kierkegaard's writings: the importance of grace and moral striving (JP, 6:6801; JP, 2:1878).

## It Is Truly Selfless

For erotic love to be a suitable instrument of Christian love, it must first be purged of the egotism that threatens all intense dyadic love relationships. Lovers typically celebrate their selfless devotion to one another, and no one can doubt that this self-transcendence is one of love's greatest joys. Yet, with keen psychological insight, Kierkegaard observes that the intense other-relatedness and seeming selflessness of erotic love frequently cloaks an intense égoïsme à deux:

> [E]rotic love and friendship are the very peak of self-esteem, the I intoxicated in the other I. The more securely one I and another I join to become one I, the more this united I selfishly cuts itself off from everyone else. At the peak of erotic love and friendship, the two actually do become one self, one I. This is explainable only because in preferential love there is a natural determinant (drive, inclination) and self-love, which selfishly can unite the two in a new selfish self. (WL, 56)

Here too, Christian love proves liberating for those in a relationship. However intoxicating this conjoint egoism may be, it ends by isolating the pair from others outside the relationship. With each partner's ego at stake, any hint of defection by one partner becomes a personal threat to the other. The most poisonous fruit of this mentality is jealousy. "Jealousy loves as it is loved. . . . Anxious and tortured by preoccupation with itself, it dares neither to believe the beloved absolutely nor to give itself wholeheartedly" (WL, 35). At this extreme, love's bond becomes a prison for each member of the pair. Against this, Christian love, by insisting on love for all one's neighbors and by demanding a genuine selflessness, breaks the chains of this intoxicating dyadic egoism and frees each party for self and others.

> The spirit's love, in contrast, takes away from myself all natural determinants and all self-love. Therefore love for the neighbor cannot make me one with the neighbor in a united self. Love for the neighbor is love between two beings eternally and independently determined as spirit; love for the neighbor is spirit's love,

but two spirits are never able to become one in a selfish sense. (WL, 56)

## God Is Present as a Third

Christian love also transforms and sustains erotic love by admitting God, as a third person into the lover's relationship:

> Worldly wisdom is of the opinion that love is a relationship between persons; Christianity teaches that love is a relationship between: a person—God—a person, that is, that God is the middle term. However beautiful a relationship of love has been between two people or among many, however complete all their desire and all their bliss have been for themselves in mutual sacrifice and devotion, even though everyone has praised this relationship—if God and the relationship with God have been omitted, then this, in the Christian sense, has not been love but a mutually enchanting defraudation of love. To love God is to love oneself truly; to help another person to love God is to love another person; to be helped by another person to love God is to be loved. (WL, 106-107)

Once again, Kierkegaard's vision of Christian love seems to assault the very foundation of erotic love. Passionate love for another, we have seen, is by its nature exclusive. How can it admit a third party, even God, without distracting the lovers' passionate attention from one another? How can it admit a goal for each party to the relationship—love of God—that seems to draw attention away from the beloved? That Kierkegaard himself appears to have sacrificed his relationship with Regine in order to fulfill his religious vocation only points up the problem.

If we keep in mind the nature of erotic love and the perils that confront it, we can see in what senses this insistence on the presence of God in an erotic relationship is the very condition for its vitality and continuity. First of all, the presence of God is the antidote to worshipful idolatry of the beloved. "[T]he relationship among human beings ought and may never be such that one worships and the other is the one worshipped" (WL, 125). Although such worship is erotic love's very instinct, it must lead inevitably to disappointment and despair, for no human being is the god that love's enchantment initially perceives. Christian love avoids this by fixing attention on God and on each member of the pair's relationship with God.

God's presence also insures the independence and freedom of each partner. Erotic love, we recall, is predicated on free choice of it by each of the parties. Although "made for one another," the lovers nevertheless choose one another freely. And yet, the perceived fatedness of love also qualifies freedom in many ways, not least of all each lover's unwillingness to see the beloved exercise freedom in ways that imperil the relationship. "You are free to do anything but reject me, reject us," is every lover's plaintive cry. By reminding us that each person stands in an independent relationship to God, Christian love creates the space, the breathing room, the "air" as Kierkegaard might say, to which erotic love aspires but which it simultaneously resists.

> [I]s it actually love, in the divine sense, to show a devotion such as the object of love demanded? Next, is it love, in the divine sense, on the part of the object of love to demand such devotion? Every person is God's bond servant; therefore he dare not belong to anyone in love unless in the same love he belongs to God and dare not possess anyone in love unless the other and he himself belong to God in this love. . . . If there was between two or among several a relationship of love so happy and perfect that the poet was bound to exult in it . . . this is by no means the end of the matter. Now Christianity steps forward and asks about the relationship to God, whether each individual is first related to God and then whether the relationship of love is related to God. If this is not the case, then Christianity, which certainly is the protector of love or because it is that, in God's name will not hesitate to split up this relationship until the lovers are willing to understand this. And if only one party understands it, then Christianity, which certainly is the protector of love, will not hesitate to lead him out into the horror of a collision such as no poet dreams of or has ventured to portray . . . : out of love and in love *to hate the beloved*. . . . Christianity does this not merely to collect, as it were, God's outstanding claim . . . but does it also out of love for the lovers, because to love God is to love oneself, to love another person as God is to deceive oneself, and to allow another person to love one as God is to deceive this other person. (WL, 107-108)

As this passage suggests, love for the other can even require doing that which appears to harm the beloved and to be motivated by hate. This can occur when the beloved must be rudely awakened from the bliss of devotion to the reality of his or her own independence, freedom, and responsibility. Since any attempt to explain or justify this "tough love" (to use a modern phrase) may only cause the beloved to love you even more (WL, 114), a sincere effort to awaken the beloved may lead unavoidably to a breach of the relationship. When there are only two parties in a relationship and when each is the other's supreme goal, truly loving the other in this way becomes impossible because it violates the relationship's essential condition, which is to please the beloved. "[S]uppose the beloved saw that the relationship would become the lover's ruin, would completely shake his distinctiveness—well, then erotic love as such does not have the power to make this sacrifice" (WL, 273). But when God is present as the third person in a love relationship and when, as Kierkegaard says, the two are related through God to the reality of loving and not merely to pleasing one another, then whatever truly is needed for the beloved's good can be accomplished.

Not only does God's presence make this kind of loving resolve necessary (because each partner is independently related to God), but also it simultaneously sustains the confidence that whatever the beloved may think or do, and whatever the world may conclude, one's conduct is nevertheless truly an expression of love. It is the tragedy of such efforts aimed at helping another person to exercise his or her freedom that these efforts must to some extent be "invisible." The goal is to help the other person become his or her own master. But, as Kierkegaard points out, to reveal one's involvement in accomplishing this contradicts the aim. If the person helped sees that they have actually become his or her own master through another's help, then "the person helped has not become his own master" (WL, 279). In a certain sense, therefore, when love succeeds in freeing its object, the one who accomplishes this will outwardly appear to have completely squandered her or his life on the existence of another. The genuine lover draws strength from the presence of God in their relationship and rests content in "simply being an active power in the hands of God" (WL, 279).

Finally, God's presence as the third party in a love relationship provides confidence that the love will survive any breach even if the beloved chooses to terminate contact. This is so because the lover is oriented not merely to the consciousness of the beloved but toward God and to love itself:

> When love ceases, when . . . in the loving relationship between
> two people something comes between them so that love ceases,
> then the two, as we human beings say, break up. . . . Christianity,
> however, does not know this use of language, does not under-
> stand it, refuses to understand it. . . . When a relationship is only
> between two, each one always has the upper hand in the
> relationship by being able to break it, because as soon as one of
> them has made the break, the *relationship* is broken. But when
> there are three, no one of them can do it. The third . . . is *love*
> itself, to which the innocent sufferer in the break can then hold—
> then the break has no power over him. (WL, 303, 304-305)

God's presence in a love relationship is thus the guarantee of
continuity. But, as we have seen, continuity—eternity—is love's
deepest ambition, from its erotic expression forward. Judge
William and his alter ego, the Married Man, who reflect the ethical
sphere of existence, appear to believe that continuity can be
attained through ethical resolve. In *Works of Love*, Kierkegaard does
not deny the importance of such resolve. "You shall love," remains
the banner under which love proceeds in the religious existence-
sphere (WL, 17-43). What Kierkegaard adds to this ethical resolve
is the understanding that unless God, and through God, the
beloved as neighbor, become central to the lovers' relationship,
even the most committed erotic love will be pulled asunder.

## Conclusion

We have tried to show that Christian love can play a decisive
role in sustaining committed erotic love in the face of the inevitable assaults that menace it. It does so in three ways: (1) by drawing
attention to what is essentially human in the beloved and thus
freeing each lover from preoccupation with the beloved's ever-
changing particularity; (2) by chastening the augmented egoism
that can makes a love relationship destructive both within and
without and that fuels jealousy and resentment; and (3) by placing
each party in independent relationship to God so as to provide
room for personal development, freedom, and courageous mutual
support.

Within the context of a loving erotic relationship or marriage,
none of these insights is easily achieved. Love's passionate attachment to the other (and fearful clinging to the relationship for one's

own sake) resists opening the duo to a third, even God. The freedom of the beloved, although a presupposition of all love, is also love's gravest threat and is typically resisted in many ways. The marital vows can themselves be used to imprison and bind the other to a destructive relationship. Thus, ethical resolve and commitment are not enough. The promise of erotic love is fulfilled only when each party's independent humanity is acknowledged, including each party's propensity toward sin and guilt. This last point is important: sin in oneself and sin in the beloved are erotic love's supreme foes. Sin as infidelity and betrayal by the other are humanly insupportable and fracture all erotic relationships or turn them into hatred. Sin in oneself, as the tendency to exalt the lover in order to control them—professing selflessness in the name of extreme selfishness—is the subtle undoing of other-regard. These are the final obstacles that erotic love must overcome to fulfill its inner drive toward permanence and genuine love for the other. But for this to happen, Kierkegaard tells us, God must enter the relationship.

This suggests that erotic love in the religious existence-sphere, like all such decisive transitions, is achieved only by a leap. It is not part of a seamless evolution from marital commitment, but is born in the crisis of some of the ethical view of marriage's more naive assumptions. Judge William in *Either/Or* and the Married Man in *Stages on Life's Way*, in their untroubled marital bliss, are still on their honeymoon. When they confront in themselves or their beloved aging, illness, ennui, betrayal, or most threatening of all, the development of a free and independent self, their feelings about love or their beloved may change. The ethical framework in which they live, premised on both parties' untroubled fidelity to their idealistic marital vows, has little room for the genuinely unconditional acceptance of the other that is the essence of erotic love in all its forms.[17] Anticipating this, Kierkegaard offers in *Works*

---

[17]"In erotic love and friendships, we rightly insist that the other's affection for us may not in any way be reducible to any moral algorithm, even if our moral behavior is a factor. And our insistence reflects a human value that is independent of intrinsic moral value." Laurence M. Thomas, "The Fragility of the Moral Self: Self-Love and Morality," Poynter Center Monograph Series, Essays on Human Institutions (Bloomington IN: The Poynter Center, October 1997).

*of Love* a guide to erotic love's survival. Having passed through aesthetic and ethical crises, erotic love in its religious expression finally achieves its promised passion for the beloved, its true equality, its freedom for each party in the love relationship, and its eternal unchangeability. In this sense, *Works of Love* is not just a study of Christian love. It is the capstone of Kierkegaard's entire philosophy of love.

# Contributors

International Kierkegaard Commentary 16
*Works of Love*

MARTIN ANDIC is associate professor of Philosophy at the University of Massachusetts in Boston.

LEE BARRETT is professor of Theology at Lancaster Theological Seminary in Lancaster, Pennsylvania.

ANTHONY T. BURGESS is associate professor of Philosophy at the University of New Mexico at Albuquerque, New Mexico.

ARNOLD COME is emeritus professor of Theology at the San Francisco Theological Seminary and the Graduate Theological Union.

MARK DOOLEY is John Henry Newman Scholar in Theology and Philosophy at University College, Dublin.

THERESA M. ELLIS is Director of Research and Public Policy at Community Anti-Drug Coalitions of America.

M. J. FERREIRA is professor of Religious Studies and Philosophy at the University of Virginia.

RONALD M. GREEN is the Cohen Professor for the Study of Ethics and Human Values at Dartmouth College in Hanover, New Hampshire.

LOUISE CARROLL KEELEY is assistant professor of Philosophy at Assumption College in Worcester, Massachusetts.

PAUL MARTENS is a graduate student at Regent College in Vancouver, Canada.

MICHAEL OPPENHEIM is associate professor of Religion at Concordia University, Montreal, Canada.

ROBERT L. PERKINS is professor of Philosophy at Stetson University in DeLand, Florida.

ANTHONY J. RUDD is lecturer in Philosophy at the University of Hertfordshire.

BEGONYA SAEZ TAJAFUERCE is a postdoctoral researcher and Coordinator of Translation Projects at the Søren Kierkegaard Research Center at the University of Copenhagen.

ERIC ZIOLKOWSKI is associate professor of Religion at Lafayette College, Easton, Pennsylvania.

# Advisory Board

*Editor*
Robert L. Perkins, Stetson University

*Advisory Board*
C. Stephen Evans, Calvin College
Sylvia Walsh, Stetson University

*Volume Consultant*
Lee Barrett

*International Advisory Board*
Julia Watkin, Australia
Poul Lübcke, Denmark
Nelly Viallaneix, France
Wolfdiedrich von Kloden, Federal Republic of Germany
J. Heywood Thomas, England
Masaru Otani, Japan
Sixtus W. Scholtens, Netherlands

# Previous Volume Consultants

Volume 1. *Early Polemical Writings*
Julia Watkin, University of Tasmania

Volume 3. *Either/Or*, Part I
George Connell, Concordia College
David Gouwens, Brite Divinity School

Volume 4. *Either/Or*, Part II
George Connell, Concordia College
Edward F. Mooney, Sonoma State University

Volume 6. *"Fear and Trembling" and "Repetition"*
Abrahim H.Kahn, University of Toronto (FT)
David Goicoechea, Brock University (R)

Volume 7. *"Philosophical Fragments" and "Johannes Climacus"*
Lee Barrett, Lancaster Theological Seminary

Volume 8. *The Concept of Anxiety*
Vincent A. McCarthy, St. Joseph's University

Volume 12. *Concluding Unscientific Postscript
to "Philosophical Fragments"*
Merold Westphal, Fordham University

Volume 13. *The Corsair Affair*
Burce H. Kirmmse, Connecticut College

Volume 14. *Two Ages*
Merold Westphal, Fordham University

Volume 19. *The Sickness unto Death*
Louis Dupré, Yale University

# Index

Abrams, M. H., 285nn.16-17
acosmism, 139, 142, 151
action, 19, 25, 34-35, 310, 315n.7
Adam, 282-83, 285
admiration, 320
Adorno, W. T., 6, 139, 148, 193, 209n., 212-16, 234n.44, 244, 247
aesthetic stage, 349
Althaus, Paul, 53
Andersen, Hans Christian, 287
Anderson, Thomas C., 80n.3, 89n.13
Andic, Martin, 3
anticonsequentialism, 148-51
Arendt, Hannah, 245
Ariès, Phillippe, 283-84, 285, 295n.31
Aristotle, 12n.4, 281, 322, 327
artistic discourse, 309, 322, 323
asymmetry, cf. symmetry, 195, 199, 201
Augustine, St., 7, 11n.3, 49, 280, 282-85, 289, 290, 335n.19
Austin, J. L., 310n.3
authority, 314-21, 331

Barrie, J. M., 302
Barth, Karl, 49, 57, 58, 76, 77
Bayle, Pierre, 134
Becker, Ernest, 231n.38
being, 47, 79, 79, 81, 81, 87, 93, 93
belief, 121-22, 126-28, 133
Bernstein, Leonard, 118
Bernasconi, Robert, 173, 259-60
Bible
    Old Testament
        Deuteronomy, 10n.1
        Exekiel, 13n.5
        Isaiah, 10n.1, 14n.7, 30n.44, 47
        Jeremiah, 10n.1
        Psalms, 11n.2, 26n.39
        2 Samuel, 19n.17

Song of Songs, 277
Apocrypha
    Ecclesiasticus (Sirach), 285
New Testament, 9-10, 13n.5, 14nn.6-7, 15n.8-9, 16-17 and n.10 18n.14, 19n.17, 26n.39, 30nn.42-44
    1 Corinthians, 255, 282, 291, 292, 293, 299, 300
    2 Corinthians, 26n.39
    Galatians, 279-80
    James, 19n.8
    John, 30n.44, 31n.46, 34n.51
    1 John, 15n.9, 16n.10, 30, 31n.45
    Luke, 181, 292,
    Mark, 281
    Matthew, 57, 59, 62, 64, 66, 68, 281, 292, 301
    1 Peter, 18n.14, 45, 52, 282, 300, 301
    Revelation, 31n.46
    Romans, 282, 283
    1 Timothy, 19n.17
Blake, William, 290-91, 293-94, 297
Blanchette, Oliva, 316n.7
Boethius, 343n.15
Bøggild, Jakob, 310n.4
Buber, Martin, 7, 138, 148, 249-50, 252-54, 256-58, 257-77, 260, 263-65, 270-71

capitalism, 2
Caputo, John D., 6, 168, 169, 171, 191
categorical imperative, 58, 59, 62, 69
Catherine of Siena, St., 30n.43
change/unchanging, 99-100, 105, 201, 202, 206